Programming in Objective-C

Fifth Edition

Developer's Library

ESSENTIAL REFERENCES FOR PROGRAMMING PROFESSIONALS

Developer's Library books are designed to provide practicing programmers with unique, high-quality references and tutorials on the programming languages and technologies they use in their daily work.

All books in the *Developer's Library* are written by expert technology practitioners who are especially skilled at organizing and presenting information in a way that's useful for other programmers.

Key titles include some of the best, most widely acclaimed books within their topic areas:

PHP & MySQL Web Development
Luke Welling & Laura Thomson
ISBN 978-0-672-32916-6

Python Essential Reference
David Beazley
ISBN-13: 978-0-672-32978-4

MySQL
Paul DuBois
ISBN-13: 978-0-672-32938-8

PostgreSQL
Korry Douglas
ISBN-13: 978-0-672-32756-8

Linux Kernel Development
Robert Love
ISBN-13: 978-0-672-32946-3

C++ Primer Plus
Stephen Prata
ISBN-13: 978-0321-77640-2

Developer's Library books are available in print and in electronic formats at most retail and online bookstores, as well as by subscription from Safari Books Online at
safari.informit.com

JAN 2013

Developer's Library
informit.com/devlibrary

Programming in Objective-C

Fifth Edition

Stephen G. Kochan

♦♦ Addison-Wesley

Upper Saddle River, NJ • Boston • Indianapolis • San Francisco
New York • Toronto • Montreal • London • Munich • Paris • Madrid
Cape Town • Sydney • Tokyo • Singapore • Mexico City

Programming in Objective-C, Fifth Edition

ISBN-13: 978-0-321-88728-3

ISBN-10: 0-321-88728-X

The Library of Congress Cataloging-in-Publication Data is on file.

Printed in the United States of America

First Printing: December 2012

Trademarks

All terms mentioned in this book that are known to be trademarks or service marks have been appropriately capitalized. Pearson cannot attest to the accuracy of this information. Use of a term in this book should not be regarded as affecting the validity of any trademark or service mark.

Warning and Disclaimer

Every effort has been made to make this book as complete and as accurate as possible, but no warranty or fitness is implied. The information provided is on an "as is" basis. The author and the publisher shall have neither liability nor responsibility to any person or entity with respect to any loss or damages arising from the information contained in this book.

Bulk Sales

Pearson offers excellent discounts on this book when ordered in quantity for bulk purchases or special sales. For more information, please contact

U.S. Corporate and Government Sales
1-800-382-3419
corpsales@pearsontechgroup.com

For sales outside of the U.S., please contact

International Sales
international@pearsoned.com

Acquisitions Editor
Mark Taber

Managing Editor
Sandra Schroeder

Project Editor
Mandie Frank

Copy Editor
Keith Cline

Indexer
Erika Millen

Proofreader
Dan Knott

Technical Editor
Michael Trent

Publishing Coordinator
Vanessa Evans

Designer
Gary Adair

Cover Designer
Chuti Prasertsith

Compositor
Tricia Bronkella

❖

To Roy and Ve, two people whom I dearly miss.

To Ken Brown, "It's just a jump to the left."

❖

Contents at a Glance

Appendixes

Table of Contents

About the Author

Stephen Kochan is the author and coauthor of several bestselling titles on the C language, including *Programming in C* (Sams, 2004), *Programming in ANSI C* (Sams, 1994), and *Topics in C Programming* (Wiley, 1991), and several UNIX titles, including *Exploring the Unix System* (Sams, 1992) and *Unix Shell Programming* (Sams, 2003). He has been programming on Macintosh computers since the introduction of the first Mac in 1984, and he wrote *Programming C for the Mac* as part of the Apple Press Library. In 2003, Kochan wrote *Programming in Objective-C* (Sams, 2003), and followed that with another Mac-related title, *Beginning AppleScript* (Wiley, 2004).

About the Technical Reviewers

Michael Trent has been programming in Objective-C since 1997—and programming Macs since well before that. He is a regular contributor to Steven Frank's www.cocoadev.com website, a technical reviewer for numerous books and magazine articles, and an occasional dabbler in Mac OS X open-source projects. Currently, he is using Objective-C and Apple Computer's Cocoa frameworks to build professional video applications for Mac OS X. Michael holds a Bachelor of Science degree in computer science and a Bachelor of Arts degree in music from Beloit College of Beloit, Wisconsin. He lives in Santa Clara, California, with his lovely wife, Angela.

Wendy Mui is a programmer and software development manager in the San Francisco Bay Area. After learning Objective-C from the second edition of Steve Kochan's book, she landed a job at Bump Technologies, where she put her programming skills to good use working on the client app and the API/SDK for Bump's third-party developers. Prior to her iOS experience, Wendy spent her formative years at Sun and various other tech companies in Silicon Valley and San Francisco. She got hooked on programming while earning a Bachelor of Arts degree in mathematics from the University of California Berkeley.

We Want to Hear from You!

As the reader of this book, *you* are our most important critic and commentator. We value your opinion and want to know what we're doing right, what we could do better, what areas you'd like to see us publish in, and any other words of wisdom you're willing to pass our way.

You can email or write directly to let us know what you did or didn't like about this book—as well as what we can do to make our books stronger.

Please note that we cannot help you with technical problems related to the topic of this book, and that due to the high volume of mail we receive, we might not be able to reply to every message.

When you write, please be sure to include this book's title and author, as well as your name and phone or email address.

Email: feedback@developers-library.info

Mail: Reader Feedback
         Addison-Wesley Developer's Library
         800 East 96th Street
         Indianapolis, IN 46240 USA

Reader Services

Visit our website and register this book at www.informit.com/register for convenient access to any updates, downloads, or errata that might be available for this book.

1

Introduction

Dennis Ritchie at AT&T Bell Laboratories pioneered the C programming language in the early 1970s. However, this programming language did not begin to gain widespread popularity and support until the late 1970s. This was because, until that time, C compilers were not readily available for commercial use outside of Bell Laboratories. Initially, this growth in popularity was also partly spurred by the equal, if not faster, growth in popularity of the UNIX operating system, which was written almost entirely in C.

Brad J. Cox designed the Objective-C language in the early 1980s. The language was based on a language called SmallTalk-80. Objective-C was *layered* on top of the C language, meaning that extensions were added to C to create a new programming language that enabled *objects* to be created and manipulated.

NeXT Software licensed the Objective-C language in 1988 and developed its libraries and a development environment called NEXTSTEP. In 1992, Objective-C support was added to the Free Software Foundation's GNU development environment. The copyrights for all Free Software Foundation (FSF) products are owned by the FSF. It is released under the GNU General Public License.

In 1994, NeXT Computer and Sun Microsystems released a standardized specification of the NEXTSTEP system, called OPENSTEP. The FSF's implementation of OPENSTEP is called GNUStep. A Linux version, which also includes the Linux kernel and the GNUStep development environment, is called, appropriately enough, LinuxSTEP.

On December 20, 1996, Apple Computer announced that it was acquiring NeXT Software, and the NEXTSTEP/OPENSTEP environment became the basis for the next major release of Apple's operating system, OS X. Apple's version of this development environment was called Cocoa. With built-in support for the Objective-C language, coupled with development tools such as Project Builder (or its successor Xcode) and Interface Builder, Apple created a powerful development environment for application development on Mac OS X.

In 2007, Apple released an update to the Objective-C language and labeled it Objective-C 2.0. That version of the language formed the basis for the second edition of the book.

When the iPhone was released in 2007, developers clamored for the opportunity to develop applications for this revolutionary device. At first, Apple did not welcome third-party application development. The company's way of placating wannabe iPhone developers was to allow them to develop Web-based applications. A Web-based application runs under the iPhone's built-in Safari Web browser and requires the user to connect to the Web site that hosts the application in order to run it. Developers were not satisfied with the many inherent limitations of Web-based applications, and Apple shortly thereafter announced that developers would be able to develop so-called *native* applications for the iPhone.

A native application is one that resides on the iPhone and runs under the iPhone's operating system, in the same way that the iPhone's built-in applications (such as Contacts, Stocks, and Weather) run on the device. The iPhone's OS is actually a version of OS X, which means that applications can be developed and debugged on a MacBook Pro, for example. In fact, Apple soon provided a powerful software development kit (SDK) that allowed for rapid iPhone application development and debugging. The availability of an iPhone simulator made it possible for developers to debug their applications directly on their development system, obviating the need to download and test the program on an actual iPhone or iPod touch device.

With the introduction of the iPad in 2010, Apple started to genericize the terminology used for the operating system and the SDK that now support different devices with different physical sizes and screen resolutions. The iOS SDK allows you to develop applications for any iOS device, and as of this writing, iOS 6 is the current release of the operating system.

What You Will Learn from This Book

When I contemplated writing a tutorial on Objective-C, I had to make a fundamental decision. As with other texts on Objective-C, I could write mine to assume that the reader already knew how to write C programs. I could also teach the language from the perspective of using the rich library of routines, such as the Foundation and UIKit frameworks. Some texts also take the approach of teaching how to use the development tools, such as the Mac's Xcode and the tool formerly known as Interface Builder to design the UI.

I had several problems adopting this approach. First, learning the entire C language before learning Objective-C is wrong. C is a *procedural* language containing many features that are not necessary for programming in Objective-C, especially at the novice level. In fact, resorting to some of these features goes against the grain of adhering to a good object-oriented programming methodology. It's also not a good idea to learn all the details of a procedural language before learning an object-oriented one. This starts the programmer in the wrong direction, and gives the wrong orientation and mindset for fostering a good object-oriented programming style. Just because Objective-C is an extension to the C language doesn't mean you have to learn C first.

So, I decided neither to teach C first nor to assume prior knowledge of the language. Instead, I decided to take the unconventional approach of teaching Objective-C and the underlying C language as a single integrated language, from an object-oriented programming perspective. The purpose of this book is, as its name implies, to teach you how to program in Objective-C.

It does not profess to teach you in detail how to use the development tools that are available for entering and debugging programs, or to provide in-depth instructions on how to develop interactive graphical applications. You can learn all that material in greater detail elsewhere, after you have learned how to write programs in Objective-C. In fact, you will find mastering that material much easier when you have a solid foundation of how to program in Objective-C. This book does not assume much, if any, previous programming experience. In fact, if you are a novice programmer, with some dedication and hard work you should be able to learn Objective-C as your first programming language. Other readers have been successful at this, based on the feedback I have received from the previous editions of this book.

This book teaches Objective-C by example. As I present each new feature of the language, I usually provide a small complete program example to illustrate the feature. Just as a picture is worth a thousand words, so is a properly chosen program example. You are strongly encouraged to run each program and compare the results obtained on your system to those shown in the text. By doing so, you will learn the language and its syntax, but you will also become familiar with the process of compiling and running Objective-C programs.

How This Book Is Organized

This book is divided into three logical parts. Part I, "The Objective-C Language," teaches the essentials of the language. Part II, "The Foundation Framework," teaches how to use the rich assortment of predefined classes that form the Foundation framework. Part III, "Cocoa, Cocoa Touch, and the iOS SDK," gives you an overview of the Cocoa and Cocoa Touch frameworks and then walks you through the process of developing a simple iOS application using the iOS SDK.

A *framework* is a set of classes and routines that have been logically grouped together to make developing programs easier. Much of the power of programming in Objective-C rests on the extensive frameworks that are available.

Chapter 2, "Programming in Objective-C," begins by teaching you how to write your first program in Objective-C.

Because this is not a book on Cocoa or iOS programming, graphical user interfaces (GUIs) are not extensively taught and are hardly even mentioned until Part III. So, an approach was needed to get input into a program and produce output. Most of the examples in this text take input from the keyboard and produce their output in a window pane: a Terminal window if you're using the command line, or a debug output pane if you're using Xcode.

Chapter 3, "Classes, Objects, and Methods," covers the fundamentals of object-oriented programming. This chapter introduces some terminology, but it is kept to a minimum. I also introduce the mechanism for defining a class and the means for sending messages to instances or objects. Instructors and seasoned Objective-C programmers will notice that I use *static* typing for declaring objects. I think this is the best way for the student to get started because the compiler can catch more errors, making the programs more self-documenting and encouraging the new programmer to explicitly declare the data types when they are known. As a result, the notion of the id type and its power is not fully explored until Chapter 9, "Polymorphism, Dynamic Typing, and Dynamic Binding."

Chapter 4, "Data Types and Expressions," describes the basic Objective-C data types and how to use them in your programs.

Chapter 5, "Program Looping," introduces the three looping statements you can use in your programs: for, while, and do.

Making decisions is fundamental to any computer programming language. Chapter 6, "Making Decisions," covers the Objective-C language's if and switch statements in detail.

Chapter 7, "More on Classes," delves more deeply into working with classes and objects. Details about methods, multiple arguments to methods, and local variables are discussed here.

Chapter 8, "Inheritance," introduces the key concept of inheritance. This feature makes the development of programs easier because you can take advantage of what comes from above. Inheritance and the notion of subclasses make modifying and extending existing class definitions easy.

Chapter 9 discusses three fundamental characteristics of the Objective-C language. Polymorphism, dynamic typing, and dynamic binding are the key concepts covered here.

Chapters 10–13 round out the discussion of the Objective-C language, covering issues such as initialization of objects, blocks, protocols, categories, the preprocessor, and some of the underlying C features, including functions, arrays, structures, and pointers. These underlying features are often unnecessary (and often best avoided) when first developing object-oriented applications. It's recommended that you skim Chapter 13, "Underlying C Language Features," the first time through the text and return to it only as necessary to learn more about a particular feature of the language. Chapter 13 also introduces a recent addition to the C language known as *blocks*. This should be learned after you learn about how to write functions, since the syntax of the former is derived from the latter.

Part II begins with Chapter 14, "Introduction to the Foundation Framework," which gives an introduction to the Foundation framework and how to use its voluminous documentation.

Chapters 15–19 cover important features of the Foundation framework. These include number and string objects, collections, the file system, memory management, and the process of copying and archiving objects.

By the time you're done with Part II, you will be able to develop fairly sophisticated programs in Objective-C that work with the Foundation framework.

Part III starts with Chapter 20, "Introduction to Cocoa and Cocoa Touch." Here you get a quick overview of the frameworks that provide the classes you need to develop sophisticated graphical applications on the Mac and on your iOS devices.

Chapter 21, "Writing iOS Applications," introduces the iOS SDK and the UIKit framework. This chapter illustrates a step-by-step approach to writing a simple iOS application, followed by a more sophisticated calculator application that enables you to use your iPhone to perform simple arithmetic calculations with fractions.

Because object-oriented parlance involves a fair amount of terminology, Appendix A, "Glossary," provides definitions of some common terms.

Appendix B, "Address Book Example Source Code," gives the source code listing for two classes that are developed and used extensively in Part II of this text. These classes define address card and address book classes. Methods enable you to perform simple operations such as adding and removing address cards from the address book, looking up someone, listing the contents of the address book, and so on.

After you've learned how to write Objective-C programs, you can go in several directions. You might want to learn more about the underlying C programming language, or you might want to start writing Cocoa programs to run on OS X, or you might want to develop more-sophisticated iOS applications.

Support

If you go to classroomM.com/objective-c, you'll find a forum rich with content. There you can get some source code (note that you won't find the "official" source code for all the examples there; I firmly believe that a big part the learning process occurs when you type in the program examples yourself and learn how to identify and correct any errors), answers to exercises, errata, and quizzes; you can also pose questions to me and fellow forum members. The forum has turned into a rich community of active members who are happy to help other members solve their problems and answer their questions. Please go, join, and participate!

Acknowledgments

I would like to acknowledge several people for their help in the preparation of the first edition of this text. First, I want to thank Tony Iannino and Steven Levy for reviewing the manuscript. I am also grateful to Mike Gaines for providing his input.

I'd also like to thank my technical editors, Jack Purdum (first edition), Wendy Mui (third edition), and Mike Trent (first, second, and fifth editions). I was particularly lucky to have Mike review the first two editions of this text. He provided the most thorough review of any book I've ever written. Not only did he point out weaknesses, but he was also generous enough to offer his suggestions. Because of Mike's comments in the first edition, I changed my approach to teaching memory management and tried to make sure that every program example in this book was "leak free." This was prior to the fourth edition, where the strong emphasis on memory management became obsolete with the introduction of ARC. Mike also provided invaluable input for my chapter on iOS programming.

From the first edition, Catherine Babin supplied the cover photograph and provided me with many wonderful pictures to choose from. Having the cover art from a friend made the book even more special.

I am so grateful to Mark Taber (for all editions) from Pearson for putting up with all delays and for being kind enough to work around my schedule and to tolerate my consistent missing of deadlines. The same kudos to Mandie Frank from Pearson. Mandie has worked tirelessly with my late deliveries to help get various editions of this book out on time. I am extremely grateful to Michael de Haan and Wendy Mui for doing an incredible, unsolicited job proofreading the first printing of the second edition.

As noted at the start of this Introduction, Dennis Ritchie invented the C language. He was also a co-inventor of the Unix operating system, which is the basis for OS X and iOS. Sadly, the world lost both Dennis Ritchie and Steve Jobs within the span of a week in 2011. These two people had a profound effect on my career; this book would not exist if not for them.

Finally, I'd like to thank the members of the forum at classroomM.com/objective-c for all their feedback, support, and kind words.

Preface to the Fifth Edition

In June 2012 Apple announced some changes to the syntax of the Objective-C language. These mostly had to do with the way number, array, and dictionary objects could be initialized and accessed. These changes were the motivation for this latest edition.

Stephen G. Kochan

November 2012

2

Programming in Objective-C

In this chapter, we dive right in and show you how to write your first Objective-C program. You won't work with objects just yet; that's the topic of the next chapter. We want you to understand the steps involved in keying in a program and compiling and running it.

To begin, let's pick a rather simple example: a program that displays the phrase "Programming is fun!" on your screen. Without further ado, Program 2.1 shows an Objective-C program to accomplish this task.

Program 2.1

```
// First program example

#import <Foundation/Foundation.h>

int main (int argc, const char * argv[])
{
    @autoreleasepool {
        NSLog (@"Programming is fun!");
    }
    return 0;
}
```

Compiling and Running Programs

Before we go into a detailed explanation of this program, we need to cover the steps involved in compiling and running it. You can both compile and run your program using Xcode, or you can use the Clang Objective-C compiler in a Terminal window. Let's go through the sequence of steps using both methods. Then you can decide how you want to work with your programs throughout the rest of this book.

> **Note**
>
> Xcode is available from the Mac App Store. However, you can also get pre-release versions of Xcode by becoming a registered Apple developer (no charge for that). Go to http://developer.apple.com to get the latest version of the Xcode development tools. There you can download Xcode and the iOS software development kit (SDK) for no charge.

Using Xcode

Xcode is a sophisticated application that enables you to easily type in, compile, debug, and execute programs. If you plan on doing serious application development on the Mac, learning how to use this powerful tool is worthwhile. We just get you started here. Later we return to Xcode and take you through the steps involved in developing a graphical application with it.

> **Note**
>
> As mentioned, Xcode is a sophisticated tool, and the introduction of Xcode 4 added even more features. It's easy to get lost using this tool. If that happens to you, back up a little and try reading the Xcode User Guide, which you can access from the Xcode Help menu, to get your bearings.

Once installed, Xcode is in your Applications folder. Figure 2.1 shows its icon.

Xcode

Figure 2.1   Xcode icon

Start Xcode. (The first time you launch the application, you have to go through some one-time things like agreeing to the license agreement.) You can then select Create a New Xcode Project from the startup screen (see Figure 2.2). Alternatively, under the File menu, select New, Project.

A window appears, as shown in Figure 2.3.

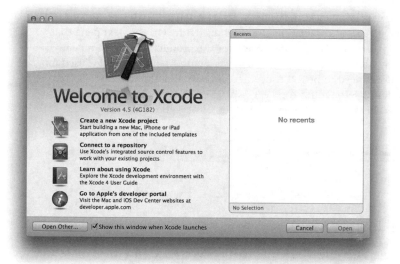

Figure 2.2   Starting a new project

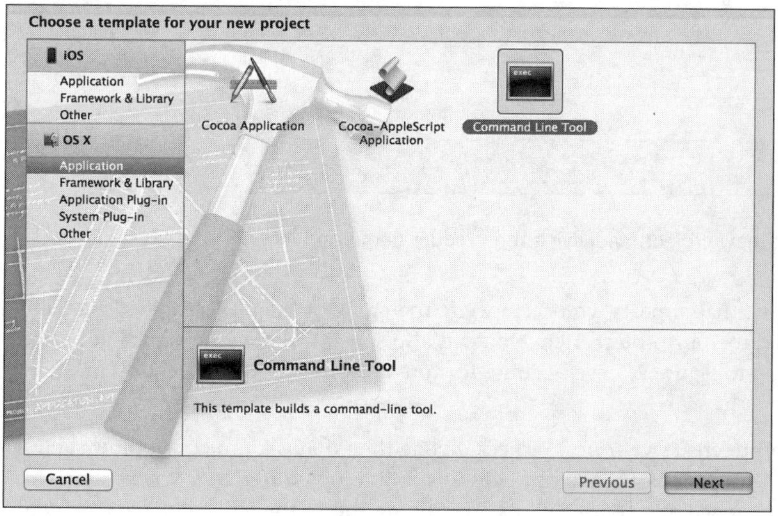

Figure 2.3   Starting a new project: selecting the application type

In the left pane, you'll see a section labeled Mac OS X. Select Application. In the upper-right pane, select Command Line Tool, as depicted in the previous figure. On the next pane that appears, you pick your application's name. Enter **prog1** for the product name and type in something in the Company Identifier and Bundle Identifier fields. The latter field is used for creating iOS apps, so we don't need to be too concerned at this point about what's entered there. Make sure Foundation is selected for the Type. Also, be sure that the Use Automatic Reference Counting box is checked. Your screen should look like Figure 2.4.

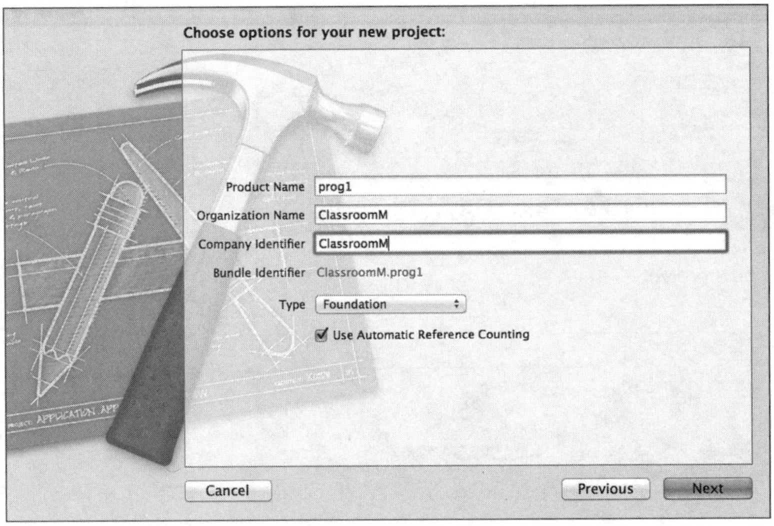

Figure 2.4   Starting a new project: specifying the product name and type

Click Next. On the sheet that appears, you can specify the name of the project folder that will contain the files related to your project. Here, you can also specify where you want that project folder stored. According to Figure 2.5, we're going to store our project on the Desktop in a folder called prog1.

Click the Create button to create your new project. Xcode then opens a project window such as the one shown in Figure 2.6. Note that your window might look different if you've used Xcode before or have changed any of its options. This figure shows the Utilities pane. You can close that pane by deselecting the third icon listed in the View category in the top right of your XCode toolbar.

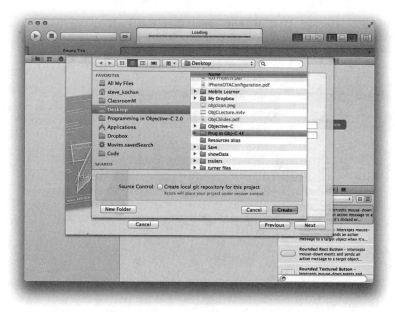

Figure 2.5   Selecting the location and name of the project folder

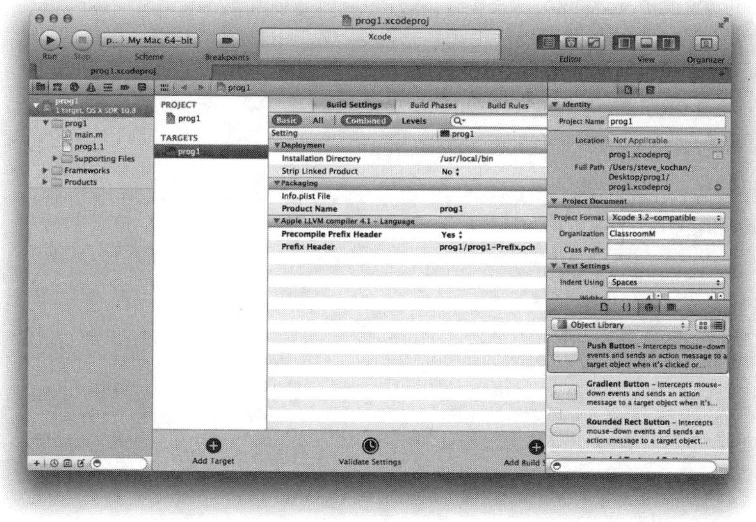

Figure 2.6   Xcode `prog1` project window

Now it's time to type in your first program. Select the file main.m in the left pane. (You might have to reveal the files under the project name by clicking the disclosure triangle.) Your Xcode window should now look like Figure 2.7.

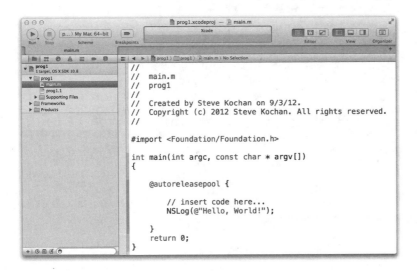

Figure 2.7   File main.m and the edit window

Objective-C source files use .m as the last two characters of the filename (known as its *extension*). Table 2.1 lists other commonly used filename extensions.

Table 2.1   **Common Filename Extensions**

Extension	Meaning
.c	C language source file
.cc, .cpp	C++ language source file
.h	Header file
.m	Objective-C source file
.mm	Objective-C++ source file
.pl	Perl source file
.o	Object (compiled) file

The right pane of your Xcode project window shows the contents of the file called main.m, which was automatically created for you as a template file by Xcode and which contains the following lines:

```
//
//   main.m
//   prog1
//
//   Created by Steve Kochan on 9/3/12.
//   Copyright (c) 2012 Steve Kochan. All rights reserved.
//
#import <Foundation/Foundation.h>

int main (int argc, const char * argv[])
{
    @autoreleasepool {

        // insert code here...
        NSLog (@"Hello World!");
    }
    return 0;
}
```

You can edit your file inside this window. Make changes to the program shown in the edit window to match Program 2.1. The lines that start with two slash characters (//) are called *comments;* we talk more about comments shortly.

Your program in the edit window should now look like this. (Don't worry if your comments don't match.)

Program 2.1

```
// First program example

#import <Foundation/Foundation.h>

int main (int argc, const char * argv[])
{
    @autoreleasepool {
        NSLog (@"Programming is fun!");
    }
    return 0;
}
```

Note

Don't worry about all the colors shown for your text onscreen. Xcode indicates values, reserved words, and so on with different colors. This will prove very valuable as you start programming more, as it can indicate the source of a potential error.

Now it's time to compile and run your first program; in Xcode terminology, it's called *building and running.* Before doing that, we need to reveal a pane that will display the results (output) from our program. You can do this most easily by selecting the middle icon under View on the toolbar. When you hover over this icon, it says Hide or Show the Debug Area. Your window should now look like Figure 2.8. Note that Xcode normally reveals the debug area automatically whenever any data is written to it.

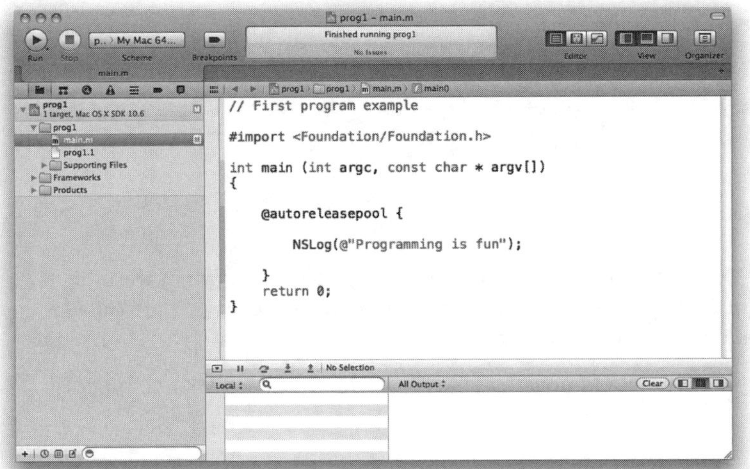

Figure 2.8   Xcode debug area revealed

Now, if you click the Run button located at the top left of the toolbar or select Run from the Product menu, Xcode goes through the two-step process of first building and then running your program. The latter occurs only if no errors are discovered in your program.

Note

The first time you click the Run button XCode displays a sheet reading Enable Developer Mode on the Mac? Click the Enable button and enter your admin password to proceed.

If you do make mistakes in your program, along the way you'll see errors denoted as red stop signs containing exclamation points; these are known as *fatal errors,* and you can't run your program without correcting these. *Warnings* are depicted by yellow triangles containing exclamation points. You can still run your program with them, but in general you should examine and correct them. After you run the program with all the errors removed, the lower-right pane displays the output from your program and should look similar to Figure 2.9.

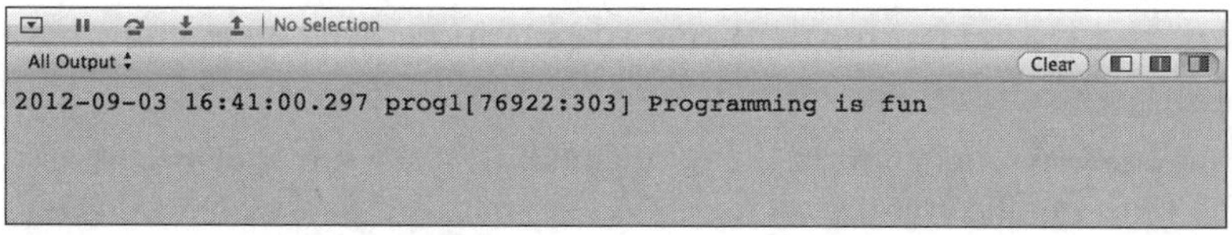

Figure 2.9   Xcode debug output

You're now done with the procedural part of compiling and running your first program with Xcode (whew!). The following summarizes the steps involved in creating a new program with Xcode:

1. Start the Xcode application.

2. If this is a new project, select File, New, New Project... or choose Create a New Xcode Project from the startup screen.

3. For the type of application, select Application, Command Line Tool, and click Next.

4. Select a name for your application and set its Type to Foundation. Make sure that Use Automatic Reference Counting is checked. Also fill in the other fields that appear on the sheet. Click Next.

5. Select a name for your project folder and a directory to store your project files in. Click Create.

6. In the left pane, you will see the file `main.m`. (You might need to reveal it from inside the folder that has the product's name.) Highlight that file. Type your program into the edit window that appears in the rightmost pane.

7. On the toolbar, select the middle icon under View to reveal the debug area. That's where you'll see your output.

8. Build and run your application by clicking the Run button on the toolbar or selecting Run from the Product menu.

Note

Xcode contains a powerful built-in tool known as the static analyzer. It does an analysis of your code and can find program logic errors. You can use it by selecting Analyze from the Product menu or from the Run button on the toolbar.

9. If you get any compiler errors or the output is not what you expected, make your changes to the program and rerun it.

Using Terminal

Some people might want to avoid having to learn Xcode to get started programming with Objective-C. If you're used to using the UNIX shell and command-line tools, you might want to edit, compile, and run your programs using the Terminal application. Here, we examine how to go about doing that.

Before attempting to compile you program from the command line, make sure that you have Xcode's Command Line Tools installed on your system. Go to Xcode, Preferences, Downloads, Components from inside Xcode. You'll see something similar to Figure 2.10. This figure indicates that the Command Line Tools have not been installed on this system. To do so, you click the Install button.

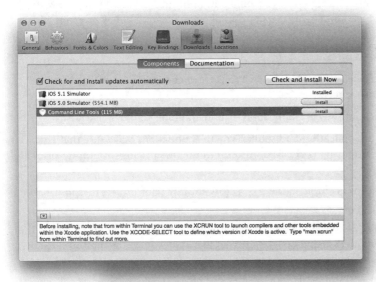

Figure 2.10   Installing the Command Line Tools

Once the Command Line Tools have been installed, the next step is to start the Terminal application on your Mac. The Terminal application is located in the Applications folder, stored under Utilities. Figure 2.11 shows its icon.

Terminal

Figure 2.11   Terminal program icon

Start the Terminal application. You'll see a window that looks like Figure 2.12.

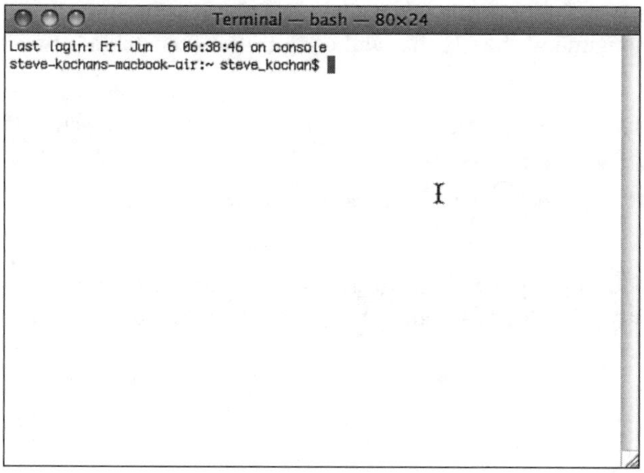

Figure 2.12   Terminal window

You type commands after the $ (or %, depending on how your Terminal application is configured) on each line. If you're familiar with using UNIX, you'll find this straightforward.

First, you need to enter the lines from Program 2.1 into a file. You can begin by creating a directory in which to store your program examples. Then, you must run a text editor, such as vi or emacs, to enter your program:

```
sh-2.05a$ mkdir Progs    Create a directory to store programs in
sh-2.05a$ cd Progs       Change to the new directory
sh-2.05a$ vi main.m      Start up a text editor to enter program
  --
```

> **Note**
>
> In the previous example and throughout the remainder of this text, commands that you, the user, enter are indicated in boldface.

For Objective-C files, you can choose any name you want; just make sure that the last two characters are .m. This indicates to the compiler that you have an Objective-C program.

After you've entered your program into a file (and we're not showing the edit commands to enter and save your text here) and have verified that you have the right tools installed, you can use the LLVM Clang Objective-C compiler, which is called clang, to compile and link your program. This is the general format of the clang command:

```
clang -fobjc-arc files -o program
```

files is the list of files to be compiled. In this example, we have only one such file, and we're calling it `main.m`. *program* is the name of the file that will contain the executable if the program compiles without any errors.

We'll call the program `prog1`; here, then, is the command line to compile your first Objective-C program:

```
$ clang -fobjc-arc main.m -o prog1      Compile main.m & call it prog1
$
```

The return of the command prompt without any messages means that no errors were found in the program. Now you can subsequently execute the program by typing the name **prog1** at the command prompt:

```
$ prog1         Execute prog1
sh: prog1: command not found
$
```

This is the result you'll probably get unless you've used Terminal before. The UNIX shell (which is the application running your program) doesn't know where `prog1` is located (we don't go into all the details of this here), so you have two options: One is to precede the name of the program with the characters `./` so that the shell knows to look in the current directory for the program to execute. The other is to add the directory in which your programs are stored (or just simply the current directory) to the shell's PATH variable. Let's take the first approach here:

```
$ ./prog1       Execute prog1
2012-09-03 18:48:44.210 prog1[7985:10b] Programming is fun!
$
```

Note that writing and debugging Objective-C programs from the Terminal is a valid approach. However, it's not a good long-term strategy. If you want to build OS X or iOS applications, there's more to just the executable file that needs to be "packaged" into an application bundle. It's not easy to do that from the Terminal application, and it's one of Xcode's specialties. Therefore, I suggest you start learning to use Xcode to develop your programs. There is a learning curve to do this, but the effort will be well worth it in the end.

Explanation of Your First Program

Now that you are familiar with the steps involved in compiling and running Objective-C programs, let's take a closer look at this first program. Here it is again:

```
// First program example

#import <Foundation/Foundation.h>

int main (int argc, const char * argv[])
{
    @autoreleasepool {
```

```
    NSLog (@"Programming is fun!");

}
    return 0;
}
```

In Objective-C, lowercase and uppercase letters are distinct. Also, Objective-C doesn't care where on the line you begin typing—you can begin typing your statement at any position on the line. You can use this to your advantage in developing programs that are easier to read.

The first seven lines of the program introduce the concept of the *comment*. A comment statement is used in a program to document a program and enhance its readability. Comments tell the reader of the program—whether it's the programmer or someone else whose responsibility it is to maintain the program—just what the programmer had in mind when writing a particular program or a particular sequence of statements.

You can insert comments into an Objective-C program in two ways. One is by using two consecutive slash characters (//). The compiler ignores any characters that follow these slashes, up to the end of the line.

You can also initiate a comment with the two characters / and *. This marks the beginning of the comment. These types of comments have to be terminated. To end the comment, you use the characters * and /, again without any embedded spaces. All characters included between the opening /* and the closing */ are treated as part of the comment statement and are ignored by the Objective-C compiler. This form of comment is often used when comments span many lines of code, as in the following:

```
/*
 This file implements a class called Fraction, which
 represents fractional numbers. Methods allow manipulation of
 fractions, such as addition, subtraction, etc.

 For more information, consult the document:
    /usr/docs/classes/Fraction.pdf
*/
```

Which style of comment you use is entirely up to you. Just note that you cannot nest the /* style comments.

Get into the habit of inserting comment statements in the program as you write it or type it into the computer, for three good reasons. First, documenting the program while the particular program logic is still fresh in your mind is much easier than going back and rethinking the logic after the program has been completed. Second, by inserting comments into the program at such an early stage of the game, you can reap the benefits of the comments during the debug phase, when program logic errors are isolated and debugged. Not only can a comment help you (and others) read through the program, but it can also help point the way to the source of the logic mistake. Finally, I haven't yet discovered a programmer who actually enjoys documenting a program. In fact, after you've finished debugging your program, you will probably not relish the idea of going back to the program to insert comments. Inserting comments while developing the program makes this sometimes-tedious task a bit easier to handle.

This next line of Program 2.1 tells the compiler to locate and process a file named Foundation.h:

```
#import <Foundation/Foundation.h>
```

This is a system file—that is, not a file that you created. #import says to import or include the information from that file into the program, exactly as if the contents of the file were typed into the program at that point. You imported the file Foundation.h because it has information about other classes and functions that are used later in the program.

In Program 2.1, this line specifies that the name of the program is main:

```
int main (int argc, const char * argv[])
```

main is a special name that indicates precisely where the program is to begin execution. The reserved word int that precedes main specifies the type of value main returns, which is an integer (more about that soon). We ignore what appears between the open and closed parentheses for now; these have to do with *command-line arguments*, a topic we address in Chapter 13, "Underlying C Language Features."

Now that you have identified main to the system, you are ready to specify precisely what this routine is to perform. This is done by enclosing all the program *statements* of the routine within a pair of curly braces. In the simplest case, a statement is just an expression that is terminated with a semicolon. The system treats all the program statements included between the braces as part of the main routine.

The next line in main reads as follows:

```
@autoreleasepool {
```

Any program statements between the { and the matching closing } are executed within a context known an *autorelease pool*. The autorelease pool is a mechanism that allows the system to efficiently manage the memory your application uses as it creates new objects. I mention it in more detail in Chapter 17, "Memory Management and Automatic Reference Counting." Here, we have one statement inside our @autoreleasepool context.

That statement specifies that a routine named NSLog is to be invoked, or *called*. The parameter, or *argument,* to be passed or handed to the NSLog routine is the following string of characters:

```
@"Programming is fun!"
```

Here, the @ sign immediately precedes a string of characters enclosed in a pair of double quotes. Collectively, this is known as a constant NSString object.

> **Note**
>
> If you have C programming experience, you might be puzzled by the leading @ character. Without that leading @ character, you are writing a constant C-style string; with it, you are writing an NSString string object. More on this topic in Chapter 15, "Numbers, Strings, and Collections."

The NSLog routine is a function that simply displays or logs its argument (or arguments, as you will see shortly). Before doing so, however, it displays the date and time the routine is executed, the program name, and some other numbers not described here. Throughout the rest of this book, we don't bother to show this text that NSLog inserts before your output.

You must terminate all program statements in Objective-C with a semicolon (;). This is why a semicolon appears immediately after the closed parenthesis of the NSLog call.

The final program statement in main looks like this:

```
return 0;
```

It says to terminate execution of main and to send back, or *return,* a status value of 0. By convention, 0 means that the program ended normally. Any nonzero value typically means some problem occurred; for example, perhaps the program couldn't locate a file that it needed.

Now that you have finished discussing your first program, let's modify it to also display the phrase "And programming in Objective-C is even more fun!" You can do this by simply adding another call to the NSLog routine, as shown in Program 2.2. Remember that every Objective-C program statement must be terminated by a semicolon. Note that we've removed the leading comment lines in all the following program examples.

Program 2.2

```
#import <Foundation/Foundation.h>

int main (int argc, const char * argv[])
{
    @autoreleasepool {
        NSLog (@"Programming is fun!");
        NSLog (@"Programming in Objective-C is even more fun!");
    }
    return 0;
}
```

If you type in Program 2.2 and then compile and execute it, you can expect the following output (again, without showing the text that NSLog normally prepends to the output).

Program 2.2   **Output**

```
Programming is fun!
Programming in Objective-C is even more fun!
```

As you will see from the next program example, you don't need to make a separate call to the NSLog routine for each line of output.

First, let's talk about a special two-character sequence. The backslash (\) and the letter n are known collectively as the *newline* character. A newline character tells the system to do precisely what its name implies: go to a new line. Any characters to be printed after the newline character then appear on the next line of the display. In fact, the newline character is very similar in concept to the carriage return key on a typewriter (remember those?).

Study the program listed in Program 2.3 and try to predict the results before you examine the output (no cheating, now!).

Program 2.3

```
#import <Foundation/Foundation.h>

int main (int argc, const char *argv[])
{
    @autoreleasepool {
        NSLog (@"Testing...\n..1\n...2\n....3");
    }
    return 0;
}
```

Program 2.3   **Output**

```
Testing...
..1
...2
....3
```

Displaying the Values of Variables

Not only can simple phrases be displayed with NSLog, but the values of variables and the results of computations can be displayed as well. Program 2.4 uses the NSLog routine to display the results of adding two numbers, 50 and 25.

Program 2.4

```
#import <Foundation/Foundation.h>

int main (int argc, const char *argv[])
{
    @autoreleasepool {
        int sum;

        sum = 50 + 25;
        NSLog (@"The sum of 50 and 25 is %i", sum);
    }

    return 0;
}
```

Program 2.4 **Output**

```
The sum of 50 and 25 is 75
```

The first program statement inside main after the autorelease pool is set up defines the variable sum to be of type integer. You must define all program variables before you can use them in a program. The definition of a variable specifies to the Objective-C compiler how the program should use it. The compiler needs this information to generate the correct instructions to store and retrieve values into and out of the variable. A variable defined as type int can be used to hold only integral values—that is, values without decimal places. Examples of integral values are 3, 5, -20, and 0. Numbers with decimal places, such as 2.14, 2.455, and 27.0, are known as *floating-point* numbers and are real numbers.

The integer variable sum stores the result of the addition of the two integers 50 and 25. We have intentionally left a blank line following the definition of this variable to visually separate the variable declarations of the routine from the program statements; this is strictly a matter of style. Sometimes adding a single blank line in a program can make the program more readable.

The program statement reads as it would in most other programming languages:

```
sum = 50 + 25;
```

The number 50 is added (as indicated by the plus sign) to the number 25, and the result is stored (as indicated by the assignment operator, the equals sign) in the variable sum.

The NSLog routine call in Program 2.4 now has two arguments enclosed within the parentheses. These arguments are separated by a comma. The first argument to the NSLog routine is always the character string to be displayed. However, along with the display of the character string, you often want to have the value of certain program variables displayed as well. In this case, you want to have the value of the variable sum displayed after these characters are displayed:

```
The sum of 50 and 25 is
```

The percent character inside the first argument is a special character recognized by the NSLog function. The character that immediately follows the percent sign specifies what type of value is to be displayed at that point. In the previous program, the NSLog routine recognizes the letter i as signifying that an integer value is to be displayed.

Whenever the NSLog routine finds the %i characters inside a character string, it automatically displays the value of the next argument to the routine. Because sum is the next argument to NSLog, its value is automatically displayed after "The sum of 50 and 25 is."

Now try to predict the output from Program 2.5.

Program 2.5

```
#import <Foundation/Foundation.h>

int main (int argc, const char *argv[])
{
   @autoreleasepool {
      int value1, value2, sum;

      value1 = 50;
      value2 = 25;
      sum = value1 + value2;

      NSLog (@"The sum of %i and %i is %i", value1, value2, sum);
   }

   return 0;
}
```

Program 2.5 **Output**

```
The sum of 50 and 25 is 75
```

The second program statement inside main defines three variables called value1, value2, and sum, all of type int. This statement could have equivalently been expressed using three separate statements, as follows:

```
int value1;
int value2;
int sum;
```

After the three variables have been defined, the program assigns the value 50 to the variable value1 and then the value 25 to value2. The sum of these two variables is then computed and the result assigned to the variable sum.

The call to the NSLog routine now contains four arguments. Once again, the first argument, commonly called the *format string,* describes to the system how the remaining arguments are to be displayed. The value of value1 displays immediately following the phrase "The sum of." Similarly, the values of value2 and sum will print at the points indicated by the next two occurrences of the %i characters in the format string.

Summary

After reading this introductory chapter on developing programs in Objective-C, you should have a good feel about what is involved in writing a program in Objective-C—and you should be able to develop a small program on your own. In the next chapter, you begin to examine some of the intricacies of this powerful and flexible programming language. But first, try your hand at the exercises that follow, to make sure you understand the concepts presented in this chapter.

Exercises

1. Type in and run the five programs presented in this chapter. Compare the output produced by each program with the output presented after each program.

2. Write a program that displays the following text:

    ```
    In Objective-C, lowercase letters are significant.
    main is where program execution begins.
    Open and closed braces enclose program statements in a routine.
    All program statements must be terminated by a semicolon.
    ```

3. What output would you expect from the following program?

    ```
    #import <Foundation/Foundation.h>
    int main (int argc, const char * argv[])
    {
        @autoreleasepool {
            int i;
            i = 1;
            NSLog (@"Testing...");
            NSLog (@"....%i", i);
            NSLog (@"...%i",  i + 1);
            NSLog (@"..%i", i + 2);
        }
        return 0;
    }
    ```

4. Write a program that subtracts the value 15 from 87 and displays the result, together with an appropriate message.

5. Identify the syntactic errors in the following program. Then type in and run the corrected program to make sure you have identified all the mistakes:

```
#import <Foundation/Foundation.h>

int main (int argc, const char *argv[]);
(
    @autoreleasepool {
        INT sum;
        /* COMPUTE RESULT //
        sum = 25 + 37 - 19
        / DISPLAY RESULTS /
        NSLog (@'The answer is %i' sum);
    }
    return 0;
}
```

6. What output would you expect from the following program?

```
#import <Foundation/Foundation.h>

int main (int argc, const char *argv[])
{
    @autoreleasepool {
        int answer, result;

        answer = 100;
        result = answer - 10;

        NSLog (@"The result is %i\n", result + 5);
    }
    return 0;
}
```

3

Classes, Objects, and Methods

In this chapter, you learn about some key concepts in object-oriented programming and start working with classes in Objective-C. You need to learn a little bit of terminology, but we keep it fairly informal. We also cover only some of the basic terms here because you can easily get overwhelmed. Refer to Appendix A, "Glossary," at the end of this book for more precise definitions of these terms.

What Is an Object, Anyway?

An object is a thing. Think about object-oriented programming as a thing and something you want to do to that thing. This is in contrast to a programming language such as C, known as a procedural programming language. In C, you typically think about what you want to do first and then you worry about the objects, almost the opposite of object orientation.

Consider an example from everyday life. Let's assume that you own a car, which is obviously an object, and one that you own. You don't have just any car; you have a particular car that was manufactured in a factory, maybe in Detroit, maybe in Japan, or maybe someplace else. Your car has a vehicle identification number (VIN) that uniquely identifies that car here in the United States.

In object-oriented parlance, your particular car is an *instance* of a car. Continuing with the terminology, car is the name of the *class* from which this instance was created. So each time a new car is manufactured, a new instance from the class of cars is created, and each instance of the car is referred to as an *object*.

Your car might be silver, have a black interior, be a convertible or hardtop, and so on. In addition, you perform certain actions with your car. For example, you drive your car, fill it with gas, (hopefully) wash it, take it in for service, and so on. Table 3.1 depicts this.

Table 3.1   **Actions on Objects**

Object	What You Do with It
Your car	Drive it
	Fill it with gas
	Wash it
	Service it

The actions listed in Table 3.1 can be done with your car, and they can be done with other cars as well. For example, your sister drives her car, washes it, fills it with gas, and so on.

Instances and Methods

A unique occurrence of a class is an *instance,* and the actions that are performed on the instance are called *methods.* In some cases, a method can be applied to an instance of the class or to the class itself. For example, washing your car applies to an instance. (In fact, all the methods listed in Table 3.1 can be considered instance methods.) Finding out how many types of cars a manufacturer makes would apply to the class, so it would be a class method.

Suppose you have two cars that came off the assembly line and are seemingly identical: They both have the same interior, same paint color, and so on. They might start out the same, but as each car is used by its respective owner, its unique characteristics or *properties* change. For example, one car might end up with a scratch on it, and the other might have more miles on it. Each instance or object contains not only information about its initial characteristics acquired from the factory but also its current characteristics. Those characteristics can change dynamically. As you drive your car, the gas tank becomes depleted, the car gets dirtier, and the tires get a little more worn.

Applying a method to an object can affect the *state* of that object. If your method is to "fill up my car with gas," after that method is performed, your car's gas tank will be full. The method then will have affected the state of the car's gas tank.

The key concepts here are that objects are unique representations from a class, and each object contains some information (data) that is typically private to that object. The methods provide the means of accessing and changing that data.

The Objective-C programming language has the following particular syntax for applying methods to classes and instances:

```
[ ClassOrInstance method ];
```

In this syntax, a left bracket is followed by the name of a class or instance of that class, which is followed by one or more spaces, which is followed by the method you want to perform. Finally, it is closed off with a right bracket and a terminating semicolon. When you ask a class or an instance to perform some action, you say that you are sending it a *message;* the recipient of that message is called the *receiver.* So another way to look at the general format described previously is as follows:

```
[ receiver message ];
```

Let's go back to the previous list and write everything in this new syntax. Before you do that, though, you need to get your new car. Go to the factory for that, like so:

```
yourCar = [Car new];      get a new car
```

You send a new message to the Car class (the receiver of the message) asking it to give you a new car. The resulting object (which represents your unique car) is then stored in the variable yourCar. From now on, yourCar can be used to refer to your instance of the car, which you got from the factory.

Because you went to the factory to get the car, the method new is called a *factory* or *class* method. The rest of the actions on your new car will be instance methods because they apply to your car. Here are some sample message expressions you might write for your car:

```
[yourCar prep];          get it ready for first-time use
[yourCar drive];         drive your car
[yourCar wash];          wash your car
[yourCar getGas];        put gas in your car if you need it
[yourCar service];       service your car

[yourCar topDown];       if it's a convertible
[yourCar topUp];
currentMileage = [yourCar odometer];
```

This last example shows an instance method that returns information—presumably, the current mileage, as indicated on the odometer. Here, we store that information inside a variable in our program called currentMileage.

Here's an example of where a method takes an *argument* that specifies a particular value that may differ from one method call to the next:

```
[yourCar setSpeed: 55];  set the speed to 55 mph
```

Your sister, Sue, can use the same methods for her own instance of a car:

```
[suesCar drive];
[suesCar wash];
[suesCar getGas];
```

Applying the same methods to different objects is one of the key concepts of object-oriented programming, and you'll learn more about it later.

You probably won't need to work with cars in your programs. Your objects will likely be computer-oriented things, such as windows, rectangles, pieces of text, or maybe even a calculator or a playlist of songs. And just like the methods used for your cars, your methods might look similar, as in the following:

`[myWindow erase];`	Clear the window
`theArea = [myRect area];`	Calculate the area of the rectangle
`[userText spellCheck];`	Spell-check some text
`[deskCalculator clearEntry];`	Clear the last entry
`[favoritePlaylist showSongs];`	Show the songs in a playlist of favorites
`[phoneNumber dial];`	Dial a phone number
`[myTable reloadData];`	Show the updated table's data
`n = [aTouch tapCount];`	Store the number of times the display was tapped

An Objective-C Class for Working with Fractions

Now it's time to define an actual class in Objective-C and learn how to work with instances of the class.

Once again, you'll learn procedure first. As a result, the actual program examples might not seem very practical. We get into more practical stuff later.

Suppose that you need to write a program to work with fractions. Maybe you need to deal with adding, subtracting, multiplying, and so on. If you didn't know about classes, you might start with a simple program that looked like this.

Program 3.1

```
// Simple program to work with fractions

#import <Foundation/Foundation.h>

int main (int argc, char * argv[])
{
    @autoreleasepool {
        int   numerator = 1;
        int   denominator = 3;
        NSLog (@"The fraction is %i/%i", numerator, denominator);
    }
    return 0;
}
```

Program 3.1 **Output**

```
The fraction is 1/3
```

In Program 3.1, the fraction is represented in terms of its numerator and denominator. After the @autoreleasepool directive, the two lines in main both declare the variables numerator and denominator as integers and assign them initial values of 1 and 3, respectively. This is equivalent to the following lines:

```
int numerator, denominator;

numerator = 1;
denominator = 3;
```

We represented the fraction 1/3 by storing 1 in the variable numerator and 3 in the variable denominator. If you needed to store a lot of fractions in your program, this could be cumbersome. Each time you wanted to refer to the fraction, you'd have to refer to the corresponding numerator and denominator. And performing operations on these fractions would be just as awkward.

It would be better if you could define a fraction as a single entity and collectively refer to its numerator and denominator with a single name, such as myFraction. You can do that in Objective-C, and it starts by defining a new class.

Program 3.2 duplicates the functionality of Program 3.1 using a new class called Fraction. Here, then, is the program, followed by a detailed explanation of how it works.

Program 3.2

```
// Program to work with fractions - class version

#import <Foundation/Foundation.h>

//---- @interface section ----

@interface Fraction: NSObject

-(void)    print;
-(void)    setNumerator: (int) n;
-(void)    setDenominator: (int) d;

@end

//---- @implementation section ----

@implementation Fraction
{
    int  numerator;
```

```
    int  denominator;
}
-(void) print
{
    NSLog (@"%i/%i", numerator, denominator);
}

-(void) setNumerator: (int) n
{
    numerator = n;
}

-(void) setDenominator: (int) d
{
    denominator = d;
}

@end

//---- program section ----


int main (int argc, char * argv[])
{
    @autoreleasepool {
        Fraction  *myFraction;

        // Create an instance of a Fraction

        myFraction = [Fraction alloc];
        myFraction = [myFraction init];

        // Set fraction to 1/3

        [myFraction setNumerator: 1];
        [myFraction setDenominator: 3];

        // Display the fraction using the print method

        NSLog (@"The value of myFraction is:");
        [myFraction print];
    }
    return 0;
}
```

Program 3.2   **Output**

```
The value of myFraction is:
1/3
```

As you can see from the comments in Program 3.2, the program is logically divided into three sections:

- @interface section

- @implementation section

- program section

The @interface section describes the class and its methods, and the @implementation section describes the data (the *instance variables* that objects from the class will store) and contains the actual code that implements the methods declared in the interface section. The program section contains the program code to carry out the intended purpose of the program.

> **Note**
>
> You can also declare the instance variables for a class in the interface section. The ability to do it in the implementation section was added as of Xcode 4.2 and is considered a better way to define a class. You learn more about why in a later chapter.

Each of these sections is a part of every Objective-C program, even though you might not need to write each section yourself. As you'll see, each section is typically put in its own file. For now, however, we keep it all together in a single file.

The @interface Section

When you define a new class, you have to tell the Objective-C compiler where the class came from. That is, you have to name its *parent* class. Next, you need to define the type of operations, or *methods,* that can be used when working with objects from this class. And, as you learn in a later chapter, you also list items known as *properties* in this special section of the program called the @interface section. The general format of this section looks like this:

```
@interface NewClassName: ParentClassName
    propertyAndMethodDeclarations;
@end
```

By convention, class names begin with an uppercase letter, even though it's not required. This enables someone reading your program to distinguish class names from other types of variables by simply looking at the first character of the name. Let's take a short diversion to talk a little about forming names in Objective-C.

Choosing Names

In Chapter 2, "Programming in Objective-C," you used several variables to store integer (int) values. For example, you used the variable sum in Program 2.4 to store the result of the addition of the two integers 50 and 25.

The Objective-C language allows you to store data types other than just integers in variables as well, as long as the proper declaration for the variable is made before it is used in the program. Variables can be used to store floating-point numbers, characters, and even objects (or, more precisely, references to objects).

The rules for forming names are quite simple: They must begin with a letter or underscore (_), and they can be followed by any combination of letters (uppercase or lowercase), underscores, or the digits 0 through 9. The following is a list of valid names:

- sum
- pieceFlag
- i
- myLocation
- numberOfMoves
- sysFlag
- ChessBoard

However, the following names are not valid for the stated reasons:

- sum$value $—Is not a valid character.
- piece flag—Embedded spaces are not permitted.
- 3Spencer—Names cannot start with a number.
- int—This is a reserved word.

int cannot be used as a variable name because its use has a special meaning to the Objective-C compiler. This use is known as a *reserved name* or *reserved word*. In general, any name that has special significance to the Objective-C compiler cannot be used as a variable name.

Always remember that uppercase and lowercase letters are distinct in Objective-C. Therefore, the variable names sum, Sum, and SUM each refer to a different variable. As noted, when naming a class, start it with a capital letter. Instance variables, objects, and method names, however, typically begin with lowercase letters. To aid readability, capital letters are used inside names to indicate the start of a new word, as in the following examples:

- AddressBook—This could be a class name.
- currentEntry—This could be an object.

- `addNewEntry`—This could be a method name.

When deciding on a name, keep one recommendation in mind: Don't be lazy. Pick names that reflect the intended use of the variable or object. The reasons are obvious. Just as with the comment statement, meaningful names can dramatically increase the readability of a program and will pay off in the debug and documentation phases. In fact, the documentation task will probably be much easier because the program will be more self-explanatory.

Here, again, is the `@interface` section from Program 3.2:

```
//---- @interface section ----

@interface Fraction: NSObject

-(void) print;
-(void) setNumerator: (int) n;
-(void) setDenominator: (int) d;

@end
```

The name of the new class is `Fraction`, and its parent class is `NSObject`. (We talk in greater detail about parent classes in Chapter 8, "Inheritance.") The `NSObject` class is defined in the file `NSObject.h`, which is automatically included in your program whenever you import `Foundation.h`.

Class and Instance Methods

You have to define methods to work with your `Fractions`. You need to be able to set the value of a fraction to a particular value. Because you won't have direct access to the internal representation of a fraction (in other words, direct access to its instance variables), you must write methods to set the numerator and denominator. You'll also write a method called `print` that will display the value of a fraction. Here's what the declaration for the `print` method looks like in the interface file:

```
-(void) print;
```

The leading minus sign (-) tells the Objective-C compiler that the method is an instance method. The only other option is a plus sign (+), which indicates a class method. A class method is one that performs some operation on the class itself, such as creating a new instance of the class.

An instance method performs some operation on a particular instance of a class, such as setting its value, retrieving its value, displaying its value, and so on. Referring to the car example, after you have manufactured the car, you might need to fill it with gas. The operation of filling it with gas is performed on a particular car, so it is analogous to an instance method.

Return Values

When you declare a new method, you have to tell the Objective-C compiler whether the method returns a value and, if it does, what type of value it returns. You do this by enclosing the return type in parentheses after the leading minus or plus sign. So this declaration specifies that the instance method called currentAge returns an integer value:

```
-(int) currentAge;
```

Similarly, this line declares a method that returns a double precision value. (You learn more about this data type in Chapter 4, "Data Types and Expressions.")

```
-(double) retrieveDoubleValue;
```

A value is returned from a method using the Objective-C return statement, similar to the way in which we returned a value from main in previous program examples.

If the method returns no value, you indicate that using the type void, as in the following:

```
-(void) print;
```

This declares an instance method called print that returns no value. In such a case, you do not need to execute a return statement at the end of your method. Alternatively, you can execute a return without any specified value, as in the following:

```
return;
```

Method Arguments

Two other methods are declared in the @interface section from Program 3.2:

```
-(void) setNumerator: (int) n;
-(void) setDenominator: (int) d;
```

These are both instance methods that return no value. Each method takes an integer argument, which is indicated by the (int) in front of the argument name. In the case of setNumerator, the name of the argument is n. This name is arbitrary and is the name the method uses to refer to the argument. Therefore, the declaration of setNumerator specifies that one integer argument, called n, will be passed to the method and that no value will be returned. This is similar for setDenominator, except that the name of its argument is d.

Notice the syntax of the declaration for these methods. Each method name ends with a colon, which tells the Objective-C compiler that the method expects to see an argument. Next, the type of the argument is specified, enclosed in a set of parentheses, in much the same way the return type is specified for the method itself. Finally, the symbolic name to be used to identify that argument in the method is specified. The entire declaration is terminated with a semicolon. Figure 3.1 depicts this syntax.

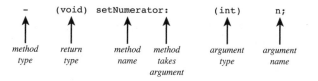

Figure 3.1   Declaring a method

When a method takes an argument, you also append a colon to the method name when refer-ring to the method. Therefore, `setNumerator:` and `setDenominator:` is the correct way to identify these two methods, each of which takes a single argument. Also, identifying the `print` method without a trailing colon indicates that this method does not take any arguments. In Chapter 7, "More on Classes," you'll see how methods that take more than one argument are identified.

The `@implementation` Section

As noted, the `@implementation` section contains the actual code for the methods you declared in the `@interface` section. You have to specify what type of data is to be stored in the objects of this class. That is, you have to describe the data that members of the class will contain. These members are called the *instance variables*. Just as a point of terminology, you say that you declare the methods in the `@interface` section and that you *define* them (that is, give the actual code) in the `@implementation` section. The general format for the `@implementation` section is as follows:

```
@implementation NewClassName
{
    memberDeclarations;
}
  methodDefinitions;
@end
```

NewClassName is the same name that was used for the class in the `@interface` section. You can use the trailing colon followed by the parent class name, as we did in the `@interface` section:

```
@implementation Fraction: NSObject
```

However, this is optional and typically not done.

The *memberDeclarations* section specifies what types of data are stored in a `Fraction`, along with the names of those data types. As you can see, this section is enclosed inside its own set of curly braces. For your `Fraction` class, these declarations say that a `Fraction` object has two integer members, called `numerator` and `denominator`:

```
int  numerator;
int  denominator;
```

The members declared in this section are known as the *instance variables*. Each time you create a new object, a new and unique set of instance variables also is created. Therefore, if you have two Fractions, one called fracA and another called fracB, each will have its own set of instance variables—that is, fracA and fracB each will have its own separate numerator and denominator. The Objective-C system automatically keeps track of this for you, which is one of the nicer things about working with objects.

The *methodDefinitions* part of the @implementation section contains the code for each method specified in the @interface section. Similar to the @interface section, each method's definition starts by identifying the type of method (class or instance), its return type, and its arguments and their types. However, instead of the line ending with a semicolon, the code for the method follows, enclosed inside a set of curly braces. It's noted here that you can have the compiler automatically generate methods for you by using a special @synthesize directive. Chapter 7 covers this in detail.

Consider the @implementation section from Program 3.2:

```
//---- @implementation section ----
@implementation Fraction
{
    int   numerator;
    int   denominator;
}

-(void) print
{
    NSLog (@"%i/%i", numerator, denominator);
}

-(void) setNumerator: (int) n
{
    numerator = n;
}

-(void) setDenominator: (int) d
{
    denominator = d;
}

@end
```

The print method uses NSLog to display the values of the instance variables numerator and denominator. But to which numerator and denominator does this method refer? It refers to the instance variables contained in the object that is the receiver of the message. That's an important concept, and we return to it shortly.

The `setNumerator:` method stores the integer argument you called n in the instance variable numerator. Similarly, `setDenominator:` stores the value of its argument d in the instance variable denominator.

The `program` Section

The `program` section contains the code to solve your particular problem, which can be spread out across many files, if necessary. Somewhere you must have a routine called main, as previously noted. That's where your program always begins execution. Here's the program section from Program 3.2:

```
//---- program section ----

int main (int argc, char * argv[])
{
   @autoreleasepool {
      Fraction  *myFraction;

      // Create an instance of a Fraction and initialize it

      myFraction = [Fraction alloc];
      myFraction = [myFraction init];

      // Set fraction to 1/3

      [myFraction setNumerator: 1];
      [myFraction setDenominator: 3];

      // Display the fraction using the print method

      NSLog (@"The value of myFraction is:");
      [myFraction print];
   }

   return 0;
}
```

Inside main, you define a variable called myFraction with the following line:

```
Fraction *myFraction;
```

This line says that myFraction is an object of type Fraction; that is, myFraction is used to store values from your new Fraction class. The asterisk that precedes the variable name is described in more detail later.

Now that you have an object to store a `Fraction`, you need to create one, just as you ask the factory to build you a new car. This is done with the following line:

```
myFraction = [Fraction alloc];
```

`alloc` is short for *allocate*. You want to allocate memory storage space for a new fraction. This expression sends a message to your newly created `Fraction` class:

```
[Fraction alloc]
```

You are asking the `Fraction` class to apply the `alloc` method, but you never defined an `alloc` method, so where did it come from? The method was inherited from a parent class. Chapter 8 deals with this topic in detail.

When you send the `alloc` message to a class, you get back a new instance of that class. In Program 3.2, the returned value is stored inside your variable `myFraction`. The `alloc` method is guaranteed to zero out all of an object's instance variables. However, that doesn't mean that the object has been properly initialized for use. You need to initialize an object after you allocate it.

This is done with the next statement in Program 3.2, which reads as follows:

```
myFraction = [myFraction init];
```

Again, you are using a method here that you didn't write yourself. The `init` method initializes the instance of a class. Note that you are sending the `init` message to `myFraction`. That is, you want to initialize a specific `Fraction` object here, so you don't send it to the class; you send it to an instance of the class. Make sure that you understand this point before continuing.

The `init` method also returns a value—namely, the initialized object. You store the return value in your `Fraction` variable `myFraction`.

The two-line sequence of allocating a new instance of class and then initializing it is done so often in Objective-C that the two messages are typically combined, as follows:

```
myFraction = [[Fraction alloc] init];
```

This inner message expression is evaluated first:

```
[Fraction alloc]
```

As you know, the result of this message expression is the actual `Fraction` that is allocated. Instead of storing the result of the allocation in a variable, as you did before, you directly apply the `init` method to it. So, again, first you allocate a new `Fraction` and then you initialize it. The result of the initialization is then assigned to the `myFraction` variable.

As a final shorthand technique, the allocation and initialization is often incorporated directly into the declaration line, as in the following:

```
Fraction *myFraction = [[Fraction alloc] init];
```

Returning to Program 3.2, you are now ready to set the value of your fraction. These program lines do just that:

```
// Set fraction to 1/3

[myFraction setNumerator: 1];
[myFraction setDenominator: 3];
```

The first message statement sends the `setNumerator:` message to `myFraction`. The argument that is supplied is the value `1`. Control is then sent to the `setNumerator:` method you defined for your `Fraction` class. The Objective-C system knows that it is the method from this class to use because it knows that `myFraction` is an object from the `Fraction` class.

Inside the `setNumerator:` method, the passed value of `1` is stored inside the variable n. The single program line in that method stores that value in the instance variable `numerator`. So, you have effectively set the numerator of `myFraction` to `1`.

The message that invokes the `setDenominator:` method on `myFraction` follows next. The argument of `3` is assigned to the variable d inside the `setDenominator:` method. This value is then stored inside the `denominator` instance variable, thus completing the assignment of the value `1/3` to `myFraction`. Now you're ready to display the value of your fraction, which you do with the following lines of code from Program 3.2:

```
// Display the fraction using the print method

NSLog (@"The value of myFraction is:");
[myFraction print];
```

The `NSLog` call simply displays the following text:

```
The value of myFraction is:
```

The following message expression invokes the `print` method:

```
[myFraction print];
```

Inside the `print` method, the values of the instance variables `numerator` and `denominator` are displayed, separated by a slash character.

Note

In the past, iOS programmers were responsible for telling the system when they were done using an object that they allocated by sending the object a `release` message. That was done in accordance with a memory management system known as *manual reference counting*. As of Xcode 4.2, programmers no longer have to worry about this and can rely on the system to take care of releasing memory as necessary. This is done through a mechanism known as *Automatic Reference Counting,* or ARC for short. ARC is enabled by default when you compile new applications using Xcode 4.2 or later.

It seems as if you had to write a lot more code to duplicate in Program 3.2 what you did in Program 3.1. That's true for this simple example here; however, the ultimate goal in working with objects is to make your programs easier to write, maintain, and extend. You'll realize that later.

Let's go back for a second to the declaration of myFraction

```
Fraction *myFraction;
```

and the subsequent setting of its values.

The asterisk (*) in front of myFraction in its declaration says that myFraction is actually a reference (or *pointer*) to a Fraction object. The variable myFraction doesn't actually store the fraction's data (that is, its numerator and denominator values). Instead, it stores a reference—which is a actually a memory address—indicating where the object's data is located in memory. When you first declare myFraction as shown, its value is undefined as it has not been set to any value and does not have a default value. We can conceptualize myFraction as a box that holds a value. Initially the box contains some undefined value, as it hasn't been assigned any value, as shown in Figure 3.2.

myFraction

Figure 3.2   Declaring Fraction *myFraction;

When you allocate a new object (using alloc, for example) enough space is reserved in memory to store the object's data, which includes space for its instance variables, plus a little more. The location of where that data is stored (the reference to the data) is returned by the alloc routine, and assigned to the variable myFraction. This all takes place when this statement is executed in Program 3.2:

```
myFraction = [Fraction alloc];
```

The allocation of the object and the storage of the reference to that object in myFraction is depicted in Figure 3.3.

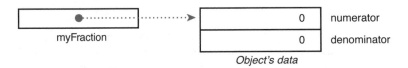

Figure 3.3   Relationship between myFraction and its data

> **Note**
>
> More data is stored with the object than just that indicated, but you don't need to worry about that here. You'll note that the instance variables are shown as being set to 0. That's currently being handled by the `alloc` method. However, the object still has not been properly initialized. You still need to use the `init` method on the newly allocated object.

Notice the directed line in Figure 3.3. This indicates the connection that has been made between the variable `myFraction` and the allocated object. (The value stored inside `myFraction` is actually a memory address. It's at that memory address that the object's data is stored.)

Subsequently in Program 3.2, the fraction's numerator and denominator are set. Figure 3.4 depicts the fully initialized `Fraction` object with its numerator set to 1 and its denominator set to 3.

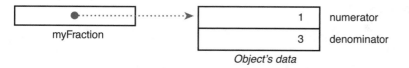

Figure 3.4   Setting the fraction's numerator and denominator

The next example shows how you can work with more than one fraction in your program. In Program 3.3, you set one fraction to `2/3`, set another to `3/7`, and display them both.

Program 3.3

```
// Program to work with fractions - cont'd

#import <Foundation/Foundation.h>

//---- @interface section ----

@interface Fraction: NSObject

-(void) print;
-(void) setNumerator: (int) n;
-(void) setDenominator: (int) d;

@end

//---- @implementation section ----

@implementation Fraction
{
    int  numerator;
```

```
      int   denominator;
}

-(void) print
{
    NSLog (@"%i/%i", numerator, denominator);
}

-(void) setNumerator: (int) n
{
    numerator = n;
}

-(void) setDenominator: (int) d
{
    denominator = d;
}

@end

//---- program section ----

int main (int argc, char * argv[])
{
    @autoreleasepool {

        Fraction  *frac1 = [[Fraction alloc] init];
        Fraction  *frac2 = [[Fraction alloc] init];

        // Set 1st fraction to 2/3

        [frac1 setNumerator: 2];
        [frac1 setDenominator: 3];

        // Set 2nd fraction to 3/7

        [frac2 setNumerator: 3];
        [frac2 setDenominator: 7];

        // Display the fractions

        NSLog (@"First fraction is:");

        [frac1 print];

        NSLog (@"Second fraction is:");
        [frac2 print];
```

```
    }
    return 0;
}
```

Program 3.3 **Output**

```
First fraction is:
2/3
Second fraction is:
3/7
```

The @interface and @implementation sections remain unchanged from Program 3.2. The program creates two Fraction objects, called frac1 and frac2, and then assigns the value 2/3 to the first fraction and 3/7 to the second. Realize that when the setNumerator: method is applied to frac1 to set its numerator to 2, the instance variable frac1 gets its instance variable numerator set to 2. Also, when frac2 uses the same method to set its numerator to 3, its distinct instance variable numerator is set to the value 3. Each time you create a new object, it gets its own distinct set of instance variables. Figure 3.5 depicts this.

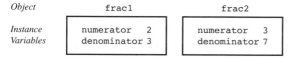

Figure 3.5   Unique instance variables

Based on which object is getting sent the message, the correct instance variables are referenced. Therefore, here frac1's numerator is referenced whenever setNumerator: uses the name numerator inside the method:

```
[frac1 setNumerator: 2];
```

That's because frac1 is the receiver of the message.

Accessing Instance Variables and Data Encapsulation

You've seen how the methods that deal with fractions can access the two instance variables numerator and denominator directly by name. In fact, an instance method can always directly access its instance variables. A class method can't, however, because it's dealing only with the class itself, not with any instances of the class. (Think about that for a second.) But what if you wanted to access your instance variables from someplace else (for example, from inside your main routine)? You can't do that directly because they are hidden. The fact that they are hidden from you is a key concept called *data encapsulation*. It enables someone writing class definitions to extend and modify the class definitions, without worrying about whether programmers (that is, users of the class) are tinkering with the internal details of the class. Data encapsulation provides a nice layer of insulation between the programmer and the class developer.

You can access your instance variables in a clean way by writing special methods to set and retrieve their values. We wrote `setNumerator:` and `setDenominator:` methods to set the values of the two instance variables in our `Fraction` class. To retrieve the values of those instance variables, you need to write two new methods. For example, create two new methods called, appropriately enough, `numerator` and `denominator` to access the corresponding instance variables of the `Fraction` that is the receiver of the message. The result is the corresponding integer value, which you return. Here are the declarations for your two new methods:

```
-(int) numerator;
-(int) denominator;
```

And here are the definitions:

```
-(int) numerator
{
    return numerator;
}

-(int) denominator
{
    return denominator;
}
```

Note that the names of the methods and the instance variables they access are the same. There's no problem doing this (although it might seem a little odd at first); in fact, it is common practice. Program 3.4 tests your two new methods.

Program 3.4

```
// Program to access instance variables - cont'd

#import <Foundation/Foundation.h>

//---- @interface section ----

@interface Fraction: NSObject

-(void) print;
-(void) setNumerator: (int) n;
-(void) setDenominator: (int) d;
-(int)  numerator;
-(int)  denominator;

@end
```

```objc
//---- @implementation section ----

@implementation Fraction
{
   int  numerator;
   int  denominator;
}

-(void) print
{
   NSLog (@"%i/%i", numerator, denominator);
}

-(void) setNumerator: (int) n
{
    numerator = n;
}

-(void) setDenominator: (int) d
{
    denominator = d;
}

-(int) numerator
{
    return numerator;
}

-(int) denominator
{
    return denominator;
}

@end

//---- program section ----

int main (int argc, char * argv[])
{
   @autoreleasepool {
      Fraction  *myFraction = [[Fraction alloc] init];

      // Set fraction to 1/3

      [myFraction setNumerator: 1];
      [myFraction setDenominator: 3];
```

```
    // Display the fraction using our two new methods

    NSLog (@"The value of myFraction is: %i/%i",
        [myFraction numerator], [myFraction denominator]);
    }

    return 0;
}
```

Program 3.4 **Output**

```
The value of myFraction is 1/3
```

This NSLog statement displays the results of sending two messages to myFraction: the first to retrieve the value of its numerator, and the second the value of its denominator:

```
NSLog (@"The value of myFraction is: %i/%i",
    [myFraction numerator], [myFraction denominator]);
```

So, in the first message call, the numerator message is sent to the Fraction object myFraction. In that method, the code returns the value of the numerator instance variable for that fraction. Remember, the context of a method while it is executing is the object that is the receiver of the message. So, when the numerator method accesses and returns the value of the numerator instance variable, it's myFraction's numerator that is accessed and returned. That returned integer value is then passed along to NSLog to be displayed.

For the second message call, the denominator method is called to access and return the value of myFraction's denominator, which is then passed to NSLog to be displayed.

Incidentally, methods that set the values of instance variables are often collectively referred to as *setters,* and methods used to retrieve the values of instance variables are called *getters*. For the Fraction class, setNumerator: and setDenominator: are the setters, and numerator and denominator are the getters. Collectively, setters and getters are also referred to as *accessor* methods.

Make sure that you understand the difference between setters and the getters. The setters don't return a value, because their purpose is to take an argument and to set the corresponding instance variable to the value of that argument. No value needs to be returned in that case. That's the purpose of a setter: to set the value of an instance variable, so setters typically do not return values. In contrast, the purpose of the getter is to "get" the value of an instance variable stored in an object and to send it back to the program. To do that, the getter must return the value of the instance variable using the return statement.

Again, the idea that you can't directly set or get the value of an instance variable from outside of the methods written for the class, but instead have to write setter and getter methods to do so is the principle of data encapsulation. So, you have to use methods to access this data that is normally hidden to the "outside world." This provides a centralized path to the instance variables and prevents some other code from indirectly changing these values, which would make your programs harder to follow, debug, and modify.

We should also point out that a method called `new` combines the actions of an `alloc` and `init`. So, this line could be used to allocate and initialize a new `Fraction`:

```
Fraction *myFraction = [Fraction new];
```

It's generally better to use the two-step allocation and initialization approach so that you conceptually understand that two distinct events are occurring: You're first creating a new object and then you're initializing it.

Summary

Now you know how to define your own class, create objects or instances of that class, and send messages to those objects. We return to the `Fraction` class in later chapters. You'll learn how to pass multiple arguments to your methods, how to divide your class definitions into separate files, and also how to use key concepts such as inheritance and dynamic binding. However, now it's time to learn more about data types and writing expressions in Objective-C. First, try the exercises that follow to test your understanding of the important points covered in this chapter.

Exercises

1. Which of the following are invalid names? Why?

Int	playNextSong	6_05
_calloc	Xx	alphaBetaRoutine
clearScreen	_1312	z
ReInitialize	_	A$

2. Based on the example of the car in this chapter, think of an object you use every day. Identify a class for that object and write five actions you do with that object.

3. Given the list in exercise 2, use the following syntax to rewrite your list in this format:

    ```
    [instance method];
    ```

4. Imagine that you own a boat and a motorcycle in addition to a car. List the actions you perform with each of these. Do you have any overlap between these actions?

5. Based on question 4, imagine that you have a class called Vehicle and an object called myVehicle that could be either Car, Motorcycle, or Boat. Suppose that you write the following:

```
[myVehicle prep];
[myVehicle getGas];
[myVehicle service];
```

Do you see any advantages of being able to apply an action to an object that could be from one of several classes?

6. In a procedural language such as C, you think about actions and then write code to perform the action on various objects. Referring to the car example, you might write a procedure in C to wash a vehicle and then inside that procedure write code to handle washing a car, washing a boat, washing a motorcycle, and so on. If you took that approach and then wanted to add a new vehicle type (see the previous exercise), do you see advantages or disadvantages to using this procedural approach over an object-oriented approach?

7. Define a class called XYPoint that will hold a Cartesian coordinate (x, y), where x and y are integers. Define methods to individually set the x and y coordinates of a point and retrieve their values. Write an Objective-C program to implement your new class and test it.

4

Data Types and Expressions

In this chapter, we take a look at the basic data types and describe some fundamental rules for forming arithmetic expressions in Objective-C.

Data Types and Constants

You have already encountered the Objective-C basic data type int. As you will recall, a variable declared to be of type int can be used to contain integral values only—that is, values that do not contain decimal digits.

The Objective-C programming language provides three other basic data types: float, double, and char. A variable declared to be of type float can be used for storing floating-point numbers (values containing decimal digits). The double type is the same as type float, typically with roughly twice the range. The char data type can be used to store a single character, such as the letter a, the digit character 6, or a semicolon (more on this later).

In Objective-C, any literal number, single character, or character string is known as a *constant*. For example, the number 58 represents a constant integer value. The string @"Programming in Objective-C is fun." is an example of a constant character string object. The expression @5 is an example of a constant number object, as you'll learn in Chapter 15, "Numbers, Strings, and Collections."

Type int

An integer constant consists of a sequence of one or more digits. A minus sign preceding the sequence indicates that the value is negative. The values 158, –10, and 0 are all valid examples of integer constants. No embedded spaces are permitted between the digits, and commas can't be used. (So, the value 12,000 is not a valid integer constant and must be written as 12000.)

Every value, whether it's a character, an integer, or a floating-point number, has a *range* of values associated with it. This range has to do with the amount of storage allocated to store a particular type of data. In general, that amount is not defined in the language; it typically depends on the computer you're running on and is therefore called *implementation* or *machine dependent.* For example, an integer variable might take 32 bits on your computer, or perhaps it might be stored in 64. If 64 bits were used, much larger numbers can be stored inside integer variables than if 32 bits were used instead.

Type `float`

You can use a variable declared to be of type `float` to store values containing decimal digits. A floating-point constant is distinguished by the presence of a decimal point. The values `3.`, `125.8`, and `-.0001` are all valid examples of floating-point constants. To display a floating-point value, the `NSLog` conversion characters `%f` or `%g` can be used.

Floating-point constants can also be expressed in so-called *scientific notation*. The value `1.7e4` is a floating-point value expressed in this notation that represents the value 1.7×10^4.

As noted, the `double` type is the same as type `float`, only with roughly twice the range.

Type `char`

You can use a `char` variable to store a single character. A character constant is formed by enclosing the character within a pair of single quotation marks. So `'a'`, `';'`, and `'0'` are all valid examples of character constants. The first constant represents the letter a, the second is a semicolon, and the third is the character zero—which is not the same as the number zero. Do not confuse a character constant, which is a single character enclosed in single quotes, with a C-style character string, which is any number of characters enclosed in double quotes. As mentioned in the last chapter, a string of characters enclosed in a pair of double quotes that is preceded by an `@` character is an `NSString` character string object.

The character constant `'\n'`, the newline character, is a valid character constant even though it seems to contradict the rule cited previously. The reason for this is that the backslash character is recognized as a special character. In other words, the Objective-C compiler treats the character `'\n'` as a single character, even though it is actually formed by two characters. Other special characters are initiated with the backslash character. The format characters `%c` can be used in an `NSLog` call to display the value of a `char` variable.

Program 4.1 uses the basic Objective-C data types.

Program 4.1

```
#import <Foundation/Foundation.h>

int main (int argc, char * argv[])
{
   @autoreleasepool {
      int    integerVar = 100;
      float  floatingVar = 331.79;
      double doubleVar = 8.44e+11;
      char   charVar = 'W';
```

```
        NSLog (@"integerVar = %i", integerVar);
        NSLog (@"floatingVar = %f", floatingVar);
        NSLog (@"doubleVar = %e", doubleVar);
        NSLog (@"doubleVar = %g", doubleVar);
        NSLog (@"charVar = %c", charVar);
    }
    return 0;
}
```

Program 4.1 **Output**

```
integerVar = 100
floatingVar = 331.790009
doubleVar = 8.440000e+11
doubleVar = 8.44e+11
charVar = W
```

In the second line of the program's output, notice that the value of 331.79, which is assigned to floatingVar, is actually displayed as 331.790009. The reason for this inaccuracy is the particular way in which numbers are internally represented inside the computer. You have probably come across the same type of inaccuracy when dealing with numbers on your calculator. If you divide 1 by 3 on your calculator, you get the result .33333333, with perhaps some additional 3s tacked on at the end. The string of 3s is the calculator's approximation to one third. Theoretically, there should be an infinite number of 3s. But the calculator can hold only so many digits, thus the inherent inaccuracy of the machine. The same type of inaccuracy applies here: Certain floating-point values cannot be exactly represented inside the computer's memory.

Qualifiers: long, long long, short, unsigned, and signed

If the qualifier long is placed directly before the int declaration, the declared integer variable is of extended range on some computer systems. An example of a long int declaration might be this:

```
long int factorial;
```

This declares the variable factorial to be a long integer variable. As with floats and doubles, the particular range of a long variable depends on your particular computer system.

To display the value of a long int using NSLog, the letter *l* is used as a modifier before the integer format characters. This means that the format characters %li can be used to display the value of a long int in decimal format.

You can also have a `long long int` variable, or even a `long double` variable to hold a floating point number with greater range.

The qualifier `short`, when placed in front of the `int` declaration, tells the Objective-C compiler that the particular variable being declared is used to store fairly small integer values. The motivation for using `short` variables is primarily one of conserving memory space, which can be an issue when the program needs a lot of memory and the amount of available memory is limited.

The final qualifier that can be placed in front of an `int` variable is used when an integer variable will be used to store only positive numbers. The following declares to the compiler that the variable `counter` is used to contain only positive values:

```
unsigned int counter;
```

Restricting the use of an integer variable to the exclusive storage of positive integers extends the range of the integer variable.

Type `id`

The `id` data type is used to store an object of any type. In a sense, it is a generic object type. For example, this line declares `graphicObject` to be a variable of type `id`:

```
id    graphicObject;
```

Methods can be declared to return values of type id, like so:

```
-(id) newObject: (int) type;
```

This declares an instance method called `newObject` that takes a single integer argument called `type` and returns a value of type `id`.

The `id` data type is an important data type used often in this book. We mention it in passing here for the sake of completeness. The `id` type is the basis for very important features in Objective-C known as *polymorphism* and *dynamic binding,* which Chapter 9, "Polymorphism, Dynamic Typing, and Dynamic Binding," discusses extensively.

Table 4.1 summarizes the basic data types and qualifiers.

Table 4.1   **Basic Data Types**

Type	Constant Examples	NSLog chars
char	'a', '\n'	%c
short int	—	%hi, %hx, %ho
unsigned short int	—	%hu, %hx, %ho
int	12, -97, 0xFFE0, 0177	%i, %x, %o
unsigned int	12u, 100U, 0XFFu	%u, %x, %o

Type	Constant Examples	NSLog chars
long int	12L, -2001, 0xffffL	%li, %lx, %lo
unsigned long int	12UL, 100ul, 0xffeeUL	%lu, %lx, %lo
long long int	0xe5e5e5e5LL, 500ll	%lli, %llx, &llo
unsigned long long int	12ull, 0xffeeULL	%llu, %llx, %llo
float	12.34f, 3.1e-5f, 0x1.5p10, 0x1P-1	%f, %e, %g, %a
double	12.34, 3.1e-5, 0x.1p3	%f, %e, %g, %a
long double	12.34L, 3.1e-51	%Lf, $Le, %Lg
id	nil	%p

> **Note**
>
> In the table, a leading zero in front of an integer constant indicates the constant is in octal (base 8) notation, whereas a leading 0x (or 0X) indicates it is in hexadecimal (base 16) notation. A number written as 0x.1p3 represents a hexadecimal floating constant. Don't worry about these formats; they're just summarized in the table here for completeness. Further, suffixes such as f, l (L), u (U), and ll (LL) can also be used to explicitly express constants as floats, longs, unsigned, and long long, respectively.

Arithmetic Expressions

In Objective-C, just as in nearly all programming languages, the plus sign (+) is used to add two values, the minus sign (-) is used to subtract two values, the asterisk (*) is used to multiply two values, and the slash (/) is used to divide two values. These operators are known as binary arithmetic operators because they operate on two values or terms.

Operator Precedence

You have seen how a simple operation such as addition can be performed in Objective-C. The following program further illustrates the operations of subtraction, multiplication, and division. The last two operations performed in the program introduce the notion that one operator can have a higher priority, or precedence, over another operator. In fact, each operator in Objective-C has a precedence associated with it.

This precedence is used to determine how an expression that has more than one operator is evaluated: The operator with the higher precedence is evaluated first. Expressions containing operators of the same precedence are evaluated either from left to right or from right to left, depending on the operator. This is known as the *associative* property of an operator.

Program 4.2

```
// Illustrate the use of various arithmetic operators

#import <Foundation/Foundation.h>

int main (int argc, char * argv[])
{
    @autoreleasepool {
        int    a = 100;
        int    b = 2;
        int    c = 25;
        int    d = 4;
        int    result;

        result = a - b;        // subtraction
        NSLog (@"a - b = %i", result);

        result = b * c;        // multiplication
        NSLog (@"b * c = %i", result);

        result = a / c;        // division
        NSLog (@"a / c = %i", result);

        result = a + b * c;  // precedence
        NSLog (@"a + b * c = %i", result);

        NSLog (@"a * b + c * d = %i", a * b + c * d);
    }
    return 0;
}
```

Program 4.2 **Output**

```
a - b = 98
b * c = 50
a / c = 4
a + b * c = 150
a * b + c * d = 300
```

After declaring the integer variables a, b, c, d, and result, the program assigns the result of subtracting b from a to result and then displays its value with an appropriate NSLog call.

The next statement has the effect of multiplying the value of b by the value of c and storing the product in result:

```
result = b * c;
```

The result of the multiplication is then displayed using an NSLog call that should be familiar to you by now.

The next program statement introduces the division operator, the slash. The NSLog statement displays the result of 4, obtained by dividing 100 by 25, immediately following the division of a by c.

Attempting to divide an integer by zero results in abnormal termination or an exception when the division is attempted. Even if the program does not terminate abnormally, the results obtained by such a division will be meaningless. In Chapter 6, "Making Decisions," you will see how you can check for division by zero before the division operation is performed. If the divisor is determined to be zero, an appropriate action can be taken and the division operation can be averted.

This expression does not produce the result of 2550 (102 × 25); instead, the result displayed by the corresponding NSLog statement is shown as 150:

```
a + b * c
```

This is because Objective-C, like most other programming languages, has rules for the order of evaluating multiple operations or terms in an expression. Evaluation of an expression generally proceeds from left to right. However, the operations of multiplication and division are given precedence over the operations of addition and subtraction. Therefore, the system evaluates the expression

```
a + b * c
```

as follows:

```
a + (b * c)
```

(This is the same way this expression would be evaluated if you applied the basic rules of algebra.)

If you want to alter the order of evaluation of terms inside an expression, you can use parentheses. In fact, the expression listed previously is a perfectly valid Objective-C expression. Thus, the following statement could have been substituted in Program 4.2 to achieve identical results:

```
result = a + (b * c);
```

However, if this expression were used instead, the value assigned to result would be 2550:

```
result = (a + b) * c;
```

This is because the value of a (100) would be added to the value of b (2) before multiplication by the value of c (25) would take place. Parentheses can also be nested, in which case evaluation of the expression proceeds outward from the innermost set of parentheses. Just be sure to have as many closed parentheses as you have open ones.

Notice from the last statement in Program 4.2 that it is perfectly valid to give an expression as an argument to NSLog without having to first assign the result of the expression evaluation to a variable. The expression

```
a * b + c * d
```

is evaluated according to the rules stated previously as

```
(a * b) + (c * d)
```

or

```
(100 * 2) + (25 * 4)
```

The result of 300 is handed to the NSLog routine.

Integer Arithmetic and the Unary Minus Operator

Program 4.3 reinforces what we have just discussed and introduces the concept of integer arithmetic.

Program 4.3

```
// More arithmetic expressions

#import <Foundation/Foundation.h>

int main (int argc, char * argv[])
{
   @autoreleasepool {
      int    a = 25;
      int    b = 2;
      float c = 25.0;
      float d = 2.0;

      NSLog (@"6 + a / 5 * b = %i", 6 + a / 5 * b);
      NSLog (@"a / b * b = %i", a / b * b);
      NSLog (@"c / d * d = %f", c / d * d);
      NSLog (@"-a = %i", -a);
   }
   return 0;
}
```

Program 4.3 **Output**

```
6 + a / 5 * b = 16
a / b * b = 24
c / d * d = 25.000000
-a = -25
```

We inserted extra blank spaces between int and the declaration of a, b, and result in the first three statements to align the declaration of each variable. This helps make the program more readable. You also might have noticed in each program presented thus far that a blank space was placed around each operator. This, too, is not required and is done solely for aesthetic reasons. In general, you can add extra blank spaces just about anywhere that a single blank space is allowed. A few extra presses of the spacebar will prove worthwhile if the resulting program is easier to read.

The expression in the first NSLog call of Program 4.3 reinforces the notion of operator precedence. Evaluation of this expression proceeds as follows:

1. Because division has higher precedence than addition, the value of a (25) is divided by 5 first. This gives the intermediate result of 5.

2. Because multiplication also has higher precedence than addition, the intermediate result of 5 is next multiplied by 2, the value of b, giving a new intermediate result of 10.

3. Finally, the addition of 6 and 10 is performed, giving a final result of 16.

The second NSLog statement introduces a new twist. You would expect that dividing a by b and then multiplying by b would return the value of a, which has been set to 25. But this does not seem to be the case, as shown by the output display of 24. Did the computer lose a bit somewhere along the way? Very unlikely. The fact of the matter is that this expression was evaluated using integer arithmetic.

If you glance back at the declarations for the variables a and b, you will recall that both were declared to be of type int. Whenever a term to be evaluated in an expression consists of two integers, the Objective-C system performs the operation using integer arithmetic. In such a case, all decimal portions of numbers are lost. Therefore, when the value of a is divided by the value of b, or 25 is divided by 2, you get an intermediate result of 12, and *not* 12.5, as you might expect. Multiplying this intermediate result by 2 gives the final result of 24, thus explaining the "lost" digit.

As you can see from the next-to-last NSLog statement in Program 4.3, if you perform the same operation using floating-point values instead of integers, you obtain the expected result.

The decision of whether to use a float variable or an int variable should be made based on the variable's intended use. If you don't need any decimal places, use an integer variable. The resulting program will be more efficient; that is, it will execute more quickly on many computers. However, if you need the decimal place accuracy, the choice is clear. The only question you then must answer is whether to use a float or a double. The answer to this question depends on the desired accuracy of the numbers you are dealing with, as well as their magnitude.

In the last NSLog statement, the value of the variable a is negated by use of the unary minus operator. A *unary* operator is one that operates on a single value, as opposed to a binary operator, which operates on two values. The minus sign actually has a dual role: As a binary operator, it is used for subtracting two values; as a unary operator, it is used to negate a value.

The unary minus operator has higher precedence than all other arithmetic operators, except for the unary plus operator (+), which has the same precedence. So the following expression results in the multiplication of -a by b:

```
c = -a * b;
```

The Modulus Operator

The last arithmetic operator to be presented in this chapter is the modulus operator, which is symbolized by the percent sign (%). Try to determine how this operator works by analyzing the output from Program 4.4.

Program 4.4

```
// The modulus operator

#import <Foundation/Foundation.h>

int main (int argc, char * argv[])
{
    @autoreleasepool {
        int a = 25, b = 5, c = 10, d = 7;

        NSLog (@"a %% b = %i", a % b);
        NSLog (@"a %% c = %i", a % c);
        NSLog (@"a %% d = %i", a % d);
        NSLog (@"a / d * d + a %% d = %i", a / d * d + a % d);
    }
    return 0;
}
```

Program 4.4   **Output**

```
a % b = 0
a % c = 5
a % d = 4
a / d * d + a % d = 25
```

Note the statement inside main that defines and initializes the variables a, b, c, and d in a single statement.

As you know, NSLog uses the character that immediately follows the percent sign to determine how to print its next argument. However, if it is another percent sign that follows, the NSLog routine takes this as an indication that you really intend to display a percent sign and inserts one at the appropriate place in the program's output.

You are correct if you concluded that the function of the modulus operator % is to give the remainder of the first value divided by the second value. In the first example, the remainder, of 25 divided by 5 is 0. If you divide 25 by 10, you would have a remainder of 5, as verified by the second line of output. Dividing 25 by 7 gives a remainder of 4, as shown in the third output line.

Let's now turn our attention to the last arithmetic expression evaluated in the last statement. You will recall that any operations between two integer values in Objective-C are performed with integer arithmetic. Therefore, any remainder resulting from the division of two integer values is simply discarded. Dividing 25 by 7, as indicated by the expression a / d, gives an intermediate result of 3. Multiplying this value by the value of d, which is 7, produces the intermediate result of 21. Finally, adding the remainder of dividing a by d, as indicated by the expression a % d, leads to the final result of 25. It is no coincidence that this value is the same as the value of the variable a. In general, this expression always equals the value of a, assuming, of course, that a and b are both integer values:

```
a / b * b + a % b
```

In fact, the modulus operator % is defined to work only with integer values.

As far as precedence is concerned, the modulus operator has equal precedence to the multiplication and division operators. This implies, of course, that an expression such as

```
table + value % TABLE_SIZE
```

will be evaluated as

```
table + (value % TABLE_SIZE)
```

Integer and Floating-Point Conversions

To effectively develop Objective-C programs, you must understand the rules used for the implicit conversion of floating-point and integer values in Objective-C. Program 4.5 demonstrates some of the simple conversions between numeric data types.

Program 4.5

```
// Basic conversions in Objective-C

#import <Foundation/Foundation.h>

int main (int argc, char * argv[])
{
    @autoreleasepool {
```

```
    float   f1 = 123.125, f2;
    int     i1, i2 = -150;

    i1 = f1;    // floating to integer conversion
    NSLog (@"%f assigned to an int produces %i", f1, i1);

    f1 = i2;    // integer to floating conversion
    NSLog (@"%i assigned to a float produces %f", i2, f1);

    f1 = i2 / 100;    // integer divided by integer
    NSLog (@"%i divided by 100 produces %f", i2, f1);

    f2 = i2 / 100.0;    // integer divided by a float
    NSLog (@"%i divided by 100.0 produces %f", i2, f2);

    f2 = (float) i2 / 100;    // type cast operator
    NSLog (@"(float) %i divided by 100 produces %f", i2, f2);
  }
  return 0;
}
```

Program 4.5 **Output**

```
123.125000 assigned to an int produces 123
-150 assigned to a float produces -150.000000
-150 divided by 100 produces -1.000000
-150 divided by 100.0 produces -1.500000
(float) -150 divided by 100 produces -1.500000
```

Whenever a floating-point value is assigned to an integer variable in Objective-C, the decimal portion of the number gets truncated. So, when the value of f1 is assigned to i1 in the previous program, the number 123.125 is *truncated,* which means that only its integer portion, or 123, is stored in i1. The first line of the program's output verifies that this is the case.

Assigning an integer variable to a floating variable does not cause any change in the value of the number; the system simply converts the value and stores it in the floating variable. The second line of the program's output verifies that the value of i2 (-150) was correctly converted and stored in the float variable f1.

The next two lines of the program's output illustrate two points to remember when forming arithmetic expressions. The first has to do with integer arithmetic, which we have already discussed in this chapter. Whenever two operands in an expression are integers (and this applies to short, unsigned, and long integers as well), the operation is carried out under the rules of integer arithmetic. Therefore, any decimal portion resulting from a division operation is discarded, even if the result is assigned to a floating variable (as we did in the program). When the integer variable i2 is divided by the integer constant 100, the system performs the division as an integer division. The result of dividing –150 by 100, which is –1, is, therefore, the value that is stored in the float variable f1.

The next division performed in the previous program involves an integer variable and a floating-point constant. Any operation between two values in Objective-C is performed as a floating-point operation if either value is a floating-point variable or constant. Therefore, when the value of i2 is divided by 100.0, the system treats the division as a floating-point division and produces the result of –1.5, which is assigned to the float variable f1.

The Type Cast Operator

You've already seen how enclosing a type inside a set of parentheses is used to declare the return and argument types when declaring and defining methods. It serves a different purpose when used inside expressions.

The last division operation from Program 4.5 that reads as follows introduces the type cast operator:

```
f2 = (float) i2 / 100;    // type cast operator
```

The type cast operator has the effect of converting the value of the variable i2 to type float for purposes of evaluating the expression. In no way does this operator permanently affect the value of the variable i2; it is a unary operator that behaves like other unary operators. Just as the expression -a has no permanent effect on the value of a, neither does the expression (float) a.

The type cast operator has a higher precedence than all the arithmetic operators except the unary minus and unary plus. Of course, if necessary, you can always use parentheses in an expression to force the terms to be evaluated in any desired order.

As another example of the use of the type cast operator, the expression

```
(int) 29.55 + (int) 21.99
```

is evaluated in Objective-C as

```
29 + 21
```

because the effect of casting a floating value to an integer is one of truncating the floating-point value. The expression

```
(float) 6 / (float) 4
```

produces a result of 1.5, as does the following expression:

```
(float) 6 / 4
```

The type cast operator is often used to coerce an object that is a generic `id` type into an object of a particular class. For example, the following lines typecast the value of the `id` variable `myNumber` to a `Fraction` object:

```
id    myNumber;
Fraction *myFraction;
  ...
myFraction = (Fraction *) myNumber;
```

The result of the casting is assigned to the `Fraction` variable `myFraction`.

Assignment Operators

The Objective-C language permits you to combine the arithmetic operators with the assignment operator using the following general format:

```
op=
```

In this format, `op` is any of the arithmetic operators, including `+`, `-`, `*`, `/`, or `%`. In addition, `op` can be any of the bit operators for shifting and masking, discussed later.

Consider this statement:

```
count += 10;
```

The effect of the "plus equals" operator `+=` is to add the expression on the right side of the operator to the expression on the left side of the operator and to store the result back into the variable on the left side of the operator. So, the previous statement is equivalent to this statement:

```
count = count + 10;
```

The following expression uses the "minus equals" assignment operator to subtract 5 from the value of counter:

```
counter -= 5
```

It is equivalent to this expression:

```
counter = counter - 5
```

This is a slightly more involved expression:

```
a /= b + c
```

It divides `a` by whatever appears to the right of the equals sign (or by the sum of `b` and `c`) and stores the result in `a`. The addition is performed first because the addition operator has higher precedence than the assignment operator. In fact, all operators but the comma operator have higher precedence than the assignment operators, which all have the same precedence.

In this case, this expression is identical to the following:

```
a = a / (b + c)
```

The motivation for using assignment operators is threefold. First, the program statement becomes easier to write because what appears on the left side of the operator does not have to be repeated on the right side. Second, the resulting expression is usually easier to read. Third, the use of these operators can result in programs that execute more quickly because the compiler can sometimes generate less code to evaluate an expression.

A Calculator Class

It's time now to define a new class. We're going to make a `Calculator` class, which will be a simple four-function calculator you can use to add, multiply, subtract, and divide numbers. Similar to a regular calculator, this one must keep track of the running total, or what's usually called the accumulator. So, methods must let you set the accumulator to a specific value, clear it (or set it to zero), and retrieve its value when you're done. Program 4.6 includes the new class definition and a test program to try your calculator.

Program 4.6

```
// Implement a Calculator class

#import <Foundation/Foundation.h>

@interface Calculator: NSObject

// accumulator methods
-(void)   setAccumulator: (double) value;
-(void)   clear;
-(double) accumulator;

// arithmetic methods
-(void) add: (double) value;
-(void) subtract: (double) value;
-(void) multiply: (double) value;
-(void) divide: (double) value;
@end

@implementation Calculator
{
    double accumulator;
}

-(void) setAccumulator: (double) value
{
```

```
        accumulator = value;
}

-(void) clear
{
        accumulator = 0;
}

-(double) accumulator
{
        return accumulator;
}

-(void) add: (double) value
{
        accumulator += value;
}

-(void) subtract: (double) value
{
        accumulator -= value;
}

-(void) multiply: (double) value
{
        accumulator *= value;
}

-(void) divide: (double) value
{
        accumulator /= value;
}
@end

int main (int argc, char * argv[])
{
    @autoreleasepool {
        Calculator *deskCalc  = [[Calculator alloc] init];

        [deskCalc setAccumulator: 100.0];
        [deskCalc add: 200.];
        [deskCalc divide: 15.0];
        [deskCalc subtract: 10.0];
        [deskCalc multiply: 5];
        NSLog (@"The result is %g", [deskCalc accumulator]);
    }
    return 0;
}
```

Program 4.6   **Output**

```
The result is 50
```

The method definitions themselves are quite straightforward. The `Calculator` class has only one instance variable, a `double` value that holds the value of the accumulator.

Notice the message that invokes the `multiply` method:

```
[deskCalc multiply: 5];
```

The argument to the method is an integer, yet the method expects a `double`. No problem arises here because numeric arguments to methods are automatically converted to match the type expected. A `double` is expected by `multiply:`, so the integer value 5 automatically is converted to a double precision floating value when the function is called. Even though this automatic conversion takes place, it's better programming practice to supply the correct argument types when invoking methods.

Realize that unlike the `Fraction` class, in which you might work with many different fractions, you might want to work with only a single `Calculator` object in your program. Yet it still makes sense to define a new class to make working with this object easy. At some point, you might want to add a graphical front end to your calculator so that the user can actually click buttons on the screen, such as the calculator application you probably have installed on your system or phone.

We discuss more about data type conversions and bit operations in Chapter 10, "More on Variables and Data Types."

In several of the exercises that follow, you'll see that one additional benefit of defining a `Calculator` class has to do with the ease of extending it.

Exercises

1. Which of the following are invalid constants? Why?

123.456	0x10.5	0X0G1
0001	0xFFFF	123L
0Xab05	0L	-597.25
123.5e2	.0001	+12
98.6F	98.7U	17777s
0996	-12E-12	07777
1234uL	1.2Fe-7	15,000
1.234L	197u	100U
0XABCDEFL	0xabcu	+123

2. Write a program that converts 27° from degrees Fahrenheit (F) to degrees Celsius (C) using the following formula:

```
C = (F - 32) / 1.8
```

Note that you don't need to define a class to perform this calculation. Simply evaluating the expression will suffice.

3. What output would you expect from the following program?

```
#import <Foundation/Foundation.h>
int main (int argc, char * argv[])
{
    @autoreleasepool {
        char c, d;

        c = 'd';
        d = c;
        NSLog (@"d = %c", d);
    }
    return 0;
}
```

4. Write a program to evaluate the polynomial shown here. (To calculate the exponents, just do straight multiplication; there is no exponentiation operator in Objective-C.)

```
3x³ - 5x² + 6
for x = 2.55
```

$3x^3 - 5x^2 + 6$
for x = 2.55

5. Write a program that evaluates the following expression and displays the results. (Remember to use exponential format to display the result.)

$(3.31 \times 10^{-8} + 2.01 \times 10^{-7}) / (7.16 \times 10^{-6} + 2.01 \times 10^{-8})$

6. *Complex* numbers are numbers that contain two components: a *real* part and an *imaginary* part. If *a* is the real component and *b* is the imaginary component, this notation is used to represent the number:

```
a + b i
```

Write an Objective-C program that defines a new class called `Complex`. Following the paradigm established for the `Fraction` class, define the following methods for your new class:

```
-(void) setReal: (double) a;
-(void) setImaginary: (double) b;
-(void) print;      // display as a + bi
-(double) real;
-(double) imaginary;
```

Write a test program to test your new class and methods.

7. Suppose you are developing a library of routines to manipulate graphical objects. Start by defining a new class called `Rectangle`. For now, just keep track of the rectangle's width and height. Develop methods to set the rectangle's width and height, retrieve these values, and calculate the rectangle's area and perimeter. Assume that these rectangle objects describe rectangles on an integral grid, such as a computer screen. In that case, assume that the width and height of the rectangle are integer values.

   Here is the `@interface` section for the `Rectangle` class:

```
@interface Rectangle: NSObject
-(void) setWidth: (int) w;
-(void) setHeight: (int) h;
-(int) width;
-(int) height;
-(int) area;
-(int) perimeter;
@end
```

   Write the implementation section and a test program to test your new class and methods.

8. The `add:`, `subtract:`, `multiply:`, and `divide:` methods from Program 4.6 do not return a value. Modify these methods to return the value of the accumulator after the computation is performed. Test the new methods.

9. After completing exercise 8, add the following methods to the `Calculator` class and test them:

```
-(double) changeSign;  // change sign of accumulator
-(double) reciprocal;  // 1/accumulator
-(double) xSquared;    // accumulator squared
```

10. Add a memory capability to the `Calculator` class from Program 4.6. Implement the following method declarations and test them:

```
-(double) memoryClear;                      // clear memory
-(double) memoryStore;                      // set memory to accumulator
-(double) memoryRecall;                     // set accumulator to memory
-(double) memoryAdd: (double) value;        // add value into memory
-(double) memorySubtract: (double) value;   // subtract value from memory
```

   The last two methods set the accumulator and perform the indicated operation on memory. Have all the methods return the value of the accumulator.

Program Looping

In Objective-C, you can repeatedly execute a sequence of code in several ways. These looping capabilities are the subject of this chapter, and they consist of the following:

- The `for` statement
- The `while` statement
- The `do` statement

We start with a simple example: counting numbers.

If you were to arrange 15 marbles into the shape of a triangle, you would end up with an arrangement that might look something like Figure 5.1.

Figure 5.1   Triangle arrangement example

The first row of the triangle contains one marble, the second row contains two marbles, and so on. In general, the number of marbles required to form a triangle containing n rows would be the sum of the integers from 1 through n. This sum is known as a *triangular number.*

If you started at 1, the fourth triangular number would be the sum of the consecutive integers 1 through 4 (1 + 2 + 3 + 4), or 10.

Suppose you wanted to write a program that calculated and displayed the value of the eighth triangular number. Obviously, you could easily calculate this number in your head, but for the sake of argument, let's assume you wanted to write a program in Objective-C to perform this task. Program 5.1 illustrates such a program.

Program 5.1

```
#import <Foundation/Foundation.h>

// Program to calculate the eighth triangular number

int main (int argc, char * argv[])
{
    @autoreleasepool {
        int triangularNumber;

        triangularNumber = 1 + 2 + 3 + 4 + 5 + 6 + 7 + 8;

        NSLog (@"The eighth triangular number is %i", triangularNumber);
    }

    return 0;
}
```

Program 5.1   **Output**

```
The eighth triangular number is 36
```

The technique of Program 5.1 works fine for calculating relatively small triangular numbers, but what would happen if you needed to find the value of the 200th triangular number, for example? It certainly would be tedious to have to modify Program 5.1 to explicitly add up all the integers from 1 to 200. Luckily, there is an easier way.

One of the fundamental properties of a computer is its capability to repetitively execute a set of statements. These looping capabilities enable programmers to develop concise programs containing repetitive processes that could otherwise require thousands or even millions of program statements to perform. The Objective-C language contains three program statements for program looping.

The `for` Statement

Let's take a look at a program that uses the `for` statement. The purpose of Program 5.2 is to calculate the 200th triangular number. See whether you can determine how the `for` statement works.

Program 5.2

```
// Program to calculate the 200th triangular number
// Introduction of the for statement
```

```
#import <Foundation/Foundation.h>

int main (int argc, char * argv[])
{
    @autoreleasepool {
        int n, triangularNumber;

        triangularNumber = 0;

        for ( n = 1; n <= 200; n = n + 1 )
            triangularNumber += n;

        NSLog (@"The 200th triangular number is %i", triangularNumber);
    }

    return 0;
}
```

Program 5.2 **Output**

```
The 200th triangular number is 20100
```

Some explanation is needed for Program 5.2. The method employed to calculate the 200th triangular number is really the same as that used to calculate the 8th triangular number in the previous program: The integers from 1 to 200 are summed.

The variable triangularNumber is set equal to 0 before the for statement is reached. In general, you need to initialize all variables to some value (just like your objects) before you use them in your program. As you'll learn later, certain types of variables are given default initial values, but it's safer not to rely on that and you should set them anyway.

The for statement enables you to avoid having to explicitly write each integer from 1 to 200. In a sense, this statement generates these numbers for you.

The general format of the for statement is as follows:

```
for ( init_expression; loop_condition; loop_expression )
    program statement
```

The three expressions enclosed within the parentheses (init_expression, loop_condition, and loop_expression) set up the environment for the program loop. The program statement that immediately follows (which is, of course, terminated by a semicolon) can be any valid Objective-C program statement and constitutes the body of the loop. This statement is executed as many times as specified by the parameters set up in the for statement.

The first component of the for statement, labeled *init_expression*, is used to set the initial values before the loop begins. In Program 5.2, this portion of the for statement is used to set the initial value of n to 1. As you can see, an assignment is a valid form of an expression.

The second component of the for statement specifies the condition or conditions necessary for the loop to continue. In other words, looping continues as long as this condition is satisfied. Again referring to Program 5.2, the *loop_condition* of the for statement is specified by the following relational expression:

```
n <= 200
```

This expression can be read as "*n* less than or equal to 200." The "less than or equal to" operator (which is the less than character [<] followed immediately by the equals sign [=]) is only one of several relational operators provided in the Objective-C programming language. These operators are used to test specific conditions. The answer to the test is yes (or true) if the condition is satisfied and no (or false) if the condition is not satisfied.

Table 5.1 lists all the relational operators available in Objective-C.

Table 5.1   **Relational Operators**

Operator	Meaning	Example
==	Equal to	count == 10
!=	Not equal to	flag != DONE
<	Less than	a < b
<=	Less than or equal to	low <= high
>	Greater than	points > POINT_MAX
>=	Greater than or equal to	j >= 0

The relational operators have lower precedence than all arithmetic operators. This means, for example, that an expression such as

```
a < b + c
```

is evaluated as

```
a < (b + c)
```

This is as you would expect. It would be true if the value of a were less than the value of b + c, and false otherwise.

Pay particular attention to the "is equal to" operator (==) and do not confuse its use with the assignment operator (=). The expression

```
a == 2
```

tests whether the value of a is equal to 2, whereas the expression

```
a = 2
```

assigns the number 2 to the variable a.

The choice of which relational operator to use depends on the particular test being made and, in some instances, on your particular preferences. For example, the relational expression

```
n <= 200
```

can be equivalently expressed as

```
n < 201
```

Returning to the previous example, the program statement that forms the body of the for loop (triangularNumber += n;) is repetitively executed *as long as* the result of the relational test is true, or in this case, as long as the value of n is less than or equal to 200. This program statement has the effect of adding the value of n to the value of triangularNumber.

When the *loop_condition* is no longer satisfied, execution of the program continues with the program statement immediately following the for loop. In this program, execution continues with the NSLog statement after the loop has terminated.

The final component of the for statement contains an expression that is evaluated each time after the body of the loop is executed. In Program 5.2, this *loop_expression* adds 1 to the value of n. Therefore, the value of n is incremented by 1 each time after its value has been added into the value of triangularNumber, and it ranges in value from 1 through 201.

It is worth noting that the last value that n attains, 201, is not added into the value of triangularNumber because the loop is terminated as soon as the looping condition is no longer satisfied, or as soon as n equals 201.

In summary, execution of the for statement proceeds as follows:

1. The initial expression is evaluated first. This expression usually sets a variable that is used inside the loop, generally referred to as an *index* variable, to some initial value (such as 0 or 1).

2. The looping condition is evaluated. If the condition is not satisfied (the expression is false), the loop immediately terminates. Execution continues with the program statement that immediately follows the loop.

3. The program statement that constitutes the body of the loop is executed.

4. The looping expression is evaluated. This expression is generally used to change the value of the index variable, frequently by adding 1 to it or subtracting 1 from it.

5. Return to step 2.

Remember that the looping condition is evaluated immediately on entry into the loop, before the body of the loop has executed one time. Also remember not to put a semicolon after the closed parenthesis at the end of the loop because this immediately ends the loop.

Program 5.2 actually generates all the first 200 triangular numbers on its way to its final goal, so it might be nice to generate a table of these numbers. To save space, however, let's assume that you want to print a table of just the first 10 triangular numbers. Program 5.3 performs this task.

Program 5.3

```
// Program to generate a table of triangular numbers

#import <Foundation/Foundation.h>

int main (int argc, char * argv[])
{
    @autoreleasepool {
        int n, triangularNumber;

        NSLog (@"TABLE OF TRIANGULAR NUMBERS");
        NSLog (@" n  Sum from 1 to n");
        NSLog (@"--  --------------");

        triangularNumber = 0;

        for ( n = 1; n <= 10; ++n ) {
            triangularNumber += n;
            NSLog (@" %i          %i", n, triangularNumber);
        }
    }

    return 0;
}
```

Program 5.3 **Output**

```
TABLE OF TRIANGULAR NUMBERS
 n  Sum from 1 to n
--  ------------------
 1          1
 2          3
 3          6
 4          10
 5          15
```

6	21
7	28
8	36
9	45
10	55

In Program 5.3, the purpose of the first three NSLog statements is simply to provide a general heading and to label the columns of the output.

After the appropriate headings have been displayed, the program calculates the first 10 triangular numbers. The variable n is used to count the current number whose sum from 1 to n you are computing, and the variable triangularNumber is used to store the value of triangular number n.

Execution of the for statement commences by setting the value of the variable n to 1. As mentioned earlier, the program statement immediately following the for statement constitutes the body of the program loop. But what happens if you want to repetitively execute not just a single program statement, but a group of program statements? You can do so by enclosing all such program statements within a pair of braces. The system then treats this group, or *block*, of statements as a single entity. In general, any place in a Objective-C program that a single statement is permitted, you can use a block of statements, provided that you remember to enclose the block within a pair of braces.

Therefore, in Program 5.3, both the expression that adds n into the value of triangularNumber and the NSLog statement that immediately follows constitute the body of the program loop. Pay particular attention to the way the program statements are indented. At a quick glance, you can easily determine which statements form part of the for loop. Note, too, that programmers use different coding styles; some prefer to type the loop this way:

```
for ( n = 1; n <= 10; ++n )
{
    triangularNumber += n;
    NSLog (@" %i %i", n, triangularNumber);
}
```

Here, the opening brace is placed on the line following the for. This is strictly a matter of taste and has no effect on the program.

The next triangular number is calculated by simply adding the value of n to the previous triangular number. The first time through the for loop, the previous triangular number is 0, so the new value of triangularNumber when n is equal to 1 is simply the value of n, or 1. The values of n and triangularNumber are then displayed, with an appropriate number of blank spaces inserted into the format string to ensure that the values of the two variables line up under the appropriate column headings.

Because the body of the loop has now been executed, the looping expression is evaluated next. The expression in this `for` statement appears a bit strange, however. Surely, you must have made a typographical mistake and meant to insert `n = n + 1` instead of this funny-looking expression:

```
++n
```

But `++n` is actually a perfectly valid Objective-C expression. It introduces a new (and rather unique) operator in the Objective-C programming language: the *increment operator.* The function of the double plus sign, or the increment operator, is to add 1 to its operand. Addition by 1 is such a common operation in programs that a special operator was created solely for this purpose. Therefore, the expression `++n` is equivalent to the expression `n = n + 1`. At first glance, it might appear that `n = n + 1` is more readable, but you will soon get used to the function of this operator and even learn to appreciate its succinctness.

Of course, no programming language that offers an increment operator to add 1 would be complete without a corresponding operator to subtract 1. As you would guess, the name of this operator is the *decrement operator,* and it is symbolized by the double minus sign. So an expression in Objective-C that reads

```
bean_counter = bean_counter - 1
```

can be equivalently expressed using the decrement operator, like so:

```
--bean_counter
```

Some programmers prefer to put the `++` or `--` after the variable name, as in `n++` or `bean_counter--`. This is a matter of personal preference in the example shown for the `for` statement. However, as you'll learn in Chapter 13, "Underlying C Language Features," the pre- or post-nature of the operator does come into play when used in more complex expressions.

You might have noticed that the last line of output from Program 5.3 doesn't line up. You can correct this minor annoyance by substituting the following `NSLog` statement in place of the corresponding statement from Program 5.3:

```
NSLog ("%2i %i", n, triangularNumber);
```

To verify that this change solves the problem, here's the output from the modified program (called Program 5.3A).

Program 5.3A **Output**

```
TABLE OF TRIANGULAR NUMBERS

 n  Sum from 1 to n
--- ---------------
 1       1
 2       3
 3       6
 4       10
```

5	15
6	21
7	28
8	36
9	45
10	55

The primary change made to the NSLog statement is the inclusion of a field width specification. The characters %2i tell the NSLog routine not only that you want to display the value of an integer at that particular point, but also that the size of the integer to be displayed should take up at least two columns in the display. Any integer that would normally take up less than two columns (that is, the integers 0 through 9) will be displayed with a leading space. This is known as *right justification*.

Therefore, by using a field width specification of %2i, you guarantee that at least two columns will be used for displaying the value of n; you also ensure that the values of triangularNumber will be aligned.

Keyboard Input

Program 5.2 calculates the 200th triangular number, and nothing more. What if you want to calculate the 50th or the 100th triangular number instead? Well, in that case, you have to change the program so that the for loop is executed the correct number of times. You also have to change the NSLog statement to display the correct message.

An easier solution might be to somehow have the program ask you which triangular number you want to calculate. Then, after you had given your answer, the program could calculate the desired triangular number. You can effect such a solution by using a routine called scanf. The scanf routine is similar in concept to the NSLog routine. Whereas the NSLog routine is used to display values, the purpose of the scanf routine is to enable the programmer to type values into the program. Of course, if you're writing an Objective-C program that uses a graphical user interface (UI), such as a Cocoa or iOS application, you likely won't be using NSLog or scanf at all in your program.

Program 5.4 asks the user which triangular number should be calculated, calculates that number, and then displays the results.

Program 5.4

```
#import <Foundation/Foundation.h>

int main (int argc, char * argv[])
{
    @autoreleasepool {
        int n, number, triangularNumber;
```

```
        NSLog (@"What triangular number do you want?");
        scanf ("%i", &number);

        triangularNumber = 0;

        for ( n = 1; n <= number; ++n )
            triangularNumber += n;

        NSLog (@"Triangular number %i is %i\n", number, triangularNumber);
    }

    return 0;
}
```

In the program output that follows, the number typed in by the user (100) is set in bold type to distinguish it from the output displayed by the program.

Program 5.4   **Output**

```
What triangular number do you want?
100
Triangular number 100 is 5050
```

According to the output, the user typed the number 100. The program then calculated the 100th triangular number and displayed the result of 5050 at the terminal. The user could have just as easily typed in the number 10 or 30, for example, if he or she wanted to calculate those particular triangular numbers.

The first NSLog statement in Program 5.4 is used to prompt the user to type in a number. Of course, it is always nice to remind the user of what you want entered. After the message is printed, the scanf routine is called. The first argument to scanf is the format string, which *does not* begin with the @ character. Unlike NSLog, whose first argument is always an NSString object, the first argument to scanf is a C-style string. As noted earlier, C-style character strings are not preceded by the @ character.

The format string tells scanf what types of values are to be read in from the console (or Terminal window, if you're compiling your programs using the Terminal application). As with NSLog, the %i characters are used to specify an integer value.

The second argument to the scanf routine specifies where the value that the user types in is to be stored. The & character before the variable number is necessary in this case. Rather than supplying the value of the variable number, we instead specify *where* we want the value that is entered to be stored. Don't worry about this right now. We discuss this character, which is actually an operator, in great detail when we talk about pointers in Chapter 13.

Given the preceding discussion, you can now see that the scanf call from Program 5.4 specifies that an integer value is to be read and stored into the variable number. This value represents the particular triangular number the user wants to have calculated.

After the user has typed in this number (and pressed the Enter key on the keyboard to signal that typing of the number is completed), the program calculates the requested triangular number. This is done in the same way as in Program 5.2; the only difference is that, instead of using 200 as the limit, number is used as the limit.

> **Note**
> Pressing the Enter key on a keyboard with a numeric keypad may not cause the number you enter to be sent to the program. Use the Return key on your keyboard instead.

After the desired triangular number has been calculated, the results display. Execution of the program is then complete.

Nested for Loops

Program 5.4 gives the user the flexibility to have the program calculate any triangular number that is desired. But suppose the user has a list of five triangular numbers to be calculated? In such a case, the user could simply execute the program five times, each time typing in the next triangular number from the list to be calculated.

Another way to accomplish the same goal, and a much more interesting method, as far as learning about Objective-C is concerned, is to have the program handle the situation. You can best accomplish this by inserting a loop into the program to repeat the entire series of calculations five times. You can use the for statement to set up such a loop. Program 5.5 and its associated output illustrate this technique.

Program 5.5

```
#import <Foundation/Foundation.h>

int main (int argc, char * argv[])
{
   @autoreleasepool {
      int n, number, triangularNumber, counter;

      for ( counter = 1; counter <= 5; ++counter ) {
         NSLog (@"What triangular number do you want?");
         scanf ("%i", &number);

         triangularNumber = 0;

         for ( n = 1; n <= number; ++n )
```

```
            triangularNumber += n;

        NSLog (@"Triangular number %i is %i", number, triangularNumber);
        }
    }

    return 0;
}
```

Program 5.5   **Output**

```
What triangular number do you want?
12
Triangular number 12 is 78

What triangular number do you want?
25
Triangular number 25 is 325

What triangular number do you want?
50
Triangular number 50 is 1275

What triangular number do you want?
75
Triangular number 75 is 2850

What triangular number do you want?
83
Triangular number 83 is 3486
```

The program consists of two levels of `for` statements. The outermost `for` statement is as follows:

```
for ( counter = 1; counter <= 5; ++counter )
```

This specifies that the program loop is to be executed precisely five times. The value of `counter` is initially set to 1 and is incremented by 1 until it is no longer less than or equal to 5 (in other words, until it reaches 6).

Unlike the previous program examples, the variable `counter` is not used anywhere else within the program. Its function is solely as a loop counter in the `for` statement. Nevertheless, because it is a variable, you must declare it in the program.

The program loop actually consists of all the remaining program statements, as indicated by the braces. You might be able to more easily comprehend the way this program operates if you conceptualize it as follows:

```
For 5 times
{
    Get the number from the user.
    Calculate the requested triangular number.
    Display the results.
}
```

The portion of the loop referred to in the preceding as `Calculate the requested triangular number` actually consists of setting the value of the variable `triangularNumber` to 0 plus the `for` loop that calculates the triangular number. Therefore, a `for` statement is actually contained within another `for` statement. This is perfectly valid in Objective-C, and nesting can continue even further to any desired level.

The proper use of indentation becomes even more critical when dealing with more sophisticated program constructs, such as nested `for` statements. At a quick glance, you can easily determine which statements are contained within each `for` statement.

`for` Loop Variants

Before leaving this discussion of the `for` loop, we should mention some of the syntactic variations that are permitted in forming this loop. When writing a `for` loop, you might discover that you want to initialize more than one variable before the loop begins, or perhaps you want to evaluate more than one expression each time through the loop. You can include multiple expressions in any of the fields of the `for` loop, as long as you separate such expressions by commas. For example, in the `for` statement that begins

```
for ( i = 0, j = 0; i < 10; ++i )
    . . .
```

the value of `i` is set to 0 and the value of `j` is set to 0 before the loop begins. The two expressions `i = 0` and `j = 0` are separated from each other by a comma, and both expressions are considered part of the *init_expression* field of the loop. As another example, the `for` loop that starts

```
for ( i = 0, j = 100; i < 10; ++i, j -= 10 )
    . . .
```

sets up two index variables: `i` and `j`, which are initialized to 0 and 100, respectively, before the loop begins. Each time after the body of the loop is executed, the value of `i` is incremented by 1 and the value of `j` is decremented by 10.

Just as you might need to include more than one expression in a particular field of the `for` statement, you also might need to omit one or more fields from the statement. You can do this simply by omitting the desired field and marking its place with a semicolon. The most common application for the omission of a field in the `for` statement occurs when no initial expression needs to be evaluated. You can simply leave the *init_expression* field blank in such a case, as long as you still include the semicolon:

```
for ( ; j != 100; ++j )
    ...
```

This statement might be used if j were already set to some initial value before the loop was entered.

A for loop that has its *looping_condition* field omitted effectively sets up an infinite loop—that is, a loop that theoretically will be executed forever. Such a loop can be used as long as some other means is used to exit from the loop (such as executing a return, break, or goto statement, as discussed later in this book).

You can also define variables as part of your initial expression inside a for loop. This is done using the typical ways we've defined variables in the past. For example, the following can be used to set up a for loop with an integer variable counter both defined and initialized to the value 1, like so:

```
for ( int counter = 1; counter <= 5; ++counter )
```

The variable counter is known only throughout the execution of the for loop (it's called a *local* variable) and cannot be accessed outside the loop.

A final for loop variant, for performing what's known as *fast enumerations* on collections of objects is described in detail in Chapter 15, "Numbers, Strings, and Collections."

The while Statement

The while statement further extends the Objective-C language's repertoire of looping capabilities. The syntax of this frequently used construct is as follows:

```
while ( expression )
    program statement
```

The *expression* specified inside the parentheses is evaluated. If the result of the *expression* evaluation is true, the *program statement* that immediately follows is executed. After execution of this statement (or statements, if enclosed in braces), *expression* is again evaluated. If the result of the evaluation is true, the *program statement* is again executed. This process continues until *expression* finally evaluates false, at which point the loop is terminated. Execution of the program then continues with the statement that follows *program statement*.

As an example of its use, the following program sets up a while loop, which merely counts from 1 to 5.

Program 5.6
```
// This program introduces the while statement

#import <Foundation/Foundation.h>

int main (int argc, char * argv[])
{
    @autoreleasepool {
        int count = 1;

        while ( count <= 5 ) {
            NSLog (@"%i", count);
            ++count;
        }
    }

    return 0;
}
```

Program 5.6 **Output**
```
1
2
3
4
5
```

The program initially sets the value of count to 1; execution of the while loop then begins. Because the value of count is less than or equal to 5, the statement that immediately follows is executed. The braces define both the NSLog statement and the statement that increments count as the body of the while loop. From the output of the program, you can see that this loop is executed five times or until the value of count reaches 5.

You might have realized from this program that you could have readily accomplished the same task by using a for statement. In fact, a for statement can always be translated into an equivalent while statement, and vice versa. For example, the general for statement

```
for ( init_expression; loop_condition; loop_expression )
    program statement
```

can be equivalently expressed in the form of a while statement, like so:

```
init_expression;
while ( loop_condition )
{
    program statement
    loop_expression;
}
```

When you become familiar with the use of the `while` statement, you will gain a better feel for when it seems more logical to use a `while` statement and when you should use a `for` statement. In general, a loop executed a predetermined number of times is a prime candidate for implementation as a `for` statement. Also, if the initial expression, looping expression, and looping condition all involve the same variable, the `for` statement is probably the right choice.

The next program provides another example of the use of the `while` statement. The program computes the greatest common divisor of two integer values. The greatest common divisor (we abbreviate it hereafter as gcd) of two integers is the largest integer value that evenly divides the two integers. For example, the gcd of 10 and 15 is 5 because 5 is the largest integer that evenly divides both 10 and 15.

A procedure, or algorithm, that can be followed to arrive at the gcd of two arbitrary integers is based on a procedure originally developed by Euclid around 300 B.C.E. It can be stated as follows:

Problem: Find the greatest common divisor of two non-negative integers u and v.

Step 1:   If v equals 0, then we are done and the gcd is equal to u.

Step 2:   Calculate temp = u % v, $u = v$, v = temp and go back to step 1.

Don't concern yourself with the details of how the previous algorithm works; just take it on faith. We are more concerned here with developing a program to find the greatest common divisor than in performing an analysis of how the algorithm works.

After expressing the solution to the problem of finding the greatest common divisor in terms of an algorithm, developing the computer program becomes a much simpler task. An analysis of the steps of the algorithm reveals that step 2 is repetitively executed as long as the value of v is not equal to 0. This realization leads to the natural implementation of this algorithm in Objective-C with the use of a `while` statement.

Program 5.7 finds the gcd of two nonnegative integer values typed in by the user.

Program 5.7

```
// Find the greatest common divisor of two nonnegative integers

#import <Foundation/Foundation.h>

int main (int argc, char * argv[])
{
    @autoreleasepool {
        unsigned int u, v, temp;

        NSLog (@"Please type in two nonnegative integers.");
        scanf ("%u%u", &u, &v);
```

```
    while ( v != 0 ) {
        temp = u % v;
        u = v;
        v = temp;
    }

    NSLog (@"Their greatest common divisor is %u", u);
}

    return 0;
}
```

Program 5.7   **Output**

```
Please type in two nonnegative integers.
150 35
Their greatest common divisor is 5
```

Program 5.7A   **Output (Rerun)**

```
Please type in two nonnegative integers.
1026 540
Their greatest common divisor is 54
```

After the two integer values have been entered and stored in the variables u and v (using the %u format characters to read in an unsigned integer value), the program enters a while loop to calculate their greatest common divisor. After the while loop is exited, the value of u, which represents the gcd of v and of the original value of u, is displayed with an appropriate message.

You will use the algorithm for finding the greatest common divisor again in Chapter 7, "More on Classes," when you return to working with fractions. There you will use the algorithm to reduce a fraction to its simplest terms.

For the next program that illustrates the use of the while statement, let's consider the task of reversing the digits of an integer that is entered from the terminal. For example, if the user types in the number 1234, the program should reverse the digits of this number and display the result of 4321.

Note

Using NSLog calls will cause each digit to appear on a separate line of the output. C programmers who are familiar with the printf function can use that routine instead to get the digits to appear consecutively.

To write such a program, you first must come up with an algorithm that accomplishes the stated task. Analyzing your own method for solving the problem often leads to an algorithm. For the task of reversing the digits of a number, the solution can be simply stated as "successively read the digits of the number from right to left." You can have a computer program successively read the digits of the number by developing a procedure to successively isolate or extract each digit of the number, beginning with the rightmost digit. The extracted digit can be subsequently displayed at the terminal as the next digit of the reversed number.

You can extract the rightmost digit from an integer number by taking the remainder of the integer after it is divided by 10. For example, `1234 % 10` gives the value `4`, which is the rightmost digit of `1234` and is also the first digit of the reversed number. (Remember that the modulus operator gives the remainder of one integer divided by another.) You can get the next digit of the number by using the same process if you first divide the number by 10, bearing in mind the way integer division works. Thus, `1234 / 10` gives a result of `123`, and `123 % 10` gives you `3`, which is the next digit of the reversed number.

You can continue this procedure until you've extracted the last digit. In the general case, you know that the last digit of the number has been extracted when the result of the last integer division by 10 is `0`.

Program 5.8 prompts the user to enter a number and then proceeds to display the digits from that number from the rightmost to leftmost digit.

Program 5.8

```
// Program to reverse the digits of a number

#import <Foundation/Foundation.h>

int main (int argc, char * argv[])
{
    @autoreleasepool {
        int    number, right_digit;

        NSLog (@"Enter your number.");
        scanf ("%i", &number);

        while ( number != 0 )  {
            right_digit = number % 10;
            NSLog (@"%i", right_digit);
            number /= 10;
        }
    }

    return 0;
}
```

Program 5.8 **Output**

```
Enter your number.
13579
9
7
5
3
1
```

The do Statement

The two looping constructs discussed thus far in this chapter both test the conditions before the loop is executed. Therefore, the body of the loop might never be executed if the conditions are not satisfied. When developing programs, you sometimes want to have the test made at the end of the loop instead of at the beginning. Naturally, the Objective-C language provides a special language construct to handle such a situation, known as the do statement. The syntax of this statement is as follows:

```
do
    program statement
while ( expression );
```

Execution of the do statement proceeds as follows: *program statement* is executed first. Next, the *expression* inside the parentheses is evaluated. If the result of evaluating *expression* is true, the loop continues and *program statement* is again executed. As long as the evaluation of *expression* continues to be true, program *statement* is repeatedly executed. When the evaluation of the expression proves false, the loop is terminated and the next statement in the program is executed in the normal sequential manner.

The do statement is simply a transposition of the while statement, with the looping conditions placed at the end of the loop instead of at the beginning.

Program 5.8 used a while statement to reverse the digits of a number. Go back to that program and try to determine what would happen if the user had typed in the number 0 instead of 13579. The loop of the while statement would never have been executed, and nothing would have been displayed for output. If you were to use a do statement instead of a while statement, you would be assured that the program loop would be executed at least once, thus guaranteeing the display of at least one digit in all cases. Program 5.9 illustrates the use of the do statement.

Program 5.9

```
// Program to reverse the digits of a number

#import <Foundation/Foundation.h>

int main (int argc, char * argv[])
{
   @autoreleasepool {
      int number, right_digit;

      NSLog (@"Enter your number.");
      scanf ("%i", &number);

      do {
         right_digit = number % 10;
         NSLog (@"%i", right_digit);
         number /= 10;
      }
      while ( number != 0 );
   }

   return 0;
}
```

Program 5.9   Output

```
Enter your number.
135
5
3
1
```

Program 5.9A   Output (Rerun)

```
Enter your number.
0
0
```

As you can see from the program's output, when 0 is keyed into the program, the program correctly displays the digit 0.

The `break` Statement

Sometimes when executing a loop, you'll want to leave the loop as soon as a certain condition occurs—for instance, maybe you detect an error condition or find the data you're looking for in a list of data. You can use the `break` statement for this purpose. Execution of the `break` statement causes the program to immediately exit from the loop it is executing, whether it's a `for`, `while`, or `do` loop. Subsequent statements in the loop are skipped and execution of the loop is terminated. Execution continues with whatever statement follows the loop.

If a `break` is executed from within a set of nested loops, only the innermost loop in which the `break` is executed is terminated.

The format of the `break` statement is simply the keyword `break` followed by a semicolon, like so:

```
break;
```

The `continue` Statement

The `continue` statement is similar to the `break` statement, except that it doesn't cause the loop to terminate. At the point that the `continue` statement is executed, any statements that appear after the `continue` statement up to the end of the loop are skipped. Execution of the loop otherwise continues as normal.

The `continue` statement is most often used to bypass a group of statements inside a loop based on some condition, but then to otherwise continue executing the loop. The format of the `continue` statement is as follows:

```
continue;
```

Don't use the `break` or `continue` statements until you become very familiar with writing program loops and gracefully exiting from them. These statements are too easy to abuse and can result in programs that are hard to follow.

Summary

Now that you are familiar with all the basic looping constructs the Objective-C language provides, you're ready to learn about another class of language statements that enables you to make decisions during the execution of a program. The next chapter describes these decision-making capabilities in detail.

Exercises

1. Write a program to generate and display a table of n and $n2$, for integer values of n ranging from 1 through 10. Be sure to print the appropriate column headings.

2. A triangular number can also be generated for any integer value of n by this formula:

   ```
   triangularNumber = n (n + 1) / 2
   ```

   For example, the 10th triangular number, 55, can be calculated by substituting 10 as the value for n into the previous formula. Write a program that generates a table of triangular numbers using the previous formula. Have the program generate every fifth triangular number between 5 and 50 (that is, 5, 10, 15, ..., 50).

3. The factorial of an integer n, written n!, is the product of the consecutive integers 1 through n. For example, 5 factorial is calculated as follows:

   ```
   5! = 5 x 4 x 3 x 2 x 1 = 120
   ```

   Write a program to generate and print a table of the first 10 factorials.

4. A minus sign placed in front of a field width specification causes the field to be displayed left-justified. Substitute the following NSLog statement for the corresponding statement in Program 5.3, run the program, and compare the outputs produced by both programs:

   ```
   NSLog (@"%-2i %i", n, triangularNumber);
   ```

5. Program 5.5 allows the user to type in only five different numbers. Modify that program so that the user can type in the number of triangular numbers to be calculated.

6. In programs 5.2 through 5.5, replace all uses of the for statement with equivalent while statements. Run each program to verify that both versions are identical.

7. What would happen if you were to type a negative number into Program 5.8? Try it and see.

8. Write a program that calculates the sum of the digits of an integer. For example, the sum of the digits of the number 2155 is 2 + 1 + 5 + 5, or 13. The program should accept any arbitrary integer the user types.

6

Making Decisions

A fundamental feature of any programming language is its capability to make decisions. Decisions were made when executing the looping statements to determine when to terminate a loop. The Objective-C programming language also provides several other decision-making constructs, which are covered in this chapter:

- The `if` statement
- The `switch` statement
- The `conditional` operator

The `if` Statement

The Objective-C programming language provides a general decision-making capability in the form of a language construct known as the `if` statement. The general format of this statement is shown here:

```
if ( expression )
    program statement
```

Imagine that you could translate a statement such as "If it is not raining, then I will go swimming" into the Objective-C language. Using the previous format for the `if` statement, this might be "written" in Objective-C as follows:

```
if ( it is not raining )
    I will go swimming
```

The `if` statement is used to stipulate execution of a program statement (or statements, if enclosed in braces) based on specified conditions. I will go swimming if it is not raining. Similarly, in the program statement

```
if ( count > MAXIMUM_SONGS )
    [playlist maxExceeded];
```

the `maxExceeded` message is sent to `playlist` *only* if the value of count is greater than the value of MAXIMUM_SONGS; otherwise, it is ignored.

An actual program example will help drive the point home. Suppose you want to write a program that accepts an integer entered from the keyboard and then displays the absolute value of that integer. A straightforward way to calculate the absolute value of an integer is to simply negate the number if it is less than zero. The phrase "if it is less than zero" in the previous sentence signals that the program must make a decision. This decision can be affected by the use of an `if` statement, as shown in the program that follows.

Program 6.1

```
// Calculate the absolute value of an integer

#import <Foundation/Foundation.h>

int main (int argc, char * argv[])
{
    @autoreleasepool {
        int number;

        NSLog (@"Type in your number: ");
        scanf ("%i", &number);

        if ( number < 0 )
            number = -number;

        NSLog (@"The absolute value is %i", number);
    }
    return 0;
}
```

Program 6.1   **Output**

```
Type in your number:
-100
The absolute value is 100
```

Program 6.1   **Output (Rerun)**

```
Type in your number:
2000
The absolute value is 2000
```

The program was run twice to verify that it is functioning properly. Of course, it might be desirable to run the program several more times to get a higher level of confidence so that you know it is indeed working correctly, but at least you know that you have checked both possible outcomes of the program's decision.

After a message is displayed to the user and the integer value that is entered is stored in `number`, the program tests the value of `number` to see whether it is less than zero. If it is, the following program statement, which negates the value of `number`, is executed. If the value of `number` is not less than zero, this program statement is automatically skipped. (If it is already positive, you don't want to negate it.) The absolute value of `number` is then displayed by the program, and program execution ends.

Let's look at another program that uses the `if` statement. We'll add one more method to the `Fraction` class, called `convertToNum`. This method will provide the value of a fraction expressed as a real number. In other words, it will divide the numerator by the denominator and return the result as a double precision value. So if you have the fraction `1/2`, you want the method to return the value `0.5`.

The declaration for such a method might look like this:

```
-(double) convertToNum;
```

This is how you could write its definition:

```
-(double) convertToNum
{
    return numerator / denominator;
}
```

Well, not quite. As it's defined, this method actually has two serious problems. Can you spot them? The first has to do with arithmetic conversions. Recall that `numerator` and `denominator` are both integer instance variables. So what happens when you divide two integers? Correct, it is done as an integer division! If you wanted to convert the fraction `1/2`, the previous code would give you zero! This is easily corrected by using the type cast operator to convert one or both of the operands to a floating-point value before the division takes place:

```
(double) numerator / denominator
```

Recalling the relatively high precedence of this operator, the value of `numerator` is first converted to `double` before the division occurs. Furthermore, you don't need to convert the `denominator` because the rules of arithmetic conversion take care of that for you.

The second problem with this method is that you should check for division by zero. (You should always check for that!) The invoker of this method could inadvertently have forgotten to set the denominator of the fraction or might have set the denominator of the fraction to zero, and you don't want your program to terminate abnormally.

The modified version of the `convertToNum` method appears here:

```
-(double) convertToNum
{
   if (denominator != 0)
      return (double) numerator / denominator;
   else
      return NAN;
}
```

We decided to return the special value NAN (which stands for Not A Number) if the denominator of the fraction is zero. This symbol is defined in a system header file called `math.h`, which gets automatically imported into your program.

Let's put this new method to use in Program 6.2.

Program 6.2

```
#import <Foundation/Foundation.h>

@interface Fraction: NSObject

-(void)    print;
-(void)    setNumerator: (int) n;
-(void)    setDenominator: (int) d;
-(int)     numerator;
-(int)     denominator;
-(double) convertToNum;
@end

@implementation Fraction
{
   int    numerator;
   int    denominator;
}

-(void) print
{
    NSLog (@" %i/%i ", numerator, denominator);
}

-(void) setNumerator: (int) n
{
    numerator = n;
}

-(void) setDenominator: (int) d
{
```

```
        denominator = d;
}

-(int) numerator
{
    return numerator;
}

-(int) denominator
{
    return denominator;
}

-(double) convertToNum
{
    if (denominator != 0)
        return (double) numerator / denominator;
    else
        return NAN;
}
@end

int main (int argc, char * argv[])
{
    @autoreleasepool {
        Fraction *aFraction = [[Fraction alloc] init];
        Fraction *bFraction = [[Fraction alloc] init];

        [aFraction setNumerator: 1];  // 1st fraction is 1/4
        [aFraction setDenominator: 4];

        [aFraction print];
        NSLog (@" =");
        NSLog (@"%g", [aFraction convertToNum]);

        [bFraction print];      // never assigned a value
        NSLog (@" =");
        NSLog (@"%g", [bFraction convertToNum]);
    }
    return 0;
}
```

Program 6.2   **Output**

```
1/4
  =
0.25
0/0
  =
nan
```

After setting `aFraction` to `1/4`, the program uses the `convertToNum` method to convert the fraction to a decimal value. This value is then displayed as 0.25.

In the second case, the value of `bFraction` is not explicitly set, so its numerator and denominator are initialized to zero, which is the default for instance variables. This explains the result from the `print` method. It also causes the `if` statement inside the `convertToNum` method to return the value `NAN`, which you will note is actually displayed by `NSLog` as nan.

The `if-else` **Construct**

If someone asks you whether a particular number is even or odd, you will most likely make the determination by examining the last digit of the number. If this digit is 0, 2, 4, 6, or 8, you will readily state that the number is even. Otherwise, you will claim that the number is odd.

An easier way for a computer to determine whether a particular number is even or odd is affected not by examining the last digit of the number to see whether it is 0, 2, 4, 6, or 8, but by simply determining whether the number is evenly divisible by 2. If it is, the number is even; otherwise, it is odd.

You have already seen how the modulus operator % is used to compute the remainder of one integer divided by another. This makes it the perfect operator to use in determining whether an integer is evenly divisible by 2. If the remainder after division by 2 is 0, it is even; otherwise, it is odd.

Now let's write a program that determines whether an integer value that the user types in is even or odd and then displays an appropriate message at the terminal; see Program 6.3.

Program 6.3

```
// Program to determine if a number is even or odd

#import <Foundation/Foundation.h>

int main (int argc, char * argv[])
{
    @autoreleasepool {
        int number_to_test, remainder;

        NSLog (@"Enter your number to be tested: ");
```

```
    scanf ("%i", &number_to_test);

    remainder = number_to_test % 2;

    if ( remainder == 0 )
        NSLog (@"The number is even.");

    if ( remainder != 0 )
        NSLog (@"The number is odd.");
    }

    return 0;
}
```

Program 6.3   **Output**

```
Enter your number to be tested:
2455
The number is odd.
```

Program 6.3   **Output (Rerun)**

```
Enter your number to be tested:
1210
The number is even.
```

After the number is typed in, the remainder after division by 2 is calculated. The first if state-ment tests the value of this remainder to see whether it is equal to zero. If it is, the message `"The number is even."` displays.

The second if statement tests the remainder to see if it's *not* equal to zero and, if that's the case, displays a message stating that the number is odd.

Whenever the first if statement succeeds the second one must fail, and vice versa. If you recall from our discussions of even/odd numbers at the beginning of this section, we said that if the number is evenly divisible by 2, it is even; otherwise, it is odd.

When writing programs, this "else" concept is so frequently required that a special construct is provided to handle this situation. In Objective-C, this is known as the if-else, and the general format is as follows:

```
if ( expression )
    program statement 1
else
    program statement 2
```

The `if-else` is actually just an extension of the general format of the `if` statement. If the result of the expression's evaluation is `true`, *program statement 1*, which immediately follows, is executed; otherwise, *program statement 2* is executed. In either case, either *program statement 1* or *program statement 2* will be executed, but not both.

You can incorporate the `if-else` statement into the previous program, replacing the two `if` statements by a single `if-else` statement. You will see how this new program construct actually helps reduce the program's complexity somewhat and also improves its readability.

Program 6.4

```
// Determine if a number is even or odd (Ver. 2)

#import <Foundation/Foundation.h>

int main (int argc, char * argv[])
{
   @autoreleasepool {
      int number_to_test, remainder;

      NSLog (@"Enter your number to be tested:");
      scanf ("%i", &number_to_test);

      remainder = number_to_test % 2;

      if ( remainder == 0 )
         NSLog (@"The number is even.");
      else
         NSLog (@"The number is odd.");
   }

   return 0;
}
```

Program 6.4   **Output**

```
Enter your number to be tested:
1234
The number is even.
```

Program 6.4   **Output (Rerun)**

```
Enter your number to be tested:
6551
The number is odd.
```

Don't forget that the double equals sign (==) is the equality test, and the single equals sign is the assignment operator. Forgetting this and inadvertently using the assignment operator inside the if statement can lead to a lot of headaches.

Compound Relational Tests

The if statements you've used so far in this chapter set up simple relational tests between two numbers. Program 6.1 compared the value of number against zero, whereas Program 6.2 compared the denominator of the fraction to zero. Sometimes it becomes desirable, if not necessary, to set up more sophisticated tests. Suppose, for example, that you want to count the number of grades from an exam that were between 70 and 79, inclusive. In such a case, you would want to compare the value of a grade not merely against one limit, but against the two limits 70 and 79 to ensure that it fell within the specified range.

The Objective-C language provides the mechanisms necessary to perform these types of compound relational tests. A *compound relational test* is simply one or more simple relational tests joined by either the logical AND or the logical OR operator. These operators are represented by the character pairs && and || (two vertical bar characters), respectively. As an example, the following Objective-C statement increments the value of grades_70_to_79 only if the value of grade is greater than or equal to 70 and less than or equal to 79:

```
if ( grade >= 70 && grade <= 79 )
    ++grades_70_to_79;
```

In a similar manner, the following statement causes execution of the NSLog statement if index is less than 0 *or* greater than 99:

```
if ( index < 0 || index > 99 )
    NSLog (@"Error - index out of range");
```

The compound operators can be used to form extremely complex expressions in Objective-C. The Objective-C language grants the programmer the ultimate flexibility in forming expressions, but this flexibility is a capability that programmers often abuse. Simpler expressions are almost always easier to read and debug.

When forming compound relational expressions, liberally use parentheses to aid readability of the expression and avoid getting into trouble because of a mistaken assumption about the precedence of the operators in the or expression. (The && operator has lower precedence than any arithmetic or relational operator but higher precedence than the || operator.) Blank spaces also can aid in the expression's readability. An extra blank space around the && and || operators visually sets these operators apart from the expressions they are joining.

To illustrate the use of a compound relational test in an actual program example, let's write a program that tests whether a year is a leap year. We all know that a year is a leap year if it is evenly divisible by 4. What you might not realize, however, is that a year that is divisible by 100 is not a leap year unless it is also divisible by 400.

Try to think how you would go about setting up a test for such a condition. First, you could compute the remainders of the year after division by 4, 100, and 400, and assign these values to appropriately named variables, such as `rem_4`, `rem_100`, and `rem_400`, respectively. Then you could test these remainders to determine whether the desired criteria for a leap year were met.

If we rephrase our previous definition of a leap year, we can say that a year is a leap year if it is evenly divisible by 4 and not by 100 or if it is evenly divisible by 400. Stop for a moment to reflect on this last sentence and to verify to yourself that it is equivalent to the previously stated definition. Now that we have reformulated our definition in these terms, it becomes a relatively straightforward task to translate it into a program statement, as follows:

```
if ( (rem_4 == 0 && rem_100 != 0) || rem_400 == 0 )
    NSLog (@"It's a leap year.");
```

The parentheses around the following subexpression are not required:

```
rem_4 == 0 && rem_100 != 0
```

This is because the expression will be evaluated that way anyway: Remember that `&&` has higher precedence than `||`.

In fact, in this particular example, the following test would work just as well:

```
if ( rem_4 == 0 && ( rem_100 != 0 || rem_400 == 0 ) )
```

If you add a few statements in front of the test to declare the variables and to enable the user to key in the year from the terminal, you end up with a program that determines whether a year is a leap year, as shown in Program 6.5.

Program 6.5

```
// This program determines if a year is a leap year

#import <Foundation/Foundation.h>

int main (int argc, char * argv[])
{
    @autoreleasepool {
        int year, rem_4, rem_100, rem_400;

        NSLog (@"Enter the year to be tested: ");
        scanf ("%i", &year);

        rem_4 = year % 4;
        rem_100 = year % 100;
        rem_400 = year % 400;

        if ( (rem_4 == 0 && rem_100 != 0) || rem_400 == 0 )
            NSLog (@"It's a leap year.");
```

```
        else
            NSLog (@"Nope, it's not a leap year.");
    }

    return 0;
}
```

Program 6.5 **Output**

```
Enter the year to be tested:
1955
Nope, it's not a leap year.
```

Program 6.5 **Output (Rerun)**

```
Enter the year to be tested:
2000
It's a leap year.
```

Program 6.5 **Output (Rerun)**

```
Enter the year to be tested:
1800
Nope, it's not a leap year.
```

The previous examples use a year that is not a leap year because it isn't evenly divisible by 4 (1955), a year that is a leap year because it is evenly divisible by 400 (2000), and a year that isn't a leap year because it is evenly divisible by 100 but not by 400 (1800). To complete the run of test cases, you should also try a year that is evenly divisible by 4 and not by 100. This is left as an exercise for you.

We mentioned that Objective-C gives the programmer a tremendous amount of flexibility in forming expressions. For instance, in the previous program, you did not have to calculate the intermediate results rem_4, rem_100, and rem_400; you could have performed the calculation directly inside the if statement, as follows:

```
if ( ( year % 4 == 0 && year % 100 != 0 ) || year % 400 == 0 )
```

Using blank spaces to set off the various operators still makes the previous expression readable. If you decided to ignore this and removed the unnecessary set of parentheses, you could end up with an expression that looked like this:

```
if(year%4==0&&year%100!=0||year%400==0)
```

This expression is perfectly valid and, believe it or not, executes identically to the expression shown immediately before it. Obviously, those extra blanks go a long way toward aiding our understanding of complex expressions.

Nested `if` Statements

In discussions of the general format of the `if` statement, we indicated that if the result of evaluating the expression inside the parentheses is `true`, the statement that immediately follows is executed. It is perfectly valid for this program statement to be another `if` statement, as in the following statement:

```
if ( [chessGame isOver] == NO )
    if ( [chessGame whoseTurn] == YOU )
        [chessGame yourMove] ;
```

If the value returned by sending the `isOver` message to `chessGame` is `NO`, the following statement is executed; this statement, in turn, is another `if` statement. This `if` statement compares the value returned from the `whoseTurn` method against `YOU`. If the two values are equal, the `yourMove` message is sent to the `chessGame` object. Therefore, the `yourMove` message is sent only if both the game is not done and it's your turn. In fact, this statement could have been equivalently formulated using compound relationals, like so:

```
if ( [chessGame isOver] == NO && [chessGame whoseTurn] == YOU )
    [chessGame yourMove] ;
```

A more practical example of nested `if` statements might involve adding an `else` clause to the previous example, as shown here:

```
if ( [chessGame isOver] == NO )
    if ( [chessGame whoseTurn] == YOU )
        [chessGame yourMove] ;
    else
        [chessGame myMove] ;
```

Executing this statement proceeds as described previously. However, if the game is not over and it's not your move, the `else` clause is executed. This sends the message `myMove` to `chessGame`. If the game is over, the entire `if` statement that follows, including its associated `else` clause, is skipped.

Notice how the `else` clause is associated with the `if` statement that tests the value returned from the `whoseTurn` method, not with the `if` statement that tests whether the game is over. The general rule is that an `else` clause is always associated with the last `if` statement that doesn't contain an `else`.

You can go one step further and add an `else` clause to the outermost `if` statement in the preceding example. This `else` clause is executed if the game is over:

```
if ( [chessGame isOver] == NO )
    if ( [chessGame whoseTurn] == YOU )
```

```
        [chessGame yourMove];
    else
        [chessGame myMove];
else
    [chessGame finish];
```

Of course, even if you use indentation to indicate the way you think a statement will be interpreted in the Objective-C language, it might not always coincide with the way the system actually interprets the statement. For instance, removing the first `else` clause from the previous
example will *not* result in the statement being interpreted as its format indicates:

```
if ( [chessGame isOver] == NO )
    if ( [chessGame whoseTurn] == YOU )
        [chessGame yourMove];
else
    [chessGame finish];
```

Instead, this statement will be interpreted as follows:

```
if ( [chessGame isOver] == NO )
    if ( [chessGame whoseTurn] == YOU )
        [chessGame yourMove];
    else
        [chessGame finish];
```

This is because the `else` clause is associated with the last un-`elsed` `if`. You can use braces to
force a different association when an innermost `if` does not contain an else but an outer `if`
does. The braces have the effect of closing off the `if` statement. Therefore, the following statement achieves the desired effect:

```
if ( [chessGame isOver] == NO ) {
    if ( [chessGame whoseTurn] == YOU )
        [chessGame yourMove];
}
else
    [chessGame finish];
```

The `else if` Construct

You have seen how the `else` statement comes into play when you have a test against two
possible conditions: Either the number is even or it is odd; either the year is a leap year or it
is not. However, programming decisions you have to make are not always so black and white.
Consider the task of writing a program that displays –1 if a number the user types is less than
zero, 0 if the number is equal to zero, and 1 if the number is greater than zero. (This is actually
an implementation of what is commonly called the *sign* function.) Obviously, you must make
three tests in this case to determine whether the number that is keyed in is negative, zero, or
positive. The simple `if-else` construct will not work. Of course, in this case, you can always

resort to three separate `if` statements, but this solution does not always work, especially if the tests are not mutually exclusive.

You can handle the situation just described by adding an `if` statement to your `else` clause. We mentioned that the statement that follows an `else` could be any valid Objective-C program statement, so why not another `if`? Thus, in the general case, you could write the following:

```
if ( expression 1 )
    program statement 1
else
    if ( expression 2 )
        program statement 2
    else
        program statement 3
```

This effectively extends the `if` statement from a two-valued logic decision to a three-valued logic decision. You can continue to add `if` statements to the `else` clauses, in the manner just shown, to effectively extend the decision to an n-valued logic decision.

The preceding construct is so frequently used that it is generally referred to as an `else if` construct and is usually formatted differently from that shown previously:

```
if ( expression 1 )
    program statement 1
else if ( expression 2 )
    program statement 2
else
    program statement 3
```

This latter method of formatting improves the readability of the statement and makes it clearer that a three-way decision is being made.

The next program illustrates the use of the `else if` construct by implementing the sign function discussed earlier.

Program 6.6

```
// Program to implement the sign function

#import <Foundation/Foundation.h>

int main (int argc, char * argv[])
{
    @autoreleasepool {
        int number, sign;

        NSLog (@"Please type in a number: ");
```

```
        scanf ("%i", &number);

        if ( number < 0 )
            sign = -1;
        else if ( number == 0 )
            sign = 0;
        else        // Must be positive
            sign = 1;

        NSLog (@"Sign = %i", sign);
    }

    return 0;
}
```

Program 6.6   **Output**

```
Please type in a number:
1121
Sign = 1
```

Program 6.6   **Output (Rerun)**

```
Please type in a number:
-158
Sign = -1
```

Program 6.6   **Output (Rerun)**

```
Please type in a number:
0
Sign = 0
```

If the number that is entered is less than zero, sign is assigned the value -1; if the number is equal to zero, sign is assigned the value 0; otherwise, the number must be greater than zero, so sign is assigned the value 1.

The next program analyzes a character that is typed in from the terminal and classifies it as either an alphabetic character (a–z or A–Z), a digit (0–9), or a special character (anything else). To read a single character from the terminal, the format characters %c are used in the scanf call.

Program 6.7

```objc
// This program categorizes a single character
//        that is entered from the keyboard

#import <Foundation/Foundation.h>

int main (int argc, char * argv[])
{
   @autoreleasepool {
      char c;

      NSLog (@"Enter a single character:");
      scanf (" %c", &c);

      if ( (c >= 'a' && c <= 'z') || (c >= 'A' && c <= 'Z') )
         NSLog (@"It's an alphabetic character.");
      else if ( c >= '0' && c <= '9' )
         NSLog (@"It's a digit.");
      else
         NSLog (@"It's a special character.");
   }

   return 0;
}
```

Program 6.7 **Output**

```
Enter a single character:
&
It's a special character.
```

Program 6.7 **Output (Rerun)**

```
Enter a single character:
8
It's a digit.
```

Program 6.7 **Output (Rerun)**

```
Enter a single character:
B
It's an alphabetic character.
```

> **Note**
>
> As shown in the program example, it's best to put a space before the `%c` in the `scanf` format string (as in `" %c"`). This causes `scanf` to "skip" over any so-called whitespace characters (for example, newlines, returns, tabs, line feeds) in the input. Omitting that space can cause `scanf` to read in a character that you don't expect. Although that might not be a problem in this example, it's good to keep this in mind when working on other examples in this chapter (including the exercises) whenever you want to read a single character.

The first test that is made after the character is read in determines whether the `char` variable `c` is an alphabetic character. This is done by testing whether the character is a lowercase letter or an uppercase letter. The former test is made by the following expression:

```
( c >= 'a' && c <= 'z' )
```

This expression is true if c is within the range of characters `'a'` through `'z'`; that is, if c is a lowercase letter. The latter test is made by this expression:

```
( c >= 'A' && c <= 'Z' )
```

This expression is true if c is within the range of characters `'A'` through `'Z'`; that is, if c is an uppercase letter. These tests work on computer systems that store characters inside the machine in a format known as ASCII.

If the variable c is an alphabetic character, the first `if` test succeeds and the message `"It's an alphabetic character."` is displayed. If the test fails, the `else if` clause is executed. This clause determines whether the character is a digit. Note that this test compares the character c against the *characters* `'0'` and `'9'` and *not* the *integers* 0 and 9. This is because a character was read in from the terminal, and the characters `'0'` to `'9'` are not the same as the numbers 0–9. In fact, in ASCII, the character `'0'` is actually represented internally as the number 48, the character `'1'` as the number 49, and so on.

If c is a digit character, the phrase `"It's a digit."` is displayed. Otherwise, if c is not alphabetic and is not a digit, the final `else` clause is executed and displays the phrase `"It's a special character."` at the terminal. Execution of the program is then complete.

Note that even though `scanf` is used here to read just a single character, you still must press the Return key after the character is typed to send the input to the program. In general, whenever you're reading data from the terminal, the program doesn't see any of the data typed on the line until the Return key is pressed.

Let's suppose for the next example that you want to write a program that allows the user to type in simple expressions of the following form:

```
number  operator  number
```

The program will evaluate the expression and display the results at the terminal. The operators you want to have recognized are the normal operators for addition, subtraction, multiplication, and division. Let's use the `Calculator` class from Program 4.6 in Chapter 4, "Data Types and Expressions," here. Each expression will be given to the calculator for computation.

The following program uses a large `if` statement with many `else if` clauses to determine which operation is to be performed.

> **Note**
> It's better to use routines in the standard library called `islower` and `isupper` and avoid the internal representation issue entirely. To do that, include the line `#import <ctype.h>` in your program. However, we've put this here for illustrative purposes only.

Program 6.8

```
// Program to evaluate simple expressions of the form
//         number operator number

// Implement a Calculator class

#import <Foundation/Foundation.h>

@interface Calculator: NSObject

// accumulator methods
-(void)  setAccumulator: (double) value;
-(void)  clear;
-(double) accumulator;

// arithmetic methods
-(void)  add: (double) value;
-(void)  subtract: (double) value;
-(void)  multiply: (double) value;
-(void)  divide: (double) value;
@end

@implementation Calculator
{
    double accumulator;
}

-(void) setAccumulator: (double) value
{
    accumulator = value;
}

-(void) clear
{
    accumulator = 0;
```

```
}

-(double) accumulator
{
    return accumulator;
}

-(void) add: (double) value
{
    accumulator += value;
}

-(void) subtract: (double) value
{
    accumulator -= value;
}

-(void) multiply: (double) value
{
    accumulator *= value;
}

-(void) divide: (double) value
{
    accumulator /= value;
}
@end

int main (int argc, char * argv[])
{
    @autoreleasepool {
        double      value1, value2;
        char        operator;
        Calculator  *deskCalc = [[Calculator alloc] init];

        NSLog (@"Type in your expression.");
        scanf ("%lf %c %lf", &value1, &operator, &value2);

        [deskCalc setAccumulator: value1];
        if ( operator == '+' )
           [deskCalc add: value2];
        else if ( operator == '-' )
           [deskCalc subtract: value2];
        else if ( operator == '*' )
           [deskCalc multiply: value2];
```

```
        else if ( operator == '/' )
            [deskCalc divide: value2];

        NSLog (@"%.2f", [deskCalc accumulator]);
    }

    return 0;
}
```

Program 6.8   **Output**

```
Type in your expression.
123.5 + 59.3
182.80
```

Program 6.8   **Output (Rerun)**

```
Type in your expression.
198.7 / 26
7.64
```

Program 6.8   **Output (Rerun)**

```
Type in your expression.
89.3 * 2.5
223.25
```

The scanf call specifies that three values are to be read into the variables value1, operator, and value2. A double value can be read in with the %lf format characters. This is the format used to read in the value of the variable value1, which is the first operand of the expression.

Next, you read in the operator. Because the operator is a character ('+', '-', '*', or '/') and not a number, you read it into the character variable operator. The %c format characters tell the system to read in the next character from the terminal. The blank spaces inside the format string indicate that an arbitrary number of blank spaces are to be permitted on the input. This enables you to separate the operands from the operator with blank spaces when you type in these values.

After the two values and the operator have been read in, the program stores the first value in the calculator's accumulator. Next, you test the value of operator against the four permissible operators. When a correct match is made, the corresponding message is sent to the calculator to perform the operation. In the last NSLog, the value of the accumulator is retrieved for display. Execution of the program is then complete.

A few words about program thoroughness are in order at this point. Although the preceding program does accomplish the task that we set out to perform, the program is not really complete because it does not account for user mistakes. For example, what would happen if the user typed in a ? for the operator by mistake? The program would simply fall through the if statement and no messages would ever appear at the terminal to alert the user that he had incorrectly typed in his expression.

Another overlooked case is when the user types in a division operation with zero as the divisor. You know by now that you should never attempt to divide a number by zero in Objective-C. The program should check for this case.

Trying to predict the ways in which a program can fail or produce unwanted results and then taking preventive measures to account for such situations are necessary parts of producing good, reliable programs. Running a sufficient number of test cases against a program can often point a finger to portions of the program that do not account for certain cases. But it goes further than that. It must become a matter of self-discipline while coding a program to always ask "What would happen if...?" and to insert the necessary program statements to handle the situation properly.

Program 6.8A, a modified version of Program 6.8, accounts for division by zero and the keying in of an unknown operator.

Program 6.8A

```
// Program to evaluate simple expressions of the form
//     value   operator   value

#import <Foundation/Foundation.h>

// Insert interface and implementation sections for
// Calculator class here

int main (int argc, char * argv[])
{
    @autoreleasepool {
        double    value1, value2;
        char      operator;
        Calculator *deskCalc = [[Calculator alloc] init];

        NSLog (@"Type in your expression.");
        scanf ("%lf %c %lf", &value1, &operator, &value2);

        [deskCalc setAccumulator: value1];

        if ( operator == '+' )
           [deskCalc add: value2];
        else if ( operator == '-' )
```

```
                    [deskCalc subtract: value2];
            else if ( operator == '*' )
                [deskCalc multiply: value2];
            else if ( operator == '/' )
                if ( value2 == 0 )
                    NSLog (@"Division by zero.");
                else
                    [deskCalc divide: value2];
            else
                NSLog (@"Unknown operator.");

            NSLog (@"%.2f", [deskCalc accumulator]);
    }

    return 0;
}
```

Program 6.8A   **Output**

```
Type in your expression.
123.5 + 59.3
182.80
```

Program 6.8A   **Output (Rerun)**

```
Type in your expression.
198.7 / 0
Division by zero.
198.7
```

Program 6.8A   **Output (Rerun)**

```
Type in your expression.
125 $ 28
Unknown operator.
125
```

When the operator that is typed in is the slash, for division, another test is made to determine whether value2 is 0. If it is, an appropriate message is displayed at the terminal; otherwise, the division operation is carried out and the results are displayed. Pay careful attention to the nesting of the if statements and the associated else clauses in this case.

The `else` clause at the end of the program catches any fall-throughs. Therefore, any value of `operator` that does not match any of the four characters tested causes this `else` clause to be executed, resulting in the display of `"Unknown operator."` at the terminal.

A better way to handle the division-by-zero problem is to perform the test inside the method that handles division. You can modify your `divide:` method as shown here:

```
-(void) divide: (double) value
{
   if (value != 0.0)
      accumulator /= value;
   else {
      NSLog (@"Division by zero.");
      accumulator = NAN;
   }
}
```

If `value` is nonzero, you perform the division; otherwise, you display the message and set the accumulator to the value NAN. In general, it's better to have the method handle special cases than rely on the resourcefulness of the programmer using the method.

The `switch` Statement

The type of `if-else` statement chain you encountered in the last program example—with the value of a variable successively compared against different values—is so commonly used when developing programs that a special program statement exists in the Objective-C language for performing precisely this function. The name of the statement is the `switch` statement, and its general format is as follows:

```
switch ( expression )
{
    case value1:
        program statement
        program statement
           . . .
        break;
    case value2:
        program statement
        program statement
           . . .
        break;
      . . .
    case valuen:
        program statement
        program statement
           . . .
        break;
```

```
        default:
            program statement
            program statement
              ...
            break;
}
```

The *expression* enclosed within parentheses is successively compared against the values *value1*, *value2*, ..., *valuen*, which must be simple constants or constant expressions. If a case is found whose value is equal to the value of *expression*, the program statements that follow the case are executed. Note that when more than one such program statement is included, they do *not* have to be enclosed within braces.

The break statement signals the end of a particular case and causes execution of the switch statement to be terminated. Remember to include the break statement at the end of every case. Forgetting to do so for a particular case causes program execution to continue into the next case whenever that case is executed. Sometimes this is done intentionally; if you elect to do so, be sure to insert comments to alert others of your purpose.

The special optional case called default is executed if the value of *expression* does not match any of the case values. This is conceptually equivalent to the catchall else used in the previous example. In fact, the general form of the switch statement can be equivalently expressed as an if statement, as follows:

```
if ( expression == value1 )
{
    program statement
    program statement
        ...
}
else if ( expression == value2 )
{
    program statement
    program statement
        ...
}
    ...
else if ( expression == valuen )
{
    program statement
    program statement
        ...
}
else
{
    program statement
    program statement
        ...
}
```

Bearing in mind the previous code, you can translate the big `if` statement from Program 6.8A into an equivalent `switch` statement, as shown in Program 6.9.

Program 6.9

```
// Program to evaluate simple expressions of the form
//      value operator  value

#import <Foundation/Foundation.h>

// Insert interface and implementation sections for
// Calculator class here

int main (int argc, char * argv[])
{
    @autoreleasepool {
        double   value1, value2;
        char     operator;
        Calculator *deskCalc = [[Calculator alloc] init];

        NSLog (@"Type in your expression.");
        scanf ("%lf %c %lf", &value1, &operator, &value2);

        [deskCalc setAccumulator: value1];

        switch ( operator ) {
            case '+':
                [deskCalc add: value2];
                break;
            case '-':
                [deskCalc subtract: value2];
                break;
            case '*':
                [deskCalc multiply: value2];
                break;
            case '/':
                [deskCalc divide: value2];
                break;
            default:
                NSLog (@"Unknown operator.");
                break;
        }

        NSLog (@"%.2f", [deskCalc accumulator]);
    }

    return 0;
}
```

Program 6.9   **Output**

```
Type in your expression.
178.99 - 326.8
-147.81
```

After the expression has been read in, the value of `operator` is successively compared against the values specified by each case. When a match is found, the statements contained inside the case are executed. The `break` statement then sends execution out of the `switch` statement, where execution of the program is completed. If none of the cases matches the value of `operator`, the `default` case, which displays "Unknown operator.", is executed.

The `break` statement in the `default` case is actually unnecessary in the preceding program because no statements follow this case inside the `switch`. Nevertheless, it is a good programming habit to remember to include the `break` at the end of every case.

When writing a `switch` statement, bear in mind that no two case values can be the same. However, you can associate more than one case value with a particular set of program statements. This is done simply by listing the multiple case values (with the keyword `case` before the value and a colon after the value in each case) before the common statements that are to be executed. For example, in the `switch` statement that follows, the `multiply:` method is executed if `operator` is equal to an asterisk or to the lowercase letter x:

```
switch ( operator )
{
    . . .
  case '*':
  case 'x':
      [deskCalc multiply: value2];
      break;
    . . .
}
```

Boolean Variables

Just about anyone learning to program soon faces the task of having to write a program to generate a table of prime numbers. To refresh your memory, a positive integer, p, is a prime number if it is not evenly divisible by any other integers other than 1 and itself. The first prime integer is defined to be 2. The next prime is 3 because it is not evenly divisible by any integers other than 1 and 3; and 4 is *not* prime because it *is* evenly divisible by 2.

You can take several approaches to generate a table of prime numbers. If you had the task of generating all prime numbers up to 50, for example, the most straightforward (and simplest) algorithm to generate such a table would simply test each integer, p, for divisibility by all integers from 2 through p-1. If any such integer evenly divided p, then p would not be prime; otherwise, it would be a prime number.

Program 6.10 generates a list of prime numbers from 2 to 50.

Program 6.10

```
// Program to generate a table of prime numbers

#import <Foundation/Foundation.h>

int main (int argc, char * argv[])
{
    @autoreleasepool {
        int    p, d, isPrime;

        for ( p = 2; p <= 50; ++p ) {
            isPrime = 1;

            for ( d = 2; d < p; ++d )
                if ( p % d == 0 )
                    isPrime = 0;

            if ( isPrime != 0 )
                NSLog (@"%i ", p);
        }
    }

    return 0;
}
```

Program 6.10 **Output**

```
2
3
5
7
11
13
17
19
23
29
31
37
41
43
47
```

Several points are worth noting about Program 6.10. The outermost for statement sets up a loop to cycle through the integers 2-50. The loop variable p represents the value you are currently testing to see whether it is prime. The first statement in the loop assigns the value 1 to the variable isPrime. The use of this variable will become apparent shortly.

A second loop is set up to divide p by the integers 2 through p-1. Inside the loop, a test is performed to see whether the remainder of p divided by d is 0. If it is, you know that p cannot be prime because an integer other than 1 and itself evenly divides it. To signal that p is no longer a candidate as a prime number, the value of the variable isPrime is set equal to 0.

When the innermost loop finishes execution, the value of isPrime is tested. If its value is not equal to 0, no integer was found that evenly divided p; therefore, p must be a prime number, and its value is displayed.

You might have noticed that the variable isPrime takes on either 0 or 1, and no other values. Its value is 1 as long as p still qualifies as a prime number. But as soon as a single even divisor is found, its value is set to 0 to indicate that p no longer satisfies the criteria for being prime. Variables used in such a manner are generally referred to as *Boolean* variables. A flag typically assumes only one of two different values. Furthermore, the value of a flag usually is tested at least once in the program to see whether it is on (true or YES) or off (false or NO), and some particular action is taken based on the results of the test.

In Objective-C, the notion of a flag being true or false is most naturally translated into the values 1 and 0, respectively. So in Program 6.10, when you set the value of isPrime to 1 inside the loop, you are effectively setting it as true to indicate that p "is prime." During the course of execution of the inner for loop, if an even divisor is found, the value of isPrime is set false to indicate that p no longer "is prime."

It is no coincidence that the value 1 is typically used to represent the true or on state and 0 is used to represent the false or off state. This representation corresponds to the notion of a single bit inside a computer. When the bit is on, its value is 1; when it is off, its value is 0. In Objective-C, however, there is an even more convincing argument in favor of these logic values. It has to do with the way the Objective-C language treats the concept of true and false.

When we began our discussions in this chapter, we noted that if the conditions specified inside the if statement are satisfied, the program statement that immediately followed is executed. But what exactly does *satisfied* mean? In the Objective-C language, *satisfied* means nonzero, and nothing more. Therefore, the statement

```
if ( 100 )
    NSLog (@"This will always be printed.");
```

results in the execution of the NSLog statement because the condition in the if statement (in this case, simply the value 100) is nonzero and, therefore, is satisfied.

In each of the programs in this chapter, we used the notions of "nonzero means satisfied" and "zero means not satisfied." This is because whenever a relational expression is evaluated in Objective-C, it is given the value 1 if the expression is satisfied and 0 if the expression is not satisfied. So, evaluation of the statement

```
if ( number < 0 )
    number = -number;
```

actually proceeds as follows: The relational expression `number < 0` is evaluated. If the condition is satisfied—that is, if `number` is less than `0`—the value of the expression is `1`; otherwise, its value is `0`.

The `if` statement tests the result of the expression evaluation. If the result is nonzero, the statement that immediately follows is executed; otherwise, the statement is skipped.

The preceding discussion also applies to the evaluation of conditions inside the `for`, `while`, and `do` statements. Evaluation of compound relational expressions such as in the following statement also proceeds as outlined previously:

```
while ( char != 'e' && count != 80 )
```

If both specified conditions are valid, the result is `1`, but if either condition is not valid, the result of the evaluation is `0`. The results of the evaluation are then checked. If the result is `0`, the `while` loop terminates; otherwise, it continues.

Returning to Program 6.10 and the notion of flags, it is perfectly valid in Objective-C to test whether the value of a flag is true using an expression such as this one:

```
if ( isPrime )
```

This expression is equivalent to the following:

```
if ( isPrime != 0 )
```

To easily test whether the value of a flag is false, you use the logical negation operator, `!`. In the expression that follows, the logical negation operator is used to test whether the value of `isPrime` is false (read this statement as "if not `isPrime`"):

```
if ( ! isPrime )
```

In general, an expression such as this one negates the logical value of *expression*:

```
! expression
```

So if *expression* is `0`, the logical negation operator produces a `1`. And if the result of the evaluation of *expression* is nonzero, the negation operator yields a `0`.

The logical negation operator can be used to easily flip the value of a flag, as in the following expression:

```
my_move = ! my_move;
```

As you might expect, this operator has the same precedence as the unary minus operator, which means that it has higher precedence than all binary arithmetic operators and all relational operators. To test whether the value of a variable `x` is not less than the value of a variable `y`, such as in

```
! ( x < y )
```

the parentheses are required to ensure proper evaluation of the expression. Of course, you could have equivalently expressed the previous statement as follows:

```
x >= y
```

A couple of built-in features in Objective-C make working with Boolean variables a little easier. One is the special type BOOL, which can be used to declare variables that will contain either a true or a false value. The other is the built-in values YES and NO. Using these predefined values in your programs can make them easier to write and read. Take a look at Program 6.10, rewritten to take advantage of these features.

Note

The type BOOL is really added by a mechanism known as the preprocessor.

Program 6.10

```
// Program to generate a table of prime numbers
// second version using BOOL type and predefined values

#import <Foundation/Foundation.h>

int main (int argc, char * argv[])
{
    @autoreleasepool {
        int     p, d;
        BOOL    isPrime;

        for ( p = 2; p <= 50; ++p ) {
            isPrime = YES;

            for ( d = 2; d < p; ++d )
                if ( p % d == 0 )
                    isPrime = NO;

            if ( isPrime == YES )
                NSLog (@"%i ", p);
        }
    }
    return 0;
}
```

Program 6.10A   **Output**

```
2
3
5
7
11
13
17
19
23
29
31
37
41
43
47
```

Many methods in the system libraries either return a value of type BOOL or take one or more arguments of this type. You'll see examples of these later in the text.

The Conditional Operator

Perhaps the most unusual operator in the Objective-C language is one called the *conditional* operator. Unlike all other operators in Objective-C—which are either unary or binary operators—the conditional operator is a *ternary* operator; that is, it takes three operands. The two symbols used to denote this operator are the question mark (?) and the colon (:). The first operand is placed before the ?, the second between the ? and the :, and the third after the :.

The general format of the conditional expression is shown here:

```
condition ? expression1 : expression2
```

In this syntax, condition is an expression, usually a relational expression, that the Objective-C system evaluates first whenever it encounters the conditional operator. If the result of the evaluation of condition is true (that is, nonzero), expression1 is evaluated and the result of the evaluation becomes the result of the operation. If condition evaluates false (that is, zero), expression2 is evaluated and its result becomes the result of the operation.

A conditional expression is often used to assign one of two values to a variable, depending on some condition. For example, suppose you have an integer variable x and another integer variable s. If you want to assign -1 to s if x is less than 0, and the value of x2 to s otherwise, you can write the following statement:

```
s = ( x < 0 ) ? -1 : x * x;
```

The condition x < 0 is first tested when the previous statement is executed. Parentheses are generally placed around the condition expression to aid in the statement's readability. This is usually not required, though, because the precedence of the conditional operator is very low (lower, in fact, than all other operators but the assignment operators and the comma operator).

If the value of x is less than zero, the expression immediately following the ? is evaluated. This expression is simply the constant integer value -1, which is assigned to the variable s if x is less than zero.

If the value of x is not less than zero, the expression immediately following the : is evaluated and assigned to s. So, if x is greater than or equal to zero, the value of x * x, or x2, is assigned to s.

As another example of the conditional operator, the following statement assigns to the variable max_value the maximum of a and b:

```
max_value = ( a > b ) ? a : b;
```

If the expression after the : (the "else" part) consists of another conditional operator, you can achieve the effects of an else if clause. For example, the sign function implemented in Program 6.6 can be written in one program line using two conditional operators, as follows:

```
sign = ( number < 0 ) ? -1 : (( number == 0 ) ? 0 : 1);
```

If number is less than zero, sign is assigned the value -1; if number is equal to zero, sign is assigned the value 0; otherwise, it is assigned the value 1. The parentheses around the "else" part of the previous expression are actually unnecessary. This is because the conditional operator associates from right to left, meaning that multiple uses of this operator in a single expression, such as in

```
e1 ? e2 : e3 ? e4 : e5
```

group from right to left and therefore are evaluated as follows:

```
e1 ? e2 : ( e3 ? e4 : e5 )
```

Conditional expressions don't have to be used on the right side of an assignment; they can be used in any situation in which expressions can be used. This means you can display the sign of the variable number without first assigning it to a variable using an NSLog statement, as shown here:

```
NSLog (@"Sign = %i", ( number < 0 ) ? -1
                          : ( number == 0 ) ? 0 : 1);
```

The conditional operator is very handy when writing preprocessor macros in Objective-C. You can see this in detail in Chapter 12, "The Preprocessor."

Exercises

1. Write a program that asks the user to type in two integer values. Test these two numbers to determine whether the first is evenly divisible by the second and then display an appropriate message at the terminal.

2. Program 6.8A displays the value in the accumulator even if an invalid operator is entered or division by zero is attempted. Fix that problem.

3. Modify the `print` method from the `Fraction` class so that whole numbers are displayed as such (so the fraction `5/1` should display as simply `5`). Also modify the method to display fractions with a numerator of `0` as simply zero.

4. Write a program that acts as a simple printing calculator. The program should allow the user to type in expressions of the following form:

   number   operator

   The program should recognize the following operators:

   `+    -    *    /    S    E`

   The `S` operator tells the program to set the accumulator to the typed-in number, and the `E` operator tells the program that execution is to end. The arithmetic operations are performed on the contents of the accumulator, with the number that was keyed in acting as the second operand. The following is a sample run showing how the program should operate:

   ```
   Begin Calculations
   10 S                Set Accumulator to 10
   = 10.000000         Contents of Accumulator
   2 /                 Divide by 2
   = 5.000000          Contents of Accumulator
   55 -                Subtract 55
   = -50.000000
   100.25 S            Set Accumulator to 100.25
   = 100.250000
   4 *                 Multiply by 4
   = 401.000000
   0 E                 End of program
   = 401.000000
   End of Calculations.
   ```

Make sure that the program detects division by zero and also checks for unknown operators. Use the `Calculator` class developed in Program 6.8 for performing your calculations. Note: Remember to use a space character in your `scanf` format string (for example, `"%f %c"`) to skip whitespace characters in the input.

5. We developed Program 5.9 to reverse the digits of an integer typed in from the terminal. However, this program does not function well if you type in a negative number. Find out what happens in such a case, and then modify the program so that negative numbers are correctly handled. By this, we mean that if the number `-8645` were typed in, for example, the output of the program should be `5468-`.

6. Write a program that takes an integer keyed in from the terminal and extracts and displays each digit of the integer in English. So if the user types in `932`, the program should display the following:

```
nine
three
two
```

(Remember to display `zero` if the user types in just `0`.) Note: This exercise is a hard one!

7. Program 6.10 has several inefficiencies. One inefficiency results from checking even numbers. Because any even number greater than 2 obviously cannot be prime, the program could simply skip all even numbers as possible primes and as possible divisors. The inner `for` loop is also inefficient because the value of `p` is always divided by all values of `d` from 2 through `p-1`. You can avoid this inefficiency if you add a test for the value of `isPrime` in the conditions of the `for` loop. In this manner, you can set up the `for` loop to continue as long as no divisor is found and the value of `d` is less than `p`. Modify Program 6.10 to incorporate these two changes; then run the program to verify its operation.

7

More on Classes

In this chapter, you continue learning how to work with classes and write methods. You also apply some of the concepts you learned in the previous chapter, such as completing program looping, making decisions, and working with expressions. First, though, we talk about splitting your program into multiple files to make working with larger programs easier.

Separate Interface and Implementation Files

It's time to get used to putting your class declarations and definitions in separate files.

If you're using Xcode, start a new project called `FractionTest`. Type the following program into the file `main.m`.

Program 7.1   **Main Test Program:** `main.m`

```
#import "Fraction.h"

int main (int argc, char * argv[])
{
    @autoreleasepool {
        Fraction  *myFraction = [[Fraction alloc] init];

        // set fraction to 1/3

        [myFraction setNumerator: 1];
        [myFraction setDenominator: 3];

        // display the fraction

        NSLog (@"The value of myFraction is:");
```

```
    [myFraction print];
}

    return 0;
}
```

Note that this file does not include the definition of the `Fraction` class. However, it does import a file called `Fraction.h`.

Typically, a class declaration (that is, the `@interface` section) is placed in its own file, called *class*`.h`. The definition (that is, the `@implementation` section that contains the code) is normally placed in a file of the same name, using the extension `.m` instead. So, let's put the declaration of the `Fraction` class in the file `Fraction.h` and the definition in `Fraction.m`.

To do this in Xcode, select New, File from the File menu. In the left pane, select Cocoa. In the top-right pane, select Objective-C class. Your window should appear as shown in Figure 7.1.

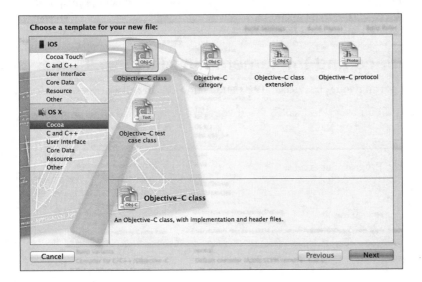

Figure 7.1   Xcode New File menu

Click Next. Type in the name of your class (**Fraction**) and choose NSObject for Subclass Of (see Figure 7.2). Click Next again.

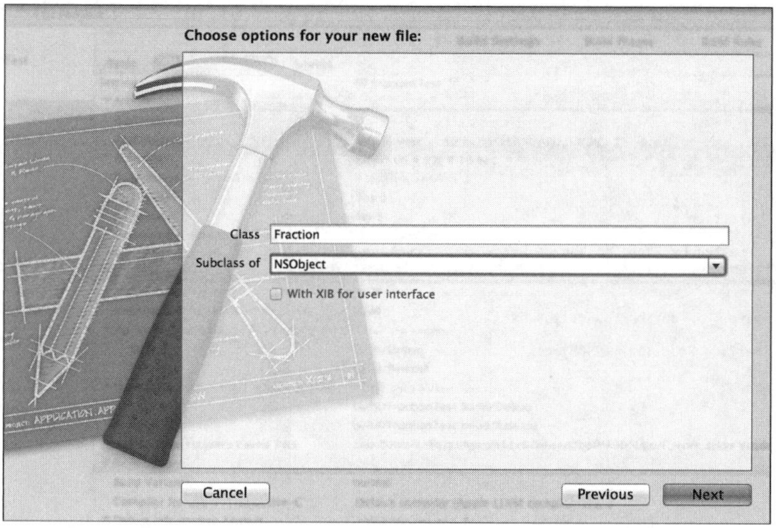

Figure 7.2   Adding a new class to your project

You should get a sheet similar to that shown in Figure 7.3 You can leave everything set as shown on your screen and simply click Create.

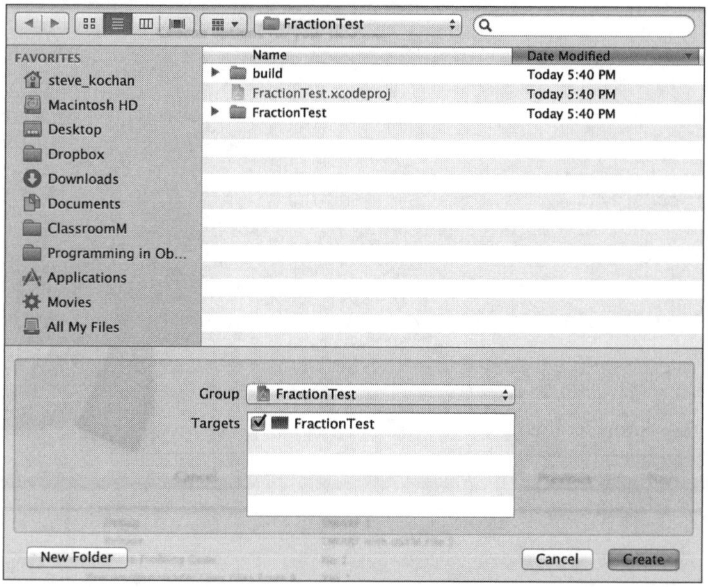

Figure 7.3   Adding a new class to your project

Xcode has added two files to your project: Fraction.h and Fraction.m. Figure 7.4 shows this.

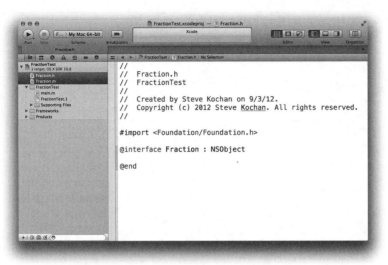

Figure 7.4   Xcode creates files for the new class

In the file Fraction.h, you will now enter your interface section for the Fraction class, as shown here.

Program 7.1   **Interface File** Fraction.h

```
//
//  Fraction.h
//  FractionTest
//
//  Created by Steve Kochan on 9/3/12.
//  Copyright (c) ClassroomM, Inc. All rights reserved.
//

#import <Foundation/Foundation.h>

// The Fraction class

@interface Fraction : NSObject

-(void)     print;
-(void)     setNumerator: (int) n;
-(void)     setDenominator: (int) d;
-(int)      numerator;
-(int)      denominator;
```

```
-(double)  convertToNum;
```

```
@end
```

The interface file tells the compiler (and other programmers, as you'll learn later) what a `Fraction` looks like: It has six instance methods: `print`, `setNumerator:`, `setDenominator:`, `numerator`, `denominator`, and `convertToNum`. The first three methods don't return a value, the next two return an `int`, and the last one returns a `double`. The `setNumerator:` and `setDenominator:` methods each take an integer argument.

The details of the implementation for the `Fraction` class should be typed into the file `Fraction.m`.

Program 7.1   **Implementation File:** `Fraction.m`

```
//
//  Fraction.m
//  FractionTest
//
//  Created by Steve Kochan on 9/3/12.
//  Copyright (c) ClassroomM, Inc. All rights reserved.
//
#import "Fraction.h"

@implementation Fraction
{
   int numerator;
   int denominator;
}

-(void) print
{
   NSLog (@"%i/%i", numerator, denominator);
}

-(void) setNumerator: (int) n
{
   numerator = n;
}

-(void) setDenominator: (int) d
{
   denominator = d;
}

-(int) numerator
{
```

```
      return numerator;
}

-(int) denominator
{
      return denominator;
}

-(double) convertToNum
{
      if (denominator != 0)
         return (double) numerator / denominator;
      else
         return NAN;
}
@end
```

Note that the interface file is imported into the implementation file with the following statement:

```
#import "Fraction.h"
```

This is done because we separated the interface and implementation sections into two separate files. The compiler will compile each file independently. When the compiler is processing the file containing the implementation section (that is, the file Fraction.m), it needs to know information from the class's interface section (such as the names and argument types of its methods). By importing the .h file, the compiler knows about the class and methods you declared for your Fraction class and can ensure consistency between the two files.

Another thing you should note is that the file that is imported is enclosed in a set of double quotes, not < and > characters, as was the case with <Foundation/Foundation.h>. The double quotes are used for *local* files (files that you create) instead of system files, and they tell the compiler where to look for the specified file. When you use double quotes, the compiler typically looks for the specified file first inside your project directory and then in a list of other places. If necessary, you can specify different places for the compiler to search.

Note again that the test program, main.m (which was shown at the start of this chapter), includes the interface file Fraction.h, and *not* the implementation file Fraction.m. The interface section provides all the information the compiler needs to know about a class when you need to use that class in another file. The implementation section contains the actual code for the methods, and Xcode takes care of including that code along with any other code you write when you build your application. Think of the interface file as containing the *public* information about a class—the information you share with the users of the class. In contrast, the implementation section contains the *private* information—the instance variables and the code.

> **Note**
>
> In fact, the code may actually be stored someplace else, such as in a framework or library.

Now you have your program split into three separate files. This might seem like a lot of work for a small program example, but the usefulness will become apparent when you start dealing with larger programs and sharing class declarations with other programmers.

You can now compile and run your program the same way you did before: Select Run from the Product menu, or simply click the Run button on the toolbar.

If you're compiling your programs from the command line, give the Objective-C compiler both .m filenames. Using `clang`, the command line looks like this:

```
clang -fobjc-arc Fraction.m main.m -o FractionTest
```

This builds an executable file called `FractionTest`. Here's the output after running the program.

Program 7.1   FractionTest **Output**

```
The value of myFraction is:
1/3
```

Synthesized Accessor Methods

As of Objective-C 2.0, you can have your setter and getter methods (collectively known as *accessor* methods) automatically generated for you. We haven't shown you how to do this up to this point because it was important for you to learn how to write these methods on your own. However, it's a nice convenience provided in the language, so it's time for you to learn how to take advantage of this feature.

The first step is to use the `@property` directive in your interface section to identify your properties. These properties are often named the same as your instance variables, although they don't have to be. In the case of our `Fraction` class, the two instance variables `numerator` and `denominator` fall into this category. Following is the new interface section with the new `@property` directive added.

```
@interface Fraction : NSObject

@property int numerator, denominator;

-(void)    print;
-(double)  convertToNum;
@end
```

Note that we no longer include the definitions for our getter and setter methods: `numerator`, `denominator`, `setNumerator:`, and `setDenominator:`. We're going to have the Objective-C compiler automatically generate or *synthesize* these for us. How is that done? Simply by using the `@synthesize` directive in the implementation section, as shown:

```
#import "Fraction.h"

@implementation Fraction

@synthesize numerator, denominator;

-(void) print
{
    NSLog (@"%i/%i", numerator, denominator);
}

-(double) convertToNum
{
    if (denominator != 0)
        return (double) numerator / denominator;
    else
        return NAN;
}
@end
```

Note that when you use the `@property` directive you no longer need to declare the corresponding instance variable in your implementation section. You can if you want to, but it's no longer necessary; the compiler takes care of that for you.

The following line tells the Objective-C compiler to generate a pair of getter and setter methods for each of the two properties, `numerator` and `denominator`:

```
@synthesize numerator, denominator;
```

In general, if you have a property called *x*, including the following line in your implementation section causes the compiler to automatically synthesize a getter method called *x* and a setter method called set*X*:.

```
@synthesize x;
```

Even though this might not seem like a big deal here, having the compiler do this for you is worthwhile because the accessor methods that are generated will be efficient and will run safely with multiple threads, on multiple machines, with multiple cores.

> **Note**
>
> As of Xcode 4.5, you no longer need to use the `@synthesize` directive. Using the `@property` directive suffices. The compiler automatically generates the setter and getter for you. We return to this topic later in this chapter.

Now go back to Program 7.1 and make the changes to the interface and implementation sections as indicated so that the accessor methods are synthesized for you. Verify that you still get the same output from the program without making any changes to `main.m`.

Accessing Properties Using the Dot Operator

The Objective-C language enables you to access properties using a more convenient syntax. To get the value of the numerator stored in `myFraction`, you could write this:

```
[myFraction numerator]
```

This sends the `numerator` message to the `myFraction` object, resulting in the return of the desired value. You can also write the following equivalent expression using the dot operator:

```
myFraction.numerator
```

The general format here is as follows:

```
instance.property
```

You can use a similar syntax to assign values as well:

```
instance.property = value
```

This is equivalent to writing the following expression: `[instance setProperty: value]`

In Program 7.1, you set the numerator and denominator of your fraction to `1/3` using the following two lines of code:

```
[myFraction setNumerator: 1];
[myFraction setDenominator: 3];
```

Here's an equivalent way to write the same two lines:

```
myFraction.numerator = 1;
myFraction.denominator = 3;
```

We use these new features for synthesizing methods and accessing properties throughout the remainder of this text.

Program 7.2 shows the use of the dot operator as just described.

Program 7.2   **Main Test Program:** `main.m` **Showing Use of the Dot Operator**

```
#import "Fraction.h"

int main (int argc, char * argv[])
{
    @autoreleasepool {
```

```
    Fraction  *myFraction = [[Fraction alloc] init];

    // set fraction to 1/3 using the dot operator

    myFraction.numerator = 1;
    myFraction.denominator = 3;

    // display the fraction's numerator and denominator

    NSLog (@"The numerator is %i, and the denominator is %i",
        myFraction.numerator, myFraction.denominator);
}

    return 0;
}
```

Program 7.2   FractionTest **Output**

```
The numerator is 1, and the denominator is 3
```

It's worth pointing out that you can use the dot operator with methods that you manually write, not just those that are synthesized. Further, if you have a getter method called `numerator`, you can still write an expression such as `myFraction.numerator` in your program, even if `numerator` has not been defined as a property.

> **Note**
>
> Based on the preceding discussion, realize that although it's syntactically correct to write a statement such as `myFraction.print`, it's not considered good programming style. The dot operator was really intended to be used with properties; typically to set/get the value of an instance variable. Methods that do work (such as calculating the sum of two fractions) are labeled as *tasks* in Apple documentation. Tasks are typically not executed using the dot operator; the traditional bracketed message expression is the preferred syntax.

> **Note**
>
> If you synthesize your accessor methods, don't start the names of the properties with the words `new`, `alloc`, `copy`, or `init`. This has to do with assumptions the compiler makes about the corresponding methods that will be synthesized and is described in greater detail in Chapter 17, "Memory Management and Automatic Reference Counting."

Multiple Arguments to Methods

Let's continue to work with the `Fraction` class and make some additions. You have defined six methods. It would be nice to have a method to set both the numerator and the denominator with a single message. You define methods that take multiple arguments simply by listing each successive argument followed by a colon. This becomes part of the method name. For example, the method named `addEntryWithName:andEmail:` takes two arguments, presumably a name and an email address. The method `addEntryWithName:andEmail:andPhone:` takes three arguments: a name, an email address, and a phone number.

A method to set both the numerator and the denominator could be named `setNumerator:andDenominator:`, and you might use it like this:

```
[myFraction setNumerator: 1 andDenominator: 3];
```

That's not bad. And that was actually the first choice for the method name. But we can come up with a more readable method name. For example, how about `setTo:over:`? That might not look too appealing at first glance, but compare this message to set `myFraction` to 1/3 with the previous one:

```
[myFraction setTo: 1 over: 3];
```

I think that reads a little better, but the choice is up to you. (Some might actually prefer the first name because it explicitly references the instance variable names contained in the class.) Again, choosing good method names is important for program readability. Writing out the actual message expression can help you pick a good one.

Let's put this new method to work. First, add the declaration of `setTo:over:` to the interface file, as shown in Program 7.2.

Program 7.2   **Interface File:** `Fraction.h`

```
#import <Foundation/Foundation.h>

// Define the Fraction class

@interface Fraction : NSObject

@property int numerator, denominator;

-(void)     print;
-(void)     setTo: (int) n over: (int) d;
-(double)   convertToNum;
@end
```

Next, add the definition for the new method to the implementation file.

Program 7.2   **Implementation File:** `Fraction.m`

```objc
#import "Fraction.h"

@implementation Fraction

@synthesize numerator, denominator;

-(void) print
{
    NSLog (@"%i/%i", numerator, denominator);
}

-(double) convertToNum
{
   if (denominator != 0)
       return (double) numerator / denominator;
   else
       return NAN;
}

-(void) setTo: (int) n over: (int) d
{
    numerator = n;
    denominator = d;
}
@end
```

The new `setTo:over:` method simply assigns its two integer arguments, n and d, to the corresponding instance variables for the fraction, `numerator`, and `denominator`.

Here's a test program to try your new method.

Program 7.2   **Test File:** `main.m`

```objc
#import "Fraction.h"

int main (int argc, char * argv[])
{
   @autoreleasepool {
      Fraction *aFraction = [[Fraction alloc] init];

      [aFraction setTo: 100 over: 200];
      [aFraction print];

      [aFraction setTo: 1 over: 3];
      [aFraction print];
```

```
    }

    return 0;
}
```

Program 7.2   **Output**

```
100/200
1/3
```

Methods without Argument Names

When creating the name for a method, the argument names are actually optional. For example, you can declare a method like this:

```
-(int) set: (int) n: (int) d;
```

Note that, unlike in previous examples, no name is given for the second argument to the method here. This method is named `set::`, and the two colons mean the method takes two arguments, even though they're not all named.

To invoke the `set::` method, you use the colons as argument delimiters, as shown here:

```
[aFraction set:1 :3];
```

It's not good programming style to omit argument names when writing new methods because it makes the program harder to follow and makes the purpose of the method's actual parameters less intuitive.

Operations on Fractions

Let's continue to work with the `Fraction` class. First, you write a method that enables you to add one fraction to another. You name the method `add:`, and you have it take a fraction as an argument. Here's the declaration for the new method:

```
-(void) add: (Fraction *) f;
```

Note the declaration for the argument `f`:

```
(Fraction *) f
```

This says that the argument to the `add:` method is a reference to an object from the `Fraction` class. The asterisk is necessary, so the following declaration is not correct:

```
(Fraction) f
```

You will be passing one fraction as an argument to your `add:` method, and you'll have the method add it to the receiver of the message; the following message expression adds the `Fraction bFraction` to the `Fraction aFraction`:

```
[aFraction add: bFraction];
```

Just as a quick math refresher, to add the fractions `a/b` and `c/d`, you perform the calculation as follows:

$$\frac{a}{b} + \frac{c}{d} = \frac{ad + bc}{bd}$$

You put this code for the new method into the `@implementation` section:

```
// add a Fraction to the receiver

- (void) add: (Fraction *) f
{
    // To add two fractions:
    // a/b + c/d = ((a*d) + (b*c)) / (b * d)

    numerator = numerator * f.denominator + denominator * f.numerator;
    denominator = denominator * f.denominator;
}
```

Don't forget that you can refer to the `Fraction` that is the receiver of the message by its fields: `numerator` and `denominator`. Stated another way, inside the `add:` method, you refer to the instance variables of the object you sent the message to directly by name.

However, you can't directly refer to the instance variables of the argument `f` that way. Instead, you have to identify that object by its name, `f`. Then you can obtain the corresponding instance variables by applying the dot operator to `f`.

So, the first statement in the `add:` method that reads

```
nuumerator = numerator * f.denominator + denominator * f.numerator;
```

says to take the numerator of the first fraction (the receiver of the message), multiply that by the denominator of the argument (`numerator * f.denominator`) and add that to the product of the receiver's denominator and the argument's numerator (`denominator * f.numerator`). The final result of the addition is then stored in the receiver's numerator.

Please reread the previous paragraph to make sure you fully grasp the operations being performed. Critical here is that you understand when the receiver is being referenced and when the argument is being referenced.

Let's assume that you added the previous declarations and definitions for your new `add:` method to your interface and implementation files. Program 7.3 shows all that plus a sample test program and output.

Program 7.3   **Interface File:** `Fraction.h`

```
#import <Foundation/Foundation.h>

// Define the Fraction class

@interface Fraction : NSObject

@property int numerator, denominator;

-(void)    print;
-(void)    setTo: (int) n over: (int) d;
-(double)  convertToNum;
-(void)    add: (Fraction *) f;
@end
```

Program 7.3   **Implementation File:** `Fraction.m`

```
#import "Fraction.h"

@implementation Fraction

@synthesize numerator, denominator;

-(void) print
{
    NSLog (@"%i/%i", numerator, denominator);
}

-(double) convertToNum
{
   if (denominator != 0)
       return (double) numerator / denominator;
   else
       return NAN;
}

-(void) setTo: (int) n over: (int) d
{
    numerator = n;
    denominator = d;
}

// add a Fraction to the receiver

- (void) add: (Fraction *) f
{
```

```
    // To add two fractions:
    // a/b + c/d = ((a*d) + (b*c)) / (b * d)

    numerator = numerator * f.denominator + denominator * f.numerator;
    denominator = denominator * f.denominator;
}

@end
```

Program 7.3   **Test File: FractionTest.m**

```
#import "Fraction.h"

int main (int argc, char * argv[])
{
    @autoreleasepool {
        Fraction *aFraction = [[Fraction alloc] init];
        Fraction *bFraction = [[Fraction alloc] init];

        // Set two fractions to 1/4 and 1/2 and add them together

        [aFraction setTo: 1 over: 4];
        [bFraction setTo: 1 over: 2];

        // Print the results

        [aFraction print];
        NSLog (@"+");
        [bFraction print];
        NSLog (@"=");

        [aFraction add: bFraction];
        [aFraction print];
    }

    return 0;
}
```

Program 7.3   **Output**

```
1/4
+
1/2
=
6/8
```

The test program is straightforward enough. Two Fractions, called aFraction and bFraction, are allocated and initialized. Then they are set to the values 1/4 and 1/2, respectively. Next, the Fraction bFraction is added to the Fraction aFraction; the result of the addition is then displayed. Note again that the add: method adds the argument to the object of the message, so the object gets modified. This is verified when you print the value of aFraction at the end of main. You had to print the value of aFraction *before* invoking the add: method to get its value displayed before the method changed it. Later in this chapter, you redefine the add: method so that add: does not affect the value of its receiver.

Local Variables

You might have noticed that the result of adding 1/4 to 1/2 was displayed as 6/8, not as 3/4, which you might have preferred (or even expected!). That's because your addition routine just does the math and no more; it doesn't worry about reducing the result. So, to continue our exercise of adding new methods to work with fractions, let's make a new reduce method to reduce a fraction to its simplest terms.

Reaching back to your high school math again, you can reduce a fraction by finding the largest number that evenly divides both the numerator and the denominator of your fraction and then dividing them by that number. Technically, you want to find the greatest common divisor (gcd) of the numerator and denominator. You already know how to do that from Program 5.7. You might want to refer to that program example just to refresh your memory.

With the algorithm in hand, you can now write your new reduce method:

```
- (void) reduce
{
   int  u = numerator;
   int  v = denominator;
   int  temp;

   while (v != 0) {
      temp = u % v;
      u = v;
      v = temp;
   }

   numerator /= u;
   denominator /= u;
}
```

Notice something new about this reduce method: It declares three integer variables called u, v, and temp. These variables are *local* variables, meaning that their values exist only during execution of the reduce method and that *they can be accessed only from within the method in which they are defined*. In that sense, they are similar to the variables you have been declaring inside your main routine; those variables were also local to main and could be accessed directly only from within the main routine. None of the methods you developed could directly access those variables defined in main.

Local variables that are basic C data types have no default initial value, so you must set them to some value before using them. The three local variables in the reduce method are set to values before they are used, so that's not a problem here. Local object variables are initialized to *nil* by default. Unlike your instance variables (which retain their values through method calls), these local variables have no memory. Therefore, after the method returns, the values of these variables disappear. Every time a method is called, each local variable defined in that method is reinitialized to the value specified (if any) with the variable's declaration.

Method Arguments

The names you use to refer to a method's arguments are also local variables. When the method is executed, whatever arguments are passed to the method are copied into these variables. Because the method is dealing with a copy of the arguments, *it cannot change the original values passed to the method*. This is an important concept. Suppose you had a method called calculate:, defined as follows:

```
-(void) calculate: (double) x
{
    x *= 2;
    ...
}
```

Also suppose that you used the following message expression to invoke it:

```
[myData calculate: ptVal];
```

Whatever value was contained in the variable ptVal would be copied into the local variable x when the calculate method was executed. So changing the value of x inside calculate: would have no effect on the value of ptVal—only on the copy of its value stored inside x.

Incidentally, in the case of arguments that are objects, you can change the instance variables stored in that object. That's because when you pass an object as an argument, you actually pass a reference to where to the data is stored. Because of that, you can modify that data. You'll learn more about that in the next chapter.

The static Keyword

You can have a local variable retain its value through multiple invocations of a method by placing the keyword static in front of the variable's declaration. For example, the following declares the integer hitCount to be a static variable:

```
static int hitCount = 0;
```

Unlike other local variables, which are basic data types, a static variable does have an initial value of 0, so the initialization shown previously is redundant. Furthermore, they are initialized only once when program execution begins and retain their values through successive method calls.

The following code sequence might appear inside a `showPage` method that wanted to keep track of the number of times it was invoked (or, in this case, perhaps the number of pages that have been printed, for example):

```
-(int) showPage
{
    static int pageCount = 0;
      . . .
    ++pageCount;
      . . .
    return pageCount;
}
```

The local static variable would be set to `0` only once when the program started and would retain its value through successive invocations of the `showPage` method.

Note the difference between making `pageCount` a local static variable and making it an instance variable. In the former case, `pageCount` could count the number of pages printed by all objects that invoked the `showPage` method. In the latter case, the variable would count the number of pages printed by each individual object because each object would have its own copy of `pageCount`.

Remember that static or local variables can be accessed only from within the method in which they're defined. So even the static `pageCount` variable can be accessed only from within `show-Page`. You can move the declaration of the variable *outside* any method declaration (typically near the beginning of your implementation file) to make it accessible to any methods, like so:

```
#import "Printer.h"
static int pageCount;

@implementation Printer
  . . .
@end
```

Now any instance or class method contained in the file can access the `pageCount` variable. Chapter 10, "More on Variables and Data Types," covers this topic of variable scope in greater detail.

Returning to fractions, you can incorporate the code for the `reduce` method into your `Fraction.m` implementation file. Don't forget to declare the `reduce` method in your `Fraction.h` interface file as well. With that done, you can test your new method in Program 7.4. Here, we show all three files: the interface file, the implementation file, and the test program file.

Program 7.4   **Interface File: Fraction.h**

```
#import <Foundation/Foundation.h>

// Define the Fraction class

@interface Fraction : NSObject

@property int numerator, denominator;

-(void)    print;
-(void)    setTo: (int) n over: (int) d;
-(double)  convertToNum;
-(void)    add: (Fraction *) f;
-(void)    reduce;
@end
```

Program 7.4   **Implementation File: Fraction.m**

```
#import "Fraction.h"

@implementation Fraction

@synthesize numerator, denominator;

-(void) print
{
    NSLog (@"%i/%i", numerator, denominator);
}

-(double) convertToNum
{
    if (denominator != 0)
        return (double) numerator / denominator;
    else
        return NAN;
}

-(void) setTo: (int) n over: (int) d
{
    numerator = n;
    denominator = d;
}

// add a Fraction to the receiver

-(void) add: (Fraction *) f
```

```
{
    // To add two fractions:
    // a/b + c/d = ((a*d) + (b*c)) / (b * d)

    numerator = numerator * f.denominator + denominator * f.numerator;
    denominator = denominator * f.denominator;
}

-(void) reduce
{
    int  u = numerator;
    int  v = denominator;
    int  temp;

    while (v != 0) {
        temp = u % v;
        u = v;
        v = temp;
    }

    numerator /= u;
    denominator /= u;
}

@end
```

Program 7.4 **Test File main.m**

```
#import "Fraction.h"

int main (int argc, char * argv[])
{
    @autoreleasepool {
        Fraction *aFraction = [[Fraction alloc] init];
        Fraction *bFraction = [[Fraction alloc] init];

        [aFraction setTo: 1 over: 4];    // set 1st fraction to 1/4
        [bFraction setTo: 1 over: 2];    // set 2nd fraction to 1/2

        [aFraction print];
        NSLog (@"+");
        [bFraction print];
        NSLog (@"=");

        [aFraction add: bFraction];
```

```
    // reduce the result of the addition and print the result

    [aFraction reduce];
    [aFraction print];
  }

  return 0;
}
```

Program 7.4 **Output**

```
1/4
+
1/2
=
3/4
```

That's better!

The `self` Keyword

In Program 7.4, we decided to reduce the fraction outside of the `add:` method. We could have done it inside `add:` as well; the decision was completely arbitrary. However, how would we go about identifying the fraction to be reduced? What fraction do we want to reduce anyway? We want to reduce the same fraction that we sent the `add:` message to.

We know how to identify instance variables inside a method directly by name, but we don't know how to directly identify the receiver of the message. Luckily, there is a way to do that.

You can use the keyword `self` to refer to the object that is the receiver of the current message. If inside your `add:` method you wrote

```
[self reduce];
```

the `reduce` method would be applied to the `Fraction` object that was the receiver of the `add:` message, which is what you want. You will see throughout this book how useful the `self` keyword can be, and it's used all the time in iOS programming. For now, you use it in your `add:` method. Here's what the modified method looks like:

```
- (void) add: (Fraction *) f
{
  // To add two fractions:
  // a/b + c/d = ((a*d) + (b*c)) / (b * d)

  numerator = numerator * f.denominator + denominator * f.numerator;
```

```
    denominator = denominator * f.denominator;

    [self reduce];
}
```

After the addition is performed, the fraction is reduced. The `reduce` message gets sent to the receiver of the `add:` message. So, if your test program contains this line of code

```
[aFraction add: bFraction];
```

then `self` refers to `aFraction` when the `add:` method executes, and so that is the fraction that will be reduced.

Allocating and Returning Objects from Methods

We noted that the `add:` method changes the value of the object that is receiving the message. Let's create a new version of `add:` that instead makes a new fraction to store the result of the addition. In this case, we need to return the new `Fraction` to the message sender. Here is the definition for the new `add:` method:

```
-(Fraction *) add: (Fraction *) f
{
    // To add two fractions:
    // a/b + c/d = ((a*d) + (b*c)) / (b * d)

    // result will store the result of the addition
    Fraction    *result = [[Fraction alloc] init];

    result.numerator = numerator * f.denominator +
                          denominator * f.numerator;
    result.denominator = denominator * f.denominator;

    [result reduce];

    return result;
}
```

The first line of your method definition is this:

```
-(Fraction *) add: (Fraction *) f
```

It says that your `add:` method will return a `Fraction` object and that it will take one as its argument as well. The argument will be added to the receiver of the message, which is also a `Fraction`. Note that you need to change your interface section to reflect the fact that the `add:` method now returns a `Fraction` object.

The method allocates and initializes a new `Fraction` object called `result` to store the result of the addition.

The method performs the addition as before, assigning the resulting numerator and denominator to your newly allocated Fraction object result. After reducing the result, you return its value to the sender of the message with the return statement. Note that this time we don't want to reduce the receiver, because we're not changing it. Instead we want to reduce result, which is why the message is sent to that object this time around.

Program 7.5 tests your new add: method.

Program 7.5 **Test File main.m**

```
#import "Fraction.h"

int main (int argc, char * argv[])
{
   @autoreleasepool {
      Fraction *aFraction = [[Fraction alloc] init];
      Fraction *bFraction = [[Fraction alloc] init];

      Fraction *resultFraction;

      [aFraction setTo: 1 over: 4];    // set 1st fraction to 1/4
      [bFraction setTo: 1 over: 2];    // set 2nd fraction to 1/2

      [aFraction print];
      NSLog (@"+");
      [bFraction print];
      NSLog (@"=");

      resultFraction = [aFraction add: bFraction];
      [resultFraction print];
   }

   return 0;
}
```

Program 7.5 **Output**

```
1/4
+
1/2
=
3/4
3/4
```

Some explanation is in order here. First, you define two Fractions (aFraction and bFraction) and set their values to 1/4 and 1/2, respectively. You also define a Fraction called resultFraction. This variable stores the result of your addition operation that follows.

The following line of code sends the add: message to aFraction, passing along the Fraction bFraction as its argument:

```
resultFraction = [aFraction add: bFraction];
```

Inside the method, a new Fraction object is allocated and the resulting addition is performed. The result that is stored in the Fraction object result is then returned by the method, where it is then stored in the variable resultFraction.

You may have noticed that we never allocated (or initialized) a Fraction object inside main for resultFraction; that's because the add: method allocated the object for us and then returned the reference to that object. That reference was then stored in resultFraction. So resultFraction ends up storing the reference to the Fraction object that we allocated in the add: method. This paragraph is important! It's worth reviewing until you fully understand it.

Extending Class Definitions and the Interface File

You might not need to work with fractions, but these examples have shown how you can continually refine and extend a class by adding new methods. You could hand your Fraction.h interface file to someone else working with fractions, and it would be sufficient for that person to be able to write programs to deal with fractions. If that person needed to add a new method, he could do so either directly, by extending the class definition, or indirectly, by defining his own subclass and adding his own new methods. You learn how to do that in the next chapter.

Exercises

1. Add the following methods to the Fraction class to round out the arithmetic operations on fractions. Reduce the result within the method in each case:

   ```
   // Subtract argument from receiver
   -(Fraction *) subtract: (Fraction *) f;
   // Multiply receiver by argument
   -(Fraction *) multiply: (Fraction *) f;
   // Divide receiver by argument
   -(Fraction *) divide: (Fraction *) f;
   ```

2. Modify the print method from your Fraction class so that it takes an additional BOOL argument that indicates whether the fraction should be reduced for display. If it is to be reduced (that is if the argument is YES), be sure not to make any permanent changes to the fraction itself.

3. Will your `Fraction` class work with negative fractions? For example, can you add `-1/4` and `-1/2` and get the correct result? When you think you have the answer, write a test program to try it.

4. Modify the `Fraction`'s print method to display fractions greater than 1 as mixed numbers. For example, the fraction `5/3` should be displayed as `1  2/3`.

5. Exercise 6 in Chapter 4, "Data Types and Expressions," defined a new class called `Complex` for working with complex imaginary numbers. Add a new method called `add:` that can be used to add two complex numbers. To add two complex numbers, you simply add the real parts and the imaginary parts, as shown here:

   ```
   (5.3 + 7i) + (2.7 + 4i) = 8 + 11i
   ```

   Have the `add:` method store and return the result as a new `Complex` number, based on the following method declaration:

   ```
   -(Complex *) add: (Complex *) complexNum;
   ```

6. Given the `Complex` class developed in exercise 6 of Chapter 4 and the extension made in exercise 6 of this chapter, create separate `Complex.h` and `Complex.m` interface and implementation files. Create a separate test program file to test everything.

Inheritance

In this chapter, you learn about one of the key principles that makes object-oriented programming so powerful. Through the concept of *inheritance*, you build on existing class definitions and customize them for your own applications.

It All Begins at the Root

You learned about the idea of a parent class in Chapter 3, "Classes, Objects, and Methods." A parent class can itself have a parent. The class that has no parent is at the top of the hierarchy and is known as a *root* class. In Objective-C, you can define your own root class, but it's something you normally won't want to do. Instead, you want to take advantage of existing classes. All the classes we've defined up to this point are descendants of the root class called NSObject, which you specified in your interface file like this:

```
@interface Fraction: NSObject
...
@end
```

The Fraction class is derived from the NSObject class. Because NSObject is at the top of the hierarchy (that is, there are no classes above it), it's called a *root* class, as shown in Figure 8.1. The Fraction class is known as a *child* class or *subclass*.

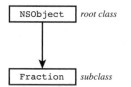

Figure 8.1   Root and subclass

From a terminology point of view, we can speak of classes, child classes, and parent classes. Analogously, we can talk about classes, subclasses, and superclasses. You should become familiar with both types of terminology.

Whenever a new class (other than a new root class) is defined, the class inherits certain things. For example, the (nonprivate) instance variables and the methods from the parent implicitly become part of the new class definition. That means the subclass can access these methods and instance variables, as if they were defined directly within the class definition.

Note that the instance variables that are to be accessed directly by a subclass must be declared in the interface section, and not in the implementation section as we have been doing throughout this book. Instance variables declared or synthesized in the implementation section are *private* instance variables and are not directly accessible by subclasses. Instead, you want to use their explicitly defined or synthesized getter and setter methods to access their values.

A simple example, albeit contrived, helps to illustrate this key concept of inheritance. Here's a declaration for an object called `ClassA` with one method called `initVar` (and note that here we are declaring the instance variable x in the interface section to make it accessible by subclasses.):

```
@interface ClassA: NSObject
{
    int    x;
}

-(void) initVar;
@end
```

The `initVar` method simply sets the value of `ClassA`'s instance variable to `100`:

```
@implementation ClassA
-(void) initVar
{
    x = 100;
}
@end
```

Now let's also define a class called `ClassB`:

```
@interface ClassB: ClassA
-(void) printVar;
@end
```

The first line of the declaration

```
@interface ClassB: ClassA
```

says that instead of `ClassB` being a subclass of `NSObject`, `ClassB` is a subclass of `ClassA`. So although `ClassA`'s parent (or superclass) is `NSObject`, `ClassB`'s parent is `ClassA`. Figure 8.2 illustrates this.

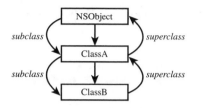

Figure 8.2   Subclasses and superclasses

As you can see from Figure 8.2, the root class has no superclass and ClassB, which is at the bottom of the hierarchy, has no subclass. Therefore, ClassA is a subclass of NSObject, and ClassB is a subclass of ClassA and also of NSObject. (Technically, it's a sub-subclass, or *grand-child*.) Also, NSObject is a superclass of ClassA, which is a superclass of ClassB. NSObject is also a superclass of ClassB because it exists farther down its hierarchy.

Here's the full declaration for ClassB, which defines one method called printVar:

```
@interface ClassB: ClassA
-(void) printVar;
@end

@implementation ClassB
-(void) printVar
{
    NSLog (@"x = %i", x);
}
@end
```

The printVar method prints the value of the instance variable x, yet you haven't defined any instance variables in ClassB. That's because ClassB is a subclass of ClassA; therefore, it inherits ClassA's public instance variables. (In this case, there's just one.) Figure 8.3 depicts this.

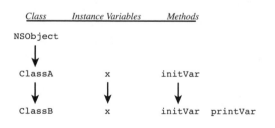

Figure 8.3   Inheriting instance variables and methods

(Of course, Figure 8.3 doesn't show any of the methods or instance variables that are inherited from the NSObject class; there are several.)

Let's see how this works by putting it all together in a complete program example. For the sake of brevity, we put all the class declarations and definitions into a single file (see Program 8.1).

Program 8.1

```
// Simple example to illustrate inheritance

#import <Foundation/Foundation.h>

// ClassA declaration and definition

@interface ClassA: NSObject
{
    int  x;
}

-(void) initVar;
@end

@implementation ClassA
-(void) initVar
{
  x = 100;
}
@end

// Class B declaration and definition

@interface ClassB : ClassA
-(void) printVar;
@end

@implementation ClassB
-(void) printVar
{
  NSLog (@"x = %i", x);
}
@end

int main (int argc, char * argv[])
{
    @autoreleasepool {
       ClassB  *b = [[ClassB alloc] init];

       [b initVar];     // will use inherited method
```

```
        [b printVar];    // reveal value of x;
    }
    return 0;
}
```

Program 8.1   **Output**

```
x = 100
```

You begin by defining b to be a ClassB object. After allocating and initializing b, you send a message to apply the initVar method to it. But looking back at the definition of ClassB, you'll notice that you never defined such a method. initVar was defined in ClassA, and because ClassA is the parent of ClassB, ClassB gets to use all of ClassA's methods. So with respect to ClassB, initVar is an *inherited* method.

> **Note**
>
> We briefly mentioned it up to this point, but alloc and init are methods you have used all along that are never defined in your classes. That's because you took advantage of the fact that they were inherited methods from the NSObject class.

After sending the initVar message to b, you invoke the printVar method to display the value of the instance variable x. The output of x = 100 confirms that printVar was capable of accessing this instance variable. That's because, as with the initVar method, it was inherited.

Remember that the concept of inheritance works all the way down the chain. So if you define a new class called ClassC, whose parent class is ClassB, like so

```
@interface ClassC: ClassB
    . . .
@end
```

then ClassC inherits all of ClassB's methods and instance variables, which in turn inherited all of ClassA's methods and instance variables, which in turn inherited all of NSObject's methods and instance variables.

Be sure you understand that each instance of a class gets its own instance variables, even if they're inherited. A ClassC object and a ClassB object would therefore each have their own distinct instance variables.

Finding the Right Method

When you send a message to an object, you might wonder how the correct method is chosen to apply to that object. The rules are actually quite simple. First, the class to which the object belongs is checked to see whether a method is explicitly defined in that class with the specific name. If it is, that's the method that is used. If it's not defined there, the parent class is checked. If the method is defined there, that's what is used. If not, the search continues.

Parent classes are checked until one of two things happens: Either you find a class that contains the specified method or you don't find the method after going all the way back to the root class. If the first occurs, you're all set; if the second occurs, you have a problem, and a warning message is generated that looks like this:

```
warning: 'ClassB' may not respond to '-inity'
```

In this case, you inadvertently are trying to send a message called `inity` to a variable of type class `ClassB`. The compiler told you that objects from that class do not know how to respond to such a method. Again, this was determined after checking `ClassB`'s methods and its parents' methods back to the root class (which, in this case, is `NSObject`).

You'll learn more about how the system checks for the right method to execute in Chapter 9, "Polymorphism, Dynamic Typing, and Dynamic Binding."

Extension through Inheritance: Adding New Methods

Inheritance often is used to extend a class. As an example, let's assume that you've just been assigned the task of developing some classes to work with 2D graphical objects such as rectangles, circles, and triangles. For now, we'll worry about just rectangles. Let's go back to exercise 7 from Chapter 4, "Data Types and Expressions," and start with the `@interface` section from that example:

```
@interface Rectangle: NSObject

@property int width, height;
-(int)   area;
-(int)   perimeter;
@end
```

You'll have synthesized methods to set the rectangle's width and height and to return those values, and your own methods to calculate its area and perimeter. Let's add a method that will allow you to set both the width and the height of the rectangle with the same message call, which is as follows:

```
-(void) setWidth: (int) w andHeight: (int) h;
```

Assume that you typed this new class declaration into a file called `Rectangle.h`. Here's what the implementation file `Rectangle.m` might look like:

```
#import "Rectangle.h"

@implementation Rectangle

@synthesize width, height;
```

```
-(void) setWidth: (int) w andHeight: (int) h
{
    width = w;
    height = h;
}

-(int) area
{
    return width * height;
}

-(int) perimeter
{
    return (width + height) * 2;
}
@end
```

Each method definition is straightforward enough. Program 8.2 shows a `main` routine to test it.

Program 8.2

```
#import "Rectangle.h"

int main (int argc, char * argv[])
{
   @autoreleasepool {
      Rectangle *myRect = [[Rectangle alloc] init];

      [myRect setWidth: 5 andHeight: 8];

      NSLog (@"Rectangle: w = %i, h = %i", myRect.width, myRect.height);
      NSLog (@"Area = %i, Perimeter = %i", [myRect area],
                 [myRect perimeter]);
   }
   return 0;
}
```

Program 8.2 Output

```
Rectangle: w = 5, h = 8
Area = 40, Perimeter = 26
```

`myRect` is allocated and initialized; then its width is set to 5 and its height to 8. The first line of output verifies this. Next, the area and the perimeter of the rectangle are calculated with the appropriate message calls, and the returned values are handed off to `NSLog` to be displayed.

Suppose that you now need to work with squares. You could define a new class called Square and define similar methods in it as in your Rectangle class. Alternately, you could recognize the fact that a square is just a special case of a rectangle whose width and height just happen to be the same.

Thus, an easy way to handle this is to make a new class called Square and have it be a subclass of Rectangle. For now, the only methods you might want to add would be to set the side of the square to a particular value and retrieve that value. Program 8.3 shows the interface and implementation files for your new Square class.

Program 8.3   Square.h **Interface File**

```
#import "Rectangle.h"

@interface Square: Rectangle

-(void) setSide: (int) s;
-(int) side;
@end
```

Program 8.3   Square.m **Implementation File**

```
#import "Square.h"

@implementation Square: Rectangle

-(void) setSide: (int) s
{
    [self setWidth: s andHeight: s];
}

-(int) side

{
   return self.width;
}
@end
```

Notice what you did here. You defined your Square class to be a subclass of Rectangle, which is declared in the header file Rectangle.h. You didn't need to add any instance variables here, but you did add new methods called setSide: and side. Note that the side method does not have direct access to the Rectangle's width instance variable; it's private and therefore not accessible by the `Square` class. However, the getter method *is* inherited from the parent class and can be used to access the value of the width. You'll recall that writing the expression

```
self.width
```

is equivalent to writing

```
[self width]
```

This sends the `width` message to the receiver of the `side` message. In other words, you execute the getter method `width` as opposed to trying to directly access the instance variable `width` (which, as discussed, you cannot do). This is an important concept that you need to understand.

A square has only one side, but you're internally representing it as two numbers; that's okay. All that is hidden from the user of the `Square` class. You can always redefine your `Square` class later, if necessary; any users of the class don't have to be concerned with the internal details because of the notion of data encapsulation discussed earlier.

The `setSide:` method takes advantage of the fact that you already have a method inherited from your `Rectangle` class to set the values of the width and height of a rectangle. So `setSide:` calls the `setWidth:andHeight:` method from the `Rectangle` class, passing the parameter s as the value for both the width and the height. You don't really have to do anything else. Someone working with a `Square` object can now set the dimensions of the square by using `setSide:` and can take advantage of the methods from the `Rectangle` class to calculate the square's area, perimeter, and so on. Program 8.3 shows the test program and output for your new `Square` class.

Program 8.3 **Test Program**

```
#import "Square.h"
#import <Foundation/Foundation.h>

int main (int argc, char * argv[])
{
    @autoreleasepool {
        Square *mySquare = [[Square alloc] init];

        [mySquare setSide: 5];

        NSLog (@"Square s = %i", [mySquare side]);
        NSLog (@"Area = %i, Perimeter = %i",
            [mySquare area], [mySquare perimeter]);
    }
    return 0;
}
```

Program 8.3   **Output**

```
Square s = 5
Area = 25, Perimeter = 20
```

The way you defined the `Square` class is a fundamental technique of working with classes in Objective-C: extending what you or someone else has already done to suit your needs. In addition, a mechanism known as *categories* enables you to add new methods to an existing class definition in a modular fashion—that is, without having to constantly add new definitions to the same interface and implementation files. This proves particularly handy when you want to do this to a class for which you don't have access to the source code. You'll learn about categories in Chapter 11, "Categories and Protocols."

A Point Class and Object Allocation

The `Rectangle` class stores only the rectangle's dimensions. In a real-world graphical application, you might need to keep track of all sorts of additional information, such as the rectangle's fill color, line color, location (origin) inside a window, and so on. You can easily extend your class to do this. For now, let's deal with the idea of the rectangle's origin. Assume that the *origin* means the location of the rectangle's lower-left corner within some Cartesian coordinate system (x, y). If you were writing a drawing application, this point might represent the location of the rectangle inside a window, as depicted in Figure 8.4.

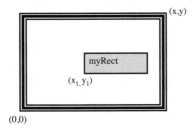

Figure 8.4   A rectangle drawn in a window

In Figure 8.4, the rectangle's origin is shown at (x_1, y_1).

You could extend your `Rectangle` class to store the x, y coordinate of the rectangle's origin as two separate values. Or you might realize that, in the development of your graphics application, you'll have to deal with a lot of coordinates and, therefore, decide to define a class called `XYPoint`. (You might recall this problem from exercise 7 in Chapter 3.)

```
#import <Foundation/Foundation.h>

@interface XYPoint: NSObject
```

```
@property int x, y;

-(void) setX: (int) xVal andY: (int) yVal;
@end
```

Now let's get back to your `Rectangle` class. You want to be able to store the rectangle's origin, so you add an instance variable, called `origin`, to the definition of your `Rectangle` class:

```
@implementation Rectangle
{
    XYPoint *origin;
}

    . . .
```

It seems reasonable to add a method to set the rectangle's origin and to retrieve it. To illustrate an important point, we won't synthesize the accessor methods for the origin now. Instead, we'll write them ourselves.

The `@class` Directive

Now you can work with rectangles (and squares as well!) with the ability to set their widths, heights, and origins. First, let's take a complete look at your `Rectangle.h` interface file:

```
#import <Foundation/Foundation.h>

@class XYPoint;

@interface Rectangle: NSObject

@property int width, height;

-(XYPoint *) origin;
-(void)   setOrigin: (XYPoint *) pt;
-(void)   setWidth: (int) w andHeight: (int) h;
-(int)    area;
-(int)    perimeter;
@end
```

You used a new directive in the `Rectangle.h` header file:

```
@class XYPoint;
```

You needed this because the compiler needs to know what an `XYPoint` is when it encounters it as one of the instance variables defined for a `Rectangle`. The class name is also used in the argument and return type declarations for your `setOrigin:` and `origin` methods, respectively. You do have another choice. You could have imported the header file instead, like so:

```
#import "XYPoint.h"
```

Using the @class directive is more efficient because the compiler doesn't need to import and therefore process the entire XYPoint.h file (even though it is quite small); it just needs to know that XYPoint is the name of a class. If you needed to reference one of the XYPoint class' methods (in the implementation section, for instance), the @class directive would not suffice because the compiler would need more information; it would need to know how many arguments the method takes, what their types are, and what the method's return type is.

So, make sure you understand the use of the @class directive here. It is simply telling the compiler that XYPoint is the name of a class. In that way, when it sees this line

```
XYPoint *origin;
```

it knows that origin is an object from a class called XYPoint. That's all the compiler needs to know at that point.

Let's fill in the blanks for your new XYPoint class and Rectangle methods so that you can test everything in a program.

First, Program 8.4 shows the new methods for the Rectangle class.

Program 8.4   Rectangle.m **Added Methods**

```
#import "XYPoint.h"

-(void) setOrigin: (XYPoint *) pt
{
    origin = pt;
}

-(XYPoint *) origin
{
    return origin;
}
@end
```

Following are the complete XYPoint and Rectangle class definitions, followed by a test program to try them out.

Program 8.4   XYPoint.h **Interface File**

```
#import <Foundation/Foundation.h>

@interface XYPoint: NSObject

@property int x, y;

-(void) setX: (int) xVal andY: (int) yVal;
@end
```

Program 8.4   XYPoint.m **Implementation File**

```
#import "XYPoint.h"

@implementation XYPoint

@synthesize x, y;

-(void) setX: (int) xVal andY: (int) yVal
{
    x = xVal;
    y = yVal;
}
@end
```

Program 8.4   Rectangle.h **Interface File**

```
#import <Foundation/Foundation.h>

@class XYPoint;
@interface Rectangle: NSObject

@property int width, height;

-(XYPoint *) origin;
-(void)   setOrigin: (XYPoint *) pt;
-(void)   setWidth: (int) w andHeight: (int) h;
-(int)    area;
-(int)    perimeter;
@end
```

Program 8.4   Rectangle.m **Implementation File**

```
#import "Rectangle.h"

@implementation Rectangle
{
   XYPoint *origin;
}

@synthesize width, height;

-(void) setWidth: (int) w andHeight: (int) h
{
   width = w;
```

```
    height = h;
}

-(void) setOrigin: (XYPoint *) pt
{
    origin = pt;
}

-(int) area
{
    return width * height;
}

-(int) perimeter
{
    return (width + height) * 2;
}

-(XYPoint *) origin
{
    return origin;
}
@end
```

Program 8.4 **Test Program**

```
#import "Rectangle.h"
#import "XYPoint.h"

int main (int argc, char * argv[])
{
    @autoreleasepool {
        Rectangle *myRect = [[Rectangle alloc] init];
        XYPoint   *myPoint = [[XYPoint alloc] init];

        [myPoint setX: 100 andY: 200];

        [myRect setWidth: 5 andHeight: 8];
        myRect.origin = myPoint;

        NSLog (@"Rectangle w = %i, h = %i", myRect.width, myRect.height);

        NSLog (@"Origin at (%i, %i)", myRect.origin.x, myRect.origin.y);

        NSLog (@"Area = %i, Perimeter = %i",
```

```
            [myRect area], [myRect perimeter]);
    }
    return 0;
}
```

Program 8.4   **Output**

```
Rectangle w = 5, h = 8
Origin at (100, 200)
Area = 40, Perimeter = 26
```

Inside the `main` routine, you allocated and initialized a rectangle identified as `myRect` and a point called `myPoint`. Using the `setX:andY:` method, you set `myPoint` to (100, 200). After setting the width and the height of the rectangle to 5 and 8, respectively, you invoked the `setOrigin` method to set the rectangle's origin to the point indicated by `myPoint`. The three `NSLog` calls then retrieve and print the values. The expression

```
myRect.origin.x
```

takes the `XYPoint` object returned by the accessor method `origin` and applies the dot operator to get the x-coordinate of the rectangle's origin. In a similar manner, the following expression retrieves the y-coordinate of the rectangle's origin:

```
myRect.origin.y
```

Remember that this expression is equivalent to this expression

```
[[myRect origin] y]
```

based on what you know about the dot operator and how it gets interpreted by the compiler.

Classes Owning Their Objects

Can you explain the output from Program 8.5?

Program 8.5

```
#import "Rectangle.h"
#import "XYPoint.h"

int main (int argc, char * argv[])
{
    @autoreleasepool {
        Rectangle *myRect = [[Rectangle alloc] init];
        XYPoint   *myPoint = [[XYPoint alloc] init];

        [myPoint setX: 100 andY: 200];
```

```
        [myRect setWidth: 5 andHeight: 8];
        myRect.origin = myPoint;

        NSLog (@"Origin at (%i, %i)", myRect.origin.x, myRect.origin.y);

        [myPoint setX: 50 andY: 50];
        NSLog (@"Origin at (%i, %i)", myRect.origin.x, myRect.origin.y);
    }
    return 0;
}
```

Program 8.5   **Output**

```
Origin at (100, 200)
Origin at (50, 50)
```

You changed myPoint from (100, 200) in the program to (50, 50), and apparently it also changed the rectangle's origin! But why did that happen? You didn't explicitly reset the rectangle's origin. So, why did the rectangle's origin change? If you go back to the definition of your setOrigin: method, perhaps you'll see why:

```
-(void) setOrigin: (XYPoint *) pt
{
    origin = pt;
}
```

When the setOrigin: method is invoked with the expression

```
myRect.origin = myPoint;
```

the value of myPoint is passed as the argument to the method. This value points to where this XYPoint object is stored in memory, as depicted in Figure 8.5.

Figure 8.5   The myPoint object reference in memory

That value stored inside myPoint, which is a pointer into memory, is copied into the local variable pt as defined inside the method. Now both pt and myPoint reference the same data stored in memory. Figure 8.6 illustrates this.

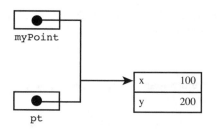

Figure 8.6   Passing the rectangle's origin to the method

When the origin variable is set to pt inside the method, the pointer stored inside pt is copied into the instance variable origin, as depicted in Figure 8.7.

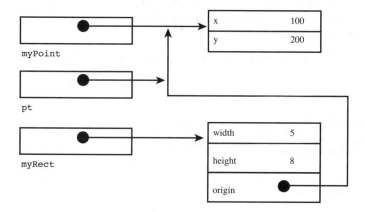

Figure 8.7   Setting the rectangle's origin

Because myPoint and the origin variable stored in myRect reference the same area in memory (as does the local variable pt), when you subsequently change the value of myPoint to (50, 50), the rectangle's origin is changed as well.

You can avoid this problem by modifying the setOrigin: method so that it allocates its own point and sets the origin to that point. This is shown here:

```
-(void) setOrigin: (XYPoint *) pt
{
    if (! origin)
        origin = [[XYPoint alloc] init];

    origin.x = pt.x;
    origin.y = pt.y;
}
```

The method first tests to see whether the instance variable origin is nonzero. (Make sure you understand that test and the use of the logical negation operator ! that's used.) Recall that all instance variables are initially set to zero. So when a new Rectangle object is allocated, its instance variables, which include origin, will be set to zero.

If the origin is zero, the setOrigin: method will allocate and initialize a new XYPoint object and store the reference to it in the origin.

The method then sets the newly allocated XYPoint object to the x, y coordinates of the argument to the method. Study this method until you fully understand how it works.

The change to the setOrigin: method means that each Rectangle instance now owns its XYPoint instance. Even though it is now responsible for allocating the memory for that XYPoint, it should also now become responsible for releasing that memory. In general, when a class contains other objects, at times you will want to have it own some or all of those objects. In the case of a rectangle, it makes sense for the Rectangle class to own its origin because that is a basic attribute of a rectangle. Only the class's accessor methods should be able to set or retrieve that origin. That's consistent with the notion of data encapsulation.

With your modified method, recompiling and rerunning Program 8.5 produces the error messages shown as Figure 8.8.

```
[origin setX: pt.x andY: pt.y];
    error: request for member 'x' in something not a structure or union
    error: request for member 'y' in something not a structure or union
    warning: no '-setX:andY:' method found
    (Messages without a matching method signature will be assumed to return 'id' and accept '...' as arguments.)
```

Figure 8.8   Compiler error messages

Oops! The problem here is that you've referenced some instance variables from the XYPoint class in your modified method, so now the compiler needs more information about it than the @class directive provides. In this case, you must go back to your Rectangle.h header file and replace that directive with an import instead, like so:

```
#import "XYPoint.h"
```

Program 8.5B   Output

```
Origin at (100, 200)
Origin at (100, 200)
```

That's better. This time, changing the value of myPoint to (50, 50) inside main had no effect on the rectangle's origin because a copy of the point was created inside the Rectangle's setOrigin: method.

Incidentally, we didn't synthesize the `origin` methods here because the synthesized setter `setOrigin:` method would have behaved just like the one you originally wrote. That is, by default, the action of a synthesized setter is to simply copy the object pointer, not the object itself.

You can synthesize a different type of setter method that instead does make a copy of the object. However, to do that, you need to learn how to write a special copying method. We revisit this topic in Chapter 18, "Copying Objects."

Before leaving this section, let's think about the getter side of the `Rectangle` class. Suppose in your test program from Program 8.4 you inserted the following lines after you had set your `Rectangle`'s values:

```
XYPoint *theOrigin =  myRect.origin;

theOrigin.x = 200;
theOrigin.y = 300;
```

What do you think would happen to the `myRect`'s origin after this code was executed? Right, its origin would be changed to `(200, 300)`. The origin object that the getter returns is "vulnerable." Anyone changing its x or y value changes the rectangle's x or y value accordingly. For this reason, the safest way to write a getter that returns an object is to actually make a copy of the object and to return that copy. In that way, you are protecting the instance variable from inadvertently getting changed. We won't make that change here, but leave that as an exercise for you. Note that you face a performance penalty if you copy your objects before returning them. You'll have to judge if that tradeoff is worth it when designing your class.

Overriding Methods

We noted earlier in this chapter that you can't remove or subtract methods through inheritance. However, you can change the definition of an inherited method by *overriding* it.

Returning to your two classes, `ClassA` and `ClassB`, assume that you want to write your own `initVar` method for `ClassB`. You already know that `ClassB` will inherit the `initVar` method defined in `ClassA`, but can you make a new method with the same name to replace the inherited method? The answer is yes, and you do so simply by defining a new method with the same name. A method defined with the same name as that of a parent class replaces, or overrides, the inherited definition. Your new method must have the same return type and take the same number and type of arguments as the method you are overriding.

Program 8.6 shows a simple example to illustrate this concept.

Program 8.6

```
// Overriding Methods

#import <Foundation/Foundation.h>

// ClassA declaration and definition
```

```objc
@interface ClassA: NSObject
{
   int x; // Will be inherited by subclasses
}

-(void) initVar;
@end
/////////////////////////////
@implementation ClassA
-(void) initVar
{
   x = 100;
}
@end

// ClassB declaration and definition

@interface ClassB: ClassA
-(void) initVar;
-(void) printVar;
@end
/////////////////////////////
@implementation ClassB
-(void) initVar     // added method
{
   x = 200;
}

-(void) printVar
{
   NSLog (@"x = %i", x);
}
@end
/////////////////////////////
int main (int argc, char * argv[])
{
   @autoreleasepool {
      ClassB  *b = [[ClassB alloc] init];

      [b initVar];  // uses overriding method in B

      [b printVar];  // reveal value of x;
   }
   return 0;
}
```

Program 8.6   **Output**

```
x = 200
```

Clearly, the message [b initVar]; causes the initVar method defined in ClassB to be used, and not the one defined in ClassA, as was the case with the previous example. Figure 8.9 illustrates this.

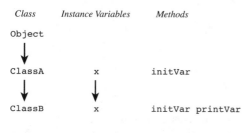

| Class | Instance Variables | Methods |

Object

ClassA   x   initVar

ClassB   x   initVar printVar

Figure 8.9   Overriding the initVar method

Which Method Is Selected?

We covered how the system searches up the hierarchy for a method to apply to an object. If you have methods in different classes with the same name, the correct method is chosen based on the class of the receiver of the message. Program 8.7 uses the same class definition for ClassA and ClassB as before.

Program 8.7

```
#import <Foundation/Foundation.h>

// insert definitions for ClassA and ClassB here

int main (int argc, char * argv[])
{
   @autoreleasepool {
      ClassA  *a = [[ClassA alloc] init];
      ClassB  *b = [[ClassB alloc] init];

      [a initVar];   // uses ClassA method
      [a printVar];  // reveal value of x;

      [b initVar];   // use overriding ClassB method
      [b printVar];  // reveal value of x;
   }
   return 0;
}
```

You'll get this warning message when you build this program:

```
warning: 'ClassA' may not respond to '-printVar'
```

What happened here? We talked about this in an earlier section. Take a look at the declaration for ClassA:

```
// ClassA declaration and definition

@interface ClassA: NSObject
{
    int  x;
}

-(void) initVar;
@end
```

Notice that no printVar method is declared. That method is declared and defined in ClassB. Therefore, even though ClassB objects and their descendants can use this method through inheritance, ClassA objects cannot because the method is defined farther down in the hierarchy.

> **Note**
>
> You can coerce the use of this method in some ways, but we don't go into that here—besides, it's not good programming practice.

Returning to our example, let's add a printVar method to ClassA so you can display the value of its instance variable:

```
// ClassA declaration and definition

@interface ClassA: NSObject
{
    int  x; // Will be inherited by subclasses
}

-(void) initVar;
-(void) printVar;
@end

@implementation ClassA
-(void) initVar
{
    x = 100;
}

-(void) printVar
```

```
{
    NSLog (@"x = %i", x);
}
```

`@end`

ClassB's declaration and definition remain unchanged. Let's try compiling and running this program again.

Program 8.7   **Output**

```
x = 100
x = 200
```

Now we can talk about the actual example. First, a and b are defined to be ClassA and ClassB objects, respectively. After allocation and initialization, a message is sent to a asking it to apply the initVar method. This method is defined in the definition of ClassA, so this method is selected. The method simply sets the value of the instance variable x to 100 and returns. The printVar method, which you just added to ClassA, is invoked next to display the value of x.

As with the ClassA object, the ClassB object b is allocated and initialized, its instance variable x is set to 200, and finally its value displayed.

Be sure that you understand how the proper method is chosen for a and b based on which class they belong to. This is a fundamental concept of object-oriented programming in Objective-C.

As an exercise, consider removing the printVar method from ClassB. Would this work? Why or why not?

When defining a subclass, not only can you add new methods to effectively extend the definition of a class, but you can also add new instance variables. In both cases, the effect is cumulative. You can never subtract methods or instance variables through inheritance; you can only add—or, in the case of methods, add or override.

So, in review, why would you want to create a subclass? Here are three reasons:

1. You want to extend the functionality of a class, perhaps by adding some new methods and/or instance variables.

2. You want to make a specialized version of a class (for example, a particular type of graphic object).

3. You need to change the default behavior of a class by overriding one or more of its methods.

Abstract Classes

What better way to conclude this chapter than with a bit of terminology? We introduce it here because it's directly related to the notion of inheritance.

Sometimes, classes are created just to make it easier for someone to create a subclass. For that reason, these classes are called *abstract* classes or, equivalently, *abstract superclasses*. Methods and instance variables are defined in the class, but no one is expected to actually create an instance from that class. For example, consider the root object NSObject. Can you think of any use for defining an object from that class?

The Foundation framework, covered in Part II, "The Foundation Framework," has several of these so-called abstract classes. As an example, the Foundation's NSNumber class is an abstract class that was created for working with numbers as objects. Integers and floating-point numbers typically have different storage requirements. Separate subclasses of NSNumber exist for each numeric type. Because these subclasses, unlike their abstract superclasses, actually exist, they are known as *concrete* subclasses. Each concrete subclass falls under the NSNumber class umbrella and is collectively referred to as a *class cluster*. When you send a message to the NSNumber class to create a new integer object, the appropriate subclass is used to allocate the necessary storage for an integer object and to set its value appropriately. These subclasses are actually private. You don't access them directly yourself; they are accessed indirectly through the abstract superclass. The abstract superclass gives a common interface for working with all types of number objects and relieves you of the burden of having to know which type of number you have stored in your number object and how to set and retrieve its value.

Admittedly, this discussion might seem a little "abstract" (sorry!). Don't worry; just a basic grasp of the concept is sufficient here.

Exercises

1. Add a new class called ClassC, which is a subclass of ClassB, to Program 8.1. Make an initVar method that sets the value of its instance variable x to 300. Write a test routine that declares ClassA, ClassB, and ClassC objects and invokes their corresponding initVar methods.

2. When dealing with higher-resolution devices, you might need to use a coordinate system that enables you to specify points as floating-point values instead of as simple integers. (iOS uses a structure called CGRect for working with rectangles. All coordinates and sizes are expressed as floating point numbers when working with such rectangles.) Modify the XYPoint and Rectangle classes from this chapter to deal with floating-point numbers. The rectangle's width, height, area, and perimeter should all work with floating-point numbers as well.

3. Modify Program 8.1 to add a new class called ClassB2 that, like ClassB, is a subclass of ClassA.

   What can you say about the relationship between ClassB and ClassB2?

   Identify the hierarchical relationship between the NSObject class, ClassA, ClassB, and ClassB2.

   What is the superclass of ClassB?

   What is the superclass of ClassB2?

   How many subclasses can a class have, and how many superclasses can it have?

4. Write a Rectangle method called translate: that takes an XYPoint object as its argument. Have it translate the rectangle's origin by the specified vector. Note: Translation simply means moving the point from one place to another.

5. Define a new class called GraphicObject, and make it a subclass of NSObject. Define instance variables in your new class as follows:

```
int    fillColor;    // 32-bit color
BOOL   filled;       // Is the object filled?
int    lineColor;    // 32-bit line color
```

   Write methods to set and retrieve the variables defined previously.

   Make the Rectangle class a subclass of GraphicObject.

   Define new classes, Circle and Triangle, which are also subclasses of GraphicObject. Write methods to set and retrieve the various parameters for these objects and also to calculate the circle's circumference and area, and the triangle's perimeter and area.

6. Write a Rectangle method called containsPoint: that takes an XYPoint object as its argument:

```
-(BOOL) containsPoint: (XYPoint *) aPoint;
```

   Have the method return the BOOL value YES if the rectangle encloses the specified point and NO if it does not.

7. Write a Rectangle method called intersect: that takes a rectangle as an argument and returns a rectangle representing the overlapping area between the two rectangles. For example, given the two rectangles shown in Figure 8.10, the method should return a rectangle whose origin is at (400, 420), whose width is 50, and whose height is 60.

   If the rectangles do not intersect, return one whose width and height are zero and whose origin is at (0, 0).

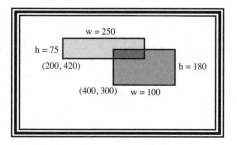

Figure 8.10   Intersecting rectangles

8. Write a method for the Rectangle class called draw that draws a rectangle using dashes and vertical bar characters. The following code sequence

```
Rectangle *myRect = [[Rectangle alloc] init];
[myRect setWidth: 10 andHeight: 3];
[myRect draw];
```

would produce the following output:

```
----------
|        |
|        |
|        |
----------
```

> **Note**
>
> You should use printf to draw your characters, since NSLog will display a new line each time it's called.

9

7

Polymorphism, Dynamic Typing, and Dynamic Binding

In this chapter, you learn about the features of the Objective-C language that make it such a powerful programming language and that distinguish it from some other object-oriented programming languages such as C++. This chapter describes three key concepts: polymorphism, dynamic typing, and dynamic binding. *Polymorphism* enables programs to be developed so that objects from different classes can define methods that share the same name. *Dynamic typing* defers the determination of the class that an object belongs to until the program is executing. *Dynamic binding* defers the determination of the actual method to invoke on an object until program execution time.

Polymorphism: Same Name, Different Class

Program 9.1 shows the interface file for a class called Complex, which is used to represent complex numbers in a program.

Program 9.1   **Interface File** Complex.h

```
// Interface file for Complex class

#import <Foundation/Foundation.h>

@interface Complex: NSObject

@property double real, imaginary;
-(void)    print;
-(void)    setReal: (double) a andImaginary: (double) b;
-(Complex *) add: (Complex *) f;
@end
```

You should have completed the implementation section for this class in exercises 5 and 6 from Chapter 7, "More on Classes." We added an additional setReal:andImaginary: method to enable you to set both the real and imaginary parts of your number with a single message and also synthesized accessor methods. This is shown in the following.

Program 9.1   **Implementation File** Complex.m

```
// Implementation file for Complex class

#import "Complex.h"

@implementation Complex

@synthesize real, imaginary;

-(void) print
{
   NSLog (@" %g + %gi ", real, imaginary);
}

-(void) setReal: (double) a andImaginary: (double) b
{
   real = a;
   imaginary = b;
}

-(Complex *) add: (Complex *) f
{
    Complex *result = [[Complex alloc] init];

    result.real = real + f.real;
    result.imaginary = imaginary + f.imaginary;

    return result;
}
@end
```

Program 9.1   **Test Program** main.m

```
// Shared Method Names: Polymorphism

#import "Fraction.h"
#import "Complex.h"

int main (int argc, char * argv[])
{
```

```
@autoreleasepool {
    Fraction *f1 = [[Fraction alloc] init];
    Fraction *f2 = [[Fraction alloc] init];
    Fraction *fracResult;
    Complex *c1 = [[Complex alloc] init];
    Complex *c2 = [[Complex alloc] init];
    Complex *compResult;

    [f1 setTo: 1 over: 10];
    [f2 setTo: 2 over: 15];

    [c1 setReal: 18.0 andImaginary: 2.5];
    [c2 setReal: -5.0 andImaginary: 3.2];

    // add and print 2 complex numbers

    [c1 print]; NSLog (@"        +"); [c2 print];
    NSLog (@"---------");
    compResult = [c1 add: c2];
    [compResult print];
    NSLog (@"\n");

    // add and print 2 fractions
    [f1 print]; NSLog (@"   +"); [f2 print];
    NSLog (@"----");
    fracResult = [f1 add: f2];
    [fracResult print];
}
    return 0;
}
```

Program 9.1   **Output**

```
18 + 2.5i
        +
-5 + 3.2i
---------
13 + 5.7i

1/10
   +
2/15
----
7/30
```

Note that both the `Fraction` and `Complex` classes contain `add:` and `print` methods. So, when executing the message expressions

```
compResult = [c1 add: c2];
[compResult print];
```

how does the system know which methods to execute? It's simple: The Objective-C runtime knows that `c1`, the receiver of the first message, is a `Complex` object. Therefore, it selects the `add:` method defined for the `Complex` class.

The Objective-C runtime system also determines that `compResult` is a `Complex` object, so it selects the `print` method defined in the `Complex` class to display the result of the addition. The same discussion applies to the following message expressions:

```
fracResult = [f1 add: f2];
[fracResult print];
```

Note

As described more completely in Chapter 13, "Underlying C Language Features," the system always carries information about the class to which an object belongs. This enables it to make these key decisions at runtime instead of at compile time.

The corresponding methods from the `Fraction` class are chosen to evaluate the message expression based on the class of `f1` and `fracResult`.

As mentioned, the capability to share the same method name across different classes is known as polymorphism. Polymorphism enables you to develop a set of classes that each can respond to the same method name. Each class definition encapsulates the code needed to respond to that particular method, and this makes it independent of the other class definitions. This also enables you to later add new classes that can respond to methods with the same name.

Dynamic Binding and the `id` Type

Chapter 4, "Data Types and Expressions," briefly touched on the `id` data type and noted that it is a generic object type. That is, `id` can be used for storing objects that belong to any class. The real power of this data type is exploited when it's used this way to store different types of objects in a variable during the execution of a program. Study Program 9.2 and its associated output.

Program 9.2   **Test Program** `main.m`

```
// Illustrate Dynamic Typing and Binding

#import "Fraction.h"
#import "Complex.h"
```

```
int main (int argc, char * argv[])
{
    @autoreleasepool {
        id      dataValue;
        Fraction *f1 = [[Fraction alloc] init];
        Complex  *c1 = [[Complex alloc] init];

        [f1 setTo: 2 over: 5];
        [c1 setReal: 10.0 andImaginary: 2.5];

        // first dataValue gets a fraction

        dataValue = f1;
        [dataValue print];

        // now dataValue gets a complex number

        dataValue = c1;
        [dataValue print];
    }
    return 0;
}
```

Program 9.2   **Output**

```
2/5
10 + 2.5i
```

The variable dataValue is declared as an id object type. Therefore, dataValue can be used to hold any type of object in the program. Note that no asterisk is used in the declaration line:

```
id dataValue;
```

The Fraction f1 is set to 2/5, and the Complex number c1 is set to (10 + 2.5i). The assignment

```
dataValue = f1;
```

stores the Fraction f1 in dataValue. Now, what can you do with dataValue? Well, you can invoke any of the methods that you can use on a Fraction object with dataValue, even though the type of dataValue is an id and not a Fraction. But if dataValue can store any type of object, how does the system know which method to invoke? That is, when it encounters the message expression

```
[dataValue print];
```

how does it know which print method to invoke? You have print methods defined for both the Fraction and Complex classes.

As noted previously, the answer lies in the fact that the Objective-C system always keeps track of the class to which an object belongs. It also lies in the concepts of dynamic typing and dynamic binding. That is, the system makes the decision about the class of the object, and, therefore, which method to invoke dynamically, at runtime rather than at compile time.

So during execution of the program, before the system sends the `print` message to `dataValue`, it first checks the class of the object stored inside `dataValue`. In the first case of Program 9.2, this variable contains a `Fraction` object, so the `print` method defined in the `Fraction` class is used. This is verified by the output from the program.

In the second case, the same thing happens. First, the `Complex` number `c1` is assigned to `dataValue`. Next, the following message expression is executed:

```
[dataValue print];
```

This time, because `dataValue` contains an object belonging to the `Complex` class, the corresponding `print` method from that class is selected for execution.

This is a simple example, but you can extrapolate this concept to more sophisticated applications. When combined with polymorphism, dynamic binding and dynamic typing enable you to easily write code that can send the same message to objects from different classes.

For example, consider a `draw` method that can be used to paint graphical objects on the screen. You might have different `draw` methods defined for each of your graphical objects, such as text, circles, rectangles, windows, and so on. If the particular object to be drawn is stored inside an `id` variable called `currentObject`, for example, you could paint it on the screen simply by sending it the `draw` message:

```
[currentObject draw];
```

You could even test it first to ensure that the object stored in `currentObject` actually responds to a draw method. You'll see how to do that later in this chapter, in the "Asking Questions about Classes" section.

Compile Time Versus Runtime Checking

Because the type of object stored inside an `id` variable can be indeterminate at compile time, some tests are deferred until runtime—that is, while the program is executing.

Consider the following sequence of code:

```
Fraction *f1 = [[Fraction alloc] init];
[f1 setReal: 10.0 andImaginary: 2.5];
```

Recalling that the `setReal:andImaginary:` method applies to complex numbers and not fractions, the following message is issued when you compile the program containing this line:

```
'Fraction' may not respond to 'setReal:andImaginary:'
```

The Objective-C compiler knows that f1 is a Fraction object because it has been declared that way. It also knows that when it sees the message expression

```
[f1 setReal: 10.0 andImaginary: 2.5];
```

the Fraction class does not have a setReal:andImaginary: method (and did not inherit one, either). Therefore, it issues the warning message shown previously.

Now consider the following code sequence:

```
id dataValue = [[Fraction alloc] init];
   ...
[dataValue setReal: 10.0 andImaginary: 2.5];
```

These lines do not produce a warning message from the compiler because the compiler doesn't know what type of object is stored inside dataValue when processing your source file. (No, the compiler doesn't see that earlier a Fraction object was stored inside that variable!)

No error message is reported until you run the program containing these lines. The program crashes, and the error contains a bunch of lines, one of which looks like this:

```
-[Fraction setReal:andImaginary:]: unrecognized selector sent to instance 0x103f00
```

When the program is executing, the system first checks the type of object stored inside dataValue. Because dataValue has a Fraction stored in it, the runtime system looks for a method setReal:andImaginary: defined for the Fraction class. Because it can't find such a method, the error message shown previously is issued and the program is terminated.

The id Data Type and Static Typing

If an id data type can be used to store any object, why don't you just declare all your objects as type id? For several reasons, you don't want to get into the habit of overusing this generic class data type.

First, when you define a variable to be an object from a particular class, you are using what's known as *static* typing. The word *static* refers to the fact that the type of object that will be stored in the variable is being explicitly declared. So the class of the object stored in that type is predeterminate, or *static*. When you use static typing, the compiler ensures, to the best of its ability, that the variable is used consistently throughout the program. The compiler can check to ensure that a method applied to an object is defined or inherited by that class; if not, it issues a warning message. Therefore, when you declare a Rectangle variable called myRect in your program, the compiler checks that any methods you invoke on myRect are defined in the Rectangle class or are inherited from its superclass.

> **Note**
>
> You can also invoke methods on an object by specifying the method name as a variable, as you'll see later in this chapter. In this case, the compiler cannot check your method argument or return types for you.

However, if this check is performed for you at runtime anyway, why do you care about static typing? You care because it's better to get your errors out during the compilation phase of your program than during the execution phase. If you leave it until runtime, you might not even be the one running the program when the error occurs. If your program is put into production, some poor unsuspecting user might discover when running the program that a particular object does not recognize a method by having the program crash on her.

Another reason for using static typing is that it makes your programs more readable. Consider the following declaration:

```
id    f1;
```

versus

```
Fraction *f1;
```

Which do you think is more understandable—that is, which makes the intended use of the variable f1 clearer? The combination of static typing and meaningful variable names (which we intentionally did not choose in the previous example) can go a long way toward making your program more self-documenting.

> **Note**
>
> You cannot use the dot operator with id variables; the compiler gives you an error if you attempt to do so.

Argument and Return Types with Dynamic Typing

If you use dynamic typing to invoke a method, note the following rule: If a method with the same name is implemented in more than one of your classes, each method must agree on the type of each argument and the type of value it returns so that the compiler can generate the correct code for your message expressions.

The compiler performs a consistency check among each class declaration it has seen. If one or more methods conflict in either argument or return type, the compiler issues a warning message. For example, both the Fraction and Complex classes contain add: methods. However, the Fraction class takes as its argument and returns a Fraction object, whereas the Complex class takes and returns a Complex object. If frac1 and myFract are Fraction objects, and comp1 and myComplex are Complex objects, statements such as

```
result = [myFract add: frac1];
```

and

```
result = [myComplex add: comp1];
```

do not cause any problems. This is because, in both cases, the receiver of the message is statically typed and the compiler can check for consistent use of the method as it is defined in the receiver's class.

If `dataValue1` and `dataValue2` are `id` variables, the statement

```
result = [dataValue1 add: dataValue2];
```

causes the compiler to generate code to pass the argument to an `add:` method and handle its returned value by making assumptions.

At runtime, the Objective-C runtime system will check the actual class of the object stored inside `dataValue1` and select the appropriate method from the correct class to execute. However, in a more general case, the compiler might generate the incorrect code to pass arguments to a method or handle its return value. This would happen if one method took an object as its argument and the other took a floating-point value, for example. Or if one method returned an object and the other returned an integer, for example. If the inconsistency between two methods is just a different type of object (for example, the `Fraction`'s `add:` method takes a `Fraction` object as its argument and returns one, and the `Complex`'s `add:` method takes and returns a `Complex` object), the compiler will still generate the correct code because memory addresses (that is, pointers) are passed as references to objects anyway.

Asking Questions about Classes

As you start working with variables that can contain objects from different classes, you might need to ask questions such as the following:

- Is this object a rectangle?
- Does this object support a `print` method?
- Is this object a member of the `Graphics` class or one of its descendants?

You can then use the answers to these questions to execute different sequences of code, avoid an error, or check the integrity of your program while it's executing.

Table 9.1 summarizes some of the basic methods that the `NSObject` class supports for asking these types of questions. In this table, `class-object` is a class object (typically generated with the `class` method), and `selector` is a value of type `SEL` (typically created with the `@selector` directive).

Table 9.1 **Methods for Working with Dynamic Types**

Method	Question or Action
-(BOOL) isKindOfClass: *class-object*	Is the object a member of *class-object* or a descendant?
-(BOOL) isMemberOfClass: *class-object*	Is the object a member of *class-object?*
-(BOOL) respondsToSelector: *selector*	Can the object respond to the method specified by *selector?*
+(BOOL) instancesRespondToSelector: *selector*	Can instances of the specified class respond to *selector?*
+(BOOL) isSubclassOfClass: *class-object*	Is the object a subclass of the specified class?
-(id) performSelector: *selector*	Apply the method specified by *selector.*
-(id) performSelector: *selector* withObject: *object*	Apply the method specified by *selector* passing the argument *object.*
-(id) performSelector: *selector* withObject: *object1* withObject: *object2*	Apply the method specified by *selector* with the arguments *object1* and *object2.*

Other methods are not covered here. One enables you to ask whether an object conforms to a protocol (see Chapter 11, "Categories and Protocols"). Others enable you to ask about dynamically resolving methods (not covered in this text).

To generate a class object from a class name or another object, you send it the class message. So to get a class object from a class named Square, you write the following:

```
[Square class]
```

If mySquare is an instance of Square object, you get its class by writing this:

```
[mySquare class]
```

To see whether the objects stored in the variables obj1 and obj2 are instances from the same class, you write this:

```
if ([obj1 class] == [obj2 class])
...
```

To see if the variable myFract is a Fraction class object, you test the result from the expression, like this:

```
[myFract isMemberOfClass: [Fraction class]]
```

To generate one of the so-called selectors listed in Table 9.1, you apply the @selector directive to a method name. For example, the following produces a value of type SEL for the method named alloc, which you know is a method inherited from the NSObject class:

```
@selector (alloc)
```

The following expression produces a selector for the `setTo:over:` method that you implemented in your `Fraction` class. (Remember those colon characters in the method names.)

```
@selector (setTo:over:)
```

To see whether an instance of the `Fraction` class responds to the `setTo:over:` method, you can test the return value from the expression, like this:

```
[Fraction instancesRespondToSelector: @selector (setTo:over:)]
```

Remember, the test covers inherited methods, not just one that is directly defined in the class definition.

The `performSelector:` method and its variants (not shown in Table 9.1) enable you to send a message to an object, where the message can be a selector stored inside a variable. For example, consider this code sequence:

```
SEL      action;
id       graphicObject;
 ...
action = @selector (draw);
 ...
[graphicObject performSelector: action];
```

In this example, the method indicated by the SEL variable action is sent to whatever graphical object is stored in `graphicObject`. Presumably, the action might vary during program execution—perhaps based on the user's input—even though we've shown the action as draw. To first ensure that the object can respond to the action, you might want to use something like this:

```
if ([graphicObject respondsToSelector: action] == YES)
    [graphicObject performSelector: action]
else
    // error handling code here
```

> **Note**
>
> The `respondsToSelector:` method is used extensively in iOS for implementing the concept of *delegation*. As you'll learn in Chapter 10, "More on Variables and Data Types," the system often gives you the option to implement one or more methods in your class to handle certain events or provide certain information (such as the number of sections in a table). For the system to determine whether you have in fact implemented a particular method, it uses `responds-ToSelector:` to see whether it can delegate the handling of the event to your method. If you didn't implement the method, it takes care of the event itself, doing whatever is defined as the default behavior.

You can employ other strategies as well: You can forward the message to another object to handle using the `forwardInvocation:` method, but covering how to do this is beyond the scope of this text.

Program 9.3 asks some questions about the Square and Rectangle classes defined in Chapter 8, "Inheritance." Try to predict the results from this program before looking at the actual output (no peeking!).

Program 9.3

```
#import "Square.h"

int main (int argc, char * argv[])
{
   @autoreleasepool {
      Square *mySquare = [[Square alloc] init];

      // isMemberOf:

      if ( [mySquare isMemberOfClass: [Square class]] == YES )
         NSLog (@"mySquare is a member of Square class");

      if ( [mySquare isMemberOfClass: [Rectangle class]] == YES )
         NSLog (@"mySquare is a member of Rectangle class");

      if ( [mySquare isMemberOfClass: [NSObject class]] == YES )
         NSLog (@"mySquare is a member of NSObject class");

      // isKindOf:

      if ( [mySquare isKindOfClass: [Square class]] == YES )
         NSLog (@"mySquare is a kind of Square");

      if ( [mySquare isKindOfClass: [Rectangle class]] == YES )
         NSLog (@"mySquare is a kind of Rectangle");

      if ( [mySquare isKindOfClass: [NSObject class]] == YES )
         NSLog (@"mySquare is a kind of NSObject");

      // respondsTo:

      if ( [mySquare respondsToSelector: @selector (setSide:)] == YES )
         NSLog (@"mySquare responds to setSide: method");

      if ( [mySquare respondsToSelector: @selector (setWidth:andHeight:)] == YES )
         NSLog (@"mySquare responds to setWidth:andHeight: method");

      if ( [Square respondsToSelector: @selector (alloc)] == YES )
         NSLog (@"Square class responds to alloc method");
```

```
    // instancesRespondTo:

    if ([Rectangle instancesRespondToSelector: @selector (setSide:)] == YES)
        NSLog (@"Instances of Rectangle respond to setSide: method");

    if ([Square instancesRespondToSelector: @selector (setSide:)] == YES)
        NSLog (@"Instances of Square respond to setSide: method");

    if ([Square isSubclassOfClass: [Rectangle class]] == YES)
        NSLog (@"Square is a subclass of a rectangle");
    }
    return 0;
}
```

Make sure that you build this program with the implementation files for the Square, Rectangle, and XYPoint classes, which were all presented in Chapter 8.

Program 9.3   **Output**

```
mySquare is a member of Square class
mySquare is a kind of Square
mySquare is a kind of Rectangle
mySquare is a kind of NSObject
mySquare responds to setSide: method
mySquare responds to setWidth:andHeight: method
Square class responds to alloc method
Instances of Square respond to setSide: method
Square is a subclass of a rectangle
```

The output from Program 9.3 should be clear. Remember that isMemberOfClass: tests for direct membership in a class, whereas isKindOfClass: checks for membership in the inheritance hierarchy. Thus, mySquare is a member of the Square class—but it's also "kind of" a Square, Rectangle, and NSObject because it exists in that class hierarchy. (Obviously, all objects should return YES for the isKindOf: test on the NSObject class, unless you've defined a new root object.)

The test

```
if ( [Square respondsToSelector: @selector (alloc)] == YES )
```

tests whether the class Square responds to the class method alloc, which it does because it's inherited from the root object NSObject. Realize that you can always use the class name directly as the receiver in a message expression, and you don't have to write this in the previous expression (although you could if you wanted):

```
[Square class]
```

That's the only place you can get away with that. In other places, you need to apply the class method to obtain the class object.

Exception Handling Using @try

Good programming practice dictates that you try to anticipate problems that can occur in your program. You can do this by testing for conditions that could cause a program to terminate abnormally and handling these situations, perhaps by logging a message and gracefully terminating the program or taking some other corrective action. For example, you saw earlier in this chapter how you can test to see if an object responds to a particular message. In the case of error avoidance, performing this test while the program is executing can enable you to avoid sending an unrecognized message to an object. When an attempt is made to send such an unrecognized message, your program will typically terminate immediately by throwing what's known as an exception.

Take a look at Program 9.4. We have no method called noSuchMethod defined in the Fraction class. When you compile the program, you will get warning messages to that effect.

Program 9.4

```
#import "Fraction.h"

int main (int argc, char * argv [])
{
    @autoreleasepool {
        Fraction *f = [[Fraction alloc] init];
        [f noSuchMethod];
        NSLog (@"Execution continues!");
    }
    return 0;
}
```

You can go ahead and run the program despite the warning messages you receive. If you do, you can expect to see your program terminate abnormally with errors similar to what's shown in Program 9.4.

Program 9.4 **Output**

```
*** Terminating app due to uncaught exception 'NSInvalidArgumentException', reason:
'-[Fraction noSuchMethod]: unrecognized selector sent to instance 0x103f00'
*** Call stack at first throw:'')
```

To avoid abnormal program termination in a case such as this, you can put one or more statements inside a special statement block, which takes the following format:

```
@try {
    statement
    statement
    ...
}
@catch (NSException *exception) {
    statement
    statement
    ...
}
```

Execution proceeds as normal with each *statement* in the @try block. However, if one of the statements in the block throws an exception, execution is not terminated but instead goes immediately to the @catch block, where it continues. Inside that block, you can handle the exception. One plausible sequence of actions here would be to log an error message, clean up, and terminate execution.

Program 9.5 illustrates exception handling. It is followed by the program's output.

Program 9.5   **Exception Handling**

```
#import <Foundation/Foundation.h>

int main (int argc, char * argv [])
{
    @autoreleasepool {
        NSArray *myArray = [NSArray array];

        @try {
            [myArray objectAtIndex: 2];
        }
        @catch (NSException *exception) {
            NSLog (@"Caught %@%@", exception.name, exception.reason);
        }

        NSLog (@"Execution continues");

    }
    return 0;
}
```

Program 9.5 **Output**

```
Caught NSRangeException*** -[__NSArrayI objectAtIndex:]: index 2 beyond bounds for
empty array
Execution continues
```

Program 9.5 sets up an array, which you'll learn how to do in Chapter 15, "Numbers, Strings, and Collections." It then tries to reference a nonexistent element from the array using the NSArray class's objectAtIndex: method. This causes an exception to occur.

When the exception occurs, the @catch block gets executed. An NSException object that contains information about the exception gets passed as the argument into this block. As you can see, the name method retrieves the name of the exception, and the reason method gives the reason (which the runtime system also previously printed automatically).

After the last statement in the @catch block is executed (we have only one here), the program continues execution with the statement immediately following the block. In this case, we execute an NSLog call to verify that execution has continued and has not been terminated.

This is a simple example to illustrate how to catch exceptions in a program. An @finally block can be used to include code to execute whether or not a statement in an @try block throws an exception.

An @throw directive enables you to throw your own exception. You can use it to throw a specific exception, or inside an @catch block to throw the same exception that took you into the block like this:

```
@throw;
```

You might want to do this after handling an exception yourself (perhaps after performing cleanup work, for example). You can then let the system handle the rest of the work for you.

You can have multiple @catch blocks that are sequenced to catch and handle different types of exceptions.

In general, you don't want exceptions to occur while your program is running. So it's considered better programming practice to test for errors before they occur rather than to catch them after they occur. It's also better to test for an error in a method and return some value as an error indicator than to throw an exception. It is strongly recommended that if you catch an exception you only do so with the intention of cleaning up and terminating your application. Why? Because Apple does not guarantee that your application will be in a well-defined state for continuing program execution once an exception is thrown.

Exercises

1. What will happen if you insert the message expression

```
[compResult reduce];
```

into Program 9.1 after the addition is performed? Try it and see.

2. Can the `id` variable `dataValue`, as defined in Program 9.2, be assigned a `Rectangle` object as you defined it in Chapter 8? That is, is the statement

```
dataValue = [[Rectangle alloc] init];
```

valid? Why or why not?

3. Add a `print` method to your `XYPoint` class defined in Chapter 8. Have it display the point in the format (x, y). Then modify Program 9.2 to incorporate an `XYPoint` object. Have the modified program create an `XYPoint` object, set its value, assign it to the `id` variable `dataValue`, and then display its value.

4. Based on the discussions about argument and return types in this chapter, modify both `add:` methods in the `Fraction` and `Complex` classes to take and return `id` objects. Then write a program that incorporates the following code sequence:

```
result = [dataValue1 add: dataValue2];
[result print];
```

Here, `result`, `dataValue1`, and `dataValue2` are `id` objects. Make sure that you set `dataValue1` and `dataValue2` appropriately in your program.

> **Note**
> You'll have to change the name of the methods to something other than `add:`. That's because the system's `NSObjectController` class also has an `add:` method. As noted in this chapter in the "Argument and Return Types with Dynamic Typing" section, if multiple methods of the same name exist in different classes and the type of the receiver isn't known at compile time, the compiler performs a consistency check to make sure the arguments and return types are consistent among the similarly named methods.

5. Given the `Fraction` and `Complex` class definitions you have been using in this text and the following definitions

```
Fraction *fraction = [[Fraction alloc] init];
Complex  *complex = [[Complex alloc] init];
id        number = [[Complex alloc] init];
```

determine the return value from the following message expressions. Then type them into a program to verify the results.

```
[fraction isMemberOfClass: [Complex class]];
[complex isMemberOfClass: [NSObject class]];
[complex isKindOfClass: [NSObject class]];
[fraction isKindOfClass: [Fraction class]];
[fraction respondsToSelector: @selector (print)];
[complex respondsToSelector: @selector (print)];
[Fraction instancesRespondToSelector: @selector (print)];
[number respondsToSelector: @selector (print)];
[number isKindOfClass: [Complex class]];
[[number class] respondsToSelector: @selector (alloc)];
```

10

More on Variables and Data Types

This chapter covers variable scope, initialization methods for objects, and data types in more detail.

The initialization of an object deserves some special attention, which we give here.

We talked briefly about the scope of instance variables as well as static and local variables in Chapter 7, "More on Classes." We talk more about static variables here and introduce the concept of global and external ones. In addition, you can give certain directives to the Objective-C compiler, to more precisely control the scope of your instance variables. We cover these directives in this chapter as well.

An *enumerated* data type enables you to define the name for a data type to be used only to store a specified list of values. The Objective-C language's `typedef` statement lets you assign your own name to a built-in or derived data type. Finally, we describe in more detail the precise steps the Objective-C compiler follows when converting data types in the evaluation of expressions.

Initializing Objects

You've seen the pattern before: You allocate a new instance of an object and then initialize it, using a familiar sequence like this:

```
Fraction *myFract = [[Fraction alloc] init];
```

We didn't write our own `init` method here; we use the one we inherited from the parent class, which is `NSObject`.

After these two methods are invoked, you typically assign some values to the new object, like this:

```
[myFract setTo: 1 over: 3];
```

The process of initializing an object followed by setting it to some initial values is often combined into a single method. For example, you can define an initWith:over: method that initializes a fraction and sets its numerator and denominator to the two supplied arguments.

A class that contains many methods and instance variables in it commonly has several initialization methods as well. For example, the Foundation framework's NSArray class contains the following six initialization methods:

```
initWithArray:
initWithArray:copyItems:
initWithContentsOfFile:
initWithContentsOfURL:
initWithObjects:
initWithObjects:count:
```

An array might be allocated and then initialized with a sequence like this:

```
myArray = [[NSArray alloc] initWithArray: myOtherArray];
```

It's common practice for all the initializers in a class to begin with init.... As you can see, the NSArray's initializers follow that convention. You should adhere to the following two strategies when writing initializers.

It might be the case that you want to do something special whenever one of the objects in your class gets initialized. For example, that's the perfect place to create the objects that your class uses and references through one or more instance variables. A perfect example of that is our Rectangle class; it is reasonable to allocate the rectangle's XYPoint origin in the init method. To do so, we just have to override the inherited init method.

You use a standard "template" overriding init, and it looks like this:

```
- (id)init
{
    self = [super init];
    if (self) {
        // Initialization code here.
    }
    return self;
}
```

This method invokes the parent initializer first. Executing the parent's initializer ensures that any inherited instance variables are properly initialized.

You must assign the result of executing the parent's init method back to self because an initializer has the right to change the location of the object in memory (meaning its reference will change).

If the parent's initialization succeeds, the value returned will be non-nil, as tested by the if statement. As the comment indicates, inside the block that follows is where you can put your own custom initialization code for your object. This often involves allocating and initializing instance variables that are in your class.

If your class contains more than one initializer, one of them should be your *designated* initializer, and all the other initialization methods should use it. Typically, that is your most complex initialization method (usually the one that takes the most arguments). Creating a designated initializer centralizes your main initialization code in a single method. Anyone subclassing your class can then override your designated initializer to ensure that new instances are properly initialized.

Based on that discussion, your initialization method `initWith:over:` for your `Fraction` class might look like this:

```
-(Fraction *) initWith: (int) n over: (int) d
{
  self = [super init];

  if (self)
     [self setTo: n over: d];

  return self;
}
```

Following the initialization of `super` (and its success, as indicated by the return of a nonzero value) you use the `setTo:over:` method to set the numerator and denominator of your `Fraction`. As with other initialization methods, you are expected to return the initialized object, which you do here.

Program 10.1 tests your new `initWith:over:` initialization method.

Program 10.1

```
#import "Fraction.h"

int main (int argc, char * argv[])
{
   @autoreleasepool {

      Fraction *a, *b;

      a = [[Fraction alloc] initWith: 1 over: 3];
      b = [[Fraction alloc] initWith: 3 over: 7];

      [a print];
      [b print];

   }
   return 0;
}
```

Program 10.1   **Output**

```
1/3
3/7
```

To adhere to the rule stated earlier about a designated initializer, you should also modify `init` in your `Fraction` class. That's particularly important if your class might be subclassed.

Here's what the `init` method could look like:

```
-(id)  init
{
    return  [self  initWith: 0 over: 0];
}
```

Note that `init` is defined to return an `id` type. That's the general rule for writing `init` methods for a class that might be subclassed. You don't want to hard-code a class name in such cases, as the subclass will not be an object from the same class as the parent. To be consistent here you should go back to the `initWith:over:` method and change its return type to `id`.

When your program begins execution, it sends the `initialize` call method to all your classes. If you have a class and associated subclasses, the parent class gets the message first. This message is sent only once to each class, and it is guaranteed to be sent before any other messages are sent to the class. The purpose is for you to perform any class initialization at that point. For example, you might want to initialize some static variables associated with that class at that time.

Scope Revisited

You can influence the scope of the variables in your program in several ways. You can do this with instance variables as well as with normal variables defined either outside or inside functions. In the following discussion, we use the term *module* to refer to any number of method or function definitions contained within a single source file.

Directives for Controlling Instance Variable Scope

You know by now that instance variables have scope that is limited to the instance methods defined for the class. So, any instance method can access its instance variables directly by name, without having to do anything special.

You also know that instance variables declared in the interface section are inherited by a subclass. Inherited instance variables can also be accessed directly by name from within any method defined in that subclass. Again, this is without having to do anything special.

You can put four directives in front of your instance variables when they are declared in the interface section, to more precisely control their scope:

- @protected—Methods defined in the class and any subclasses can directly access the instance variables that follow. This is the default for instance variables defined in the interface section.

- @private—Methods defined in the class can directly access the instance variables that follow, but subclasses cannot. This is the default for instance variables defined in the implementation section.

- @public—Methods defined in the class and any other classes or modules can directly access the instance variables that follow.

- @package—For 64-bit images, the instance variable can be accessed anywhere within the image that implements the class.

If you want to define a class called Printer that keeps two instance variables, called pageCount and tonerLevel private, and is accessible only by methods in the Printer class, you might use an interface section that looks like this:

```
@interface Printer
{
@private
    int   pageCount;
    int   tonerLevel;
@protected
    // other instance variables
}
  . . .
@end
```

Anyone subclassing Printer would be incapable of accessing these two instance variables because they were made private.

These special directives act like "switches"; all variables that appear after one of these directives (until the right curly brace that marks the end of the variable declarations) have the specified scope unless another directive is used. In the previous example, the @protected directive ensures that instance variables that follow, up to the }, will be accessible by subclasses and by the Printer class methods.

The @public directive makes instance variables accessible by other methods or functions through the use of the pointer operator (->), which is covered in Chapter 13, "Underlying C Language Features." Making an instance variable public is not considered good programming practice because it defeats the concept of data encapsulation (that is, a class hiding its instance variables).

More on Properties, Synthesized Accessors, and Instance Variables

The current trend in coding conventions (which Xcode 4 has adopted) is to use an underscore (_) as the leading character for an instance variable name. So any references you see in the template code generated by Xcode to variables starting with a _ are referencing the instance variables directly by name.

When you see an @synthesize directive that looks like this

```
@synthesize window=_window;
```

it says to synthesize the getter and setter for the property named window and to associate that property with an instance variable called _window (which does not have to be explicitly declared). This helps to distinguish the use of the instance variable from the property and to encourage you to set and retrieve the value of the instance variable through the setter and getter methods. That is, writing something like this

```
[window makeKeyAndVisible];  // This won't work
```

will fail, as there is no instance variable named window. Instead, you have to either call out the instance variable directly by its name, such as

```
[_window makeKeyAndVisible];
```

or, preferably, use the accessor method:

```
[self.window makeKeyAndVisible];
```

As you know, instance variables declared either explicitly in the implementation section (or implicitly by using the @synthesize directive) are made private, meaning they're not accessible to subclasses directly by name. So, subclasses have no choice but to use the inherited accessor methods in order to access their values.

Remember, the synthesized methods might be doing additional work based on their attributes (for example, managing memory, copying values, and so on) that won't occur when assigning or retrieving values directly to/from the instance variable. So, there's an extra level of abstraction between the property and the instance variable. This level of abstraction gives the system an opportunity to do extra work (that you don't necessarily need to be aware of) when accessing instance variables.

As noted in Chapter 7, as of Xcode 4.5 you no longer needed to use an @synthesize directive to have your accessor methods synthesized. The compiler generates those methods in the absence of such a directive when you simply declare them as properties. When the compiler does this, it adheres to the coding convention mentioned previously. That is, if you write this in your @interface section

```
@property BOOL isFinishedFlag;
```

it's as if you included the following in your @implementation section:

```
@synthesize isFinishedFlag = _isFinishedFlag;
```

So, in this case, the underlying instance variable is named `_isFinishedFlag` and can be referenced directly by name in the implementation section as such. For example

```
_isFinishedFlag = NO;
```

And to instead set the same value through the property's setter method, you write this:

```
self.isFinishedFlag = NO;
```

Global Variables

If you write the statement

```
int gMoveNumber = 0;
```

at the beginning of your program—outside any method, class definition, or function—its value can be referenced from anywhere in that module. In such a case, we say that gMoveNumber is defined as a *global* variable. By convention, a lowercase *g* is commonly used as the first letter of a global variable, to indicate its scope to the program's reader.

Actually, this same definition of the variable gMoveNumber also makes its value accessible from other files. Specifically, the preceding statement defines the variable gMoveNumber not just as a global variable, but as an *external* global variable.

An *external* variable is one whose value can be accessed and changed by any other methods or functions. Inside the module that wants to access the external variable, the variable is declared in the normal fashion and the keyword `extern` is placed before the declaration. This signals to the system that a globally defined variable from another file is to be accessed. The following is an example of how to declare the variable gMoveNumber as an external variable:

```
extern int gMoveNumber;
```

The module in which the preceding declaration appeared can now access and modify the value of gMoveNumber. Other modules can also access the value of gMoveNumber by using a similar `extern` declaration in the file.

Consider this important rule to follow when working with external variables: The variable must be defined someplace among your source files. This is done by declaring the variable outside any method or function and is *not* preceded by the keyword `extern`, like this:

```
int gMoveNumber;
```

Here, an initial value can be optionally assigned to the variable, as shown previously.

The second way to define an external variable is to declare the variable outside any function, placing the keyword `extern` in front of the declaration and explicitly assigning an initial value to it, like this:

```
extern int gMoveNumber = 0;
```

However, this is not the preferred way to do this, and the compiler warns you that you've declared the variable `extern` and assigned it a value at the same time. That's because using the word `extern` makes it a declaration for the variable, not a definition. Remember, a declaration doesn't cause storage for a variable to be allocated, but a definition does. The previous example violates this rule by forcing a declaration to be treated as a definition (by assigning it an initial value).

When dealing with external variables, you can declare a variable as `extern` in many places, but you can define it only once.

Consider a small program example to illustrate the use of external variables. Suppose we have defined a class called `Foo`, and we type the following code into a file called `main.m`:

```
#import "Foo.h"

int gGlobalVar = 5;

int main (int argc, char *argc[])
{
    @autoreleasepool {
      Foo *myFoo = [[Foo alloc] init];
      NSLog (@"%i ", gGlobalVar);

      [myFoo setgGlobalVar: 100];
      NSLog (@"%i", gGlobalVar);
    }
    return 0;
}
```

The definition of the global variable `gGlobalVar` in the previous program makes its value accessible by any method (or function) that uses an appropriate extern declaration. Suppose your `Foo` method `setgGlobalVar:` looks like this:

```
-(void) setgGlobalVar: (int) val
{
    extern int gGlobalVar;
    gGlobalVar = val;
}
```

This program produces the following output:

```
5
100
```

This verifies that the method `setgGlobalVar:` can access and change the value of the external variable `gGlobalVar`.

If many methods needed to access the value of `gGlobalVar`, making the `extern` declaration just once at the front of the file would be easier. However, if only one method or a small number of methods needs to access this variable, there is something to be said for making separate `extern` declarations in each such method; it makes the program more organized and isolates the use of the particular variable to those functions that actually use it. Note that if the variable is defined inside the file containing the code that accesses the variable, the individual `extern` declarations are not required.

Static Variables

The example just shown goes against the notion of data encapsulation and good object-oriented programming techniques. However, you might need to work with variables whose values are shared across different method invocations. Even though it might not make sense to make `gGlobalVar` an instance variable in the `Foo` class, a better approach might be to "hide" it within the `Foo` class by restricting its access to setter and getter methods defined for that class.

You now know that any variable defined outside a method is not only a global variable, but an external one as well. Many situations arise in which you want to define a variable to be global but not external. In other words, you want to define a global variable to be local to a particular module (file). It would make sense to want to define a variable this way if no methods other than those contained inside a particular class definition needed access to the particular variable. You can accomplish this by defining the variable to be *static* inside the file that contains the implementation for the particular class.

If made outside any method (or function), the following statement makes the value of `gGlobalVar` accessible from any subsequent point in the file in which the definition appears, but not from methods or functions contained in other files:

```
static int gGlobalVar = 0;
```

Recall that class methods do not have access to instance variables. (You might want to think about why that's the case again.) However, you might want a class method to be capable of setting and accessing variables. A simple example is a class allocator method that you want to keep track of the number of objects it has allocated. You would accomplish this task by setting up a static variable inside the implementation file for the class. The allocation method could then access this variable directly because it would not be an instance variable. The users of the class would not need to know about this variable. Because it's defined as a static variable in the implementation file, its scope is restricted to that file. Users therefore do not have direct access to it, and the concept of data encapsulation is not violated. You could write a method to retrieve the value of this variable if access is needed from outside the class.

Program 10.2 extends the `Fraction` class definition with the addition of two new methods. The `allocF` class method allocates a new `Fraction` and keeps track of how many `Fractions` it has allocated, whereas the `count` method returns that count. Note that this latter method is also a class method. It could have been implemented as an instance method as well, but it makes more sense to ask the class how many instances it has allocated instead of sending the message to a particular instance of the class.

These are the declarations for the two new class methods to be added to the `Fraction.h` header file:

```
+(Fraction *) allocF;
+(int)  count;
```

Notice that the inherited `alloc` method wasn't overridden here; instead, you defined your own allocator method. Your method will take advantage of the inherited `alloc` method. Place this code in your `Fraction.m` implementation file:

```
static int gCounter;

@implementation Fraction

+(Fraction *) allocF
{
    extern int gCounter;
    ++gCounter;

    return [Fraction alloc];
}

+(int)  count
{
    extern int gCounter;

    return gCounter;
}
// other methods from Fraction class go here
    ...

@end
```

> **Note**
>
> It's not considered good programming practice to override `alloc`, because this method deals with the physical allocation of the memory. You shouldn't have to get involved at that level.

The static declaration of gCounter makes it accessible to any method defined in the implementation section, yet it does not make it accessible from outside the file. The `allocF` method simply increments the gCounter variable and then uses the `alloc` method to create a new `Fraction`, returning the result. The count method simply returns the value of the counter, thus isolating its direct access from the user.

Recall that the `extern` declarations are not required in the two methods because the gCounter variable is defined within the file. It simply helps the reader of the method understand that a variable defined outside the method is being accessed. The g prefix for the variable name also serves the same purpose for the reader; for that reason, most programmers typically do not include the `extern` declarations.

Program 10.2 tests the new methods.

Program 10.2

```
#import "Fraction.h"

int main (int argc, char * argv[])
{
    @autoreleasepool {
        Fraction *a, *b, *c;

        NSLog (@"Fractions allocated: %i", [Fraction count]);

        a = [[Fraction allocF] init];
        b = [[Fraction allocF] init];
        c = [[Fraction allocF] init];

        NSLog (@"Fractions allocated: %i", [Fraction count]);
    }
    return 0;
}
```

Program 10.2   **Output**

```
Fractions allocated: 0
Fractions allocated: 3
```

When the program begins execution, the value of gCounter is automatically set to 0. (Recall that you can override the inherited class initialize method if you want to perform any special initialization of the class as a whole, such as set the value of other static variables to some nonzero values.) After allocating (and then initializing) three Fractions using the allocF method, the count method retrieves the counter variable, which is correctly set to 3. You could also add a setter method to the class if you want to reset the counter or set it to a particular value. You don't need that for this application, though.

Enumerated Data Types

The Objective-C language enables you to specify a range of values that can be assigned to a variable. An enumerated data type definition is initiated by the keyword enum. Immediately following this keyword is the name of the enumerated data type, followed by a list of identifiers (enclosed in a set of curly braces) that define the permissible values that can be assigned to the type. For example, the following statement defines a data type flag:

```
enum flag { false, true };
```

In theory, this data type can be assigned the values true and false inside the program, and no other values. Unfortunately, the Objective-C compiler does not generate warning messages if this rule is violated.

To declare a variable to be of type `enum flag`, you again use the keyword `enum`, followed by the enumerated type name, followed by the variable list. So, the following statement defines the two variables `endOfData` and `matchFound` to be of type `flag`:

```
enum flag endOfData, matchFound;
```

The only values (in theory, that is) that can be assigned to these variables are the names `true` and `false`. Thus, statements such as

```
endOfData = true;
```

and

```
if ( matchFound == false )
    . . .
```

are valid.

If you want to have a specific integer value associated with an enumeration identifier, you can assign the integer to the identifier when the data type is defined. Enumeration identifiers that subsequently appear in the list are assigned sequential integer values beginning with the specified integer value plus one.

In the following definition, an enumerated data type, `direction`, is defined with the values up, down, `left`, and `right`:

```
enum direction { up, down, left = 10, right };
```

The compiler assigns the value 0 to up because it appears first in the list, assigns 1 to down because it appears next, assigns 10 to left because it is explicitly assigned this value, and assigns 11 to right because it is the incremented value of the preceding enum in the list.

Enumeration identifiers can share the same value. For example, in

```
enum boolean { no = 0, false = 0, yes = 1, true = 1 };
```

assigning either the value no or false to an `enum boolean` variable assigns it the value 0; assigning either yes or true assigns it the value 1.

As another example of an enumerated data type definition, the following defines the type enum month, with permissible values that can be assigned to a variable of this type being the names of the months of the year:

```
enum month { january = 1, february, march, april, may, june, july,
        august, september, october, november, december };
```

The Objective-C compiler actually treats enumeration identifiers as integer constants. If your program contains these two lines, the value 2 is assigned to thisMonth (and not the name february):

```
enum month thisMonth;
  ...
thisMonth = february;
```

Program 10.3 shows a simple program using enumerated data types. The program reads a month number and then enters a switch statement to see which month was entered. Recall that the compiler treats enumeration values as integer constants, so they're valid case values. The variable days is assigned the number of days in the specified month, and its value is displayed after the switch is exited. A special test is included to see whether the month is February.

Program 10.3

```
#import <Foundation/Foundation.h>

// print the number of days in a month
int main (int argc, char * argv[])
{
    @autoreleasepool {
        enum month { january = 1, february, march, april, may, june,
                    july, august, september, october, november,
                    december };
        enum month amonth;
        int     days;

        NSLog (@"Enter month number: ");
        scanf ("%i", &amonth);

        switch (amonth) {
            case january:
            case march:
            case may:
            case july:
            case august:
            case october:
            case december:
                    days = 31;
                    break;
            case april:
            case june:
            case september:
            case november:
                    days = 30;
```

```
                    break;
            case february:
                    days = 28;
                    break;
            default:
                    NSLog (@"bad month number");
                    days = 0;
                    break;
        }

    if ( days != 0 )
        NSLog (@"Number of days is %i", days);

    if ( amonth == february )
        NSLog (@"...or 29 if it's a leap year");
    }
    return 0;
}
```

Program 10.3   **Output**

Enter month number:
5
Number of days is 31

Program 10.3   **Output (Rerun)**

Enter month number:
2
Number of days is 28
...or 29 if it's a leap year

You can explicitly assign an integer value to an enumerated data type variable; you should do this using the type cast operator. Therefore, if monthValue were an integer variable that had the value 6, for example, this expression would be permissible:

```
lastMonth = (enum month) (monthValue - 1);
```

If you don't use the type cast operator, the compiler (unfortunately) won't complain about it.

When using programs with enumerated data types, try not to rely on the fact that the enumerated values are treated as integers. Instead, treat them as distinct data types. The enumerated data type gives you a way to associate a symbolic name with an integer number. If you subsequently need to change the value of that number, you must change it only in the place where the enumeration is defined. If you make assumptions based on the actual value of the enumerated data type, you defeat this benefit of using an enumeration.

As of Xcode 4.4, you can associate an integer data type with an enumerated name when the enumeration is defined. For example the following defines the enumeration type iPhoneModels to have an `unsigned short int` as its underlying data type:

```
enum iPhoneModels : unsigned short int { iPhone, iPhone3G,
        iPhone3GS, iPhone4 iPhone4S, iPhone5, Wednesday,
```

Compiler options (`-WConversion`) and (`-Wswitch`) have been added to provide better type checking when assigning and using enumerations in expressions and when using enumeration constants in switch statements.

Some variations are permitted when defining an enumerated data type: The name of the data type can be omitted, and variables can be declared to be of the particular enumerated data type when the type is defined. As an example showing both of these options, the statement

```
enum { east, west, south, north } direction;
```

defines an (unnamed) enumerated data type with values `east`, `west`, `south`, or `north` and declares a variable (`direction`) to be of that type.

Defining an enumerated data type within a block limits the scope of that definition to the block. However, defining an enumerated data type at the beginning of the program, outside any block, makes the definition global to the file.

When defining an enumerated data type, you must make certain that the enumeration identifiers are unique with respect to other variable names and enumeration identifiers defined within the same scope.

The `typedef` Statement

Objective-C provides a capability that enables the programmer to assign an alternative name to a data type. This is done with a statement known as `typedef`. The following statement defines the name `Counter` to be equivalent to the Objective-C data type `int`:

```
typedef int Counter;
```

You can subsequently declare variables to be of type `Counter`, as in the following statement:

```
Counter  j, n;
```

The Objective-C compiler treats the declaration of the variables `j` and `n`, shown previously, as normal integer variables. The main advantage of the use of the `typedef` in this case is in the added readability it lends to the definition of the variables. The definition of `j` and `n` makes clear the intended purpose of these variables in the program. Declaring them to be of type `int` in the traditional fashion would not have made the intended use of these variables clear.

The following `typedef` defines a type named `NumberObject` to be an `NSNumber` object:

```
typedef NSNumber *NumberObject;
```

Variables subsequently declared to be of type NumberObject, as in

```
NumberObject myValue1, myValue2, myResult;
```

are treated as if they were declared in the normal way in your program:

```
NSNumber *myValue1, *myValue2, *myResult;
```

To define a new type name with typedef, follow this procedure:

1. Write the statement as if a variable of the desired type were being declared.

2. Where the name of the declared variable would normally appear, substitute the new type name.

3. In front of everything, place the keyword typedef.

As an example of this procedure, to define a type called Direction to be an enumerated data type that consists of the directions east, west, north, and south, write out the enumerated type definition and substitute the name Direction where the variable name would normally appear. Before everything, place the keyword typedef:

```
typedef enum { east, west, south, north } Direction;
```

With this typedef in place, you can subsequently declare variables to be of type Direction, as in the following:

```
Direction step1, step2;
```

Data Type Conversions

Chapter 4, "Data Types and Expressions," briefly addressed the fact that sometimes the system implicitly makes conversions when expressions are evaluated. You examined a case with the data types float and int. You saw how an operation that involves a float and an int was carried out as a floating-point operation, with the integer data item automatically converted to a floating point.

You also saw how the type cast operator can be used to explicitly dictate a conversion. So given that total and n are both integer variables

```
average = (float) total / n;
```

the value of the variable total is converted to type float before the operation is performed, thereby guaranteeing that the division will be carried out as a floating-point operation.

Conversion Rules

The Objective-C compiler adheres to very strict rules when it comes to evaluating expressions that consist of different basic data types.

The following summarizes the order in which conversions take place in the evaluation of two operands in an expression:

1. If either operand is of type `long double`, the other is converted to `long double`, and that is the type of the result.

2. If either operand is of type `double`, the other is converted to `double`, and that is the type of the result.

3. If either operand is of type `float`, the other is converted to `float`, and that is the type of the result.

4. If either operand is of type `_Bool`, `char`, `short int`, or bitfield, or of an enumerated data type, it is converted to `int`.

5. If either operand is of type `long long int`, the other is converted to `long long int`, and that is the type of the result.

6. If either operand is of type `long int`, the other is converted to `long int`, and that is the type of the result.

7. If this step is reached, both operands are of type `int`, and that is the type of the result.

This is actually a simplified version of the steps involved in converting operands in an expression. The rules get more complicated when `unsigned` operands are involved, but this is detailed enough for this text.

Realize from this series of steps that whenever you reach a step that says "that is the type of the result," you're done with the conversion process.

As an example of how to follow these steps, let's see how the following expression would be evaluated, where f is defined to be a `float`, i an `int`, l a `long int`, and s a `short int` variable:

```
f * i + l / s
```

Consider first the multiplication of f by i, which is the multiplication of a `float` by an `int`. From Step 3, you know that, because f is of type `float`, the other operand (i) will also be converted to type `float`, and that will be the type of the result of the multiplication.

Next, l is divided by s, which is the division of a `long int` by a `short int`. Step 4 tells you that the `short int` will be promoted to an `int`. Continuing, Step 6 shows that because one of the operands (l) is a `long int`, the other operand will be converted to a `long int`, which will also be the type of the result. This division therefore produces a value of type `long int`, with any fractional part resulting from the division truncated.

Finally, Step 3 indicates that, if one of the operands in an expression is of type `float` (as is the result of multiplying f * i), the other operand will be converted to type `float`, which will be the type of the result. Therefore, *after* the division of l by s, the result of the operation is converted to type `float` and then added into the product of f and i. The final result of the preceding expression will therefore be a value of type `float`.

Remember, the type cast operator can always be used to explicitly force conversions and thereby control the way in which a particular expression is evaluated.

Therefore, if you do not want the result of dividing l by s to be truncated in the preceding expression evaluation, you can type-cast one of the operands to type `float`, thereby forcing the evaluation to be performed as a floating-point division:

```
f * i + (float) l / s
```

In this expression, l is converted to `float` before the division operation is performed because the type cast operator has higher precedence than the division operator. Because one of the operands of the division is then of type `float`, the other (s) is automatically converted to type `float`, and that is the type of the result.

Bit Operators

Various operators in the Objective-C language work with the particular bits used to represent an integer value. Table 10.1 presents these operators.

Table 10.1   **Bit Operators**

Symbol	Operation
&	Bitwise AND
|	Bitwise inclusive-OR
^	Bitwise OR
~	Ones complement
<<	Left shift
>>	Right shift

> **Note**
>
> You won't use bitwise operators much, if at all, in your Objective-C programs, although you will come across them in framework header files. Because this material may be a little dense for new programmers, you can just skim this section and refer back to it later, if necessary.

All the operators listed in Table 10.1, with the exception of the ones that complement operator (~), are binary operators and, as such, take two operands. Bit operations can be performed on any type of integer value but cannot be performed on floating-point values.

In the examples that follow, you'll want to learn how to convert between binary notation and hexadecimal notation. A hexadecimal (base 16) digit is composed of 4 bits. Table 10.2 shows how to convert between these two bases.

Table 10.2   **Binary, Decimal, and Hexadecimal Equivalents**

Binary Value	Decimal Value	Hexadecimal Value
0000	0	0
0001	1	1
0010	2	2
0011	3	3
0100	4	4
0101	5	5
0110	6	6
0111	7	7
1000	8	8
1001	9	9
1010	10	a
1011	11	b
1100	12	c
1101	13	d
1110	14	e
1111	15	f

The Bitwise AND Operator

When two values are ANDed, the binary representations of the values are compared bit by bit. Each corresponding bit that is a 1 in the first value and a 1 in the second value produce a 1 in the corresponding bit position of the result; anything else produces a 0. If b1 and b2 represent corresponding bits of the two operands, the following table, called a *truth table*, shows the result of b1 ANDed with b2 for all possible values of b1 and b2.

b1	b2	b1 & b2
0	0	0
0	1	0
1	0	0
1	1	1

For example, if w1 and w2 are defined as short ints, and w1 is set equal to hexadecimal 15 and w2 is set equal to hexadecimal 0c, the following C statement assigns the value 0x04 to w3:

```
w3 = w1 & w2;
```

You can see this more easily by treating the values of w1, w2, and w3 as binary numbers. Assume that you are dealing with a short int size of 16 bits:

```
w1    0000 0000 0001 0101     0x15
w2    0000 0000 0000 1100   & 0x0c
      ─────────────────────────────
w3    0000 0000 0000 0100     0x04
```

Bitwise ANDing is frequently used for masking operations. That is, this operator can be used to easily set specific bits of a data item to 0. For example, the following statement assigns to w3 the value of w1 bitwise ANDed with the constant 3.

```
w3 = w1 & 3;
```

This has the effect of setting all the bits in w3, other than the rightmost 2 bits, to 0, and of preserving the rightmost 2 bits from w1.

As with all binary arithmetic operators in Objective-C, the binary bit operators can also be used as assignment operators by tacking on an equals sign. So, the statement

```
word &= 15;
```

performs the same function as

```
word = word & 15;
```

and has the effect of setting all but the rightmost 4 bits of word to 0.

The Bitwise Inclusive-OR Operator

When two values are bitwise inclusive-ORed in Objective-C, the binary representation of the two values is once again compared bit by bit. This time, each bit that is a 1 in the first value or a 1 in the second value produces a 1 in the corresponding bit of the result. The truth table for the inclusive-OR operator is shown next.

b1	b2	b1 | b2
0	0	0
0	1	1
1	0	1
1	1	1

So if w1 is a short int equal to hexadecimal 19, and w2 is a short int equal to hexadecimal 6a, a bitwise inclusive-OR of w1 and w2 produces a result of hexadecimal 7b, as shown:

```
w1    0000 0000 0001 1001     0x19
w2    0000 0000 0110 1010   | 0x6a
      ─────────────────────────────
      0000 0000 0111 1011     0x7b
```

Bitwise inclusive-ORing, often called just bitwise ORing, is used to set some specified bits of a word to 1. For example, the following statement sets the three rightmost bits of w1 to 1, regardless of the state of these bits before the operation was performed.

```
w1 = w1 | 07;
```

Of course, you could have used a special assignment operator in the statement, as in this statement:

```
w1 |= 07;
```

We defer a program example that illustrates the use of the inclusive-OR operator until later.

The Bitwise Exclusive-OR Operator

The bitwise exclusive-OR operator, which is often called the XOR operator, works as follows: For corresponding bits of the two operands, if either bit is a 1 (but not both bits), the corresponding bit of the result is a 1; otherwise, it is a 0. The truth table for this operator is as shown.

b1	b2	b1 ^ b2
0	0	0
0	1	1
1	0	1
1	1	0

If w1 and w2 were set equal to hexadecimal 5e and d6, respectively, the result of w1 exclusive-ORed with w2 would be hexadecimal e8, as illustrated:

```
w1    0000 0000 0101  1110      0x5e
w2    0000 0000 1011  0110   ^  0xd6
      ─────────────────────────────
      0000 0000 1110  1000      0xe8
```

The Ones Complement Operator

The ones complement operator is a unary operator, and its effect is to simply "flip" the bits of its operand. Each bit of the operand that is a 1 is changed to a 0, and each bit that is a 0 is changed to a 1. The truth table is provided here simply for the sake of completeness.

b1	~b1
0	1
1	0

If w1 is a short int that is 16 bits long and is set equal to hexadecimal a52f, taking the ones complement of this value produces a result of hexadecimal 5ad0:

```
w1    1010   0101   0010   1111      0xa52f

~w1   0101   1010   1101   0000      0x5ad0
```

The ones complement operator proves useful when you don't know the precise bit size of the quantity that you are dealing with in an operation, and its use can help make a program less dependent on the particular size of an integer data type. For example, to set the low-order bit of an int called w1 to 0, you can AND w1 with an int consisting of all 1s except for a single 0 in the rightmost bit. So, a statement in C such as this one works fine on machines on which an integer is represented by 32 bits:

```
w1 &= 0xFFFFFFFE;
```

If you replace the preceding statement with this one, w1 will be ANDed with the correct value on any machine:

```
w1 &= ~1;
```

This is because the ones complement of 1 will be calculated and will consist of as many left-most 1 bits as necessary to fill the size of an int (63 leftmost bits on a 64-bit integer system).

Now it is time to show an actual program example that illustrates the use of the various bit operators (see Program 10.4).

Program 10.4

```
// Bitwise operators illustrated

#import <Foundation/Foundation.h>

int main (int argc, char * argv[])
{
    @autoreleasepool {
        unsigned int w1 = 0xA0A0A0A0, w2 = 0xFFFF0000,
                     w3 = 0x00007777;

        NSLog (@"%x %x %x", w1 & w2, w1 | w2, w1 ^ w2);
        NSLog (@"%x %x %x", ~w1, ~w2, ~w3);
        NSLog (@"%x %x %x", w1 ^ w1, w1 & ~w2, w1 | w2 | w3);
        NSLog (@"%x %x", w1 | w2 & w3, w1 | w2 & ~w3);
        NSLog (@"%x %x", ~(~w1 & ~w2), ~(~w1 | ~w2));
    }
    return 0;
}
```

Program 10.4   **Output**

```
a0a00000 ffffa0a0 5f5fa0a0
5f5f5f5f ffff ffff8888
0 a0a0 fffff7f7
a0a0a0a0 ffffa0a0
ffffa0a0 a0a00000
```

Work out each of the operations from Program 10.4 to verify that you understand how the results were obtained.

In the fourth NSLog call, it is important to note that the bitwise AND operator has higher precedence than the bitwise OR because this fact influences the resulting value of the expression.

The fifth NSLog call illustrates DeMorgan's rule: ~(~a & ~b) is equal to a | b, and ~(~a | ~b) is equal to a & b.

The Left-Shift Operator

When a left-shift operation is performed on a value, the bits contained in the value are literally shifted to the left. Associated with this operation is the number of places (bits) that the value is to be shifted. Bits that are shifted out through the high-order bit of the data item are lost, and 0s are always shifted in through the low-order bit of the value. So, if w1 is equal to 3, the expression

```
w1 = w1 << 1;
```

which can also be expressed as

```
w1 <<= 1;
```

results in 3 being shifted one place to the left, which will result in 6 being assigned to w1:

```
w1         ... 0000 0011    0x03
w1 << 1 ... 0000 0110    0x06
```

The operand on the left of the << operator is the value to be shifted, whereas the operand on the right is the number of bit positions the value is to be shifted by. If we were to shift w1 one more place to the left, we would end up with hexadecimal 0c:

```
w1         ... 0000 0110    0x06
w1 << 1 ... 0000 1100    0x0c
```

The Right-Shift Operator

As implied from its name, the right-shift operator >> shifts the bits of a value to the right. Bits shifted out of the low-order bit of the value are lost. Right-shifting an unsigned value always results in 0s being shifted in on the left—that is, through the high-order bits. What is shifted in on the left for signed values depends on the sign of the value that is being shifted and also on how this operation is implemented. If the sign bit is 0 (meaning the value is positive), 0s will be shifted in no matter what machine is used. However, if the sign bit is 1, on some machines 1s will be shifted in, and on others 0s will be shifted in. This former type of operation is known as an arithmetic right shift, while the latter is known as a logical right shift.

> **Caution**
>
> Never make any assumptions about whether a system implements an arithmetic or a logical right shift. A program that shifts signed values right might work correctly on one system and then fail on another due to this type of assumption.

If w1 is an unsigned int, which is represented in 32 bits, and w1 is set equal to hexadecimal F777EE22, shifting w1 one place to the right with the statement

```
w1 >>= 1;
```

sets w1 equal to hexadecimal 7BBBF711, as shown:

```
w1        1111 0111 0111 0111 1110 1110 0010 0010    0xF777EE22
w1 >> 1   0111 1011 1011 1011 1111 0111 0001 0001    0x7BBBF711
```

If w1 were declared to be a (signed) short int, the same result would be produced on some computers; on others, the result would be FBBBF711 if the operation were performed as an arithmetic right shift.

Note that the Objective-C language does not produce a defined result if an attempt is made to shift a value to the left or right by an amount that is greater than or equal to the number of bits in the size of the data item. So, on a machine that represents integers in 64 bits, for example, shifting an integer to the left or right by 64 or more bits is not guaranteed to produce a defined result in your program. Also note that if you shift a value by a negative amount, the result is similarly undefined.

Exercises

1. Using the Rectangle class from Chapter 8, "Inheritance," add an initializer method according to the following declaration. (Note: Be sure to override init to use this initializer.)

    ```
    -(id) initWithWidth: (int) w andHeight: (int) h;
    ```

2. Given that you label the method developed in Exercise 1 the designated initializer for the Rectangle class, and based on the Square and Rectangle class definitions from Chapter 8, add an initializer method to the Square class according to the following declaration:

    ```
    -(id) initWithSide: (int) side;
    ```

3. Add a counter to the `Fraction` class's `add:` method to count the number of times it is invoked. How can you retrieve the value of the counter?

4. Using `typedef` and enumerated data types, define a type called `Day` with the possible values `Sunday`, `Monday`, `Tuesday`, `Wednesday`, `Thursday`, `Friday`, and `Saturday`.

5. Using `typedef`, define a type called `FractionObj` that enables you to write statements such as the following:

```
FractionObj f1 = [[Fraction alloc] init],
            f2 = [[Fraction alloc] init];
```

6. Based on the following definitions

```
float     f = 1.00;
short int i = 100;
long int  l = 500L;
double    d = 15.00;
```

and the seven steps outlined in this chapter for the conversion of operands in expressions, determine the type and value of the following expressions:

```
f + i
l / d
i / l + f
l * i
f / 2
i / (d + f)
l / (i * 2.0)
l + i / (double) l
```

11

Categories and Protocols

In this chapter, you learn how to add methods to a class in a modular fashion through the use of categories and how to create a standardized list of methods for others to implement.

Categories

Sometimes you might be working with a class definition and want to add some new methods to it. For example, you might decide for your `Fraction` class that, in addition to the `add:` method for adding two fractions, you want to have methods to subtract, multiply, and divide two fractions.

As another example, suppose that you are working on a large programming project and, as part of that project, your group is defining a new class that contains many different methods. You have been assigned the task of writing methods for the class that work with files. Other project members have been assigned methods responsible for creating and initializing instances of the class, performing operations on objects in the class, and drawing representations of objects from the class on the screen.

As a final example, suppose you've learned how to use a class from a framework library (for example, the Foundation framework's array class called `NSArray`) and realize that you wished that the class had implemented one or more methods. Of course, you could write a new subclass of the `NSArray` class and implement the new methods, but perhaps an easier way exists.

A practical solution for all these situations is *categories*. A category provides an easy way for you to modularize the definition of a class into groups or categories of related methods. It also gives you an easy way to extend an existing class definition without even having access to the original source code for the class and without having to create a subclass. This is a powerful yet easy concept for you to learn.

Let's get back to the first case and show how to add a new category to the Fraction class to handle the four basic math operations. We first show you the original Fraction interface section:

```
#import <Foundation/Foundation.h>
// Define the Fraction class

@interface Fraction : NSObject

@property int numerator, denominator;

-(void)    setTo: (int) n over: (int) d;
-(Fraction *) add: (Fraction *) f;
-(void)    reduce;
-(double) convertToNum;
-(void)    print;
@end
```

Next, let's remove the add: method from this interface section and add it to a new category, along with the other three math operations you want to implement. Here's what the interface section would look like for your new MathOps category:

```
#import "Fraction.h"

@interface Fraction (MathOps)
-(Fraction *) add: (Fraction *) f;
-(Fraction *) mul: (Fraction *) f;
-(Fraction *) sub: (Fraction *) f;
-(Fraction *) div: (Fraction *) f;
@end
```

Realize that even though this is an interface section definition, it is an extension to an existing one. Therefore, you must import the original interface section so that the compiler knows about the Fraction class (unless you incorporate the new category directly into the original Fraction.h header file, which is an option).

After the #import, you see the following line:

```
@interface Fraction (MathOps)
```

This tells the compiler that you are defining a new category for the Fraction class and that its name is MathOps. The category name is enclosed in parentheses after the class name. Notice that you don't list the Fraction's parent class here; the compiler already knows it from Fraction.h. Also, you don't tell it about the properties, as you've done in the previous interface sections you've defined. This interface section tells the compiler you are adding an extension to the class called Fraction under the category named MathOps. The MathOps category contains four instance methods: add:, mul:, sub:, and div:. Each method takes a fraction as its argument and returns one as well.

You can put the definitions for all your methods into a single implementation section. That is, you could define all the methods from the interface section in `Fraction.h` plus all the methods from the `MathOps` category in one implementations section. Alternatively, you could define your category's methods in a separate implementation section. In such a case, the implementation section for these methods must also identify the category to which the methods belong. As with the interface section, you do this by enclosing the category name inside parentheses after the class name, like this:

```
@implementation Fraction (MathOps)
    // code for category methods
    ...

@end
```

In Program 11.1, the interface and implementation sections for the new `MathOps` category are grouped together, along with a test routine, into a single file.

Program 11.1   **MathOps Category and Test Program**

```
#import "Fraction.h"

@interface Fraction (MathOps)
-(Fraction *) add: (Fraction *) f;
-(Fraction *) mul: (Fraction *) f;
-(Fraction *) sub: (Fraction *) f;
-(Fraction *) div: (Fraction *) f;
@end

@implementation Fraction (MathOps)
-(Fraction *) add: (Fraction *) f
{
   // To add two fractions:
   // a/b + c/d = ((a*d) + (b*c)) / (b * d)

   Fraction *result = [[Fraction alloc] init];

   result.numerator = (self.numerator * f.denominator) +
       (self.denominator * f.numerator);
   result.denominator = self.denominator * f.denominator;
   [result reduce];

   return result;
}

-(Fraction *) sub: (Fraction *) f
{
   // To sub two fractions:
```

```objc
    // a/b - c/d = ((a*d) - (b*c)) / (b * d)

    Fraction *result = [[Fraction alloc] init];

    result.numerator = (self.numerator * f.denominator) -
            (self.denominator * f.numerator);
    result.denominator = self.denominator * f.denominator;
    [result reduce];

    return result;
}

-(Fraction *) mul: (Fraction *) f
{
    Fraction  *result = [[Fraction alloc] init];

    result.numerator = self.numerator * f.numerator;
    result.denominator = self.denominator * f.denominator;
    [result reduce];

    return result;
}

-(Fraction *) div: (Fraction *) f
{
    Fraction  *result = [[Fraction alloc] init];

    result.numerator = self.numerator * f.denominator;
    result.denominator = self.denominator * f.numerator;
    [result reduce];

    return result;
}
@end

int main (int argc, char * argv[])
{
    @autoreleasepool {
        Fraction *a = [[Fraction alloc] init];
        Fraction *b = [[Fraction alloc] init];
        Fraction *result;

        [a setTo: 1 over: 3];
        [b setTo: 2 over: 5];

        [a print]; NSLog (@"  +"); [b print]; NSLog (@"-----");
        result = [a add: b];
```

```
        [result print];
        NSLog (@"\n");

        [a print]; NSLog (@"  -"); [b print]; NSLog (@"-----");
        result = [a sub: b];
        [result print];
        NSLog (@"\n");

        [a print]; NSLog (@"  *"); [b print]; NSLog (@"-----");
        result = [a mul: b];
        [result print];
        NSLog (@"\n");

        [a print]; NSLog (@"  /"); [b print]; NSLog (@"-----");
        result = [a div: b];
        [result print];
        NSLog (@"\n");
    }
    return 0;
}
```

Program 11.1 **Output**

```
 1/3
  +
 2/5
-----
11/15

 1/3
  -
 2/5
-----
-1/15

1/3
 *
2/5
-----
2/15

1/3
 /
2/5
-----
5/6
```

Program 11.1 puts the interface and implementation sections for the new category into the same file with the test program. As mentioned previously, the interface section for this category could go either in the original `Fraction.h` header file so that all methods would be declared in one place or in its own header file.

Note

By convention, the base name of the `.h` and `.m` files for a category is the class name followed by a plus sign, followed by the category name. In our example, we would put the interface section for the category in a file named `Fraction+MathOps.h` and the implementation section in a file called `Fraction+MathOps.m`.

If you put your category into a master class definition file, all users of the class have access to the methods in the category. If you don't have the capability to modify the original header file directly (consider adding a category to an existing class from a library, as shown in Part II, "The Foundation Framework"), you have no choice but to keep it separate.

Class Extensions

A special case allows creating a category without a name; that is, no name is specified between the (and). This special syntax defines what is known as a *class extension*. When you define an unnamed category like this, you can extend the class by adding additional instance variables and properties. This is not allowed for named categories. Methods declared in a class extension are implemented in the main implementation section for the class and not in a separate implementation section.

Class extensions are useful, because their methods are private. So, if you need to write a class that has data and methods that can be used only within the class itself, a class extension might just fit the bill.

Note

The methods are private in the sense that they're not advertised in the interface section. However, if someone knows the name of a private method, she can still call it.

Recall the `reduce` method from our `Fraction` class. Suppose you only want the methods defined in the implementation section of the `Fraction` class to have access to that `reduce` method; that is, you do not want to make it directly accessible by users of the class. You could define that method to be private by removing its declaration from the original `Fraction.h` header file and putting the following into the `Fraction.m` implementation file:

```
#import "Fraction.h"

// Make the reduce method private
```

```
@interface  Fraction ()
-(void) reduce;
@end

// Define the public methods for the Fraction class

@implementation Fraction
@synthesize numerator, denominator;

-(void) setNumerator: (int) n and Denominator: (int) d
{
    ...
]
...
@end
```

Some Notes about Categories

A category can override another method in the class, but this is considered poor programming practice. For one thing, after you override a method, you can no longer access the original method. Therefore, you must be careful to duplicate all the functionality of the overridden method in your replacement. If you do need to override a method, subclassing might be the right choice. If you override a method in a subclass, you can still reference the parent's method by sending a message to super. So, you don't have to understand all the intricacies of the method you are overriding; you can just invoke the parent's method and add your own functionality to the subclass's method.

You can have as many categories as you like, following the rules we've outlined here. If a method is defined in more than one category, the language does not specify which one will be used.

Remember that extending a class by adding new methods with a category affects not just that class, but all its subclasses as well. This can be potentially dangerous if you add new methods to the root object NSObject, for example, because everyone will inherit those new methods, whether or not that was your intention.

The new methods you add to an existing class through a category can serve your purposes just fine, but they might be inconsistent with the original design or intentions of the class. Turning a Square into a Circle (admittedly, an exaggeration), for example, by adding a new category and some methods muddies the definition of the class and is not good programming practice.

Also, object/category named pairs must be unique. Only one NSString category named Utilities can exist in a given Objective-C namespace. This can prove tricky because the Objective-C namespace is shared between the program code and all the libraries, frameworks, and plug-ins. This is especially important for Objective-C programmers writing screensavers, preference panes, and other plug-ins because their code will be injected into application or framework code that they do not control.

Protocols and Delegation

A *protocol* is a list of methods that is shared among classes. The methods listed in the protocol do not have corresponding implementations; they're meant to be implemented by someone else (like you). A protocol provides a way to define a set of methods that are somehow related with a specified name. The methods are typically documented so that you know how they are to perform and so that you can implement them in your own class definitions, if desired.

A protocol lists a set of methods, some of which you can optionally implement, and others that you are required to implement. If you decide to implement all of the *required* methods for a particular protocol, you are said to *conform to* or *adopt* that protocol. You are allowed to define a protocol where all methods are optional, or one where all are required.

Defining a protocol is easy: You simply use the @protocol directive followed by the name of the protocol, which is up to you. After that, you declare methods just as you did with your interface section. All the method declarations, up to the @end directive, become part of the protocol.

When you work with the Foundation framework, you'll find that several protocols are defined. One of them, called NSCopying, declares a method that you need to implement if your class is to support copying of objects through the copy (or copyWithZone:) method. (Chapter 18, "Copying Objects," covers the topic of copying objects in detail.)

Here's how the NSCopying protocol is defined in the standard Foundation header file NSObject.h:

```
@protocol NSCopying
- (id)copyWithZone: (NSZone *)zone;
@end
```

If you adopt the NSCopying protocol in your class, you must implement a method called copyWithZone:. You tell the compiler that you are adopting a protocol by listing the protocol name inside a pair of angular brackets (<...>) on the @interface line. The protocol name comes after the name of the class and its parent class, as in the following:

```
@interface AddressBook: NSObject <NSCopying>
```

This says that AddressBook is an object whose parent is NSObject and states that it conforms to the NSCopying protocol. Because the system already knows about the methods previously defined for the protocol (in this example, it knows from the header file NSObject.h), you don't need to declare the methods in the interface section. However, you need to define them in your implementation section.

In this example, in the implementation section for AddressBook, the compiler expects to see the copyWithZone: method defined.

If your class adopts more than one protocol, just list them inside the angular brackets, separated by commas:

```
@interface AddressBook: NSObject <NSCopying, NSCoding>
```

This tells the compiler that the `AddressBook` class adopts the `NSCopying` and `NSCoding` protocols. Again, the compiler expects to see all the required methods listed for those protocols implemented in the `AddressBook` implementation section.

If you define your own protocol, you don't have to actually implement it yourself. However, you're alerting other programmers that if they want to adopt the protocol, they do have to implement the required methods. Those methods can be inherited from a superclass. Thus, if one class conforms to the `NSCopying` protocol, its subclasses do as well (although that doesn't mean the methods are correctly implemented for that subclass).

You can use a protocol to define methods that you want other people who subclass your class to implement. Perhaps you could define a `Drawing` protocol for your `GraphicObject` class; in it, you could define paint, erase, and outline methods:

```
@protocol Drawing
-(void) paint;
-(void) erase;
@optional
-(void) outline;
@end
```

As the creator of the `GraphicObject` class, you don't necessarily want to implement these painting methods. However, you want to specify the methods that someone who subclasses the `GraphicObject` class needs to implement to conform to a standard for drawing objects he's trying to create.

Note the use of the `@optional` directive here. Any methods that are listed following that directive are optional. That is, an adopter of the `Drawing` protocol does not have to implement the `outline` method to conform to the protocol. (And you can subsequently switch back to listing required methods by using the `@required` directive inside the protocol definition.)

> **Note**
>
> Well that's the intent, anyway. The compiler lets you say that you conform to a protocol and only issues warning messages if you don't implement the methods.

So, if you create a subclass of `GraphicObject` called `Rectangle` and advertise (that is, *document*) that your `Rectangle` class conforms to the `Drawing` protocol, users of the class will know that they can send paint, erase, and (possibly) outline messages to instances from that class.

Notice that the protocol doesn't reference any classes; it's *classless*. Any class can conform to the `Drawing` protocol, not just subclasses of `GraphicObject`.

You can check to see whether an object conforms to a protocol by using the `conformsToProtocol:` method. For example, if you have an object called `currentObject` and want to see whether it conforms to the Drawing protocol so that you can send it drawing messages, you could write this:

```
id currentObject;
  ...
if ([currentObject conformsToProtocol: @protocol (Drawing)] == YES)
{
  // Send currentObject paint, erase and/or outline msgs
  ...
}
```

The special @protocol directive as used here takes a protocol name and produces a protocol object, which is what the conformsToProtocol: method expects as its argument.

To test to see whether currentObject has implemented the optional outline method, you could write this:

```
if ([currentObject respondsToSelector: @selector (outline)] == YES)
   [currentObject outline];
```

You can enlist the aid of the compiler to check for conformance with your variables by including the protocol name inside angular brackets after the type name, like this:

```
id <Drawing> currentObject;
```

This tells the compiler that currentObject will reference objects that conform to the Drawing protocol. If you assign a statically typed object to currentObject that does not conform to the Drawing protocol (say that you have a Square class that does not conform), the compiler issues a warning message that looks like this:

```
warning: class 'Square' does not implement the 'Drawing' protocol
```

This is a compiler check here, so assigning an id variable to currentObject would not generate this message because the compiler has no way of knowing whether the object stored inside an id variable conforms to the Drawing protocol.

You can list more than one protocol if the variable will hold an object conforming to more than one protocol, as in this line:

```
id <NSCopying, NSCoding> myDocument;
```

When you define a protocol, you can extend the definition of an existing one. This protocol declaration says that the Drawing3D protocol also adopts the Drawing protocol:

```
@protocol Drawing3D <Drawing>
```

Thus, whichever class adopts the Drawing3D protocol must implement the methods listed for that protocol, as well as the methods from the Drawing protocol.

Finally, a category also can adopt a protocol, like this:

```
@interface Fraction (Stuff) <NSCopying, NSCoding>
```

Here `Fraction` has a category, `Stuff` (okay, not the best choice of names), that adopts the `NSCopying` and `NSCoding` protocols.

As with class names, protocol names must be unique.

Delegation

You can also think of a protocol as an *interface* definition between two classes. The class that defines the protocol can be thought of as *delegating* the work defined by the methods in the protocol to the class that implements them. In that way, the class can be defined to be more general, with specific actions taken by the delegate class in response to certain events or to define specific parameters. Cocoa and iOS rely heavily on this concept of delegation. For example, when you set up a table on the iPhone's display, you'll use the `UITableView` class. But that class doesn't know the title of the table, how many sections or rows it contains, or what to put in each row (cell) of the table. So, it delegates that responsibility to you by defining a protocol called `UITableViewDataSource`. When it needs information (for example, how many rows are in each section of the table), it calls the appropriate method that you've defined in your class in accordance with the protocol. The `UITableView` class also defines another protocol called `UITableViewDelegate`. The methods in this protocol define, among other things, what to do when a particular row from a table is selected. This class doesn't know what action to take, so it delegates that responsibility to you.

Informal Protocols

You might come across the notion of an *informal* protocol in your readings. This is really a category that lists a group of methods but does not implement them. Everyone (or just about everyone) inherits from the same root object, so informal categories are often defined for the root class. Sometimes informal protocols are also referred to as *abstract* protocols.

If you look at the header file `<NSScriptWhoseTests.h>`, you might find some method declarations that look like this:

```
@interface NSObject (NSComparisonMethods)
- (BOOL)isEqualTo:(id)object;
- (BOOL)isLessThanOrEqualTo:(id)object;
- (BOOL)isLessThan:(id)object;
- (BOOL)isGreaterThanOrEqualTo:(id)object;
- (BOOL)isGreaterThan:(id)object;
- (BOOL)isNotEqualTo:(id)object;
- (BOOL)doesContain:(id)object;
- (BOOL)isLike:(NSString *)object;
- (BOOL)isCaseInsensitiveLike:(NSString *)object;
@end
```

This defines a category called `NSComparisonMethods` for the `NSObject` class. This informal protocol lists a group of methods (here, nine are listed) that can be implemented as part of this protocol. An informal protocol is really no more than a grouping of methods under a name. This can help somewhat from the point of documentation and modularization of methods.

The class that declares the informal protocol doesn't implement the methods in the class itself, and a subclass that chooses to implement the methods needs to redeclare them in its interface section, as well as implement one or more of them. Unlike formal protocols, the compiler gives no help with informal protocols; there's no concept of conformance or testing by the compiler.

If an object adopts a formal protocol, the object must conform to all the required messages in the protocol. This can be enforced at runtime as well as compile time. If an object adopts an informal protocol, the object might not need to adopt all methods in the protocol, depending on the protocol. Conformance to an informal protocol can be enforced at runtime (via `respondsToSelector:`) but not at compile time.

Note

The previously described `@optional` directive that was added to the Objective-C 2.0 language is meant to replace the use of informal protocols. You can see this used for several of the UIKit classes. (UIKit is part of the Cocoa Touch framework.)

Composite Objects

You've learned several ways to extend the definition of a class through techniques such as subclassing and using categories. Another technique involves defining a class that consists of one or more objects from other classes. An object from this new class is known as a *composite* object because it is composed of other objects.

For example, consider the `Square` class you defined in Chapter 8, "Inheritance." You defined this as a subclass of a `Rectangle` because you recognized that a square was just a rectangle with equal sides. When you define a subclass, it inherits all the instance variables and methods of the parent class. In some cases, this is undesirable (for example, some of the methods defined in the parent class might not be appropriate for use by the subclass). The `Rectangle`'s `setWidth:andHeight:` method is inherited by the `Square` class but really does not apply to a square (even though it will work properly). Furthermore, when you create a subclass, you must ensure that all the inherited methods work properly because users of the class will have access to them. Finally, a subclass is dependent on the parent class. Changes to the parent class might unintentionally make methods in the subclass cease to work.

As an alternative to subclassing, you can define a new class that contains as one of its instance variables an object from the class you want to extend. Then you have to define only those methods in the new class that are appropriate for that class. Getting back to the `Square` example, here's an alternative way to define a `Square`:

```
@interface Square: NSObject
{
    Rectangle *rect;
```

```
}
-(int) setSide: (int) s;
-(int) side;
-(int) area;
-(int) perimeter;
@end
```

The `Square` class is defined here with four methods. Unlike the subclass version, which gives you direct access to the `Rectangle`'s methods (`setWidth:`, `setHeight:`, `setWidth:andHeight:`, width, and height), those methods are not in this definition for a `Square`. That makes sense here because those methods really don't fit in when you deal with squares.

If you define your `Square` this way, it becomes responsible for allocating the memory for the rectangle it contains. For example, without overriding methods, the statement

```
Square *mySquare = [[Square alloc] init];
```

allocates a new `Square` object but does not allocate a `Rectangle` object stored in its instance variable, `rect`.

A solution is to override `init` or add a new method such as `initWithSide:` to do the allocation. That method can allocate the `Rectangle rect` and set its side appropriately.

When defining your methods in your `Square` class, you can still take advantage of the `Rectangle`'s methods. For example, here's how you could implement the `area` method:

```
-(int) area
{
  return [rect area];
}
```

Implementing the remaining methods is left as an exercise for you (see Exercise 5, which follows).

Exercises

1. Extend the `MathOps` category from Program 11.1 to also include an `invert` method, which returns a `Fraction` that is an inversion of the receiver.

2. Add a category to the `Fraction` class called `Comparison`. In this category, add two methods according to these declarations:

   ```
   -(BOOL) isEqualTo: (Fraction *) f;
   -(int) compare: (Fraction *) f;
   ```

   The first method should return YES if the two fractions are identical and should return NO otherwise. Be careful about comparing fractions. (For example, comparing 3/4 to 6/8 should return YES.)

The second method should return -1 if the receiver compares less than the fraction represented by the argument, return 0 if the two are equal, and return 1 if the receiver is greater than the argument.

3. Extend the `Fraction` class by adding methods that conform to the informal protocol `NSComparisonMethods`, as listed earlier in this chapter. Implement the first six methods from that protocol (`isEqualTo:`, `isLessThanOrEqualTo:`, `isLessThan:`, `isGreaterThanOrEqualTo:`, `isGreaterThan:`, `isNotEqualTo:`) and test them.

4. The functions `sin()`, `cos()`, and `tan()` are part of the C Standard Library (as `scanf ()` is). These functions are declared in the system header file `math.h`, which is automatically imported into your program when you import `Foundation.h`.

   You can use these functions to calculate the sine, cosine, or tangent, respectively, of their `double` argument, which is expressed in radians. The result is also returned as a double precision floating-point value. So, you can use this line to calculate the sine of `d`, with the angle `d` expressed in radians:

   ```
   result = sin (d);
   ```

   Add a category called `Trig` to the `Calculator` class defined in Chapter 6, "Making Decisions." Add methods to this category to calculate the sine, cosine, and tangent based on these declarations:

   ```
   -(double) sin;
   -(double) cos;
   -(double) tan;
   ```

5. Given the discussion on composite objects from this chapter and the following interface and implementation sections

   ```
   @interface Square: NSObject
   -(Square *) initWithSide: (int) s;
   -(void) setSide: (int) s;
   -(int) side;
   -(int) area;
   -(int) perimeter;
   @end

   #import "Rectangle.h"
   @implementation Square
   {
        Rectangle    *rect;
   }
   // Insert Square methods here
   ...
   @end
   ```

   complete the implementation section for a `Square` and a test program to check its methods. Note: Make sure you remember to override `init`, as well, because `initWithSide:` will be your designated initializer.

12

The Preprocessor

The preprocessor provides the tools that enable you to develop programs that are easier to develop, read, modify, and port to different systems. You can also use the preprocessor to literally customize the Objective-C language to suit a particular programming application or your own programming style.

The preprocessor is a part of the Objective-C compilation process that recognizes special statements that can be interspersed throughout a program. As its name implies, the preprocessor actually processes these statements before analysis of the Objective-C program itself takes place. Preprocessor statements are identified by the presence of a pound sign (#), which must be the first nonspace character on the line. As you will see, preprocessor statements have a syntax that differs slightly from that of normal Objective-C statements. We begin by examining the `#define` statement.

The `#define` Statement

One of the primary uses of the `#define` statement is to assign symbolic names to program constants. The preprocessor statement

```
#define   TRUE   1
```

defines the name TRUE and makes it equivalent to the value 1. The name TRUE can subsequently be used anywhere in the program where the constant 1 could be used. Whenever this name appears, the preprocessor automatically substitutes its defined value of 1 into the program. For example, you might have the following Objective-C statement that uses the defined name TRUE:

```
gameOver = TRUE;
```

This statement assigns the value of TRUE to gameOver. You don't need to concern yourself with the actual value you defined for TRUE, but because you do know that you defined it to be 1, the preceding statement would have the effect of assigning 1 to gameOver. The preprocessor statement

```
#define   FALSE   0
```

defines the name FALSE and makes its subsequent use in the program equivalent to specifying the value 0. Therefore, the statement

```
gameOver = FALSE;
```

assigns the value of FALSE to gameOver, and the statement

```
if ( gameOver == FALSE )
    ...
```

compares the value of gameOver against the defined value of FALSE.

A defined name is *not* a variable. Therefore, you cannot assign a value to it unless the result of substituting the defined value is a variable. Whenever a defined name is used in a program, the preprocessor automatically substitutes into the program whatever appears to the right of the defined name in the #define statement. It's analogous to doing a search and replace with a text editor; in this case, the preprocessor replaces all occurrences of the defined name with its associated text.

Notice that the #define statement has a special syntax: No equals sign is used to assign the value 1 to TRUE. Furthermore, a semicolon does *not* appear at the end of the statement. Soon you will understand why this special syntax exists.

#define statements are often placed toward the beginning of the program, after #import or #include statements. This is not required; they can appear anywhere in the program. However, a name must be defined before it is referenced by the program. Defined names do not behave like variables: There is no such thing as a local define. After a name has been defined, it can subsequently be used *anywhere* in the program. Most programmers place their defines inside header files so they can be used by more than one source file.

As another example of the use of a defined name, suppose you wanted to write two methods to find the area and circumference of a Circle object. Because both of these methods need to use the constant π, which is not a particularly easy constant to remember, it might make sense to define the value of this constant once at the start of the program and then use this value where necessary in each method.

So, you could include the following in your program:

```
#define PI    3.141592654
```

Then you could use it in your two Circle methods (this assumes that the Circle class has an instance variable called radius) like this:

```
-(double) area
{
    return PI * radius * radius;
}

-(double) circumference
{
    return 2.0 * PI * radius;
}
```

(Note that we acknowledge that there is already a predefined symbol called M_PI that you can use whenever you need the value of π.) Assigning a constant to a symbolic name frees you from having to remember the particular constant value every time you want to use it in a program. Furthermore, if you ever need to change the value of the constant (if perhaps you found out that you were using the wrong value, for example), you would have to change the value in only one place in the program: in the #define statement. Without this approach, you would have to search throughout the program and explicitly change the value of the constant whenever it was used.

You might have realized that all the defines shown so far (TRUE, FALSE, and PI) have been written in capital letters. This is done to visually distinguish a defined value from a variable. Some programmers adopt the convention that all defined names be capitalized, so that determining when a name represents a variable or an object, a class name, or a defined name is easy. Another common convention is to prefix the define with the letter *k*. In that case, the following characters of the name are not capitalized. kMaximumValues and kSignificantDigits are examples of two defined names that adhere to this convention.

Using a defined name for a constant value helps make programs more readily extendable. For example, when you learn how to work with arrays, instead of hard-coding in the size of the array you want to allocate, you can define a value as follows:

```
#define MAXIMUM_DATA_VALUES  1000
```

Then you can base all references on the array's size (such as allocation of the array in memory) and valid indexes into this array on this defined value.

Also, if the program were written to use MAXIMUM_DATA_VALUES in all cases where the size of the array was used, the preceding definition could be the only statement in the program that would have to be changed if you later needed to change the array size.

More Advanced Types of Definitions

A definition for a name can include more than a simple constant value. It can include an expression and, as you will see shortly, just about anything else!

The following defines the name TWO_PI as the product of 2.0 and 3.141592654:

```
#define TWO_PI  2.0 * 3.141592654
```

You can subsequently use this defined name anywhere in a program where the expression 2.0 * 3.141592654 would be valid. So, you could replace the return statement of the circumference method from the previous example with the following statement:

```
return TWO_PI * radius;
```

Whenever a defined name is encountered in an Objective-C program, everything that appears to the right of the defined name in the #define statement is literally substituted for the name at that point in the program. Thus, when the preprocessor encounters the name TWO_PI in the return statement shown previously, it substitutes for this name whatever appeared in

the #define statement for this name. Therefore, the preprocessor literally substitutes 2.0 *
3.141592654 whenever the defined name TWO_PI occurs in the program.

The fact that the preprocessor performs a literal text substitution whenever the defined name
occurs explains why you don't usually want to end your #define statement with a semicolon.
If you did, the semicolon would also be substituted into the program wherever the defined
name appeared. If you had defined PI as

```
#define PI    3.141592654;
```

and then written

```
return 2.0 * PI * r;
```

the preprocessor would replace the occurrence of the defined name PI by 3.141592654;. The
compiler would therefore see this statement as

```
return 2.0 * 3.141592654; * r;
```

after the preprocessor had made its substitution, which would result in a syntax error.
Remember not to put a semicolon at the end of your define statements unless you're really sure
you want one there.

A preprocessor definition does not have to be a valid Objective-C expression in its own right, as
long as the resulting expression is valid wherever it is used. For instance, you could set up these
definitions:

```
#define AND    &&
#define OR     ||
```

Then you could write expressions such as

```
if ( x > 0 AND x < 10 )
    ...
```

and

```
if ( y == 0 OR y == value )
    ...
```

You could even include a #define for the equality test:

```
#define EQUALS   ==
```

Then, you could write the following statement:

```
if ( y EQUALS 0 OR y EQUALS value )
    ...
```

This removes the very real possibility of mistakenly using a single equals sign for the equality
test.

Although these examples illustrate the power of the #define, you should note that it is commonly considered bad programming practice to redefine the syntax of the underlying language in such a manner. Plus, it makes it harder for someone else to understand your code.

To make things even more interesting, a defined value can itself reference another defined value. So these two #define lines are perfectly valid:

```
#define PI      3.141592654
#define TWO_PI  2.0 * PI
```

The name TWO_PI is defined in terms of the previously defined name PI, thus obviating the need to spell out the value 3.141592654 again.

Reversing the order of the defines, as in this example, is also valid:

```
#define TWO_PI  2.0 * PI
#define PI      3.141592654
```

The rule is that you can reference other defined values in your definitions as long as everything is defined at the time the defined name is used in the program.

Good use of #defines often reduces the need for comments within the program. Consider the following statement:

```
if ( year % 4 == 0 && year % 100 != 0 || year % 400 == 0 )
  ...
```

This expression tests whether the variable year is a leap year. Now consider the following #define statement and the subsequent if statement:

```
#define IS_LEAP_YEAR  year % 4 == 0 && year % 100 != 0 \
                      || year % 400 == 0
  ...
if ( IS_LEAP_YEAR )
  ...
```

Normally, the preprocessor assumes that a definition is contained on a single line of the program. If a second line is needed, the last character on the line must be a backslash character. This character signals a continuation to the preprocessor and is otherwise ignored. The same holds true for more than one continuation line; each line to be continued must end with a backslash character.

The preceding if statement is much easier to understand than the one shown directly before it. No comment is needed because the statement is self-explanatory. Of course, the definition restricts you to testing the variable year to see whether it's a leap year. It would be nice if you could write a definition to see whether any year were a leap year, not just the variable year. Actually, you can write a definition to take one or more arguments, which leads us to our next point of discussion.

IS_LEAP_YEAR can be defined to take an argument called y, as follows:

```
#define IS_LEAP_YEAR(y)   y % 4 == 0 && y % 100 != 0 \
                   || y % 400 == 0
```

Unlike in a method definition, you do not define the type of the argument y here because you are merely performing a literal text substitution; you are not calling a function. Note that when defining a name with arguments, no spaces are permitted between the defined name and the left parenthesis of the argument list.

With the previous definition, you can write a statement such as the following:

```
if ( IS_LEAP_YEAR (year) )
   . . .
```

This tests whether the value of year is a leap year. Or you could write this to test whether the value of nextYear is a leap year:

```
if ( IS_LEAP_YEAR (nextYear) )
   . . .
```

In the preceding statement, the definition for IS_LEAP_YEAR is directly substituted inside the if statement, with the argument nextYear replacing y wherever it appears in the definition. So the compiler would actually see the if statement as follows:

```
if ( nextYear % 4 == 0 && nextYear % 100 != 0 || nextYear % 400 == 0 )
   . . .
```

Definitions are often called *macros*. This terminology is more often applied to definitions that take one or more arguments.

This macro, called SQUARE, simply squares its argument:

```
#define SQUARE(x) x * x
```

Although the macro definition for SQUARE is straightforward, you must avoid an interesting pitfall when defining macros. As we have described, the statement

```
y = SQUARE (v);
```

assigns the value of v2 to y. Think about what would happen in the case of the following statement:

```
y = SQUARE (v + 1);
```

This statement does *not* assign the value of $(v + 1)2$ to y, as you would expect. Because the preprocessor performs a literal text substitution of the argument into the macro definition, the preceding expression is actually evaluated as follows:

```
y = v + 1 * v + 1;
```

This obviously does not produce the expected results. To handle this situation properly, parentheses are needed in the definition of the SQUARE macro:

```
#define SQUARE(x)   ( (x) * (x) )
```

Even though the previous definition might look strange, remember that the entire expression as given to the SQUARE macro is literally substituted wherever x appears in the definition. With your new macro definition for SQUARE, the statement

```
y = SQUARE (v + 1);
```

is then correctly evaluated as

```
y = ( (v + 1) * (v + 1) );
```

The following macro lets you easily create new fractions from your Fraction class on-the-fly:

```
#define MakeFract(x,y) ([[Fraction alloc] initWith: x over: y])
```

Then you can write expressions such as

```
myFract = MakeFract (1, 3);  // Make the fraction 1/3
```

The conditional expression operator can be particularly handy when defining macros. The following defines a macro called MAX that gives the maximum of two values:

```
#define MAX(a,b)   ( ((a) > (b)) ? (a) : (b) )
```

This macro enables you to subsequently write statements such as this:

```
limit = MAX (x + y, minValue);
```

This assigns to limit the maximum of x + y and minValue. Parentheses are placed around the entire MAX definition to ensure that an expression such as this is evaluated properly:

```
MAX (x, y) * 100
```

Parentheses are individually placed around each argument to ensure that expressions such as the following are correctly evaluated:

```
MAX (x & y, z)
```

The & operator is the bitwise AND operator, and it has lower precedence than the > operator used in the macro. Without the parentheses in the macro definition, the > operator would be evaluated before the bitwise AND, producing the incorrect result.

The following macro tests whether a character is a lowercase letter:

```
#define IS_LOWER_CASE(x) ( ((x) >= 'a') && ((x) <= 'z') )
```

It thereby permits you to write expressions such as this:

```
if ( IS_LOWER_CASE (c) )
    ...
```

You can even use this macro in another macro definition to convert a character from lowercase to uppercase, leaving any nonlowercase character unchanged:

```
#define TO_UPPER(x) ( IS_LOWER_CASE (x) ? (x) - 'a' + 'A' : (x) )
```

Again, you are dealing with a standard ASCII character set here. When you learn about Foundation string objects in Part II, "The Foundation Framework," you'll see how to perform case conversion that will work for international (Unicode) character sets as well.

The #import **Statement**

When you have programmed in Objective-C for a while, you will find yourself developing your own set of macros, which you will want to use in each of your programs. But instead of having to type these macros into each new program you write, the preprocessor enables you to collect all your definitions into a separate file and then include them in your program, using the #import statement. These files—similar to the ones you've previously encountered but haven't written yourself—normally end with the characters .h and are referred to as *header* or *include* files.

Suppose that you are writing a series of programs for performing various metric conversions. You might want to set up some #define statements for the various constants you need for performing your conversions:

```
#define INCHES_PER_CENTIMETER   0.394
#define CENTIMETERS_PER_INCH   (1 / INCHES_PER_CENTIMETER)

#define QUARTS_PER_LITER        1.057
#define LITERS_PER_QUART        (1 / QUARTS_PER_LITER)

#define OUNCES_PER_GRAM         0.035
#define GRAMS_PER_OUNCE         (1 / OUNCES_PER_GRAM)
    ...
```

Suppose that you enter the previous definitions into a separate file on the system called metric.h. Any program that subsequently needs to use any of the definitions contained in the metric.h file can do so by simply issuing this preprocessor directive:

```
#import "metric.h"
```

This statement must appear before any of the #define statements contained in metric.h are referenced and is typically placed at the beginning of the source file. The preprocessor looks for the specified file on the system and effectively copies the contents of the file into the program at the precise point at which the #import statement appears. So, any statements inside the file are treated just as if they had been directly typed into the program at that point.

The double quotation marks around the header filename instruct the preprocessor to look for the specified file in one or more file directories (typically, first in the directory that contains the source file, but the actual places the preprocessor searches can be specified in Xcode).

Enclosing the filename within the characters < and > instead, as in

```
#import <Foundation/Foundation.h>
```

causes the preprocessor to look for the include file only in the special "system" header file directory or directories; the current directory will not be searched. Again, with Xcode, you can specify the directories to be searched.

One of the nicest things about the import file capability is that it enables you to centralize your definitions, thus ensuring that all programs reference the same value. Furthermore, errors discovered in one of the values contained in the include file need be corrected in only that one spot, thus eliminating the need to correct every program that uses the value. Any program that referenced the incorrect value would simply have to be recompiled and would not have to be edited.

Conditional Compilation

The Objective-C preprocessor offers a feature known as *conditional compilation*. Conditional compilation is often used to create one program that can be compiled to run on different computer systems. It is also often used to switch on or off various statements in the program, such as debugging statements that print the values of variables or trace the flow of program execution.

The #ifdef, #endif, #else, and #ifndef Statements

Unfortunately, a program sometimes must rely on system-dependent parameters that need to be specified differently on different devices (for example, an iPhone versus an iPad) or on a particular version of the operating system (for example, Leopard versus Snow Leopard).

If you have a large program that has many such dependencies on the particular hardware or software of the computer system (you should minimize this as much as possible), you might end up with many values that would have to be changed to run in the other environment.

You can help reduce the problem of having to change these values and can incorporate into the program the values of these defines for each different machine by using the conditional compilation capabilities of the preprocessor. As a simple example, the following statements have the effect of defining kImageFile to @"barnHD.png" if the symbol IPAD has been previously defined, and to @"barn.png" otherwise:

```
#ifdef IPAD
#   define kImageFile  @"barnHD.png"
#else
#   define kImageFile  @"barn.png"
#endif
```

As you can see here, you are allowed to put one or more spaces after the # that begins a preprocessor statement.

The #ifdef, #else, and #endif statements behave as you would expect. If the symbol speci-fied on the #ifdef line has been already defined—through a #define statement or through the command line when the program is compiled—the compiler processes lines that follow up to a #else, #elif, or #endif; otherwise, they are ignored.

To define the symbol IPAD to the preprocessor, the statement

```
#define IPAD   1
```

or even just

```
#define IPAD
```

will suffice. As you can see, no text at all has to appear after the defined name to satisfy the #ifdef test. The compiler also permits you to define a name to the preprocessor when the program is compiled by using a special option to the compiler command. The command line

```
clang -fobjc-arc -D IPAD program.m
```

defines the name IPAD to the preprocessor, causing all #ifdef IPAD statements inside program.m to evaluate as TRUE. (Note that you must type the -D IPAD before the program name on the command line.) This technique enables you to define names without having to edit the source program.

In Xcode, you add new defined names and specify their values by selecting Build Settings, All, Apple LLVM compiler x.x – Preprocessing, Preprocessor Macros. You can see a screenshot of the symbols IPAD and DEBUG (defined as 1) set in Xcode 4 in Figure 12.1.

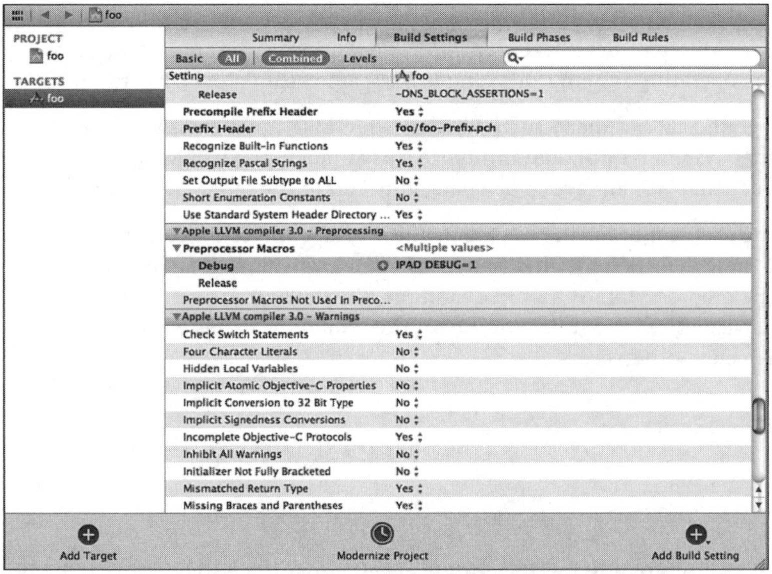

Figure 12.1   Defining the preprocessor identifier IPAD

The #ifndef statement follows along the same lines as the #ifdef. This statement is used in a similar way, except that it causes the subsequent lines to be processed if the indicated symbol is *not* defined.

As already mentioned, conditional compilation is useful when debugging programs. You might have many NSLog calls embedded in your program that are used to display intermediate results and trace the flow of execution. You can turn on these statements by conditionally compiling them into the program if a particular name, such as DEBUG, is defined. For example, you could use a sequence of statements such as the following to display the value of some variables only if the program had been compiled with the name DEBUG defined:

```
#ifdef DEBUG
  NSLog (@"User name = %@, id = %i", userName, userId);
#endif
```

You might have many such debugging statements throughout the program. Whenever the program is being debugged, it can be compiled with DEBUG defined to have all the debugging statements compiled. When the program is working correctly, it can be recompiled without DEBUG defined. This has the added benefit of reducing the size of the program because all your debugging statements are not compiled in.

The #if and #elif Preprocessor Statements

The #if preprocessor statement offers a more general way of controlling conditional compilation. The #if statement can be used to test whether a constant expression evaluates to nonzero. If the result of the expression is nonzero, subsequent lines up to a #else, #elif, or #endif are processed; otherwise, they are skipped.

As an example of how this can be used, the following lines appear in the Foundation header file NSString.h:

```
#if MAC_OS_X_VERSION_MIN_REQUIRED < MAC_OS_X_VERSION_10_5
#define NSMaximumStringLength   (INT_MAX-1)
#endif
```

This tests the value of the defined variable MAC_OS_X_VERSION_MIN_REQUIRED against the defined variable MAC_OS_X_VERSION_10_5. If the former is less than the latter, the #define that follows is processed; otherwise, it is skipped. Presumably, this sets the maximum length of a string to the maximum size of an integer minus 1 if the program is being compiled on Mac OS X 10.5 or later versions.

The special operator

```
defined (name)
```

can also be used in #if statements. This set of preprocessor statements does the same thing:

```
#if defined (DEBUG)
  ...
```

```
#endif
```

and

```
#ifdef DEBUG
  ...
#endif
```

The following statements appear in the NSObjcRuntime.h header file for the purpose of defining NS_INLINE (if it's not previously defined) based on the particular compiler that is being used:

```
#if !defined(NS_INLINE)
    #if defined(__GNUC__)
        #define NS_INLINE static __inline__attribute__((always_inline))
    #elif defined(__MWERKS__) || defined(__cplusplus)
        #define NS_INLINE static inline
    #elif defined(_MSC_VER)
        #define NS_INLINE static __inline
    #elif defined(__WIN32__)
        #define NS_INLINE static __inline__
    #endif
#endif
```

Another common use of #if is in code sequences that look like this:

```
#if defined (DEBUG) && DEBUG
...
#endif
```

This causes the statements after the #if and up to the #endif to be processed only if DEBUG is defined and has a nonzero value.

Because expressions can be used and because 0 is always false, programmers (myself included) often comment out a block of code by enveloping it inside a #if 0 ... #endif pair of preprocessor statements.

The #undef Statement

Sometimes you need to cause a defined name to become undefined. You do this with the #undef statement. To remove the definition of a particular name, you write the following:

```
#undef name
```

Therefore, this statement removes the definition of IPAD:

```
#undef IPAD
```

Subsequent #ifdef IPAD or #if defined (IPAD) statements evaluate to FALSE.

This concludes our discussion on the preprocessor.

Exercises

1. Locate the system header files `limits.h` and `float.h` on your machine. Examine the files to see what's in them. If these files include other header files, be sure to track them down as well to examine their contents.

2. Define a macro called `MIN` that gives the minimum of two values. Then write a program to test the macro definition.

3. Define a macro called `MAX3` that gives the maximum of three values. Write a program to test the definition.

4. Write a macro called `IS_UPPER_CASE` that gives a nonzero value if a character is an uppercase letter.

5. Write a macro called `IS_ALPHABETIC` that gives a nonzero value if a character is an alphabetic character. Have the macro use the `IS_LOWER_CASE` macro defined in the chapter text and the `IS_UPPER_CASE` macro defined in Exercise 4.

6. Write a macro called `IS_DIGIT` that gives a nonzero value if a character is a digit 0 through 9. Use this macro in the definition of another macro called `IS_SPECIAL`, which gives a nonzero result if a character is a special character (that is, not alphabetic and not a digit). Be sure to use the `IS_ALPHABETIC` macro developed in Exercise 5.

7. Write a macro called `ABSOLUTE_VALUE` that computes the absolute value of its argument. Make sure that the macro properly evaluates an expression such as this:

   `ABSOLUTE_VALUE (x + delta)`

13

Underlying C Language Features

This chapter describes features of the Objective-C language that you don't necessarily need to know to write Objective-C programs. In fact, most of these come from the underlying C programming language. Features such as functions, structures, pointers, unions, and arrays are best learned on a need-to-know basis. Because C is a procedural language, some of these features go against the grain of object-oriented programming. They can also interfere with some of the strategies implemented by the Foundation framework, such as the memory-allocation methodology or work with character strings containing multibyte characters.

> **Note**
>
> There are ways to work with multibyte characters at the C level, but Foundation provides a much more elegant solution with its NSString class.

However, some applications can require you to use a lower-level approach, perhaps for the sake of optimization. If you're working with large arrays of data, for example, you might want to use the built-in data structures of C instead of the array objects of Foundation (which are described in Chapter 15, "Numbers, Strings, and Collections"). Functions also come in handy if used properly to group repetitive operations and modularize a program.

Skim this chapter to get an overview of the material, and come back after you've finished reading Part II, "The Foundation Framework." Or you can skip it altogether and go on to Part II. If you end up supporting someone else's code or start digging through some of the Foundation framework header files, you will encounter some of the constructs covered in this chapter. Several of the Foundation data types, such as NSRange, NSPoint, and NSRect, require a rudimentary understanding of structures, which are described here. In such cases, you can return to this chapter and read the appropriate section to gain an understanding of the concepts.

Arrays

The Objective-C language enables the user to define a set of ordered data items known as an *array*. This section describes how to define and manipulate arrays. Later sections illustrate how arrays work together with functions, structures, character strings, and pointers.

Suppose you wanted to read a set of grades into the computer and then perform some operations on these grades, such as rank them in ascending order, compute their average, or find their median. In the process of ranking a set of grades, you cannot perform such an operation until you enter every grade.

In Objective-C, you can define a variable called `grades` that represents not a single value of a grade, but an entire set of grades. You can then reference each element of the set using a number called an *index* number, or *subscript*. Whereas in mathematics a subscripted variable, x_i, refers to the ith element x in a set, in Objective-C the equivalent notation is this:

```
x[i]
```

So the expression

```
grades[5]
```

(read as "grades sub 5") refers to element number 5 in the array called grades. In Objective-C, array elements begin with the number 0, so

```
grades[0]
```

actually refers to the first element of the array.

You can use an individual array element anywhere that you can use a normal variable. For example, you can assign an array value to another variable with a statement such as this:

```
g = grades[50];
```

This statement assigns the value contained in `grades[50]` to g. More generally, if i is declared to be an integer variable, the statement

```
g = grades[i];
```

assigns the value contained in element number i of the `grades` array to g.

A value can be stored in an element of an array simply by specifying the array element on the left side of an equals sign. In the statement

```
grades[99] = 95;
```

the value 95 is stored in element number 99 of the `grades` array.

You can easily sequence through the elements in the array by varying the value of a variable that is used as a subscript into the array. Therefore, the `for` loop

```
for ( i = 0; i < 100; ++i )
    sum += grades[i];
```

sequences through the first 100 elements of the array grades (elements 0–99) and adds the value of each grade into sum. When the for loop is finished, the variable sum contains the total of the first 100 values of the grades array (assuming that sum was set to 0 before the loop was entered).

As with other types of variables, you must declare arrays before you can use them. Declaring an array involves declaring the type of element that will be contained in the array, such as int, float, or an object, as well as the maximum number of elements that will be stored inside the array.

The definition

```
Fraction *fracts [100];
```

defines fracts to be an array containing 100 fractions. You can make valid references to this array by using subscripts 0–99.

The expression

```
fracts[2] = [fracts[0] add: fracts[1]];
```

invokes the Fraction's add: method to add the first two fractions from the fracts array and stores the result in the third location of the array.

Program 13.1 generates a table of the first 15 Fibonacci numbers. Try to predict its output. What relationship exists between each number in the table?

Program 13.1

```
// Program to generate the first 15 Fibonacci numbers
#import <Foundation/Foundation.h>

int main (int argc, char * argv[])
{
   @autoreleasepool {
      int Fibonacci[15], i;

      Fibonacci[0] = 0;  /* by definition */
      Fibonacci[1] = 1;  /*   ditto    */

      for ( i = 2; i < 15; ++i )
         Fibonacci[i] = Fibonacci[i-2] + Fibonacci[i-1];

      for ( i = 0; i < 15; ++i )
         NSLog (@"%i", Fibonacci[i]);
   }
   return 0;
}
```

Program 13.1   **Output**

```
0
1
1
2
3
5
8
13
21
34
55
89
144
233
377
```

The first two Fibonacci numbers, which we call $F0$ and $F1$, are defined to be 0 and 1, respectively. Thereafter, each successive Fibonacci number Fi is defined to be the sum of the two preceding Fibonacci numbers Fi-2 and Fi-1. So $F2$ is calculated by adding the values of $F0$ and $F1$. In the preceding program, this corresponds directly to calculating `Fibonacci[2]` by adding the values `Fibonacci[0]` and `Fibonacci[1]`. This calculation is performed inside the `for` loop, which calculates the values of $F2$–$F14$ (or, equivalently, `Fibonacci[2]` through `Fibonacci[14]`).

Initializing Array Elements

Just as you can assign initial values to variables when they are declared, you can assign initial values to the elements of an array. This is done by simply listing the initial values of the array, starting from the first element. Values in the list are separated by commas, and the entire list is enclosed in a pair of braces.

The statement

```c
int integers[5] = {  0, 1, 2, 3, 4 } ;
```

sets the value of `integers[0]` to 0, `integers[1]` to 1, `integers[2]` to 2, and so on.

Arrays of characters are initialized in a similar manner; thus, the statement

```c
char letters[5] = {  'a', 'b', 'c', 'd', 'e' } ;
```

defines the character array `letters` and initializes the five elements to the characters `'a'`, `'b'`, `'c'`, `'d'`, and `'e'`, respectively.

You don't have to completely initialize an entire array. If fewer initial values are specified, only an equal number of elements are initialized; the remaining values in the array are set to zero. Thus, the declaration

```
float sample_data[500] = {  100.0, 300.0, 500.5 } ;
```

initializes the first three values of sample_data to 100.0, 300.0, and 500.5 and sets the remaining 497 elements to 0.

By enclosing an element number in a pair of brackets, you can initialize specific array elements in any order. For example,

```
int x = 1233;
int a[] = {  [9] = x + 1, [2] = 3, [1] = 2, [0] = 1 } ;
```

defines a 10-element array called a (based on the highest index in the array) and initializes the last element to the value of x + 1 (1234). In addition, it initializes the first three elements to 1, 2, and 3, respectively.

Character Arrays

Program 13.2 illustrates how you can use a character array. However, one point is worthy of discussion. Can you spot it?

Program 13.2

```
#import <Foundation/Foundation.h>

int main (int argc, char * argv[])
{
    @autoreleasepool {
        char word[] = {  'H', 'e', 'l', 'l', 'o', '!' } ;
        int  i;

        for ( i = 0; i < 6; ++i )
            NSLog (@"%c", word[i]);
    }
    return 0;
}
```

Program 13.2   **Output**

```
H
e
l
l
o
!
```

In this case, the size of the array is determined automatically based on the number of initialization elements. Because Program 13.2 has six initial values listed for the array word, the Objective-C language implicitly dimensions the array to six elements.

This approach works fine as long as you initialize every element in the array at the point that the array is defined. If this is not to be the case, you must explicitly dimension the array.

If you put a terminating null character (`'\0'`) at the end of a character array, you create what is often called a *character string*. If you substituted the initialization of word in Program 13.2 with this line

```
char word[] = {  'H', 'e', 'l', 'l', 'o', '!', '\0' } ;
```

you could have subsequently displayed the string with a single NSLog call, like this:

```
NSLog (@"%s", word);
```

This works because the `%s` format characters tell NSLog to keep displaying characters until a terminating null character is reached. That's the character you put at the end of your word array.

Multidimensional Arrays

The types of arrays you've seen thus far are all linear arrays; that is, they all deal with a single dimension. The language enables you to define arrays of any dimension. This section takes a look at two-dimensional arrays.

One of the most natural applications for a two-dimensional array arises in the case of a matrix. Consider the 4 × 5 matrix shown here:

10	5	−3	17	82
9	0	0	8	−7
32	20	1	0	14
0	0	8	7	6

In mathematics, an element of a matrix commonly is referred to by using a double subscript. If the preceding matrix were called M, the notation $M_{i,j}$ would refer to the element in the *i*th row, *j*th column, where *i* ranges from 1 through 4 and *j* ranges from 1 through 5. The notation $M_{3,2}$ would refer to the value 20, which is found in the third row, second column of the matrix. In a similar fashion, $M_{4,5}$ would refer to the element contained in the fourth row, fifth column (the value 6).

In Objective-C, an analogous notation is used when referring to elements of a two-dimensional array. However, because Objective-C likes to start numbering things at 0, the first row of the matrix is actually row 0 and the first column of the matrix is column 0. The preceding matrix would then have row and column designations as shown in the following diagram.

Row (i)	Column (j)				
	0	1	2	3	4
0	10	5	−3	17	82
1	9	0	0	8	−7
2	32	20	1	0	14
3	0	0	8	7	6

Whereas in mathematics the notation $M_{i,j}$ is used, in Objective-C the equivalent notation is as follows:

```
M[i][j]
```

Remember, the first index number refers to the row number, whereas the second index number references the column. Therefore, the statement

```
sum = M[0][2] + M[2][4];
```

adds the value contained in row 0, column 2 (which is -3) to the value contained in row 2, column 4 (which is 14) and assigns the result of 11 to the variable sum.

Two-dimensional arrays are declared the same way that one-dimensional arrays are; thus,

```
int M[4][5];
```

declares the array M to be a two-dimensional array consisting of 4 rows and 5 columns, for a total of 20 elements. Each position in the array is defined to contain an integer value.

Two-dimensional arrays can be initialized in a manner analogous to their one-dimensional counterparts. When listing elements for initialization, the values are listed by row. Brace pairs are used to separate the list of initializers for one row from the next. Therefore, to define and initialize the array M to the elements listed in the preceding table, you can use a statement such as the following:

```
int M[4][5] = {
            { 10, 5, -3, 17, 82 } ,
            { 9, 0, 0, 8, -7 } ,
            { 32, 20, 1, 0, 14 } ,
            { 0, 0, 8, 7, 6 }
    } ;
```

Pay particular attention to the syntax of the previous statement. Note that commas are required after each brace that closes off a row, except in the case of the last row. The use of the inner pairs of braces is actually optional. If these aren't supplied, initialization proceeds by row. Therefore, the previous statement could also have been written as follows:

```
int M[4][5] = { 10, 5, -3, 17, 82, 9, 0, 0, 8, -7, 32,
            20, 1, 0, 14, 0, 0, 8, 7, 6 } ;
```

As with one-dimensional arrays, the entire array need not be initialized. A statement such as the following initializes only the first three elements of each row of the matrix to the indicated values:

```
int M[4][5] = {
        {  10, 5, -3 } ,
        {  9, 0, 0 } ,
        {  32, 20, 1 } ,
        {  0, 0, 8 }
    } ;
```

The remaining values are set to 0. Note that, in this case, the inner pairs of braces are required to force the correct initialization. Without them, the first two rows and the first two elements of the third row would have been initialized instead. (Verify for yourself that this would be the case.)

Functions

The NSLog routine is an example of a function that you have used in every program so far. Indeed, every program also has used a function called main. Let's go back to the first program you wrote (Program 2.1), which displayed "Programming is fun." at the terminal:

```
#import <Foundation/Foundation.h>

int main (int argc, char * argv[])
{
    @autoreleasepool {
        NSLog (@"Programming is fun.");
    }
    return 0;
}
```

This function, called printMessage, produces the same output:

```
void printMessage (void)
{
    NSLog (@"Programming is fun.");
}
```

The first line of a function definition tells the compiler four things about the function:

- Who can call it
- The type of value it returns
- Its name
- The number and type of arguments it takes

The first line of the `printMessage` function definition tells the compiler that `printMessage` is the name of the function and that it returns no value (the first use of the keyword `void`). Unlike methods, you don't put the function's return type inside a set of parentheses. In fact, you get a compiler error message if you do.

After telling the compiler that `printMessage` doesn't return a value, the second use of the keyword `void` says that it takes no arguments.

Recall that `main` is a specially recognized name in the Objective-C system that always indicates where the program is to begin execution. There always must be a `main`. So you can add a `main` function to the preceding code to end up with a complete program, as shown in Program 13.3.

Program 13.3

```
#import <Foundation/Foundation.h>

void printMessage (void)
{
    NSLog (@"Programming is fun.");
}

int main (int argc, char * argv[])
{
    @autoreleasepool {
        printMessage ();
    }
    return 0;
}
```

Program 13.3   **Output**

```
Programming is fun.
```

Program 13.3 consists of two functions: `printMessage` and `main`. As mentioned earlier, the idea of calling a function is not new. Because `printMessage` takes no arguments, you call it simply by listing its name followed by a pair of open and close parentheses.

Arguments and Local Variables

In Chapter 5, "Program Looping," you developed programs for calculating triangular numbers. Here you define a function to generate a triangular number and call it, appropriately enough, `calculateTriangularNumber`. As an argument to the function, you specify which triangular number to calculate. The function then calculates the desired number and displays the results. Program 13.4 shows the function to accomplish the task and a `main` routine to try it.

Program 13.4

```
#import <Foundation/Foundation.h>

// Function to calculate the nth triangular number

void calculateTriangularNumber (int n)
{
   int i, triangularNumber = 0;

   for ( i = 1; i <= n; ++i )
       triangularNumber += i;

   NSLog (@"Triangular number %i is %i", n, triangularNumber);
}

int main (int argc, char * argv[])
{
    @autoreleasepool {
       calculateTriangularNumber (10);
       calculateTriangularNumber (20);
       calculateTriangularNumber (50);
    }
    return 0;
}
```

Program 13.4   **Output**

```
Triangular number 10 is 55
Triangular number 20 is 210
Triangular number 50 is 1275
```

The first line of the calculateTriangularNumber function is this:

```
void calculateTriangularNumber (int n)
```

It tells the compiler that calculateTriangularNumber is a function that returns no value (the keyword void) and that it takes a single argument, called n, which is an int. Note again that you can't put the argument type inside parentheses, as you are accustomed to doing when you write methods.

The opening curly brace indicates the beginning of the function's definition. Because you want to calculate the *n*th triangular number, you must set up a variable to store the value of the triangular number as it is being calculated. You also need a variable to act as your loop index. The variables TriangularNumber and i are defined for these purposes and are declared to be of type int. You define and initialize these variables in the same manner that you defined and initialized your variables inside the main routine in previous programs.

Local variables in functions behave the same way they do in methods: If an initial value is given to a variable inside a function, that initial value is assigned to the variable each time the function is called. And if using Automatic Reference Counting (ARC), note that local object variables are also by default initialized to zero each time a function (or method) is called.

Variables defined inside a function (as in methods) are known as *automatic local* variables because they are automatically "created" each time the function is called and their values are local to the function.

Static local variables are declared with the keyword `static`, retain their values through function calls, and have default initial values of `0`.

The value of a local variable can be accessed only by the function in which the variable is defined. Its value cannot be directly accessed from outside the function.

Returning to our program example, after the local variables have been defined, the function calculates the triangular number and displays the results at the terminal. The closed brace then defines the end of the function.

Inside the `main` routine, the value `10` is passed as the argument in the first call to `calculateTriangularNumber`. Execution then transfers directly to the function where the value `10` becomes the value of the formal parameter `n` inside the function. The function then calculates the value of the 10th triangular number and displays the result.

The next time `calculateTriangularNumber` is called, the argument `20` is passed. In a similar process, as described earlier, this value becomes the value of `n` inside the function. The function then calculates the value of the 20th triangular number and displays the answer.

Returning Function Results

As with methods, a function can return a value. The type of value returned with the `return` statement must be consistent with the return type declared for the function. A function declaration that starts like this

```
float kmh_to_mph (float km_speed)
```

begins the definition of a function `kmh_to_mph`, which takes one `float` argument called `km_speed` and returns a floating-point value. Similarly,

```
int gcd (int u, int v)
```

defines a function called `gcd` with integer arguments `u` and `v` and returns an integer value.

Let's rewrite the greatest common divisor algorithm used in Program 5.7 in function form. The two arguments to the function are the two numbers whose greatest common divisor (`gcd`) you want to calculate (see Program 13.5).

Program 13.5
___

```
#import <Foundation/Foundation.h>

// This function finds the greatest common divisor of two
//  nonnegative integer values and returns the result

int gcd (int u, int v)
{
    int temp;

    while ( v != 0 )
    {
       temp = u % v;
       u = v;
       v = temp;
    }

   return u;
}

main ()
{
    @autoreleasepool {
       int result;

       result = gcd (150, 35);
       NSLog (@"The gcd of 150 and 35 is %i", result);

       result = gcd (1026, 405);
       NSLog (@"The gcd of 1026 and 405 is %i", result);

       NSLog (@"The gcd of 83 and 240 is %i", gcd (83, 240));
    }
    return 0;
}
```
___

Program 13.5 **Output**
___

```
The gcd of 150 and 35 is 5
The gcd of 1026 and 405 is 27
The gcd of 83 and 240 is 1
```
___

The function gcd is defined to take two integer arguments. The function refers to these arguments through their formal parameter names: u and v. After declaring the variable temp to be of type int, the program displays the values of the arguments u and v, together with an appropriate message at the terminal. The function then calculates and returns the greatest common divisor of the two integers.

The statement

```
result = gcd (150, 35);
```

says to call the function gcd with the arguments 150 and 35, and to store the value that this function returns in the variable result.

If the return type declaration for a function is omitted, the compiler assumes that the function will return an integer (if it returns a value at all). Many programmers take advantage of this fact and omit the return type declaration for functions that return integers. However, you should avoid this bad programming habit. The compiler will warn you that the return type defaults to int, which is an indication that you're doing something wrong!

The default return type for functions differs from that for methods. Recall that if no return type is specified for a method, the compiler assumes that it returns a value of type id. Again, you should always declare the return type for a method instead of relying on this fact.

Declaring Return Types and Argument Types

As mentioned earlier, the Objective-C compiler assumes that a function returns a value of type int as the default case. More specifically, whenever a call is made to a function, the compiler assumes that the function returns a value of type int unless either of the following has occurred:

- The function has been defined in the program before the function call is encountered.
- The value returned by the function has been declared before the function call is encountered. Declaring the return and argument types for a function is known as a *prototype* declaration.

The function declaration not only is used to declare the function's return type, but it also is used to tell the compiler how many arguments the function takes and what their types are. This is analogous to declaring methods inside the @interface section when defining a new class.

To declare absoluteValue as a function that returns a value of type float and that takes a single argument, also of type float, you could use the following prototype declaration:

```
float absoluteValue (float);
```

As you can see, you have to specify just the argument type inside the parentheses, not its name. You can optionally specify a "dummy" name after the type, if you like:

```
float absoluteValue (float x);
```

This name doesn't have to be the same as the one used in the function definition—the compiler ignores it anyway.

A foolproof way to write a prototype declaration is to simply make a copy of the first line from the actual definition of the function. Remember to place a semicolon at the end.

If the function takes a variable number of arguments (such as is the case with NSLog and scanf), the compiler must be informed. The declaration

```
void NSLog (NSString *format, ...);
```

tells the compiler that NSLog takes an NSString object as its first argument and is followed by any number of additional arguments (the use of the ...). NSLog is declared in the special file Foundation/Foundation.h[1], which is one reason why you have been placing the following line at the start of each of your programs:

```
#import <Foundation/Foundation.h>
```

Without this line, the compiler can assume that NSLog takes a fixed number of arguments, which can result in incorrect code being generated.

The compiler automatically converts your numeric arguments to the appropriate types when a function is called only if you have placed the function's definition or have declared the function and its argument types before the call.

Consider some reminders and suggestions about functions:

- By default, the compiler assumes that a function returns an int.
- When defining a function that returns an int, define it as such.
- When defining a function that doesn't return a value, define it as void.
- The compiler converts your arguments to agree with the ones the function expects only if you have previously defined or declared the function.

To be safe, declare all functions in your program, even if they are defined before they are called. (You might decide later to move them someplace else in your file or even to another file.) A good strategy is to put your function declarations inside a header file and then just import that file into your modules.

Functions are *external* by default. That is, the default scope for a function is that it can be called by any functions or methods contained in any files that are linked with the function. You can limit the scope of a function by making it static. You do this by placing the keyword static in front of the function declaration, as shown here:

```
static int gcd (int u, int v)
{
   ...
}
```

[1] Technically speaking, its defined in the file NSObjCRuntime.h, which is imported from inside the file Foundation.h.

A static function can be called only by other functions or methods that appear in the same file that contains the function's definition.

Functions, Methods, and Arrays

To pass a single array element to a function or method, you specify the array element as an argument in the normal fashion. So if you had a `squareRoot` function to calculate square roots and wanted to take the square root of `averages[i]` and assign the result to a variable called `sq_root_result`, a statement such as this one would work:

```
sq_root_result = squareRoot (averages[i]);
```

Passing an entire array to a function or method is an entirely new ballgame. To pass an array, you need to list only the name of the array, without any subscripts, inside the call to the function or method invocation. For example, if you assume that `grade_scores` has been declared as an array containing 100 elements, the expression

```
minimum (grade_scores)
```

passes the entire 100 elements contained in the array `grade_scores` to the function called `minimum`. Naturally, the `minimum` function must be expecting an entire array to be passed as an argument and must make the appropriate formal parameter declaration.

This function finds the minimum integer value in an array containing a specified number of elements:

```
// Function to find the minimum in an array

int minimum (int values[], int numElements)
{
    int minValue, i;

    minValue = values[0];

    for ( i = 1; i < numElements; ++i )
        if ( values[i] < minValue )
            minValue = values[i];

    return (minValue);
}
```

The function `minimum` is defined to take two arguments: first, the array whose minimum you want to find and, second, the number of elements in the array. The open and close brackets that immediately follow `values` in the function header inform the Objective-C compiler that `values` is an array of integers. The compiler doesn't care how large it is.

The formal parameter `numElements` serves as the upper limit inside the `for` statement. Thus, the `for` statement sequences through the array from `values[1]` through the last element of the array, which is `values[numElements - 1]`.

If a function or method changes the value of an array element, that change is made to the original array that was passed to the function or method. This change remains in effect even after the function or method has completed execution.

The reason an array behaves differently from a simple variable or an array element—whose value a function or method cannot change—is worthy of a bit of explanation. We stated that when a function or method is called, the values passed as arguments are copied into the corresponding formal parameters. This statement is still valid. However, when dealing with arrays, the entire contents of the array are not copied into the formal parameter array. Instead, a pointer is passed indicating where in the computer's memory the array is located. So, any changes made to the formal parameter array are actually made to the original array, not to a copy of the array. Therefore, when the function or method returns, these changes remain in effect.

Blocks

Blocks are a recent extension to the C language. They are not part of the standard ANSI C definition and were added to the language by Apple, Inc. Blocks look and act a lot like functions. The syntax takes some getting used to. You can pass arguments to blocks, just like you can to functions. You can also return a value from a block. Unlike a function, a block can be defined inside a function or method, and gets to access any variables defined outside the block that are within its scope. In general, such variables can be accessed, but their values cannot be changed. There is a special __block modifier (two underscore characters precede the word block) that enables you to modify the value of a variable from inside the block, and you'll see shortly how to use it.

Blocks can be passed as arguments to functions and methods, and in Part II you learn about some of the methods that expect to see a block passed as an argument. One of the advantages of blocks is that they can be dispatched by the system for execution by other processors or by other threads within your application.

Let's get started with a simple example. Recall the first function we wrote in this chapter, called printMessage:

```
void printMessage (void)
{
    NSLog (@"Programming is fun.");
}
```

Here's a block that accomplishes the same task:

```
^(void)
{
    NSLog (@"Programming is fun.");
}
```

A block is identified by a leading caret (^) character. It's followed by the parenthesized argument list that the block takes. In our case, our block takes no arguments, so we write `void` just as we did in the function definition.

You can assign this block to a variable called `printMessage`, as long as the variable is properly declared (and here's where the syntax gets tough):

```
void (^printMessage)(void) =
    ^(void){
        NSLog (@"Programming is fun.");
    } ;
```

To the left of the equal sign we specify that `printMessage` is a pointer to a block that takes no arguments and returns no value. Note that the assignment statement is terminated by a semicolon.

Executing a block referenced by a variable is done the same way a function is called:

```
printMessage ();
```

Program 13.6 puts this all together into an example.

Program 13.6

```
#import <Foundation/Foundation.h>

int main (int argc, char * argv[])
{
   @autoreleasepool {
      void (^printMessage)(void) =
         ^(void) {
             NSLog (@"Programming is fun.");
          } ;

      printMessage ();
   }
   return 0;
}
```

Program 13.6   **Output**

```
Programming is fun.
```

Program 13.7 is Program 13.4 rewritten to use a block rather than a function. A block can be defined globally or locally. In this case, we define our block outside of `main`, making it external and global in scope.

Program 13.7

```
#import <Foundation/Foundation.h>

// Block to calculate the nth triangular number

void (^calculateTriangularNumber) (int) =
    ^(int n) {
        int i, triangularNumber = 0;

        for ( i = 1; i <= n; ++i )
            triangularNumber += i;

        NSLog (@"Triangular number %i is %i", n, triangularNumber);
    } ;

int main (int argc, char * argv[])
{
    @autoreleasepool {
        calculateTriangularNumber (10);
        calculateTriangularNumber (20);
        calculateTriangularNumber (50);
    }
    return 0;
}
```

Program 13.7   **Output**

```
Triangular number 10 is 55
Triangular number 20 is 210
Triangular number 50 is 1275
```

Compare the syntax of the function in Program 13.4 to the block defined in Program 13.7. The block pointer variable `calculateTriangularNumber` is defined to take an `int` argument and returns no value.

As noted at the start of this section, a block can return a value. Here's the `gcd` function of Program 13.5 rewritten in block form:

```
int (^gcd) (int, int) =
    ^(int u, int v){
        int temp;

        while ( v != 0 )
        {
            temp = u % v;
            u = v;
```

```
            v = temp;
        }

        return u;
    } ;
```

A block can access variables within the scope in which it's defined. The value of that variable is the value it has *at the time the block is defined,* as illustrated in Program 13.8.

Program 13.8

```
#import <Foundation/Foundation.h>

int main (int argc, char * argv[])
{
    @autoreleasepool {
        int foo = 10;

        void (^printFoo)(void) =
            ^(void) {
                NSLog (@"foo = %i", foo);
            } ;

        foo = 15;

        printFoo ();
    }
    return 0;
}
```

Program 13.8   **Output**

```
foo = 10
```

The printFoo block can access the value of the local variable foo. Note that the value displayed is 10, and not 15. That's because the value of foo is the value it had at the time the block was defined, and not at the time it was executed.

You can't by default modify the value of a variable defined outside a block. So, if you try to change the value of foo inside the block (see Program 13.9) you'll get this error message from the compiler: Assignment of read-only variable 'foo.'

Program 13.9
```
#import <Foundation/Foundation.h>

int main (int argc, char * argv[])
{
   @autoreleasepool {
      int foo = 10;

      void (^printFoo)(void) =
         ^(void) {
            NSLog (@"foo = %i", foo);
            foo = 20;   // ** THIS LINE GENERATES A COMPILER ERROR
         } ;

      foo = 15;

      printFoo ();
      NSLog (@"foo = %i", foo);
   }
   return 0;
}
```

If you insert the __ block modifier before the definition of the local variable foo in Program 13.9 so that it reads like this:

```
__ block int foo = 10;
```

and run the program, you'll get these two lines of output:

```
foo = 15
foo = 20
```

The first line shows that the value of foo is now its value at the time the block is called. The second line verifies that the block was able to change the value of foo to 20.

This concludes our introduction on blocks. In Chapter 15, you'll find more examples of how they're used.

Structures

The Objective-C language provides another tool besides arrays for grouping elements. You also can use *structures,* which form the basis for the discussions in this section.

Suppose you wanted to store a date—say, 7/18/11—inside a program, perhaps to be used for the heading of some program output or even for computational purposes. A natural method for storing the date is to simply assign the month to an integer variable called `month`, the day to an integer variable `day`, and the year to an integer variable `year`. So, the statements

```
int month = 7, day = 18, year = 2011;
```

would work just fine. This is a totally acceptable approach. But what if your program also needed to store several dates? It would be much better to somehow group these sets of three variables.

You can define a structure called `date` in the Objective-C language that consists of three components that represent the month, day, and year. The syntax for such a definition is rather straightforward:

```
struct date
{
    int month;
    int day;
    int year;
} ;
```

The `date` structure just defined contains three integer members, called `month`, `day`, and `year`. Essentially, the definition of `date` defines a new type in the language, in that variables can subsequently be declared to be of type `struct date`, as in the following definition:

```
struct date today;
```

You can also define a variable called `purchaseDate` to be of the same type with a separate definition:

```
struct date purchaseDate;
```

Or you can simply include the two definitions on the same line:

```
struct date today, purchaseDate;
```

Unlike variables of type `int`, `float`, or `char`, a special syntax is needed when dealing with structure variables. A member of a structure is accessed by specifying the variable name, followed by a period and then the member name. For example, to set the value of `day` in the variable `today` to `21`, you would write this:

```
today.day = 21;
```

Note that no spaces are permitted between the variable name, the period, and the member name.

Now, wait a second! Wasn't this the same operator we used to access a property on an object? Recall that we could write the statement

```
myRect.width = 12;
```

to invoke the Rectangle object's setter method (called setWidth:), passing it the argument value of 12. No confusion arises here: The compiler determines whether it's a structure or an object to the left of the dot operator and handles the situation properly.

Returning to the struct date example, to set year in today to 2011, you can use this expression:

```
today.year = 2011;
```

Finally, to test the value of month to see whether it is equal to 12, you can use a statement such as this:

```
if ( today.month == 12 )
   next_month = 1;
```

Program 13.10 incorporates the preceding discussions into an actual program.

Program 13.10

```
#import <Foundation/Foundation.h>

int main (int argc, char * argv[])
{
    @autoreleasepool {

        struct date
        {
            int month;
            int day;
            int year;
        } ;

        struct date today;

        today.month = 9;
        today.day = 25;
        today.year = 2011;

        NSLog (@"Today's date is %i/%i/%.2i.", today.month,
                today.day, today.year % 100);
    }
    return 0;
}
```

Program 13.10 Output

```
Today's date is 9/25/11.
```

The first statement inside `main` defines the structure called `date` to consist of three integer members, called `month`, `day`, and `year`. In the second statement, the variable `today` is declared to be of type `struct date`. So the first statement simply defines what a `date` structure looks like to the Objective-C compiler and causes no storage to be reserved inside the computer. The second statement declares a variable to be of type `struct date` and, therefore, does reserve memory for storing the three integer members of the structure variable `today`.

After the assignments, an appropriate `NSLog` call displays the values contained inside the structure. The remainder of `today.year` divided by 100 is calculated before being passed to the `NSLog` function so that just `11` displays for the year. The `%.2i` format characters in the `NSLog` call specify a minimum of two characters to be displayed, thus forcing the display of the leading zero for the year.

When it comes to the evaluation of expressions, structure members follow the same rules as ordinary variables in the Objective-C language. Division of an integer structure member by another integer is performed as an integer division, as shown here:

```
century = today.year / 100 + 1;
```

Suppose that you want to write a simple program that accepts today's date as input and displays tomorrow's date to the user. At first glance, this seems a perfectly simple task to perform. You can ask the user to enter today's date and then calculate tomorrow's date by a series of statements, like so:

```
tomorrow.month = today.month;
tomorrow.day   = today.day + 1;
tomorrow.year  = today.year;
```

Of course, the previous statements would work fine for most dates, but the following two cases would not be properly handled:

- If today's date fell at the end of a month
- If today's date fell at the end of a year (that is, if today's date were December 31)

One way to easily determine whether today's date falls at the end of a month is to set up an array of integers that corresponds to the number of days in each month. A lookup inside the array for a particular month would then give the number of days in that month.

Initializing Structures

Initializing structures is similar to initializing arrays; the elements are simply listed inside a pair of braces, with a comma separating each element.

To initialize the `date` structure variable `today` to July 2, 2011, you can use this statement:

```
struct date today = {  7, 2, 2011 } ;
```

As with the initialization of an array, fewer values can be listed than the structure contains. So the statement

```
struct date today = {  7 } ;
```

sets `today.month` to 7 but gives no initial value to `today.day` or `today.year`. In such a case, their default initial values are undefined.

Specific members can be designated for initialization in any order with the notation

```
.member = value
```

in the initialization list, as in

```
struct date today = {  .month = 7, .day = 2, .year = 2011 } ;
```

and

```
struct date today = {  .year = 2011 } ;
```

The last statement just sets the year in the structure to 2011. As you know, the other two members are undefined.

Structures within Structures

Objective-C provides an enormous amount of flexibility in defining structures. For instance, you can define a structure that itself contains other structures as one or more of its members, or you can define structures that contain arrays.

You learned about the `typedef` statement in Chapter 10, "More on Variables and Data Types." In your iOS programs, you will often need to work with rectangles. Rectangles define the size and location of a window on an iPhone's or iPad's screen, for example. They also define the location and size of subwindows (or what are called subviews). There are three basic data types that are used and are defined using `typedef`:

1. `CGPoint`, which describes an (x,y) point

2. `CGSize`, which describes a width and height

3. `CGRect`, which is a rectangle that contains an origin (a `CGPoint`) and a size (a `CGSize`)

Here are the `typedef` definitions from Apple's `CGGeometry.h` header file:

```
/* Points. */

struct CGPoint {
   CGFloat x;
   CGFloat y;
} ;
typedef struct CGPoint CGPoint;

/* Sizes. */
```

```
struct CGSize {
   CGFloat width;
   CGFloat height;
} ;
typedef struct CGSize CGSize;

/* Rectangles. */

struct CGRect {
   CGPoint origin;
   CGSize size;
} ;
typedef struct CGRect CGRect;
```

The `typedefs` provide a convenient way to declare variables without having to use the keyword `struct`. `CGFloat` is just a `typedef` for a basic float data type. So, if you want to declare a `CGPoint` variable and set its x member to `100` and y member to `200`, respectively, you could write this code sequence:

```
CGPoint startPt;

startPt.x = 100;
startPt.y = 200;
```

Remember that `startPt` is a structure and not an object. (A good indication of that is often the lack of an asterisk in front of the variable name.) Apple also provides convenience functions for creating `CGRect`, `CGSize`, and `CGRect` structures. For example

```
CGPoint startPt = CGPointMake (100.0, 200.0);
```

There's also `CGSizeMake` and `CGRectMake` functions that perform tasks as their names imply.

So, suppose that you want to define a new rectangle and set its size to `200` x `100`. You could specify its size this way:

```
CGSize rectSize;

rectSize.width = 200;
rectSize.height = 100;
```

You could use the `CGSizeMake` function like so:

```
CGSize rectSize = CGSizeMake (200.0, 100.0);
```

Now let's go ahead and create a rectangle with the indicated size and origin:

```
CGRect theFrame;

theFrame.origin = startPt;
theFrame.size = rectSize;
```

(We won't show the use of the `CGRectMake` function here.)

Suppose later you want to get the rectangle's width (maybe it changed?). You could do so by writing this expression:

```
theFrame.size.width
```

And to change its width to `175`, you could write this:

```
theFrame.size.width = 175;
```

Finally, to set the rectangle's origin to `(0,0)`, these statements would do the trick:

```
theFrame.origin.x = 0.0;
theFrame.origin.y = 0.0;
```

These are just a few examples of working with these structures. As noted, you'll likely be using them often in your applications.

Additional Details about Structures

We should mention that you have some flexibility in defining a structure. First, you can declare a variable to be of a particular structure type at the same time that the structure is defined. You do this simply by including the variable names before the terminating semicolon of the structure definition. For example, the following statement defines the structure `date` and also declares the variables `todaysDate` and `purchaseDate` to be of this type:

```
struct date
{
    int month;
    int day;
    int year;
} todaysDate, purchaseDate;
```

You can also assign initial values to the variables in the normal fashion. Therefore, the following defines the structure `date` and the variable `todaysDate` with initial values as indicated:

```
struct date
{
    int month;
    int day;
    int year;
} todaysDate = {  9, 25, 2011 } ;
```

If all the variables of a particular structure type are defined when the structure is defined, you can omit the structure name. So the following statement defines an array called `dates` to consist of 100 elements:

```
struct
{
    int month;
    int day;
```

```
    int year;
} dates[100];
```

Each element is a structure containing three integer members: month, day, and year. Because you did not supply a name to the structure, the only way to subsequently declare variables of the same type is to explicitly define the structure again.

Don't Forget about Object-Oriented Programming!

Now you know how to define a structure to store a date, and you've written various routines to manipulate that date structure. But what about object-oriented programming? Shouldn't you have made a class called Date instead and then developed methods to work with a Date object? Wouldn't that be a better approach? Well, yes. Hopefully, that entered your mind when we discussed storing dates in your program.

Certainly, if you have to work with a lot of dates in your programs, defining a class and methods to work with dates is a better approach. In fact, the Foundation framework has a couple of classes, called NSDate and NSCalendarDate, defined for such purposes. We leave it as an exercise for you to implement a Date class to deal with dates as objects instead of as structures.

Pointers

Pointers enable you to effectively represent complex data structures, change values passed as arguments to functions and methods, and more concisely and efficiently deal with arrays. At the end of this chapter, we also clue you in about how important they are to the implementation of objects in the Objective-C language.

We introduced the concept of a pointer in Chapter 8, "Inheritance," when we talked about the Point and Rectangle classes and stated that you can have multiple references to the same object.

To understand the way pointers operate, you first must understand the concept of *indirection*. We witness this concept in our everyday life. For example, suppose that I need to buy a new toner cartridge for my printer. In the company that I work for, the purchasing department handles all purchases. So, I call Jim in purchasing and ask him to order the new cartridge for me. Jim then calls the local supply store to order the cartridge. To obtain my new cartridge, I take an indirect approach because I do not order the cartridge directly from the supply store.

This same notion of indirection applies to the way pointers work in Objective-C. A pointer provides an indirect means of accessing the value of a particular data item. And just as there are reasons it makes sense to go through the purchasing department to order new cartridges (I don't have to know which particular store the cartridges are being ordered from, for example), good reasons exist for why sometimes it makes sense to use pointers in Objective-C.

But enough talk; it's time to see how pointers actually work. Suppose you've defined a variable called count as follows:

```
int count = 10;
```

You can define another variable, called intPtr, that enables you to indirectly access the value of count with the following declaration:

```
int *intPtr;
```

The asterisk defines to the Objective-C system that the variable intPtr is of type pointer to int. This means that the program will use intPtr to indirectly access the value of one or more integer variables.

You have seen how we used the & operator in the scanf calls of previous programs. This unary operator, known as the *address* operator, makes a pointer to a variable in Objective-C. So if x is a variable of a particular type, the expression &x is a pointer to that variable. If you want, you can assign the expression &x to any pointer variable that has been declared to be a pointer of the same type as x.

Therefore, with the definitions of count and intPtr as given, you can write a statement such as

```
intPtr = &count;
```

to set up the indirect reference between intPtr and count. The address operator assigns to the variable intPtr not the value of count, but a pointer to the variable count. Figure 13.1 illustrates the link made between intPtr and count. The directed line illustrates the idea that intPtr does not directly contain the value of count, but contains a pointer to the variable count.

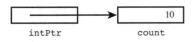

Figure 13.1   Pointer to an integer

To reference the contents of count through the pointer variable intPtr, you use the indirection operator, which is the asterisk (*). If x were defined to be of type int, the statement

```
x = *intPtr;
```

would assign the value that is indirectly referenced through intPtr to the variable x. Because intPtr was previously set pointing to count, this statement would have the effect of assigning the value contained in the variable count (which is 10) to the variable x.

Program 13.11 incorporates the previous statements and illustrates the two fundamental pointer operators: the address operator (&) and the indirection operator (*).

Program 13.11

```
// Program to illustrate pointers

#import <Foundation/Foundation.h>

int main (int argc, char * argv[])
{
    @autoreleasepool {
        int   count = 10, x;
        int   *intPtr;

        intPtr = &count;
        x = *intPtr;

        NSLog (@"count = %i, x = %i", count, x);
    }
    return 0;
}
```

Program 13.11 **Output**

```
count = 10, x = 10
```

The variables count and x are declared to be integer variables in the normal fashion. On the next line, the variable intPtr is declared to be of type "pointer to int." Note that you can combine the two lines of declarations into a single line:

```
int count = 10, x, *intPtr;
```

Next, the address operator is applied to the variable count, which has the effect of creating a pointer to this variable, which the program then assigns to the variable intPtr.

Execution of the next statement in the program

```
x = *intPtr;
```

proceeds as follows: The indirection operator tells the Objective-C system to treat the variable intPtr as containing a pointer to another data item. This pointer is then used to access the desired data item, whose type is specified by the declaration of the pointer variable. Because you told the compiler when you declared the variable that intPtr points to integers, the compiler knows that the value referenced by the expression *intPtr is an integer. Also, because you set intPtr to point to the integer variable count in the previous program statement, this expression indirectly accesses the value of count.

Program 13.12 illustrates some interesting properties of pointer variables. This program uses a pointer to a character.

Program 13.12

```
#import <Foundation/Foundation.h>

int main (int argc, char * argv[])
{
    @autoreleasepool {
        char c = 'Q';
        char *charPtr = &c;

        NSLog (@"%c %c", c, *charPtr);

        c = '/';
        NSLog (@"%c %c", c, *charPtr);

        *charPtr = '(';
        NSLog (@"%c %c", c, *charPtr);
    }
    return 0;
}
```

Program 13.12   **Output**

```
Q Q
/ /
( (
```

The character variable c is defined and initialized to the character 'Q'. In the next line of the program, the variable charPtr is defined to be of type "pointer to char," meaning that whatever value is stored inside this variable should be treated as an indirect reference (pointer) to a character. Notice that you can assign an initial value to this variable in the normal fashion. The value you assign to charPtr in the program is a pointer to the variable c, which is obtained by applying the address operator to the variable c. (Note that this initialization would have generated a compiler error had c been defined after this statement because a variable must always be declared before its value can be referenced in an expression.)

The declaration of the variable charPtr and the assignment of its initial value could have been equivalently expressed in two separate statements, as follows

```
char *charPtr;
charPtr = &c;
```

(and not by the statements

```
char *charPtr;
*charPtr = &c;
```

as might be implied from the single line declaration).

Remember that the value of a pointer in Objective-C is meaningless until it is set to point to something.

The first NSLog call simply displays the contents of the variable c and the contents of the variable referenced by charPtr. Because you set charPtr to point to the variable c, the value displayed is the contents of c, as verified by the first line of the program's output.

In the next line of the program, the character '/' is assigned to the character variable c. Because charPtr still points to the variable c, displaying the value of *charPtr in the subsequent NSLog call correctly displays this new value of c at the terminal. This is an important concept. Unless the value of charPtr changes, the expression *charPtr always accesses the value of c. Therefore, as the value of c changes, so does the value of *charPtr.

The previous discussion can help you understand how the program statement that appears next in the program works. We mentioned that unless charPtr were changed, the expression *charPtr would always reference the value of c. Therefore, in the expression

```
*charPtr = '(';
```

the left parenthesis character is being assigned to c. More formally, the character '(' is assigned to the variable that charPtr points to. You know that this variable is c because you placed a pointer to c in charPtr at the beginning of the program.

The previous concepts are the key to your understanding of pointer operation. Review them at this point if they still seem a bit unclear.

Pointers and Structures

You have seen how to define a pointer to point to a basic data type such as an int or a char. But you can also define a pointer to point to a structure. Earlier in this chapter, you defined your date structure as follows:

```
struct date
{
    int month;
    int day;
    int year;
} ;
```

Just as you defined variables to be of type struct date, as in

```
struct date  todaysDate;
```

you can define a variable to be a pointer to a struct date variable:

```
struct date *datePtr;
```

You can then use the variable datePtr, as just defined, in the expected fashion. For example, you can set it to point to todaysDate with the following assignment statement:

```
datePtr = &todaysDate;
```

After such an assignment, you can indirectly access any of the members of the date structure that datePtr points to in the following way:

```
(*datePtr).day = 21;
```

This statement sets the day of the date structure pointed to by datePtr to 21. The parentheses are required because the structure member operator period (.) has higher precedence than the indirection operator asterisk (*).

To test the value of month stored in the date structure that datePtr points to, you can use a statement such as this:

```
if ( (*datePtr).month == 12 )
    . . .
```

Pointers to structures are so often used that the language has a special operator. The structure pointer operator ->, which is a hyphen followed by the greater-than sign, permits expressions that would otherwise be written as

```
(*x).y
```

to be more clearly expressed as

```
x->y
```

So, you can conveniently write the previous if statement as follows:

```
if ( datePtr->month == 12 )
    . . .
```

We rewrote Program 13.10, the first program to illustrate structures, using the concept of structure pointers. Program 13.13 presents this program.

Program 13.13

```
// Program to illustrate structure pointers
#import <Foundation/Foundation.h>

int main (int argc, char * argv[])
{
    @autoreleasepool {

        struct date
        {
            int month;
            int day;
            int year;
        } ;

        struct date today, *datePtr;
```

```
        datePtr = &today;
        datePtr->month = 9;
        datePtr->day = 25;
        datePtr->year = 2011;

        NSLog (@"Today's date is %i/%i/%.2i.",
                datePtr->month, datePtr->day, datePtr->year % 100);
    }
    return 0;
}
```

Program 13.13   **Output**

```
Today's date is 9/25/11.
```

Pointers, Methods, and Functions

You can pass a pointer as an argument to a method or function in the normal fashion, and you can have a function or method return a pointer as its result. When you think about it, that's what your `alloc` and `init` methods have been doing all along—returning pointers. We cover that in more detail at the end of this chapter.

Now consider Program 13.14.

Program 13.14

```
// Pointers as arguments to functions
#import <Foundation/Foundation.h>

void exchange (int *pint1, int *pint2)
{
    int temp;

    temp = *pint1;
    *pint1 = *pint2;
    *pint2 = temp;
}

int main (int argc, char * argv[])
{
    @autoreleasepool {
        void exchange (int *pint1, int *pint2);
        int  i1 = -5, i2 = 66, *p1 = &i1, *p2 = &i2;

        NSLog (@"i1 = %i, i2 = %i", i1, i2);
```

```
    exchange (p1, p2);
    NSLog (@"i1 = %i, i2 = %i", i1, i2);

    exchange (&i1, &i2);
    NSLog (@"i1 = %i, i2 = %i", i1, i2);
  }
  return 0;
}
```

Program 13.14   **Output**

```
i1 = -5, i2 = 66
i1 = 66, i2 = -5
i1 = -5, i2 = 66
```

The purpose of the `exchange` function is to interchange the two integer values that its two arguments point to. The local integer variable `temp` is used to hold one of the integer values while the exchange is made. Its value is set equal to the integer that `pint1` points to. The integer that `pint2` points to is then copied into the integer that `pint1` points to, and the value of `temp` is then stored in the integer that `pint2` points to, thus making the exchange complete.

The `main` routine defines integers `i1` and `i2` with values of `-5` and `66`, respectively. Two integer pointers, `p1` and `p2`, are then defined and set to point to `i1` and `i2`, respectively. The program next displays the values of `i1` and `i2` and calls the `exchange` function, passing the two pointers (`p1` and `p2`) as arguments. The `exchange` function exchanges the value contained in the integer that `p1` points to with the value contained in the integer that `p2` points to. Because `p1` points to `i1`, and `p2` to `i2`, the function exchanges the values of `i1` and `i2`. The output from the second `NSLog` call verifies that the exchange worked properly.

The second call to `exchange` is a bit more interesting. This time, the arguments passed to the function are pointers to `i1` and `i2` that are manufactured on the spot by applying the address operator to these two variables. Because the expression `&i1` produces a pointer to the integer variable `i1`, this is in line with the type of argument your function expects for the first argument (a pointer to an integer). The same applies for the second argument. As you can see from the program's output, the exchange function did its job and switched the values of `i1` and `i2` to their original values.

Study Program 13.14 in detail. It illustrates with a small example the key concepts when dealing with pointers in Objective-C.

Pointers and Arrays

If you have an array of 100 integers called `values`, you can define a pointer called `valuesPtr`, which you can use to access the integers contained in this array with the following statement:

```
int *valuesPtr;
```

When you define a pointer that will be used to point to the elements of an array, you don't designate the pointer as type "pointer to array"; instead, you designate the pointer as pointing to the type of element contained in the array.

If you had an array of `Fraction` objects called `fracts`, you could similarly define a pointer to be used to point to elements in `fracts` with the following statement:

```
Fraction **fractsPtr;
```

To set `valuesPtr` to point to the first element in the `values` array, you just write this:

```
valuesPtr = values;
```

The address operator is not used in this case because the Objective-C compiler treats the occurrence of an array name without a subscript as a pointer to the first element of the array. Therefore, simply specifying `values` without a subscript produces a pointer to the first element of values.

An equivalent way of producing a pointer to the start of `values` is to apply the address operator to the first element of the array. Therefore, the statement

```
valuesPtr = &values[0];
```

serves the same purpose of placing a pointer to the first element of `values` in the pointer variable `valuesPtr`.

To display the `Fraction` object in the array `fracts` that `fractsPtr` points to, you would write this statement:

```
[*fractsPtr print];
```

The real power of using pointers to arrays comes into play when you want to sequence through the elements of an array. If `valuesPtr` is defined as mentioned previously and is set pointing to the first element of `values`, you can use the expression

```
*valuesPtr
```

to access the first integer of the `values` array (that is, `values[0]`). To reference `values[3]` through the `valuesPtr` variable, you can add 3 to `valuesPtr` and then apply the indirection operator:

```
*(valuesPtr + 3)
```

In general, you can use the expression

```
*(valuesPtr + i)
```

to access the value contained in `values[i]`.

So, to set `values[10]` to 27, you write the following expression:

```
values[10] = 27;
```

Or, using `valuesPtr`, you write this:

```
*(valuesPtr + 10) = 27;
```

To set `valuesPtr` to point to the second element of the `values` array, you apply the address operator to `values[1]` and assign the result to `valuesPtr`:

```
valuesPtr = &values[1];
```

If `valuesPtr` points to `values[0]`, you can set it to point to `values[1]` by simply adding 1 to the value of `valuesPtr`:

```
valuesPtr += 1;
```

This is a perfectly valid expression in Objective-C and can be used for pointers to any data type.

In general, if `a` is an array of elements of type `x`, `px` is of type "pointer to `x`," and `i` and `n` are integer constants of variables, the statement

```
px = a;
```

sets `px` to point to the first element of `a`, and the expression

```
*(px + i)
```

subsequently references the value contained in `a[i]`. Furthermore, the statement

```
px += n;
```

sets `px` to point to n elements further in the array, no matter what type of element the array contains.

Suppose that `fractsPtr` points to a fraction stored inside an array of fractions. Further suppose that you want to add it to the fraction contained in the next element of the array and assign the result to the `Fraction` object `result`. You could do this by writing the following:

```
result = [*fractsPtr add: *(fractsPtr + 1)];
```

The increment and decrement operators (`++` and `--`) are particularly handy when dealing with pointers. Applying the increment operator to a pointer has the same effect as adding 1 to the pointer, whereas applying the decrement operator has the same effect as subtracting 1 from the pointer (here 1 means one unit, or the size of the data item the pointer is declared to point to). So, if `textPtr` were defined as a `char` pointer and were set to point to the beginning of an array of `chars` called `text`, the statement

```
++textPtr;
```

would set `textPtr` to point to the next character in `text`, which is `text[1]`. In a similar fashion, the statement

```
--textPtr;
```

sets `textPtr` to point to the previous character in `text` (assuming, of course, that `textPtr` was not pointing to the beginning of `text` before this statement executed).

Comparing two pointer variables in Objective-C is perfectly valid. This is particularly useful when comparing two pointers in the same array. For example, you could test the pointer `valuesPtr` to see whether it points past the end of an array containing 100 elements by comparing it to a pointer to the last element in the array. So, the expression

```
valuesPtr > &values[99]
```

would be TRUE (nonzero) if `valuesPtr` was pointing past the last element in the `values` array, and it would be FALSE (zero) otherwise. From our earlier discussions, you can replace the previous expression with its equivalent:

```
valuesPtr > values + 99
```

This is possible because `values` used without a subscript is a pointer to the beginning of the `values` array. (Remember that it's the same as writing `&values[0]`.)

Program 13.15 illustrates pointers to arrays. The `arraySum` function calculates the sum of the elements contained in an array of integers.

Program 13.15

```
// Function to sum the elements of an integer array

#import <Foundation/Foundation.h>

int arraySum (int array[], int n)
{
    int sum = 0, *ptr;
    int *arrayEnd = array + n;

    for ( ptr = array; ptr < arrayEnd; ++ptr )
        sum += *ptr;

    return (sum);
}

int main (int argc, char * argv[])
{
    @autoreleasepool {
        int arraySum (int array[], int n);
        int values[10] = {  3, 7, -9, 3, 6, -1, 7, 9, 1, -5 } ;

        NSLog (@"The sum is %i", arraySum (values, 10));
    }
    return 0;
}
```

Program 13.15   **Output**

```
The sum is 21
```

Inside the `arraySum` function, the integer pointer `arrayEnd` is defined and set pointing imme-diately after the last element of `array`. A `for` loop is then set up to sequence through the elements of `array`; then the value of `ptr` is set to point to the beginning of `array` when the loop is entered. Each time through the loop, the element of `array` that `ptr` points to is added into `sum`. The `for` loop then increments the value of `ptr` to set it to point to the next element in `array`. When `ptr` points past the end of `array`, the `for` loop is exited and the value of `sum` is returned to the caller.

Is It an Array, or Is It a Pointer?

To pass an array to a function, you simply specify the name of the array, as you did previously with the call to the `arraySum` function. But we also mentioned in this section that to produce a pointer to an array, you need only specify the name of the array. This implies that in the call to the `arraySum` function, a pointer to the array `values` was passed to the function. This is precisely the case and explains why you can change the elements of an array from within a function.

But if a pointer to the array is passed to the function, why isn't the formal parameter inside the function declared to be a pointer? In other words, in the declaration of `array` in the `arraySum` function, why isn't this declaration used?

```
int *array;
```

Shouldn't all references to an array from within a function be made using pointer variables?

To answer these questions, we must first reiterate what we have already said about pointers and arrays. We mentioned that if `valuesPtr` points to the same type of element as contained in an array called `values`, the expression `*(valuesPtr + i)` is an equivalent to the expression `values[i]`, assuming that `valuesPtr` has been set to point to the beginning of `values`. What follows from this is that you can also use the expression `*(values + i)` to reference the `i`th element of the array `values`—and, in general, if `x` is an array of any type, the expression `x[i]` can always be equivalently expressed in Objective-C as `*(x + i)`.

As you can see, pointers and arrays are intimately related in Objective-C, which is why you can declare `array` to be of type "array of `int`s" inside the `arraySum` function or to be of type "pointer to `int`." Either declaration works fine in the preceding program. Try it and see.

If you will be using index numbers to reference the elements of an array, declare the corre-sponding formal parameter to be an array. This more correctly reflects the function's use of the array. Similarly, if you will be using the argument as a pointer to the array, declare it to be of type pointer.

Pointers to Character Strings

One of the most common applications of using a pointer to an array is as a pointer to a character string. The reasons are ones of notational convenience and efficiency. To show how easily you can use pointers to character strings, let's write a function called `copyString` to copy one string into another. If you were writing this function using your normal array-indexing methods, you might code the function as follows:

```
void copyString (char to[], char from[])
{
    int i;

    for ( i = 0; from[i] != '\0'; ++i )
        to[i] = from[i];

    to[i] = '\0';
}
```

The `for` loop is exited before the null character is copied into the `to` array, thus explaining the need for the last statement in the function.

If you write `copyString` using pointers, you no longer need the index variable `i`. Program 13.16 shows a pointer version.

Program 13.16

```
#import <Foundation/Foundation.h>
void copyString (char *to, char *from)
{
    for ( ; *from != '\0'; ++from, ++to )
        *to = *from;

    *to = '\0';
}

int main (int argc, char * argv[])
{
    @autoreleasepool {
        void copyString (char *to, char *from);
        char string1[] = "A string to be copied.";
        char string2[50];

        copyString (string2, string1);
        NSLog (@"%s", string2);

        copyString (string2, "So is this.");
        NSLog (@"%s", string2);
    }
}
```

```
    return 0;
}
```

Program 13.16   **Output**

```
A string to be copied.
So is this.
```

The `copyString` function defines the two formal parameters, `to` and `from`, as character pointers and not as character arrays, as was done in the previous version of `copyString`. This reflects how the function will use these two variables.

A `for` loop is then entered (with no initial conditions) to copy the string that `from` points to into the string that `to` points to. Each time through the loop, the `from` and `to` pointers are each incremented by 1. This sets the `from` pointer pointing to the next character that is to be copied from the source string and sets the `to` pointer pointing to the location in the destination string where the next character is to be stored.

When the `from` pointer points to the null character, the `for` loop is exited. The function then places the null character at the end of the destination string.

In the `main` routine, the `copyString` function is called twice—the first time to copy the contents of `string1` into `string2`, and the second time to copy the contents of the constant character string `"So is this."` into `string2`.[2]

Constant Character Strings and Pointers

The fact that the call

```
copyString (string2, "So is this.");
```

works in the previous program implies that when a constant character string is passed as an argument to a function, that character string is actually passed to a pointer. Not only is this true in this case, but it can also be generalized by saying that whenever a constant character string is used in Objective-C, a pointer to that character string is produced.

This point might sound a bit confusing now, but as we briefly noted in Chapter 4, "Data Types and Expressions," constant character strings that we mention here are called C-style strings. These are not objects. As you know, a constant character string object is created by putting an @ sign in front of the string, as in `@"This is okay."`. You can't substitute one for the other.

---

[2] Note the use of the strings `"A string to be copied."` and `"So is this."` in the program. These are not string objects, but C-style character strings, as distinguished by the fact that an @ character does not precede the string. The two types are not interchangeable. If a function expects an array of char as an argument, you may pass it either an array of type `char` or a literal C-style character string, but not a character string object.

So, if `textPtr` is declared to be a character pointer, as in

```
char *textPtr;
```

then the statement

```
textPtr = "A character string.";
```

assigns to `textPtr` a pointer to the constant character string "`A character string.`" Be careful to make the distinction here between character pointers and character arrays because the type of assignment shown previously is not valid with a character array. For example, if text were defined instead to be an array of `chars`, with a statement such as

```
char text[80];
```

you could not write a statement such as this:

```
text = "This is not valid.";
```

The only time Objective-C lets you get away with performing this type of assignment to a character array is when initializing it:

```
char text[80] = "This is okay.";
```

Initializing the `text` array in this manner does not have the effect of storing a pointer to the character string `"This is okay."` inside `text`. Instead, the actual characters themselves are followed by a terminating null character inside corresponding elements of the `text` array.

If `text` were a character pointer, initializing `text` with the statement

```
char *text = "This is okay.";
```

would assign to it a pointer to the character string "`This is okay.`"

The Increment and Decrement Operators Revisited

Up to this point, whenever you used the increment or decrement operator, that was the only operator that appeared in the expression. When you write the expression ++x, you know that this adds 1 to the value of the variable x. And as you have just seen, if x is a pointer to an array, this sets x to point to the next element of the array.

You can use the increment and decrement operators in expressions where other operators also appear. In such cases, it becomes important to know more precisely how these operators work.

Whenever you used the increment and decrement operators, you always placed them before the variables that were being incremented or decremented. So, to increment a variable i, you simply wrote the following:

```
++i;
```

You can also place the increment operator after the variable, like so:

```
i++;
```

292 Chapter 13 Underlying C Language Features

Both expressions are valid, and both achieve the same result: incrementing the value of i. In the first case, where the ++ is placed before its operand, the increment operation is more precisely identified as a *pre-increment*. In the second case, where the ++ is placed after its operand, the operation is identified as a *post-increment*.

The same discussion applies to the decrement operator. So, the statement

```
--i;
```

technically performs a pre-decrement of i, whereas the statement

```
i--;
```

performs a post-decrement of i. Both have the same net result of subtracting 1 from the value of i.

When the increment and decrement operators are used in more complex expressions, the distinction between the pre and post nature of these operators is realized.

Suppose that you have two integers, called i and j. If you set the value of i to 0 and then write the statement

```
j = ++i;
```

the value assigned to j is 1 (not 0, as you might expect). In the case of the pre-increment operator, the variable is incremented before its value is used in an expression. Therefore, in the previous expression, the value of i is first incremented from 0 to 1, and then its value is assigned to j, as if the following two statements had been written instead:

```
++i;
j = i;
```

If you use the post-increment operator in the statement

```
j = i++;
```

i is incremented after its value has been assigned to j. So, if i were 0 before the previous statement were executed, 0 would be assigned to j and then i would be incremented by 1, as if these statements were used instead:

```
j = i;
++i;
```

As another example, if i is equal to 1, the statement

```
x = a[--i];
```

has the effect of assigning the value of a[0] to x because the variable i is decremented before its value is used to index into a. The statement

```
x = a[i--];
```

used instead assigns the value of a[1] to x because i would be decremented after its value was used to index into a.

As a third example of the distinction between the pre- and post-increment and pre- and post-decrement operators, the function call

```
NSLog (@"%i", ++i);
```

increments i and then sends its value to the NSLog function, whereas the call

```
NSLog (@"%i", i++);
```

increments i after its value has been sent to the function. So, if i were equal to 100, the first NSLog call would display 101 at the terminal, whereas the second NSLog call would display 100. In either case, the value of i would be equal to 101 after the statement had been executed.

As a final example on this topic before we present a program, if textPtr is a character pointer, the expression

```
*(++textPtr)
```

first increments textPtr and then fetches the character it points to, whereas the expression

```
*(textPtr++)
```

fetches the character that textPtr points to before its value is incremented. In either case, the parentheses are not required because the * and ++ operators have equal precedence but associate from right to left.

Let's go back to the copyString function from Program 13.16 and rewrite it to incorporate the increment operations directly into the assignment statement.

Because the to and from pointers are incremented each time after the assignment statement inside the for loop is executed, they should be incorporated into the assignment statement as post-increment operations. The revised for loop of Program 13.16 then becomes this:

```
for ( ; *from != '\0'; )
    *to++ = *from++;
```

Execution of the assignment statement inside the loop would proceed as follows. The character that from points to would be retrieved, and then from would be incremented to point to the next character in the source string. The referenced character would be stored inside the location that to points to; then to would be incremented to point to the next location in the destination string.

The previous for statement hardly seems worthwhile because it has no initial expression and no looping expression. In fact, the logic is better served when expressed in the form of a while loop, as done in Program 13.17, which presents the new version of the copyString function. The while loop uses the fact that the null character is equal to the value 0, as experienced Objective-C programmers commonly do.

Program 13.17

```
// Function to copy one string to another
//          pointer version 2

#import <Foundation/Foundation.h>
void copyString (char *to, char *from)
{
    while ( *from )
            *to++ = *from++;
    *to = '\0';
}

int main (int argc, char * argv[])
{
   @autoreleasepool {
      void copyString (char *to, char *from);
      char string1[] = "A string to be copied.";
      char string2[50];

      copyString (string2, string1);
      NSLog (@"%s", string2);

      copyString (string2, "So is this.");
      NSLog (@"%s", string2);
   }
   return 0;
}
```

Program 13.17   **Output**

```
A string to be copied.
So is this.
```

Operations on Pointers

As you have seen in this chapter, you can add or subtract integer values from pointers. Furthermore, you can compare two pointers to see whether they are equal or whether one pointer is less than or greater than another pointer. The only other operation permitted on pointers is the subtraction of two pointers of the same type. The result of subtracting two pointers in Objective-C is the number of elements contained between the two pointers. Thus, if a points to an array of elements of any type and b points to another element somewhere further along in the same array, the expression b - a represents the number of elements between these two pointers. For example, if p points to some element in an array x, the statement

```
n = p - x;
```

assigns to the variable n (assumed here to be an integer variable) the index number of the element inside x that p points to. Therefore, if p had been set pointing to the 100th element in x by a statement such as

```
p = &x[99];
```

the value of n after the previous subtraction was performed would be 99.

Pointers to Functions

Of a slightly more advanced nature, but presented here for the sake of completeness, is the notion of a pointer to a function. When working with pointers to functions, the Objective-C compiler needs to know not only that the pointer variable points to a function, but also the type of value returned by that function, as well as the number and types of its arguments. To declare a variable, fnPtr, to be of type "pointer to function that returns an int and that takes no arguments," you write this declaration:

```
int (*fnPtr) (void);
```

The parentheses around *fnPtr are required; otherwise, the Objective-C compiler treats the preceding statement as the declaration of a function called fnPtr that returns a pointer to an int (because the function call operator () has higher precedence than the pointer indirection operator *).

To set your function pointer to point to a specific function, you simply assign the name of the function to it. Therefore, if lookup were a function that returned an int and that took no arguments, the statement

```
fnPtr = lookup;
```

would store a pointer to this function inside the function pointer variable fnPtr. Writing a function name without a subsequent set of parentheses is treated in an analogous way to writing an array name without a subscript. The Objective-C compiler automatically produces a pointer to the specified function. An ampersand is permitted in front of the function name, but it's not required.

If the lookup function has not been previously defined in the program, you must declare the function before the previous assignment can be made. A statement such as

```
int lookup (void);
```

would be needed before a pointer to this function could be assigned to the variable fnPtr.

You can call the function indirectly referenced through a pointer variable by applying the function call operator to the pointer, listing any arguments to the function inside the parentheses. For example

```
entry = fnPtr ();
```

calls the function that fnPtr points to, storing the returned value inside the variable entry.

One common application for pointers to functions is passing them as arguments to other functions. The Standard Library uses this in the function qsort, which performs a *quick sort* on an array of data elements. This function takes as one of its arguments a pointer to a function that is called whenever qsort needs to compare two elements in the array being sorted. In this manner, qsort can be used to sort arrays of any type because the actual comparison of any two elements in the array is made by a user-supplied function, not by the qsort function itself.

In the Foundation framework, some methods take a function pointer as an argument. For example, the method sortUsingFunction:context: is defined in the NSMutableArray class and calls the specified function whenever two elements in an array to be sorted need to be compared.

Another common application for function pointers is to create *dispatch* tables. You can't store functions themselves inside the elements of an array. However, you can store function pointers inside an array. Given this, you can create tables that contain pointers to functions to be called. For example, you might create a table for processing different commands that a user will enter. Each entry in the table could contain both the command name and a pointer to a function to call to process that particular command. Now, whenever the user entered a command, you could look up the command inside the table and invoke the corresponding function to handle it.

Pointers and Memory Addresses

Before we end this discussion of pointers in Objective-C, we should point out the details of how they are actually implemented. A computer's memory can be conceptualized as a sequential collection of storage cells. Each cell of the computer's memory has a number, called an *address,* associated with it. Typically, the first address of a computer's memory is numbered 0. On most computer systems, a *cell* is 1 byte.

The computer uses memory to store the instructions of your computer program and to store the values of the variables associated with a program. So if you declare a variable called count to be of type int, the system assigns locations in memory to hold the value of count while the program is executing. For example, this location might be at address $1000FF_{16}$ inside the computer's memory.

Luckily, you don't need to concern yourself with the particular memory addresses assigned to variables; the system automatically handles them. However, the knowledge that each variable is associated with a unique memory address will help you understand the way pointers operate.

Whenever you apply the address operator to a variable in Objective-C, the value generated is the actual address of that variable inside the computer's memory. (Obviously, this is where the address operator gets its name.) So the statement

```
intPtr = &count;
```

assigns to intPtr the address in the computer's memory that has been assigned to the variable count. Thus, if count were located at address $1000FF_{16}$, this statement would assign the value 0x1000FF to intPtr.

Applying the indirection operator to a pointer variable, as in the expression

```
*intPtr
```

has the effect of treating the value contained in the pointer variable as a memory address. The value stored at that memory address is then fetched and interpreted in accordance with the type declared for the pointer variable. So if `intPtr` were of type pointer to `int`, the system would interpret the value stored in the memory address given by `*intPtr` as an integer.

They're Not Objects!

Now you know how to define arrays, structures, character strings, and unions, and how to manipulate them in your program. Remember one fundamental thing: *They're not objects.* Thus, you can't send messages to them. You also can't use them to take maximum advantage of nice things such as the memory-allocation strategy that the Foundation framework provides. That's one of the reasons I encouraged you to skip this chapter and return to it later. In general, you're better served learning how to use the Foundation's classes that define arrays and strings as objects than using the ones built in to the language. Resort to using the types defined in this chapter only if you really need to—and hopefully you won't!

Miscellaneous Language Features

Some language features didn't fit well into any of the other chapters, so we've included them here.

Compound Literals

A *compound literal* is a type name enclosed in parentheses followed by an initialization list. It creates an unnamed value of the specified type, which has scope limited to the block in which it is created or global scope if defined outside any block. In the latter case, the initializers must all be constant expressions.

Consider an example:

```
(struct date) { .month = 7, .day = 2, .year = 2011}
```

This expression produces a structure of type `struct date` with the specified initial values. You can assign this to another `struct date` structure, like so:

```
theDate = (struct date) { .month = 7, .day = 2, .year = 2011} ;
```

Or you can pass it to a function or method that expects an argument of `struct date`, like so:

```
setStartDate ((struct date) { .month = 7, .day = 2, .year = 2011} );
```

In addition, you can define types other than structures. For example, if `intPtr` is of type `int *`, the statement

```
intPtr = (int [100]) { [0] = 1, [50] = 50, [99] = 99 } ;
```

(which can appear anywhere in the program) sets `intptr` pointing to an array of 100 integers, whose 3 elements are initialized as specified.

If the size of the array is not specified, the initializer list determines it.

The `goto` Statement

Executing a `goto` statement causes a direct branch to be made to a specified point in the program. To identify where in the program the branch is to be made, a label is needed. A *label* is a name formed with the same rules as variable names; it must be immediately followed by a colon. The label is placed directly before the statement to which the branch is to be made and must appear in the same function or method as the `goto`.

For example, the statement

```
goto out_of_data;
```

causes the program to branch immediately to the statement that is preceded by the label `out_of_data;`. This label can be located anywhere in the function or method, before or after the `goto`, and might be used as shown here:

```
out_of_data: NSLog (@"Unexpected end of data.");
   ...
```

Lazy programmers often abuse the `goto` statement to branch to other portions of their code. The `goto` statement interrupts the normal sequential flow of a program. As a result, programs are harder to follow. Using many `goto`s in a program can make it impossible to decipher. For this reason, `goto` statements are not considered part of good programming style.

The Null Statement

Objective-C permits you to place a solitary semicolon wherever a normal program statement can appear. The effect of such a statement, known as the *null statement,* is that nothing is done. This might seem quite useless, but programmers often do this in `while`, `for`, and `do` statements. For example, the purpose of the following statement is to store all the characters read in from *standard input* (your terminal, by default) in the character array that `text` points to until a newline character is encountered. This statement uses the library routine `getchar`, which reads and returns a single character at a time from standard input:

```
while ( (*text++ = getchar ()) != '' )
   ;
```

All the operations are performed inside the looping conditions part of the `while` statement. The null statement is needed because the compiler takes the statement that follows the looping expression as the body of the loop. Without the null statement, the compiler would treat whatever statement follows in the program as the body of the program loop.

The Comma Operator

At the bottom of the precedence totem pole, so to speak, is the comma operator. In Chapter 5, we pointed out that inside a `for` statement, you can include more than one expression in any of the fields by separating each expression with a comma. For example, the `for` statement that begins

```
for ( i = 0, j = 100; i != 10; ++i, j -= 10 )
    ...
```

initializes the value of i to 0 and j to 100 before the loop begins, and it increments the value of i and subtracts 10 from the value of j after the body of the loop is executed.

Because all operators in Objective-C produce a value, the value of the comma operator is that of the rightmost expression.

The `sizeof` Operator

Although you should never make assumptions about the size of a data type in your program, sometimes you need to know this information. This might be when performing dynamic memory allocation using library routines such as `malloc`, or when writing or archiving data to a file. Objective-C provides an operator called `sizeof` that you can use to determine the size of a data type or object. The `sizeof` operator returns the size of the specified item in bytes. The argument to the `sizeof` operator can be a variable, an array name, the name of a basic data type, an object, the name of a derived data type, or an expression. For example, writing

```
sizeof (int)
```

gives the number of bytes needed to store an integer. On my MacBook Air, this produces a result of 4 (or 32 bits). If x is declared as an array of 100 `int`s, the expression

```
sizeof (x)
```

would give the amount of storage required to store the 100 integers of x.

Given that `myFract` is a `Fraction` object that contains two `int` instance variables (`numerator` and `denominator`), the expression

```
sizeof (myFract)
```

produces the value 4 on any system that represents pointers using 4 bytes. In fact, this is the value that `sizeof` yields for any object because here you are asking for the size of the pointer to the object's data. To get the size of the actual data structure to store an instance of a Fraction object, you instead write the following:

```
sizeof (*myFract)
```

On my MacBook Air, this gives me a value of 12. That's 4 bytes each for the numerator and denominator, plus another 4 bytes for the inherited isa member mentioned in the section "How Things Work," at the end of this chapter.

The expression

```
sizeof (struct data_entry)
```

has as its value the amount of storage required to store one data_entry structure. If data is defined as an array of struct data_entry elements, the expression

```
sizeof (data) / sizeof (struct data_entry)
```

gives the number of elements contained in data (data must be a previously defined array, not a formal parameter or externally referenced array). The expression

```
sizeof (data) / sizeof (data[0])
```

produces the same result.

Use the sizeof operator wherever possible, to avoid having to calculate and hard-code sizes into your programs.

Command-Line Arguments

Often a program is developed that requires the user to enter a small amount of information at the terminal. This information might consist of a number indicating the triangular number you want to have calculated or a word you want to have looked up in a dictionary.

Instead of having the program request this type of information from the user, you can supply the information to the program at the time the program is executed. *Command-line arguments* provide this capability.

We have pointed out that the only distinguishing quality of the function main is that its name is special; it specifies where program execution is to begin. In fact, the runtime system actually calls upon the function main at the start of program execution, just as you would call a function from within your own program. When main completes execution, control returns to the runtime system, which then knows that your program has completed.

When the runtime system calls main, two arguments are passed to the function. The first argument, called argc by convention (for *argument c*ount), is an integer value that specifies the number of arguments typed on the command line. The second argument to main is an array of character pointers, called argv by convention (for ar*gument v*ector). In addition, argc + 1 character pointers are contained in this array. The first entry in this array is either a pointer to the name of the program that is executing or a pointer to a null string if the program name is not available on your system. Subsequent entries in the array point to the values specified in the same line as the command that initiated execution of the program. The last pointer in the `argv` array, `argv[argc]`, is defined to be null.

To access the command-line arguments, the `main` function must be appropriately declared as taking two arguments. The conventional declaration we have used in all the programs in this book suffices:

```
int main (int argc, char * argv[])
{
    ...
}
```

Remember, the declaration of `argv` defines an array that contains elements of type "pointer to `char`." As a practical use of command-line arguments, suppose that you had developed a program that looks up a word inside a dictionary and prints its meaning. You can use command-line arguments so that the word whose meaning you want to find can be specified at the same time that the program is executed, as in the following command:

```
lookup aerie
```

This eliminates the need for the program to prompt the user to enter a word because it is typed on the command line.

If the previous command were executed, the system would automatically pass to the `main` function a pointer to the character string `"aerie"` in `argv[1]`. Recall that `argv[0]` would contain a pointer to the name of the program, which, in this case, would be `"lookup"`.

The `main` routine might appear as shown:

```
#include <Foundation/Foundation.h>

int main (int argc, char * argv[])
{
    struct entry dictionary[100] =
        { { "aardvark", "a burrowing African mammal"    } ,
          { "abyss",   "a bottomless pit"           } ,
          { "acumen",  "mentally sharp; keen"        } ,
          { "addle",   "to become confused"         } ,
          { "aerie",   "a high nest"            } ,
          { "affix",   "to append; attach"         } ,
          { "agar",    "a jelly made from seaweed"    } ,
          { "ahoy",    "a nautical call of greeting"   } ,
          { "aigrette", "an ornamental cluster of feathers" } ,
          { "ajar",    "partially opened"          } } ;

    int   entries = 10;
    int   entryNumber;
    int   lookup (struct entry dictionary [], char search[],
                  int entries);
```

```
if ( argc != 2 )
{
    NSLog (@"No word typed on the command line.");
    return (1);
}

entryNumber = lookup (dictionary, argv[1], entries);

if ( entryNumber != -1 )
    NSLog (@"%s", dictionary[entryNumber].definition);
else
    NSLog (@"Sorry, %s is not in my dictionary.", argv[1]);

return (0);
}
```

The main routine tests to ensure that a word was typed after the program name when the program was executed. If it wasn't, or if more than one word was typed, the value of argc is not equal to 2. In that case, the program writes an error message to standard error and terminates, returning an exit status of 1.

If argc is equal to 2, the lookup function is called to find the word that argv[1] points to in the dictionary. If the word is found, its definition is displayed.

Remember that command-line arguments are always stored as character strings. So execution of the program power with the command-line arguments 2 and 16, as in

power 2 16

stores a pointer to the character string "2" inside argv[1] and a pointer to the string "16" inside argv[2]. If the program is to interpret arguments as numbers (as we suspect is the case in the power program), the program itself must convert them. Several routines are available in the program library for doing such conversions: sscanf, atof, atoi, strtod, and strtol. In Part II, you learn how to use a class called NSProcessInfo to access the command-line arguments as string objects instead of as C strings.

How Things Work

We would be remiss if we finished this chapter without first tying a couple things together. Because the Objective-C language has the C language underneath, it's worth mentioning some of the connections between the two. You can ignore these implementation details or use them to better understand how things work, in the same way that learning about pointers as memory addresses can help you better understand pointers. We don't get too detailed here; we just state four facts about the relationship between Objective-C and C.

Fact 1: Instance Variables Are Stored in Structures

When you define a new class and its instance variables, those instance variables are actually stored inside a structure. That's how you can manipulate objects; they're really structures whose members are your instance variables. So, the inherited instance variables plus the ones you added in your class comprise a single structure. When you allocate a new object using `alloc`, enough space is reserved to hold one of these structures.

One of the inherited members (it comes from the root object) of the structure is a protected member called `isa` that identifies the class to which the object belongs. Because it's part of the structure (and, therefore, part of the object), it is carried around with the object. In that way, the runtime system can always identify the class of an object (even if you assign it to a generic `id` object variable) by just looking at its `isa` member.

You can gain direct access to the members of an object's structure by making them `@public` (see the discussion in Chapter 10). If you did that with the `numerator` and `denominator` members of your `Fraction` class, for example, you could write expressions such as

```
myFract->numerator
```

in your program to directly access the `numerator` member of the `Fraction` object `myFract`. But we strongly advise against doing that. As mentioned in Chapter 10, it goes against the grain of data encapsulation.

Fact 2: An Object Variable Is Really a Pointer

When you define an object variable such as a `Fraction`, as in

```
Fraction *myFract;
```

you're really defining a pointer variable called `myFract`. This variable is defined to point to something of type `Fraction`, which is the name of your class. When you allocate a new instance of a `Fraction`, with

```
myFract = [Fraction alloc];
```

you're allocating space to store a new `Fraction` object in memory (that is, space for a structure) and then storing the pointer to that structure that is returned inside the pointer variable `myFract`.

When you assign one object variable to another, as in

```
myFract2 = myFract1;
```

you're simply copying pointers. Both variables end up pointing to the same structure stored somewhere in memory. Making a change to one of the members referenced (that is, pointed to) by `myFract2` therefore changes the same instance variable (that is, structure member) that `myFract1` references.

Fact 3: Methods Are Functions, and Message Expressions Are Function Calls

Methods are really functions. When you invoke a method, you call a function associated with the class of the receiver. The arguments passed to the function are the receiver (self) and the method's arguments. So all the rules about passing arguments to functions, return values, and automatic and static variables are the same whether you're talking about a function or a method. The Objective-C compiler creates a unique name for each function using a combination of the class name and the method name.

Fact 4: The id Type Is a Generic Pointer Type

Because objects are referenced through pointers, which are just memory addresses, you can freely assign them between id variables. A method that returns an id type consequently just returns a pointer to some object in memory. You can then assign that value to any object variable. Because the object carries its isa member wherever it goes, its class can always be identified, even if you store it in a generic object variable of type id.

Exercises

1. Write a function that calculates the average of an array of 10 floating-point values and returns the result.

2. The reduce method from your Fraction class finds the greatest common divisor of the numerator and denominator to reduce the fraction. Modify that method so that it uses the gcd function from Program 13.5 instead. Where do you think you should place the function definition? Are there any benefits to making the function static? Which approach do you think is better, using a gcd function or incorporating the code directly into the method as you did previously? Why?

3. An algorithm known as the Sieve of Erastosthenes can generate prime numbers. The algorithm for this procedure is presented here. Write a program that implements this algorithm. Have the program find all prime numbers up to $n = 150$. What can you say about this algorithm as compared to the ones used in the text for calculating prime numbers?

   Step 1: Define an array of integers P. Set all elements Pi to 0, $2 <= i <= n$.

   Step 2: Set i to 2.

   Step 3: If $i > n$, the algorithm terminates.

   Step 4: If Pi is 0, i is prime.

   Step 5: For all positive integer values of j, such that $i \times j <= n$, set Pixj to 1.

   Step 6: Add 1 to i and go to Step 3.

4. Write a function to add all the `Fractions` passed to it in an array and to return the result as a `Fraction`.

5. Write a `typedef` definition for a `struct date` called `Date` that enables you to make declarations such as

```
Date todaysDate;
```

in your program.

6. As noted in the text, defining a `Date` class instead of a `date` structure is more consistent with the notion of object-oriented programming. Define such a class with appropriate setter and getter methods. Also add a method called `dateUpdate` to return the day after its argument.

Do you see any advantages of defining a `Date` as a class instead of as a structure? Do you see any disadvantages?

7. Given the following definitions

```
char *message = "Programming in Objective-C is fun";
char message2[] = "You said it";
int  x = 100;
```

determine whether each `NSLog` call from the following sets is valid and produces the same output as other calls from the set.

```
/*** set 1 ***/
NSLog (@"Programming in Objective-C is fun");
NSLog (@"%s", "Programming in Objective-C is fun");
NSLog (@"%s", message);

/*** set 2 ***/
NSLog (@"You said it");
NSLog (@"%s", message2);
NSLog (@"%s", &message2[0]);

/*** set 3 ***/
NSLog (@"said it");
NSLog (@"%s", message2 + 4);
NSLog (@"%s", &message2[4]);
```

8. Write a program that prints all its command-line arguments, one per line at the terminal. Notice the effect of enclosing arguments that contain space characters inside quotation marks.

9. Which of the following statements produce the output This is a test? Explain.

```
NSLog (@"This is a test");
NSLog ("This is a test");

NSLog (@"%s", "This is a test");
NSLog (@"%s", @"This is a test");

NSLog ("%s", "This is a test");
NSLog ("%s", @"This is a test");

NSLog (@"%@", @"This is a test");
NSLog (@"%@", "This is a test");
```

10. Rewrite the exchange function from Program 13.14 as a block and test it.

14

Introduction to the Foundation Framework

A framework is a collection of classes, methods, functions, and documentation logically grouped together to make developing programs easier. On OS X, more than 90 frameworks are available for developing applications so that you can easily work with the Mac's Address Book structure, burn CDs, play back DVDs, play movies with QuickTime, play songs, and so on.

The framework that provides the base or foundation for all your program development is called the Foundation framework. This framework, the subject of the second part of this book, enables you to work with basic objects, such as numbers and strings, and with collections of objects, such as arrays, dictionaries, and sets. Other capabilities provide for working with dates and times, using automated memory management, working with the underlying file system, storing (or *archiving*) objects, and working with geometric data structures such as points and rectangles.

The Application Kit framework contains an extensive collection of classes and methods to develop interactive graphical applications. These provide the capability to easily work with text, menus, toolbars, tables, documents, the pasteboard, and windows. In OS X, the term *Cocoa* collectively refers to the Foundation framework, the Application Kit framework, and a third framework known as Core Data. The term *Cocoa Touch* collectively refers to the Foundation, Core Data, and UIKit frameworks. Part III, "Cocoa, Cocoa Touch, and the iOS SDK," provides some more detail on this subject.

Foundation Documentation

You should take advantage of the Foundation framework documentation that is stored on your system (if you elected to download local copies) and that is also available online at Apple's website. Most documentation exists in the form of HTML files for viewing by a browser or as Acrobat PDF files. Contained in this documentation is a description of all the Foundation classes and all the implemented methods and functions. I keep the URL to the Foundation documentation as a bookmark in my browser so that I can easily look up information about a Foundation class.

If you're using Xcode to develop your programs, you have easy access to documentation in several different ways. You can get to the main Documentation window Xcode Help from the Help menu. This window enables you to easily search and access documentation that is stored locally on your computer or is available online. Figure 14.1 shows the results of searching for the string "NSString" in the Xcode Help window.

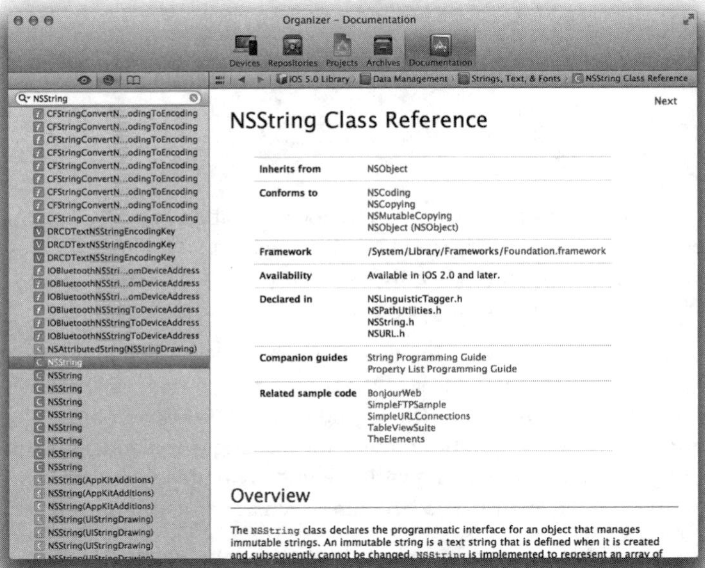

Figure 14.1   Using Xcode for reference documentation

If you're editing a file in Xcode and you want to get immediate access to the documentation for a particular header file, method, or class, you can simply place your cursor over the class, method, or variable you want to search for, hold down the Option key, and click. Doing so gives you a quick summary of whatever you selected. Figure 14.2 shows the pane that appears when the mouse cursor is located in the text NSString and you hold the Option key while clicking the mouse.

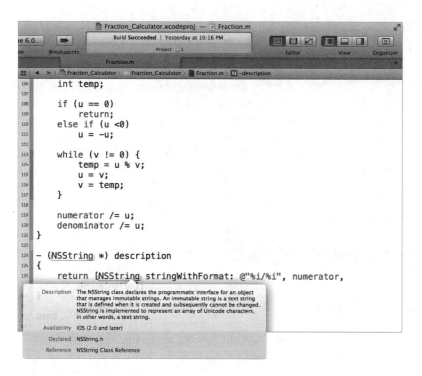

```
      int temp;

      if (u == 0)
          return;
      else if (u <0)
          u = -u;

      while (v != 0) {
          temp = u % v;
          u = v;
          v = temp;
      }

      numerator /= u;
      denominator /= u;
  }

  - (NSString *) description
  {
      return [NSString stringWithFormat: @"%i/%i", numerator,
```

Description The NSString class declares the programmatic interface for an object
             that manages immutable strings. An immutable string is a text string
             that is defined when it is created and subsequently cannot be changed.
             NSString is implemented to represent an array of Unicode characters,
             in other words, a text string.

Availability iOS (2.0 and later)

Declared NSString.h

Reference NSString Class Reference

Figure 14.2   Quick reference for NSString

You can get direct access to the NSString.h header file, or the class reference for the class, by clicking on the appropriate link in the help pane. It's really a great and convenient tool that you should get used to using!

You can also turn on the Quick Help pane so that it always appears and is automatically updated as you type or select items in your program. Just select View, Utilities, Quick Help to open a window layout like that shown in Figure 14.3, with the Quick Help menu appearing in the rightmost pane by default.

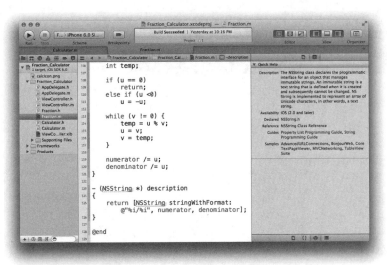

Figure 14.3   Quick Help displayed in the view pane

You can access the Mac OS X reference library online at http://developer.apple.com/library/ mac/navigation/index.html and navigate your way to the appropriate reference. At this address, you'll also find a wide assortment of documents covering specific programming issues, such as memory management, strings, and file management.

Unless you subscribe to automatic updates of your documentation with Xcode (look at Xcode, Preferences, Downloads, Documentation), the online documentation might be more current than that stored on your disk.

This concludes our brief introduction to the Foundation framework. Now it's time to learn about some of its classes and how you can put them to good use in your applications.

15

Numbers, Strings, and Collections

This chapter describes how to work with some of the basic objects provided in the Foundation framework. These include numbers, strings, and collections, which refer to the capability to work with groups of objects in the form of arrays, dictionaries, and sets.

The Foundation framework contains a plethora of classes, methods, and functions for you to use. Approximately 125 header files are available under OS X. As a convenience, you can simply use the following import:

```
#import <Foundation/Foundation.h>
```

Because the `Foundation.h` file imports nearly all the other Foundation header files, you don't have to worry about whether you are importing the correct header file. Xcode automatically inserts this header file into your program, as you've seen in each example throughout this book.

Using this statement can add significant time to your compiles. However, you can avoid this extra time by using *precompiled* headers (files that the compiler has preprocessed). By default, all Xcode projects benefit from precompiled headers.

Number Objects

All the numeric data types we've dealt with up to now, such as integers, floats, and longs, are basic data types in the Objective-C language; that is, they are not objects. For example, you cannot send messages to them. Sometimes, though, you need to work with these values as objects. For example, the Foundation object `NSArray` enables you to set up an array in which you can store values. These values have to be objects, so you cannot directly store any of your basic data types in these arrays. Instead, to store any of the basic numeric data types (including the `char` data type), you can use the `NSNumber` class to create objects from these data types (see Program 15.1).

Program 15.1
_____

```
// Working with Numbers

#import <Foundation/Foundation.h>

int main (int argc, char * argv[])
{
    @autoreleasepool {
        NSNumber            *myNumber, *floatNumber, *intNumber;
        NSInteger           myInt;

        // integer value

        intNumber = [NSNumber numberWithInteger: 100];
        myInt = [intNumber integerValue];
        NSLog (@"%li", (long) myInt);

        // long value

        myNumber = [NSNumber numberWithLong: 0xabcdef];
        NSLog (@"%lx", [myNumber longValue]);

        // char value

        myNumber = [NSNumber numberWithChar: 'X'];
        NSLog (@"%c", [myNumber charValue]);

        // float value

        floatNumber = [NSNumber numberWithFloat: 100.00];
        NSLog (@"%g", [floatNumber floatValue]);

        // double

        myNumber = [NSNumber numberWithDouble: 12345e+15];
        NSLog (@"%lg", [myNumber doubleValue]);

        // Wrong access here

        NSLog (@"%li", (long) [myNumber integerValue]);

        // Test two Numbers for equality

        if ([intNumber isEqualToNumber: floatNumber] == YES)
            NSLog (@"Numbers are equal");
        else
```

```
        NSLog (@"Numbers are not equal");

    // Test if one Number is <, ==, or > second Number

    if ([intNumber compare: myNumber] == NSOrderedAscending)
        NSLog (@"First number is less than second");
    }
    return 0;
}
```

Program 15.1 **Output**

```
100
abcdef
X
100
1.2345e+19
-9223372036854775808
0
Numbers are equal
First number is less than second
```

The NSNumber class contains many methods that allow you to create NSNumber objects with initial values. For example, the line

```
intNumber = [NSNumber numberWithInteger: 100];
```

creates an object from an integer whose value is 100.

The value retrieved from an NSNumber object must be consistent with the type of value that was stored in it. So, in the statement that follows in the program

```
myInt = [intNumber integerValue];
```

retrieves the integer value stored inside intNumber and stores it inside the NSInteger variable myInt. Note that NSInteger is not an object, but a typedef for a basic data type. It is typedef'ed either to a long for 64-bit builds or to an int for 32-bit builds. A similar typedef for NSUInteger exists for working with unsigned integers in your program.

In the NSLog call, we cast the NSInteger myInt to a long and use the format characters %li to ensure that the value will be passed and displayed correctly even if the program is compiled for a 32-bit architecture.

For each basic data type, a class method exists that allocates an NSNumber object and sets it to a specified value. These methods begin with numberWith followed by the type, as in numberWithLong:, numberWithFloat:, and so on. In addition, instance methods can be used to set a previously alloc'ed NSNumber object to a specified value. These all begin with initWith, as in initWithLong: and initWithFloat:.

Table 15.1 lists the class and instance methods for setting values for NSNumber objects and the corresponding instance methods for retrieving their values.

> **Note**
>
> In versions of Xcode earlier than 4.2, it mattered more which version of the method you used. The class method would create an object that was *autoreleased*, whereas the alloc'ed versions created objects whose memory you were responsible for releasing when you were done using them (under iOS). The introduction of Automatic Reference Counting (ARC) to Objective-C means that a strong motivation no longer exists to use one form of a method over the other because memory management is now handled automatically.

Table 15.1 NSNumber **Creation and Retrieval Methods**

Creation and Initialization Class Method	Initialization Instance Method	Retrieval Instance Method
numberWithChar:	initWithChar:	charValue
numberWithUnsignedChar:	initWithUnsignedChar:	unsignedCharValue
numberWithShort:	initWithShort:	shortValue
numberWithUnsignedShort:	initWithUnsignedShort:	unsignedShortValue
numberWithInteger:	initWithInteger:	integerValue
numberWithUnsignedInteger:	initWithUnsignedInteger:	unsignedIntegerValue
numberWithInt:	initWithInt:	intValue
numberWithUnsignedInt:	initWithUnsignedInt:	unsignedIntValue
numberWithLong:	initWithLong:	longValue
numberWithUnsignedLong:	initWithUnsignedLong:	unsignedLongValue
numberWithLongLong:	initWithLongLong:	longlongValue
numberWithUnsignedLongLong:	initWithUnsignedLongLong:	unsignedLongLongValue
numberWithFloat:	initWithFloat:	floatValue
numberWithDouble:	initWithDouble:	doubleValue
numberWithBool:	initWithBool:	boolValue

Returning to Program 15.1, the program next uses the class methods to create long, char, float, and double NSNumber objects. Notice what happens after you create a double object with the line

```
myNumber = [NSNumber numberWithDouble: 12345e+15];
```

and then try to (incorrectly) retrieve and display its value with the following line:

```
NSLog (@"%li", (long) [myNumber integerValue]);
```

We show the output as -9223372036854775808, but you may get a different result because the access is not valid. Also, you get no error message from the system. In general, it's up to you to ensure that if you store a value in an NSNumber object, you retrieve it in a consistent manner.

Inside the if statement, the message expression

```
[intNumber isEqualToNumber: floatNumber]
```

uses the isEqualToNumber: method to numerically compare two NSNumber objects. The program tests the returned BOOL value to see whether the two numbers are equal.

You can use the compare: method to test whether one numeric value is numerically less than, equal to, or greater than another. The message expression

```
[intNumber compare: myNumber]
```

returns the value NSOrderedAscending if the numeric value stored in intNumber is less than the numeric value contained in myNumber, returns the value NSOrderedSame if the two numbers are equal, and returns the value NSOrderedDescending if the first number is greater than the second. These values are defined in the header file NSObject.h, which is included when you import Foundation.h.

Note that you *cannot change the value of a previously created* NSNumber object. For example, this does not work:

```
NSNumber *myNumber = [[NSNumber alloc] initWithInt: 50];
...
[myNumber initWithInt: 1000];
```

This last statement will cause your program to crash when it is run. All number objects must be newly created, meaning that you must invoke either one of the methods listed in the first column of Table 15.1 on the NSNumber class or one of the methods listed in the second column using the result from the alloc method, as shown in the first line of the previous example.

Just to make sure you understand the distinction in using numberWithInt: versus numberWithInteger:, just follow these rules:

1. If you create an integer using numberWithInt:, you should retrieve its value using intValue, and you can display its value using %i as the format characters.

2. If you create an integer using numberWithInteger:, you should retrieve its value using integerValue, and you should cast it to a long if it is displayed or used to format a string with a method like stringWithFormat:. The format characters to use would be %li in such cases.

A similar discussion applies to using numberWithUnsignedInt: versus numberWithUnsignedInteger:.

A recent extension to the Objective-C language allows number objects to be created within your program by using the notation @*expression*. Take a look at Program 15.2 to see how you can use this syntax.

Program 15.2

```
// Working with Literal Number Objects

#import <Foundation/Foundation.h>

int main (int argc, char * argv[])
{
    @autoreleasepool {
        NSNumber            *myNumber, *floatNumber, *intNumber;
        NSInteger           myInt;

        // integer

        intNumber = @100;
        myInt = [intNumber integerValue];
        NSLog (@"%li", (long) myInt);

        // long value

        myNumber = @0xabcdefL;
         NSLog (@"%lx", [myNumber longValue]);

        myNumber = @'X';
        NSLog (@"%c", [myNumber charValue]);

        // float value

        floatNumber = @100.0f;
        NSLog (@"%g", [floatNumber floatValue]);
    }

    return 0;
}
```

Program 15.2   **Output**

```
100
abcdef
X
100
```

Program 15.2 shows number objects created from simple objects, but you could also write an expression such as the following:

```
NSNumber *center = @((start + end) / 2.0);
```

Note that you need to use parenthesis after the @ if the value that follows is an expression or a variable. You will encounter NSNumber objects again in programs throughout the remainder of this chapter. You might want to look at the documentation for the NSDecimalNumber class before moving on to the next section. That class is a subclass of NSNumber and provides methods for doing arithmetic with numbers at the object level.

String Objects

You have encountered string objects in your programs before. Whenever you enclosed a sequence of character strings inside a pair of double quotes, as in

```
@"Programming is fun"
```

you created a character string object in Objective-C. The Foundation framework supports a class called NSString for working with character string objects. Whereas C-style strings consist of char characters, NSString objects consist of unichar characters. A unichar character is a multibyte character according to the Unicode standard. This enables you to work with character sets that can contain literally millions of characters. Luckily, you don't have to worry about the internal representation of the characters in your strings because the NSString class automatically handles this for you.[1] By using the methods from this class, you can more easily develop applications that can be *localized*—that is, made to work in different languages around the world.

As you know, you create a constant character string object in Objective-C by putting the @ character in front of the string of double-quoted characters. So, the expression

```
@"Programming is fun"
```

creates a constant character string object. In particular, it is a constant character string that belongs to the class NSConstantString. NSConstantString is a subclass of the string object class NSString.

More on the NSLog Function

Program 15.3, which follows, shows how to define an NSString object and assign an initial value to it. It also shows how to use the format characters %@ to display an NSString object.

---

[1] Currently, unichar characters occupy 16 bits, but the Unicode standard provides for characters larger than that size. So in the future, unichar characters might be larger than 16 bits. The bottom line is to never make an assumption about the size of a Unicode character.

Program 15.3

```
#import <Foundation/Foundation.h>

int main (int argc, char * argv[])
{
    @autoreleasepool {
        NSString *str = @"Programming is fun";

        NSLog (@"%@", str);
    }
    return 0;
}
```

Program 15.3   **Output**

```
Programming is fun
```

In the line

```
NSString *str = @"Programming is fun";
```

the constant string object Programming is fun is assigned to the NSString variable str. Its value is then displayed using NSLog.

The NSLog format characters %@ can be used to display not just NSString objects, but other objects as well. For example, given the following

```
NSNumber *intNumber = @100;
```

the NSLog call

```
NSLog (@"%@", intNumber);
```

produces the following output:

```
100
```

The description Method

You can also use the %@ format characters to display the entire contents of arrays, dictionaries, and sets. In fact, you can use them to display objects from your own classes, as well, as long as you override the description method inherited by your class. If you do not override the method, NSLog simply displays the name of the class the object belongs to and the address of the object in memory. That is the default implementation for the description method inherited from the NSObject class.

Following is an example of a description method that you could add to your Fraction class's implementation section to have it format a Fraction object. This uses NSString's stringWithFormat: method; a method that resembles NSLog but, unlike the function, the purpose of this method is to return the formatted string as the result, rather than writing it to the console:

```
-(NSString *) description
{
    return [NSString stringWithFormat: @"%i/%i", numerator, denominator];
}
```

> **Note**
>
> Methods such as stringWithFormat: allow a variable number of arguments to be provided (in this case, the format string and the data to be formatted). Such arguments are provided to the method as a comma-separated list of values.

With this method defined in your Fraction class (statements and with two Fraction objects f1 and f2 set appropriately), you could then write statements like the following in your program:

```
sum = [f1 add: f2];
NSLog (@"The sum of %@ and %@ is %@", f1, f2, sum);
```

Which result in a single line of output like this:

```
The sum of 1/2 and 1/4 is 3/4
```

Adding your own description method to your classes is a good debugging tool; it allows you to display your objects in a meaningful way.

Mutable Versus Immutable Objects

When you create a string object by writing an expression such as

```
@"Programming is fun"
```

you create an object whose contents cannot be changed. This is referred to as an *immutable* object. The NSString class deals with immutable strings. You will often want to deal with strings whose characters you can change. For example, you might want to delete some characters from a string or perform a search-and-replace operation on a string. You handle these types of strings through the NSMutableString class.

Program 15.4 shows basic ways to work with immutable character strings in your programs.

Program 15.4

```
// Basic String Operations

#import <Foundation/Foundation.h>
```

```
int main (int argc, char * argv[])
{
   @autoreleasepool {
      NSString  *str1 = @"This is string A";
      NSString  *str2 = @"This is string B";
      NSString  *res;
      NSComparisonResult  compareResult;

      // Count the number of characters

      NSLog (@"Length of str1: %lu", [str1 length]);

      // Copy one string to another

      res = [NSString stringWithString: str1];
      NSLog (@"copy: %@", res);

      // Copy one string to the end of another

      str2 = [str1 stringByAppendingString: str2];
      NSLog (@"Concatenation: %@", str2);
      // Test if two strings are equal

      if ([str1 isEqualToString: res] == YES)
         NSLog (@"str1 == res");
      else
         NSLog (@"str1 != res");

      // Test if one string is <, == or > than another

      compareResult = [str1 compare: str2];

      if  (compareResult == NSOrderedAscending)
         NSLog (@"str1 < str2");
      else if (compareResult == NSOrderedSame)
         NSLog (@"str1 == str2");
      else  // must be NSOrderedDescending
         NSLog (@"str1 > str2");

      // Convert a string to uppercase

      res = [str1 uppercaseString];
      NSLog (@"Uppercase conversion: %s", [res UTF8String]);

      // Convert a string to lowercase

      res = [str1 lowercaseString];
```

```
    NSLog (@"Lowercase conversion: %@", res);

    NSLog (@"Original string: %@", str1);
  }
  return 0;
}
```

Program 15.4 **Output**

```
Length of str1: 16
Copy: This is string A
Concatenation: This is string AThis is string B
str1 == res
str1 < str2
Uppercase conversion: THIS IS STRING A
Lowercase conversion: this is string a
Original string: This is string A
```

Program 15.4 first declares three immutable NSString objects: str1, str2, and res. The first two are initialized to constant character string objects. The declaration

```
NSComparisonResult compareResult;
```

declares compareResult to hold the result of the string comparison that will be performed later in the program.

You can use the length method to count the number of characters in a string. It returns an unsigned integer value of type NSUInteger. The output verifies that the string

```
@"This is string A"
```

contains 16 characters. The statement

```
res = [NSString stringWithString: str1];
```

shows how to create a new character string with the contents of another. The resulting NSString object is assigned to res and is then displayed to verify the results. An actual copy of the string contents is made here, not just another reference to the same string in memory. That means that str1 and res refer to two different string objects, which is different from just performing a simple assignment like this:

```
res = str1;
```

As previously discussed, this statement just creates another reference to the same object in memory.

The stringByAppendingString: method can join two character strings. So, the expression

```
[str1 stringByAppendingString: str2]
```

creates a new string object that consists of the characters str1 followed by str2, returning the result. The original string objects, str1 and str2, are not affected by this operation. (They cannot be because they are both immutable string objects.)

The isEqualToString: method is used next in the program to test to see whether two character strings are equal—that is, whether they contain the same characters. You can use the compare: method instead if you need to determine the ordering of two character strings (for example, if you want to sort an array of them). Similar to the compare: method you used earlier for comparing two NSNumber objects, the result of the comparison is NSOrderedAscending if the first string is lexically less than the second string, NSOrderedSame if the two strings are equal, and NSOrderedDescending if the first string is lexically greater than the second. If you don't want to perform a case-sensitive comparison, use the caseInsensitiveCompare: method instead of compare: to compare two strings. In such a case, the two string objects @"Gregory" and @"gregory" compare as equal with caseInsensitiveCompare.

The uppercaseString and lowercaseString are the last two NSString methods used in Program 15.4 to convert strings to uppercase and lowercase, respectively. Again, the conversion does not affect the original strings, as the last line of output verifies.

Make sure that you understand that str1 and str2 are declared as immutable string objects, which means the characters in the string objects they reference cannot be changed. However, the references, str1 and str2, *can be changed*. That is, these two variables can be reassigned to reference different immutable string objects. This is a very important point. Let's look at this again with some figures. Figure 15.1 shows the variables res and str1 just after they've just been declared and initialized. The variable res is not set to any initial value, so its contents appear empty. In contrast, str1 is set to point to the constant character string object @"This is string A" that is stored somewhere in memory.

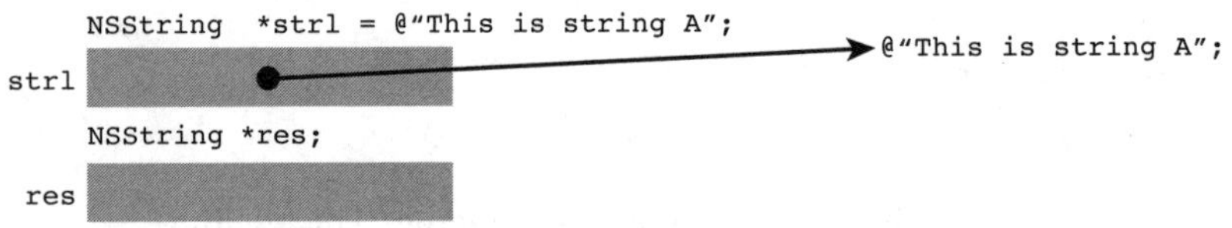

Figure 15.1   Immutable string object declaration and initialization

When we send the uppercaseString message to str1 in Program 15.3, we get a new string created from the character str1, with any lowercase characters in that string object replaced by uppercase characters, as shown in Figure 15.2.

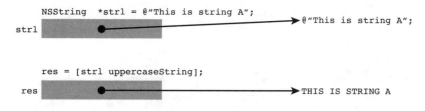

Figure 15.2   Sending the `uppercaseString` message to a string object

Note that `str1` still points to the original string object and that a new string object has been created.

Sending the `lowercaseString` message to `str1` works the same way: A new string object is created that consists of all the uppercase characters from `str1` converted to lowercase. The reference to that newly created string object is then stored in the variable `res`. This is depicted in Figure 15.3. Note that a reference to the uppercase string that was created in the previous step no longer exists. You do not have to worry about that; the system's memory management cleans that up for you.

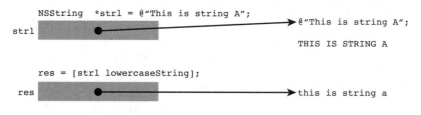

Figure 15.3   Sending the `lowercaseString` message to a string object

Program 15.5 illustrates additional methods for dealing with strings. These methods enable you to extract substrings from a string and to search one string for the occurrence of another.

Some methods require that you identify a substring by specifying a range. A *range* consists of a starting index number plus a character count. Index numbers begin with zero, so you specify the first three characters in a string by the pair of numbers {0, 3}. Some methods of the `NSString` class (and other Foundation classes, too) use the special data type `NSRange` to create a range specification. It is actually a `typedef` definition for a structure that has two members, `location` and `length`, each defined as type `NSUInteger`. Program 15.5 uses this data type.

Note

You can read about structures in Chapter 13, "Underlying C Language Features." However, you can probably gain enough information to work with them from the discussion that follows in this chapter.

Program 15.5

```
// Basic String Operations - Continued

#import <Foundation/Foundation.h>

int main (int argc, char * argv[])
{
   @autoreleasepool {
      NSString  *str1 = @"This is string A";
      NSString  *res;
      NSRange    subRange;

      // Extract first 3 chars from string

      res = [str1 substringToIndex: 3];
      NSLog (@"First 3 chars of str1: %@", res);

      // Extract chars to end of string starting at index 5

      res = [str1 substringFromIndex: 5];
      NSLog (@"Chars from index 5 of str1: %@", res);

      // Extract chars from index 8 through 13 (6 chars)

      res = [[str1 substringFromIndex: 8] substringToIndex: 6];
      NSLog (@"Chars from index 8 through 13: %@", res);

      // An easier way to do the same thing

      res = [str1 substringWithRange: NSMakeRange (8, 6)];
      NSLog (@"Chars from index 8 through 13: %@", res);

      // Locate one string inside another

      subRange = [str1 rangeOfString: @"string A"];
      NSLog (@"String is at index %lu, length is %lu",
         subRange.location, subRange.length);


      subRange = [str1 rangeOfString: @"string B"];

      if (subRange.location == NSNotFound)
         NSLog (@"String not found");
      else
         NSLog (@"String is at index %lu, length is %lu",
```

```
            subRange.location, subRange.length);

    }
    return 0;
}
```

Program 15.5 **Output**

```
First 3 chars of str1: Thi
Chars from index 5 of str1: is string A
Chars from index 8 through 13: string
Chars from index 8 through 13: string
String is at index 8, length is 8
String not found
```

The substringToIndex: method creates a substring from the leading characters in a string up to but not including the specified index number. Because indexing begins at zero, the argument of 3 extracts characters 0, 1, and 2 from the string and returns the resulting string object. For any of the string methods that take an index number as one of its arguments, you get a "Range or index out of bounds" error message if you provide an invalid index number in the string.

The substringFromIndex: method returns a substring from the receiver beginning with the character at the specified index and up through the end of the string.

The expression

```
res = [[str1 substringFromIndex: 8] substringToIndex: 6];
```

shows how the two methods can be combined to extract a substring of characters from inside a string. The substringFromIndex: method is first used to extract characters from index number 8 through the end of the string; then substringToIndex: is applied to the result to get the first six characters. The net result is a substring representing the range of characters {8, 6} from the original string.

The substringWithRange: method does in one step what we just did in two: It takes a range and returns a character in the specified range. The special function

```
NSMakeRange (8, 6)
```

creates a range from its argument and returns the result. This is given as the argument to the substringWithRange: method.

To locate one string inside another, you can use the rangeOfString: method. If the specified string is found inside the receiver, the returned range specifies precisely where in the string it was found. However, if the string is not found, the range returned has its location member set to NSNotFound.

So, the statement

```
subRange = [str1 rangeOfString: @"string A"];
```

assigns the NSRange structure returned by the method to the NSRange variable subRange. Be sure to remember that subRange is not an object variable, but a *structure* variable. (The declaration for subRange in the program also does not contain an asterisk; that is often a good clue that you are not dealing with an object. A notable exception is the id type.) You can retrieve its members by using the structure member operator dot (.). So, the expression subRange.location gives the value of the location member of the structure, and subRange.length gives the length member. These values are passed to the NSLog function to be displayed.

Mutable Strings

You can use the NSMutableString class to create string objects whose characters can be changed. Because this class is a subclass of NSString, you can use all of NSString's methods as well.

When we speak of mutable versus immutable string objects, we are talking about changing the actual characters within the string. Either a mutable or an immutable string object can always be set to a completely different string object during execution of the program. This was stressed in the discussion of Program 15.4. So, for example, consider the following:

```
str1 = @"This is a string";
   ...
str1 = [str1 substringFromIndex: 5];
```

In this case, str1 is first set to a constant character string object. Later in the program, it is set to a substring. In such a case, str1 could be declared as either a mutable or an immutable string object. Be sure that you understand this point.

Program 15.6 shows some ways to work with mutable strings in your programs.

Program 15.6

```
// Basic String Operations - Mutable Strings

#import <Foundation/Foundation.h>

int main (int argc, char * argv[])
{
    @autoreleasepool {
        NSString    *str1 = @"This is string A";
        NSString    *search, *replace;
        NSMutableString  *mstr;
        NSRange     substr;
```

```
// Create mutable string from nonmutable

mstr = [NSMutableString  stringWithString: str1];
NSLog (@"%@", mstr);

// Insert characters

[mstr insertString: @" mutable" atIndex: 7];
NSLog (@"%@", mstr);

// Effective concatenation if insert at end

[mstr insertString: @" and string B" atIndex: [mstr length]];
NSLog (@"%@", mstr);

//  Or can use appendString directly

[mstr appendString: @" and string C"];
NSLog (@"%@", mstr);

// Delete substring based on range

[mstr deleteCharactersInRange: NSMakeRange (16, 13)];
NSLog (@"%@", mstr);

// Find range first and then use it for deletion

substr = [mstr  rangeOfString: @"string B and "];

if (substr.location != NSNotFound) {
   [mstr deleteCharactersInRange: substr];
   NSLog (@"%@", mstr);
}

// Set the mutable string directly

[mstr setString: @"This is string A"];
NSLog (@"%@", mstr);

// Now let's replace a range of chars with another

[mstr replaceCharactersInRange: NSMakeRange(8, 8)
                  withString: @"a mutable string"];
NSLog (@"%@", mstr);

// Search and replace
```

```
        search = @"This is";
        replace = @"An example of";

        substr = [mstr  rangeOfString: search];

        if (substr.location != NSNotFound) {
           [mstr replaceCharactersInRange: substr
                               withString: replace];
           NSLog (@"%@", mstr);
        }

        // Search and replace all occurrences

        search = @"a";
        replace = @"X";

        substr = [mstr rangeOfString: search];

        while (substr.location != NSNotFound) {
           [mstr replaceCharactersInRange: substr
                               withString: replace];
             substr = [mstr rangeOfString: search];
        }

        NSLog (@"%@", mstr);

    }
    return 0;
}
```

Program 15.6   **Output**

```
This is string A
This is mutable string A
This is mutable string A and string B
This is mutable string A and string B and string C
This is mutable string B and string C
This is mutable string C
This is string A
This is a mutable string
An example of a mutable string
An exXmple of X mutXble string
```

The declaration

```
NSMutableString *mstr;
```

declares `mstr` to be a variable that holds a character string object whose contents might change during execution of the program. The line

```
mstr = [NSMutableString stringWithString: str1];
```

sets `mstr` to the string object whose contents are a copy of the characters in str1, or "This is string A". When the `stringWithString:` method is sent to the `NSMutableString` class, a mutable string object is returned. When it is sent to the `NSString` class, as in Program 15.5, you get an immutable string object instead.

The `insertString:atIndex:` method inserts the specified character string into the receiver beginning at the specified index number. In this case, you insert the string @" mutable" into the string beginning at index number 7, or in front of the eighth character in the string. Unlike the immutable string object methods, no value is returned here because the receiver is modified; you can do that because it is a mutable string object.

The second `insertString:atIndex:` invocation uses the `length` method to insert one character string at the end of another. The `appendString:` method makes this task a little simpler.

By using the `deleteCharactersInRange:` method, you can remove a specified number of characters from a string. The range {16, 13}, when applied to the string

```
This is mutable string A and string B and string C
```

deletes the 13 characters "string A and " beginning with index number 16 (or the 17th character in the string), as shown in Figure 15.4.

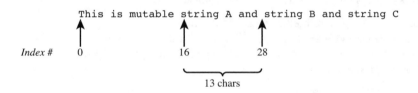

Figure 15.4   Indexing into a string

The `rangeOfString:` method is used in the lines that follow in Program 15.5 to show how a string can first be located and then deleted. After first verifying that the string @"string B and" does exist in `mstr`, the `deleteCharactersInRange:` method is used to delete the characters, using the range returned from the `rangeOfString:` method as its argument.

You can use the `setString:` method to directly set the contents of a mutable string object. After using this method to set `mstr` to the string @"This is string A", the `replaceCharactersInRange:withString:` method replaces some of the characters in the string with another string. The sizes of the strings do not have to be the same; you can replace one string with another of equal or unequal sizes. So, in the statement

```
[mstr replaceCharactersInRange: NSMakeRange(8, 8)
                      withString: @"a mutable string"];
```

the 8 characters `"string A"` are replaced with the 16 characters `"a mutable string"`.

The remaining lines in the program example show how to perform search and replace operations. In the first case, you locate the string `@"This is"` inside the string `mstr`, which has been set to `@"This is a mutable string"`. This string is found inside the search string and gets replaced by the string `@"An example of"`. The net result is that `mstr` gets changed to the string `@"An example of a mutable string"`.

The program next sets up a loop to illustrate how to implement a search-and-replace-all operation. The search string is set to `@"a"` and the replacement string is set to `@"X"`.

Note that if the replacement string also contains the search string (for example, consider replacing the string `"a"` with the string `"aX"`), you end up with an infinite loop.

Second, if the replacement string is empty (that is, if it contains no characters), you effectively delete all occurrences of the search string. An empty constant character string object is specified by an adjacent pair of quotation marks, with no intervening spaces:

```
replace = @"";
```

Of course, if you just want to delete an occurrence of a string, you could use the `deleteCharactersInRange:` method instead, as you have already seen.

Finally, the `NSMutableString` class also contains a method called `replaceOccurrencesOfString:withString:options:range:` that you can use to do a search-and-replace-all on a string. In fact, you could have replaced the `while` loop from Program 15.5 with this single statement:

```
[mstr replaceOccurrencesOfString: search
                      withString: replace
                         options: nil
                           range: NSMakeRange (0, [mstr length])];
```

This achieves the same result and averts the potential of an infinite loop because the method prevents such a thing from happening.

The `NSString` class contains more than 100 methods that can work with string objects. Table 15.2 summarizes some of the more commonly used ones, and Table 15.3 lists some of the additional methods that the `NSMutableString` class provides. Some other `NSString` methods (such as working with pathnames and reading the contents of a file into a string) are introduced to you throughout the remainder of this book. You should look at the documentation for the `NSString` class to just get a better idea of the wide variety of methods that are at your disposal.

Table 15.2   **Common** `NSString` **Methods**

Method	Description
+(id) stringWithContentsOfFile: *path* encoding: *enc* error: *err*	Creates a new string and sets it to the *path* contents of a file specified by *path* using character encoding *enc*, returning error in *err* if non-nil
+(id) stringWithContentsOfURL: *url* encoding: *enc* error: *err*	Creates a new string and sets it to the contents of *url* using character encoding *enc*, returning error in *err* if non-nil
+(id) string	Creates a new empty string
+(id) stringWithString: *nsstring*	Creates a new string, setting it to *nsstring*
+(NSString *) stringWithFormat: *format, arg1, arg2, arg3* ...	Creates a new string according to the specified *format* and arguments *arg1, arg2, arg3* ...
-(id) initWithString: *nsstring*	Sets a newly allocated string to *nsstring*
-(id) initWithContentsOfFile: *path* encoding: *enc* error: *err*	Sets a string to the contents of a file specified by *path*
-(id) initWithContentsOfURL: *url* encoding: *enc* error: *err*	Sets a string to the contents of *url* (NSURL *) *url* using character encoding enc, returning error in *err* if non-nil
-(NSUInteger) length	Returns the number of characters in the string
-(unichar) characterAtIndex: *i*	Returns the Unicode character at index *i*
-(NSString *) substringFromIndex: *i*	Returns a substring from the character at *i* to the end
-(NSString *) substringWithRange: *range*	Returns a substring based on a specified range
-(NSString *) substringToIndex: *i*	Returns a substring from the start of the string up to the character at index *i*
-(NSComparator *) caseInsensitiveCompare: *nsstring*	Compares two strings, ignoring case
-(NSComparator *) compare: *nsstring*	Compares two strings
-(BOOL) hasPrefix: *nsstring*	Tests whether a string begins with *nsstring*
-(BOOL) hasSuffix: *nsstring*	Tests whether a string ends with *nsstring*
-(BOOL) isEqualToString: *nsstring*	Tests whether two strings are equal
-(NSString *) capitalizedString	Returns a string with the first letter of every word capitalized (and the remaining letters in each word converted to lowercase)
-(NSString *) lowercaseString	Returns a string converted to lowercase
-(NSString *) uppercaseString	Returns a string converted to uppercase

Method	Description
`-(const char *) UTF8String`	Returns a string converted to a UTF-8 C-style character string
`-(double) doubleValue`	Returns a double precision floating-point representation of the string
`-(float) floatValue`	Returns a floating-point representation of the string
`-(NSInteger) integerValue`	Returns an `NSInteger` representation of the string
`-(int) intValue`	Returns the integer representation of the string

In Tables 15.2 and 15.3, `url` is an `NSURL` object, `path` is an `NSString` object specifying the path to a file, `nsstring` is an `NSString` object, `i` is an `NSUInteger` value representing a valid character number in a string, `enc` is an `NSStringEncoding` object that specifies the character encoding, `err` is an `NSError` object that describes an error if one occurs, `size` and `opts` are `NSUIntegers`, and `range` is an `NSRange` structure indicating a valid range of characters within a string.

The methods in Table 15.3 either create or modify `NSMutableString` objects.

Table 15.3   **Common** `NSMutableString` **Methods**

Method	Description
`+(id) stringWithCapacity: size`	Creates a string initially containing `size` characters.
`-(id) initWithCapacity: size`	Initializes a string with an initial capacity of `size` characters.
`-(void) setString: nsstring`	Sets a string to `nsstring`.
`-(void) appendString: nsstring`	Appends `nsstring` to the end of the receiver.
`-(void) deleteCharactersInRange: range`	Deletes characters in a specified `range`.
`-(void) insertString: nsstring atIndex: i`	Inserts `nsstring` into the receiver starting at index i.
`-(void) replaceCharactersInRange: range withString: nsstring`	Replaces characters in a specified `range` with `nsstring`.

Method	Description
-(void) replaceOccurrencesOfString: *nsstring* withString: *nsstring2* options: *opts* range: *range*	Replaces all occurrences of *nsstring* with *nsstring2* within a specified *range* and according to options *opts*. Options can include a bitwise-ORed combination of NSBackwardsSearch (the search starts from the end of range), NSAnchoredSearch (*nsstring* must match from the beginning of the range only), NSLiteralSearch (performs a character-by-character comparison), and NSCaseInsensitiveSearch.

NSString objects are used extensively throughout the remainder of this text. If you need to parse strings into tokens, you can take a look at Foundation's NSScanner class.

Array Objects

A Foundation array is an ordered collection of objects. Most often, elements in an array are of one particular type, but that's not required. Just as there are mutable and immutable strings, there are mutable and immutable arrays. *Immutable* arrays are handled by the NSArray class, whereas *mutable* ones are handled by NSMutableArray. The latter is a subclass of the former, which means it inherits its methods.

Program 15.7 sets up an array to store the names of the months of the year and then prints them.

Program 15.7

```
#import <Foundation/Foundation.h>

int main (int argc, char * argv[])
{
    int    i;
    @autoreleasepool {
        // Create an array to contain the month names

        NSArray  *monthNames = [NSArray  arrayWithObjects:
            @"January", @"February", @"March", @"April",
            @"May", @"June", @"July", @"August", @"September",
            @"October", @"November", @"December", nil];

        // Now list all the elements in the array
```

```
        NSLog (@"Month     Name");
        NSLog (@"=====     ====");

        for (i = 0; i < 12; ++i)
            NSLog (@" %2i      %@", i + 1, [monthNames objectAtIndex: i]);
    }
    return 0;
}
```

Program 15.7 **Output**

Month	Name
=====	====
1	January
2	February
3	March
4	April
5	May
6	June
7	July
8	August
9	September
10	October
11	November
12	December

You can use the class method `arrayWithObjects:` to create an array with a list of objects as its elements. In such a case, the objects are listed in order and are separated by commas. This is a special syntax used by methods that can take a variable number of arguments. To mark the end of the list, `nil` must be specified as the last value in the list; it is not actually stored inside the array.

Program 15.7 `monthNames` is set to the 12 string values specified by the arguments to `arrayWithObjects:`.

Elements are identified in an array by their index numbers. Similar to `NSString` objects, indexing begins with zero. So, an array containing 12 elements has valid index numbers 0–11. To retrieve an element of an array using its index number, you use the `objectAtIndex:` method.

The program simply executes a `for` loop to extract each element from the array using the `objectAtIndex:` method. Each retrieved element is displayed with `NSLog`.

Objective-C enables you to easily set up an `NSArray` of objects using the following syntax:

`@[elem1, elem2, ... elemn]`

In this case, you do not put `nil` at the end of the list of elements.

Objective-C allows you to reference array elements using this syntax:

array[*index*]

Which is equivalent to writing the following expression:

[*array* objectAtIndex: *index*]

You can also store a reference to an object inside an array using this syntax:

array[index] = object

which is the same as writing this:

[*array* setObject: *object* forIndex: *index*]

Program 15.8 is a rewrite of Program 15.7 illustrating the alternate syntax for defining arrays and referencing elements.

Program 15.8

```
#import <Foundation/Foundation.h>

int main (int argc, char * argv[])
{
   int    i;
   @autoreleasepool {
      // Create an array to contain the month names

      NSArray  *monthNames =  @[@"January", @"February", @"March", @"April",
          @"May", @"June", @"July", @"August", @"September",
          @"October", @"November", @"December"];

      // Now list all the elements in the array

      NSLog (@"Month    Name");
      NSLog (@"=====    ====");

      for (i = 0; i < 12; ++i)
         NSLog (@" %2i      %@", i + 1, monthNames[i]);
   }
   return 0;
}
```

Program 15.9 simply creates an array of 10 number objects, whose values range from 0 through 9. The values are retrieved for display using a simple `for` loop and then the entire array is displayed again using just the `%@` format characters in the `NSLog` format string. Later in this chapter, you learn another technique known as *fast enumeration* that you can also use to sequence through the elements of your array.

Program 15.9

```
#import <Foundation/Foundation.h>

int main (int argc, char * argv[])
{
    @autoreleasepool {
        NSMutableArray   *numbers = [NSMutableArray array];
        int              i;

        // Create an array with the number 0-9

        for (i = 0; i < 10; ++i )
            numbers[i] = @(i);

        // Sequence through the array and display the values

        for (i = 0; i < 10; ++i )
            NSLog (@"%@", numbers[i]);

        // Look how NSLog can display it with a single %@ format

        NSLog (@"====== Using a single NSLog");
        NSLog (@"%@", numbers);
    }
    return 0;
}
```

Program 15.9   Output

```
2010-11-12 15:25:42.701 prog15.7[6379:903] 0
2010-11-12 15:25:42.704 prog15.7[6379:903] 1
2010-11-12 15:25:42.704 prog15.7[6379:903] 2
2010-11-12 15:25:42.704 prog15.7[6379:903] 3
2010-11-12 15:25:42.705 prog15.7[6379:903] 4
2010-11-12 15:25:42.705 prog15.7[6379:903] 5
2010-11-12 15:25:42.705 prog15.7[6379:903] 6
2010-11-12 15:25:42.706 prog15.7[6379:903] 7
2010-11-12 15:25:42.706 prog15.7[6379:903] 8
2010-11-12 15:25:42.706 prog15.7[6379:903] 9
2010-11-12 15:25:42.707 prog15.7[6379:903] ====== Using a single NSLog
2010-11-12 15:25:42.707 prog15.7[6379:903] (
    0,
```

```
        1,
        2,
        3,
        4,
        5,
        6,
        7,
        8,
        9
)
```

(Here we left in all NSLog output just to distinguish the difference in appearance between the first and second sets of output.)

The NSMutableArray method array simply creates an empty mutable array object for you. The number of elements in the array is not specified and the array can grow as large as you like.

Recall that you cannot store a basic data type like an integer into a collection such as an array. So, we make an NSNumber object out of each values of i, which ranged from 0 through 9.

If you want to add an object to the end of an array, you can use the addObject: method. So, in Program 15.9, we could have written

```
[numbers addObject: @(i)];
```

to add each NSNumber object that is created, in turn, to the end of the array numbers.

The program then enters a for loop to display each of the number objects stored in the array.

Finally, in Program 15.9, you see how a single %@ can be used in NSLog's format string to display the entire numbers array at once.

> **Note**
>
> How does NSLog know how to display the objects stored in the array? For each element in the array, NSLog uses the description method from the class the element belongs to. If it is the default method inherited from NSObject, you just get the object's class and address, as previously noted. In this case, however, you get a meaningful display, indicating that a customized description method has been implemented in the NSNumber class.

The Foundation classes for working with arrays provide many conveniences. However, in the case of manipulating large arrays of numbers with complex algorithms, learning how to perform such a task using the lower-level array constructs provided by the underlying C language might be more efficient, in terms of both memory usage and execution speed. Refer to the section titled "Arrays" in Chapter 13 for more information.

Making an Address Book

Let's take a look at an example that starts to combine a lot of what you have learned to this point by creating an address book.[2] Your address book will contain address cards. For the sake of simplicity, your address cards will contain only a person's name and email address. Extending this concept to other information, such as address and phone number, is straightforward, but we leave that as an exercise for you at the end of this chapter.

The two classes we create, an `AddressBook` and an `AddressCard` class, and the relationship between the two are depicted in Figure 15.5.

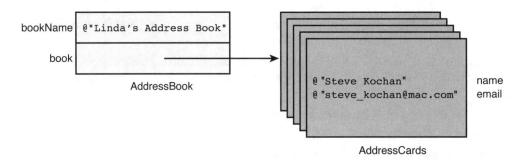

Figure 15.5   An `AddressBook` that contains `AddressCards`

Creating an Address Card

We start by defining the `AddressCard` class. You want the capability to create a new address card, set its name and email fields, retrieve those fields, and print the card. In a graphics environment, you could use some handy methods to draw your card on your computer's screen or iOS device's window. But here you stick to a simple Console interface to display your address cards.

Program 15.8 shows the interface file for your new `AddressCard` class. We're not going to synthesize the accessor methods yet; writing them yourself offers valuable lessons.

Program 15.10   **Interface File** `AddressCard.h`

```
#import <Foundation/Foundation.h>

@interface AddressCard: NSObject

-(void) setName: (NSString *) theName;
-(void) setEmail: (NSString *) theEmail;
```

---

[2]   OS X and iOS provide an entire Address Book framework that offers extremely powerful capabilities for working with address books.

```
-(NSString *) name;
-(NSString *) email;

-(void) print;

@end
```

This is straightforward, as is the implementation file in Program 15.10.

Program 15.10   **Implementation File** AddressCard.m

```
#import "AddressCard.h"

@implementation AddressCard
{
    NSString *name;
    NSString *email;
}

-(void) setName: (NSString *) theName
{
   name = [NSString stringWithString: theName];
}

-(void) setEmail: (NSString *) theEmail
{
   email = [NSString stringWithString: theEmail];
}

-(NSString *) name
{
    return name;
}

-(NSString *) email
{
    return email;
}

-(void) print
{
    NSLog (@"===================================");
    NSLog (@"|                                 |");
    NSLog (@"|  %-31s |", [name UTF8String]);
    NSLog (@"|  %-31s |", [email UTF8String]);
    NSLog (@"|                                 |");
```

```
      NSLog (@"|                                   |");
      NSLog (@"|                                   |");
      NSLog (@"|          O                  O     |");
      NSLog (@"====================================");
   }
}
@end
```

You could have the `setName:` and `setEmail:` methods store the objects directly in their respective instance variables with method definitions like these:

```
-(void) setName: (NSString *) theName
{
   name = theName;
}

-(void) setEmail: (NSString *) theEmail
{
   email = theEmail;
}
```

But the `AddressCard` object would not own its member objects. (It would contain only references to the arguments passed into the methods.) We talked about the motivation for an object to take ownership with respect to the `Rectangle` class owning its origin object in Chapter 8, "Inheritance."

The `print` method tries to present the user with a nice display of an address card in a format resembling a Rolodex card. (Anyone remember those?) The `%-31s` characters to `NSLog` indicate to display a UTF8 C-string within a field width of 31 characters, left-justified. This ensures that the right edges of your address card line up in the output. It's used in this example strictly for cosmetic reasons.

With your `AddressCard` class in hand, you can write a test program to create an address card, set its values, and display it (see Program 15.10).

Program 15.10   **Test Program**

```
#import "AddressCard.h"

int main (int argc, char * argv[])
{
   @autoreleasepool {
      NSString   *aName = @"Julia Kochan";
      NSString   *aEmail = @"jewls337@axlc.com";
      AddressCard   *card1 = [[AddressCard alloc] init];

      [card1 setName: aName];
      [card1 setEmail: aEmail];
```

```
        [card1 print];
    }
    return 0;
}
```

Program 15.10   **Output**

```
========================================
|                                      |
| Julia Kochan                         |
| jewls337@axlc.com                    |
|                                      |
|                                      |
|                                      |
|        O               O             |
========================================
```

Here are new `setName:` and `setEmail:` methods that can save a little work:

```
-(void)  setName: (NSString *) theName
{
    if (name != theName)
        name = [NSString stringWithString: theName];
}

-(void)  setEmail: (NSString *) theEmail
{
    if (email != theEmail)
        email = [NSString stringWithString: theEmail];
}
```

The `if` test is there in case someone sends into the setter the same object that's already stored in the instance variable. If the object being passed in is the same as what's stored, we don't have to do any work at all.

Synthesized `AddressCard` Methods

Now that we've discussed the correct way to write the accessor methods `setName:` and `setEmail:`, and you understand the important principles, we can go back and let the system generate the accessor methods for you. Consider the second version of the `AddressCard` interface file:

```
#import <Foundation/Foundation.h>

@interface AddressCard: NSObject

@property (copy, nonatomic) NSString *name, *email;
```

```
-(void) print;
@end
```

The line

```
@property (copy, nonatomic) NSString *name, *email;
```

lists the *attributes* `copy` and `nonatomic` for the properties. The `copy` attribute says to make a copy of the instance variable in its setter method, as you did in the version you wrote. The default action is to not make a copy, but to instead perform a simple assignment (that's the default attribute `assign`), an incorrect approach in this case, as we recently discussed.

The `nonatomic` attribute says that you don't need to worry about race conditions that could occur from multiple threads trying to access the instance variable at the same time. Chapter 18, "Copying Objects," discusses this topic in greater detail.

Program 15.11 is the new `AddressCard` implementation file that specifies that the accessor methods be synthesized. (Note that we removed the explicit declaration of our instance variables here because we now have properties listed for them.)

Program 15.11　**Implementation File** `AddressCard.m` **with Synthesized Methods**

```
#import "AddressCard.h"

@implementation AddressCard

@synthesize name, email;

-(void) print
{
    NSLog (@"===================================");
    NSLog (@"|                                 |");
    NSLog (@"|   %-31s |", [name UTF8String]);
    NSLog (@"|   %-31s |", [email UTF8String]);
    NSLog (@"|                                 |");
    NSLog (@"|                                 |");
    NSLog (@"|                                 |");
    NSLog (@"|        O              O         |");
    NSLog (@"===================================");

}
@end
```

Now let's add another method to your `AddressCard` class. You might want to set both the name and email fields of your card with one call. To do so, add a new method, `setName:andEmail:`.[3] The new method looks like this:

```
-(void) setName: (NSString *) theName andEmail: (NSString *) theEmail
{
   self.name = theName;
   self.email = theEmail;
}
```

Recall that writing

```
self.name = theName;
```

is the same as writing

```
[self setName: theName];
```

and therefore uses the setter method for the instance variable. Contrast that to writing

```
name = theName;
```

which instead bypasses the setter and assigns the argument's value directly to the instance variable.

By relying on the synthesized setter methods to set the appropriate instance variables (instead of setting them directly inside the method yourself), you add a level of abstraction and, therefore, make the program slightly more independent of its internal data structures. You also take advantage of the synthesized property's attributes, which, in this case, copy instead of assign the value to the instance variable.

Program 15.11 tests your new method.

Program 15.11   **Test Program**

```
#import "AddressCard.h"

int main (int argc, char * argv[])
{
   @autoreleasepool {
      NSString   *aName = @"Julia Kochan";
      NSString   *aEmail = @"jewls337@axlc.com";
      NSString   *bName = @"Tony Iannino";
      NSString   *bEmail = @"tony.iannino@techfitness.com";

      AddressCard   *card1 = [[AddressCard alloc] init];
```

[3]   You also might want an `initWithName:andEmail:` initialization method, but we don't show that here.

```
        AddressCard   *card2 = [[AddressCard alloc] init];

        [card1 setName: aName andEmail: aEmail];
        [card2 setName: bName andEmail: bEmail];

        [card1 print];
        [card2 print];
    }
    return 0;
}
```

Program 15.11   **Output**

```
======================================
|                                    |
| Julia Kochan                       |
| jewls337@axlc.com                  |
|                                    |
|                                    |
|                                    |
|        o            o              |
======================================


======================================
|                                    |
| Tony Iannino                       |
| tony.iannino@techfitness.com       |
|                                    |
|                                    |
|                                    |
|        o            o              |
======================================
```

The AddressBook **Class**

Your AddressCard class seems to be working okay. What if you want to work with a lot of AddressCards? It would make sense to collect them together, which is exactly what you will do by defining a new class called AddressBook. The AddressBook class will store the name of an address book and a collection of AddressCards, which you will store in an array object. To start, you want the ability to create a new address book, add new address cards to it, find out how many entries are in it, and list its contents. Later, you want to be able to search the address book, remove entries, possibly edit existing entries, sort it, or even make a copy of its contents.

Let's get started with a simple interface file (see Program 15.12).

Program 15.12   AddressBook.h **Interface File**

```
#import <Foundation/Foundation.h>
#import "AddressCard.h"

@interface AddressBook: NSObject

@property (nonatomic, copy) NSString *bookName;
@property (nonatomic, strong) NSMutableArray *book;

-(id)    initWithName: (NSString *) name;
-(void) addCard: (AddressCard *) theCard;
-(NSUInteger)   entries;
-(void) list;

@end
```

The strong attribute for a property says to make an additional reference to the object whenever the setter method is used. This influences the life span of the object. Chapter 17, "Memory Management and Automatic Reference Counting," describes it in greater detail.

The initWithName: method sets up the initial array to hold the address cards and store the name of the book, whereas the addCard: method adds an AddressCard to the book. The entries method reports the number of address cards in your book, and the list method gives a concise listing of its entire contents. Program 15.12 shows the implementation file for your AddressBook class.

Program 15.12   AddressBook.m **Implementation File**

```
#import "AddressBook.h"

@implementation AddressBook

@synthesize bookName, book;

// set up the AddressBook's name and an empty book

-(id) initWithName: (NSString *) name
{
   self = [super init];

   if (self) {
      bookName = [NSString stringWithString: name];
      book = [NSMutableArray array];
   }

   return self;
```

```
}

-(id) init
{
    return [self initWithName: @"NoName"];
}

-(void) addCard: (AddressCard *) theCard
{
    [book addObject: theCard];
}

-(NSUInteger) entries
{
    return [book count];
}

-(void) list
{
    NSLog (@"======== Contents of: %@ =========", bookName);

    for ( AddressCard *theCard in book )
        NSLog (@"%-20s    %-32s", [theCard.name UTF8String],
                    [theCard.email UTF8String]);

    NSLog (@"==================================================");
}
@end
```

The initWithName: method first calls the init method for the superclass to perform its initialization. Next, it makes a copy of the string passed in as the argument to the method and stores it in the bookName instance variable. This is followed by the creation of an empty NSMutableArray object that we assign to book.

You defined initWithName: to return an id object, instead of an AddressBook one. If AddressBook is subclassed, the receiver to the initWithName: message (and therefore the return value) is not an AddressBook object; its type is that of the subclass. For that reason, you define the return type as a generic object type.

We override the init method here to make sure that if someone does an alloc followed by an init that they still get the address book set up okay, albeit with a default name of NoName. So here, the initWithName: method is our designated initializer, and we want to make sure that init uses it.

The addCard: method takes the AddressCard object given as its argument and adds it to the address book.

The count method gives the number of elements in an array. The entries method uses this to return the number of address cards stored in the address book.

Fast Enumeration

The list method's for loop shows a construct you haven't seen before:

```
for ( AddressCard *theCard in book )
     NSLog (@"%-20s    %-32s", [theCard.name UTF8String],
                 [theCard.email UTF8String]);
```

This uses a technique known as *fast enumeration* to sequence through each element of the book array. The syntax is simple enough: You define a variable that will hold each element in the array in turn (AddressCard *theCard). You follow that with the keyword in, and then you list the name of the array. When the for loop executes, it assigns the first element in the array to the specified variable and then executes the body of the loop. Then it assigns the second element in the array to the variable and again executes the body of the loop. This continues in sequence until all elements of the array have been assigned to the variable and the body of the loop executed for each such element.

Note that if theCard had been previously defined as an AddressCard object, the for loop would more simply become this:

```
for ( theCard in book )

    . . .
```

Program 15.12 is a test program for your new AddressBook class.

Program 15.12 **Test Program**

```
#import "AddressBook.h"

int main (int argc, char * argv[])
{
   @autoreleasepool {
      NSString  *aName = @"Julia Kochan";
      NSString  *aEmail = @"jewls337@axlc.com";
      NSString  *bName = @"Tony Iannino";
      NSString  *bEmail = @"tony.iannino@techfitness.com";
      NSString  *cName = @"Stephen Kochan";
      NSString  *cEmail = @"steve@classroomM.com";
      NSString  *dName = @"Jamie Baker";
      NSString  *dEmail = @"jbaker@classroomM.com";

      AddressCard *card1 = [[AddressCard alloc] init];
      AddressCard *card2 = [[AddressCard alloc] init];
      AddressCard *card3 = [[AddressCard alloc] init];
      AddressCard *card4 = [[AddressCard alloc] init];
```

```
    // Set up a new address book

    AddressBook   *myBook = [[AddressBook alloc]
                    initWithName: @"Linda's Address Book"];

    NSLog (@"Entries in address book after creation: %li",
            [myBook entries]);

    // Now set up four address cards

    [card1 setName: aName andEmail: aEmail];
    [card2 setName: bName andEmail: bEmail];
    [card3 setName: cName andEmail: cEmail];
    [card4 setName: dName andEmail: dEmail];

    // Add the cards to the address book

    [myBook addCard: card1];
    [myBook addCard: card2];
    [myBook addCard: card3];
    [myBook addCard: card4];

    NSLog (@"Entries in address book after adding cards: %li",
            [myBook entries]);

    // List all the entries in the book now

    [myBook list];
    }
    return 0;
}
```

Program 15.12   **Output**

```
Entries in address book after creation: 0
Entries in address book after adding cards: 4


======== Contents of: Linda's Address Book =========
Julia Kochan          jewls337@axlc.com
Tony Iannino          tony.iannino@techfitness.com
Stephen Kochan        steve@classroomM.com
Jamie Baker           jbaker@classroomM.com
====================================================
```

The program creates a new address book called Linda's Address Book and then sets up four address cards. The four cards are then added to the address book using the `addCard:` method, and the `list` method is used to list and verify the contents of the address book.

Looking Up Someone in the Address Book

When you have a large address book, you don't want to list its complete contents each time you want to look up someone. Therefore, adding a method to do that for you makes sense. Let's call the method `lookup:` and have it take as its argument the name to locate. The method searches the address book for a match (ignoring case) and returns the matching entry, if found. If the name does not appear in the phone book, you have it return `nil`.

Here's our new `lookup:` method:

```
// lookup address card by name -- assumes an exact match

-(AddressCard *) lookup: (NSString *) theName
{
    for ( AddressCard *nextCard in book )
      if ( [nextCard.name caseInsensitiveCompare: theName] == NSOrderedSame )
        return nextCard;

    return nil;
}
```

If you put the declaration for this method in your interface file and the definition in the implementation file, you can write a test program to try your new method. Program 15.13 shows such a program, followed immediately by its output.

Program 15.13 **Test Program**

```
#import "AddressBook.h"

int main (int argc, char * argv[])
{

   @autoreleasepool {
      NSString   *aName = @"Julia Kochan";
      NSString   *aEmail = @"jewls337@axlc.com";
      NSString   *bName = @"Tony Iannino";
      NSString   *bEmail = @"tony.iannino@techfitness.com";
      NSString   *cName = @"Stephen Kochan";
      NSString   *cEmail = @"steve@classroomM.com";
      NSString   *dName = @"Jamie Baker";
      NSString   *dEmail = @"jbaker@classroomM.com";
      AddressCard   *card1 = [[AddressCard alloc] init];
      AddressCard   *card2 = [[AddressCard alloc] init];
      AddressCard   *card3 = [[AddressCard alloc] init];
```

```
        AddressCard   *card4 = [[AddressCard alloc] init];

        AddressBook   *myBook = [[AddressBook alloc]
                                    initWithName: @"Linda's Address Book"];
        AddressCard   *myCard;

        // Now set up four address cards

        [card1 setName: aName andEmail: aEmail];
        [card2 setName: bName andEmail: bEmail];
        [card3 setName: cName andEmail: cEmail];
        [card4 setName: dName andEmail: dEmail];

        // Add some cards to the address book

        [myBook addCard: card1];
        [myBook addCard: card2];
        [myBook addCard: card3];
        [myBook addCard: card4];

        // Look up a person by name

        NSLog (@"Stephen Kochan");
        myCard = [myBook lookup: @"stephen kochan"];

        if (myCard != nil)
           [myCard print];
        else
           NSLog (@"Not found!");

        // Try another lookup

        NSLog (@"Haibo Zhang");
        myCard = [myBook lookup: @"Haibo Zhang"];

        if (myCard != nil)
           [myCard print];
        else
           NSLog (@"Not found!");
    }
    return 0;
}
```

Program 15.13   **Output**

```
Lookup: Stephen Kochan
=====================================
|                             |
| Stephen Kochan              |
| steve@classroomM.com        |
|                             |
|                             |
|                             |
|      O           O          |
=====================================

Lookup: Haibo Zhang
Not found!
```

When the `lookup:` method located Stephen Kochan in the address book (taking advantage of the fact that a non-case-sensitive match was made), the method returned the matching card immediately by executing the `return` statement, which terminates the loop and sends back the value of `nextCard`. That matching card was then given to the `AddressCard`'s `print` method for display. In the case of the second lookup, the name Haibo Zhang was not found.

This `lookup:` method is very primitive because it needs to find an exact match of the entire name. A better method would perform partial matches and be able to handle multiple matches. For example, the message expression

`[myBook lookup: @"steve"]`

could match entries for Steve Kochan, Fred Stevens, and steven levy. Because multiple matches might exist, a good approach might be to create an array containing all the matches and return the array to the method caller (see Exercise 2 at the end of this chapter), like so:

`matches = [myBook lookup: @"steve"];`

Removing Someone from the Address Book

No address book manager that enables you to add an entry is complete without the capability to also remove an entry. You can make a `removeCard:` method to remove a particular `AddressCard` from the address book. Another possibility is to create a `remove:` method that removes someone based on name. (See Exercise 6 at the end of this chapter.)

Because you've made a couple of changes to your interface file, Program 15.14 shows it again with the new `removeCard:` method. It's followed by the implementation of your new method.

Program 15.14   `Addressbook.h` **Interface File**

```
#import "AddressCard.h"

@interface AddressBook: NSObject

@property (nonatomic, copy) NSString *bookName;
@property (nonatomic, strong) NSMutableArray *book;

-(id) initWithName: (NSString *) name;

-(void) addCard: (AddressCard *) theCard;
-(void) removeCard: (AddressCard *) theCard;

-(AddressCard *) lookup: (NSString *) theName;
-(int) entries;
-(void) list;

@end
```

Here's the new `removeCard:` method:

```
-(void) removeCard: (AddressCard *) theCard
{
    [book removeObjectIdenticalTo: theCard];
}
```

For purposes of what's considered an *identical* object, we are using the idea of the same exact object, that is, it's an object with the same location in memory. So the `removeObjectIdenticalTo:` method does *not* consider two address cards that contain the same information but are located in different places in memory (which might happen if you made a copy of an `AddressCard`, for example) to be identical.

Incidentally, the `removeObjectIdenticalTo:` method removes all objects identical to its argument. However, that is an issue only if you have multiple occurrences of the same object in your arrays.

You can get more sophisticated with your approach to equal objects by using the `removeObject:` method and then writing your own `isEqual:` method for testing whether two objects are equal. If you use `removeObject:`, the system automatically invokes the `isEqual:` method for each element in the array, giving it the two elements to compare. In this case, because your address book contains `AddressCard` objects as its elements, you would have to add an `isEqual:` method to *that* class. (You would be overriding the method that the class inherits from `NSObject`.) The method could then decide for itself how to determine equality. It would make sense to compare the two corresponding names and emails. If both were equal, you could return YES from the method; otherwise, you could return NO. Your method might look like this:

```
-(BOOL) isEqual: (AddressCard *) theCard
{
```

```
   if ([name isEqualToString: theCard.name] == YES &&
          [email isEqualToString: theCard.email] == YES)
      return YES;
   else
      return NO;
}
```

Note that other NSArray methods, such as containsObject: and indexOfObject:, also rely on this isEqual: strategy for determining whether two objects are considered equal.

Program 15.14 tests the new removeCard: method.

Program 15.14   Test Program

```
#import "AddressBook.h"

int main (int argc, char * argv[])
{
   @autoreleasepool {
      NSString  *aName = @"Julia Kochan";
      NSString  *aEmail = @"jewls337@axlc.com";
      NSString  *bName = @"Tony Iannino";
      NSString  *bEmail = @"tony.iannino@techfitness.com";
      NSString  *cName = @"Stephen Kochan";
      NSString  *cEmail = @"steve@classroomM.com";
      NSString  *dName = @"Jamie Baker";
      NSString  *dEmail = @"jbaker@classroomM.com";

      AddressCard *card1 = [[AddressCard alloc] init];
      AddressCard *card2 = [[AddressCard alloc] init];
      AddressCard *card3 = [[AddressCard alloc] init];
      AddressCard *card4 = [[AddressCard alloc] init];

      AddressBook  *myBook = [[AddressBook alloc]
                      initWithName: @"Linda's Address Book"];

      AddressCard  *myCard;

      // Now set up four address cards

      [card1 setName: aName andEmail: aEmail];
      [card2 setName: bName andEmail: bEmail];
      [card3 setName: cName andEmail: cEmail];
      [card4 setName: dName andEmail: dEmail];

      // Add some cards to the address book
```

```
        [myBook addCard: card1];
        [myBook addCard: card2];
        [myBook addCard: card3];
        [myBook addCard: card4];

        // Look up a person by name

        NSLog (@"Lookup: Stephen Kochan");
        myCard = [myBook lookup: @"Stephen Kochan"];

        if (myCard != nil)
            [myCard print];
        else
            NSLog (@"Not found!");

        // Now remove the entry from the phone book

        [myBook removeCard: myCard];
        [myBook list];      // verify it's gone
    }

    return 0;
}
```

Program 15.14 **Output**

```
Lookup: Stephen Kochan
======================================
|                                    |
| Stephen Kochan                     |
| steve@classroomM.com               |
|                                    |
|                                    |
|                                    |
|       O             O              |
======================================

======== Contents of: Linda's Address Book =========
Julia Kochan     jewls337@axlc.com
Tony Iannino     tony.iannino@techfitness.com
Jamie Baker      jbaker@classroomM.com
===================================================
```

After looking up Stephen Kochan in the address book and verifying that he is there, you pass the resulting `AddressCard` to your new `removeCard:` method to be removed. The resulting listing of the address book verifies the removal.

Sorting Arrays

If your address book contains a lot of entries, alphabetizing it might be convenient. You can easily do this by adding a `sort` method to your `AddressBook` class and by taking advantage of an `NSMutableArray` method called `sortUsingSelector:`. This method takes as its argument a selector that the `sortUsingSelector:` method uses to compare two elements. Arrays can contain any type of objects in them, so the only way to implement a generic sorting method is to have you decide whether elements in the array are in order. To do this, you must add a method to compare two elements in the array.[4] The result returned from that method is to be of type `NSComparisonResult`. It should return `NSOrderedAscending` if you want the sorting method to place the first element before the second in the array, return `NSOrderedSame` if the two elements are considered equal, or return `NSOrderedDescending` if the first element should come after the second element in the sorted array.

First, here's the new sort method from your `AddressBook` class:

```
-(void) sort
{
    [book sortUsingSelector: @selector(compareNames:)];
}
```

As you learned in Chapter 9, "Polymorphism, Dynamic Typing, and Dynamic Binding," the expression

```
@selector (compareNames:)
```

creates a selector, which is of type `SEL`, from a specified method name; this is the method `sortUsingSelector:` uses to compare two elements in the array. When it needs to make such a comparison, it invokes the specified method, sending the message to the first element in the array (the receiver) to be compared against its argument. The returned value should be of type `NSComparisonResult`, as previously described.

Because the elements of your address book are `AddressCard` objects, the comparison method must be added to the `AddressCard` class. (Make sure that you fully understand that.) You must go back to your `AddressCard` class and add a `compareNames:` method to it, as shown here:

```
// Compare the two names from the specified address cards

-(NSComparisonResult) compareNames: (id) element
{
    return [name compare: [element name]];
}
```

[4] A method called `sortUsingFunction:context:` lets you use a function rather than a method to perform the comparison.

Because you are doing a string comparison of the two names from the address book, you can use the NSString compare: method to do the work for you.

If you add the sort method to the AddressBook class and the compareNames: method to the AddressCard class, you can write a test program to test it (see Program 15.15).

Program 15.15 **Test Program**

```
#import "AddressBook.h"

int main (int argc, char * argv[])
{

    @autoreleasepool {
        NSString   *aName = @"Julia Kochan";
        NSString   *aEmail = @"jewls337@axlc.com";
        NSString   *bName = @"Tony Iannino";
        NSString   *bEmail = @"tony.iannino@techfitness.com";
        NSString   *cName = @"Stephen Kochan";
        NSString   *cEmail = @"steve@classroomM.com";
        NSString   *dName = @"Jamie Baker";
        NSString   *dEmail = @"jbaker@classroomM.com";

        AddressCard   *card1 = [[AddressCard alloc] init];
        AddressCard   *card2 = [[AddressCard alloc] init];
        AddressCard   *card3 = [[AddressCard alloc] init];
        AddressCard   *card4 = [[AddressCard alloc] init];

        AddressBook    *myBook = [AddressBook alloc];

        // First set up four address cards

        [card1 setName: aName andEmail: aEmail];
        [card2 setName: bName andEmail: bEmail];
        [card3 setName: cName andEmail: cEmail];
        [card4 setName: dName andEmail: dEmail];

        myBook = [myBook initWithName: @"Linda's Address Book"];

        // Add some cards to the address book

        [myBook addCard: card1];
        [myBook addCard: card2];
        [myBook addCard: card3];
        [myBook addCard: card4];
```

```
    // List the unsorted book

    [myBook list];

    // Sort it and list it again

    [myBook sort];
    [myBook list];
  }
  return 0;
}
```

Program 15.15 **Output**

```
======== Contents of: Linda's Address Book =========
Julia Kochan          jewls337@axlc.com
Tony Iannino          tony.iannino@techfitness.com
Stephen Kochan        steve@classroomM.com
Jamie Baker           jbaker@classroomM.com
===================================================


======== Contents of: Linda's Address Book =========
Jamie Baker           jbaker@classroomM.com
Julia Kochan          jewls337@axlc.com
Stephen Kochan        steve@classroomM.com
Tony Iannino          tony.iannino@techfitness.com
===================================================
```

Note that the sort is an ascending one. However, you can easily perform a descending sort by modifying the `compareNames:` method in the `AddressCard` class to reverse the sense of the values returned.

Sorting Using Blocks

Some sorting methods in the `NSArray` and `NSMutableArray` classes take blocks as arguments for comparing elements in an array in lieu of selectors.

The general format of the `NSArray` method is this:

```
-(NSArray *) sortedArrayUsingComparator: (NSComparator) block
```

That of the `NSMutableArray` method, which does the sort in place, looks like this:

```
-(void) sortUsingComparator:(NSComparator) block
```

NSComparator is defined this way as a typedef in one of the system header files:

```
typedef NSComparisonResult (^NSComparator)(id obj1, id obj2);
```

Translating this into English, it says that NSComparator is a block that takes two objects as its arguments and that returns a value of type NSComparisonResult. This method, because it uses blocks, will probably run faster for sorting large arrays. So, consider using it in your applications for that reason.

So, the block takes the two objects to compare as its arguments and is expected to return an indicator of whether the first object should be considered, less than, equal to, or greater than the second object. This is consistent with the method that gets called by the nonblock versions of the array sort methods.

The block we supply as the argument to the sortUsingComparator: method can just call our compareNames: method to compare the address cards like so:

```
-(void) sort
{
    [book sortUsingComparator:
        ^(id obj1, id obj2) {
            return [obj1 compareNames: obj2];
        } ];
}
```

This works okay, but when you think about, it does not offer any performance improvement at all, because the block we specified calls the same compareNames: method as the sortUsingSelector: method does. So, a better approach is to do more of the work inside the block; that could help to speed things up:

```
-(void) sort
{
    [book sortUsingComparator:
        ^(id obj1, id obj2) {
            return [[obj1 name] compare: [obj2 name]];
        } ];
}
```

Go back to Program 15.15 and replace the AddressBook's sort method with the one we just developed. Verify that the program still runs and correctly sorts your address book.

One of the nice aspects of the block version of the sort method is that you don't have to add a comparison method to the class whose objects are being compared. That would be the AddressCard class, which is where, as you'll recall, we placed the compareNames: method used by the previous version of the sort method.

Another nice advantage is that if you decide to change the way your address cards are compared you can do it directly in your sort method, meaning you do not have to make the change to the AddressCard class.

More than 50 methods are available for working with array objects. Tables 15.4 and 15.5 list some commonly used methods for working with immutable and mutable arrays, respectively. Because NSMutableArray is a subclass of NSArray, the former inherits the methods of the latter.

In Tables 15.4 and 15.5, *obj*, *obj1*, and *obj2* are any objects; *i* is an NSUInteger integer representing a valid index number into the array; *selector* is a selector object of type SEL; and *size* is an NSUInteger integer.

Table 15.4   **Common NSArray Methods**

Method	Description
+(id) arrayWithObjects: *obj1*, *obj2*, ... nil	Creates a new array with *obj1*, *obj2*, ... as its elements.
-(BOOL) containsObject: *obj*	Determines whether the array contains *obj* (uses the isEqual: method).
-(NSUInteger) count	Indicates the number of elements in the array.
-(NSUInteger) indexOfObject: *obj*	Specifies the index number of the first element that contains *obj* (uses the isEqual: method).
-(NSUInteger) indexOfObjectPassingTest: (BOOL(^)(id *obj*, NSUInteger *idx*, BOOL *stop*)) *block*	Passes each object *obj* (with index number *idx*) into the block *block*, which should return YES if *obj* passes the test, NO if it doesn't. Set variable pointed to by *stop* to YES to end processing.
-(id) lastObject	Returns the last object in the array
-(id) objectAtIndex: *i*	Indicates the object stored in element *i*.
-(void) makeObjectsPerform Selector: (SEL) *selector*	Sends the message indicated by *selector* to every element of the array.
-(void) enumerateObjectsUsingBlock: (void (^)(id *obj*, NSUInteger *idx*, BOOL *stop*)) *block*	Execute block for each element in the array, passing in the array object *obj*, and its index number *idx*. Processing continues until all elements have been enumerated or the variable pointed to by *stop* is set to YES.
-(NSArray *) sortedArrayUsing Selector: (SEL) *selector*	Sorts the array according to the comparison method specified by *selector*.
-(NSArray *) sortedArrayUsingComparator: (NSComparator) *block*	Sorts the array according to the comparison performed by the block *block*.
-(BOOL) writeToFile: *path* atomically: (BOOL) *flag*	Writes the array to the specified file, creating a temporary file first if *flag* is YES.

Table 15.5   **Common** `NSMutableArray` **Methods**

Method	Description
`+(id) array`	Creates an empty array
`+(id) arrayWithCapacity: size`	Creates an array with a specified initial `size`
`-(id) initWithCapacity: size`	Initializes a newly allocated array with a specified initial `size`
`-(void) addObject: obj`	Adds `obj` to the end of the array
`-(void) insertObject: obj atIndex: i`	Inserts `obj` into element `i` of the array
`-(void) replaceObjectAtIndex: i withObject: obj`	Replaces element `i` of the array with `obj`
`-(void) removeObject: obj`	Removes all occurrences of `obj` from the array
`-(void) removeObjectAtIndex: i`	Removes element `i` from the array, moving down elements `i+1` through the end of the array
`-(void) sortUsingSelector: (SEL) selector`	Sorts the array based on the comparison method indicated by `selector`
`-(void) sortUsingComparator: (NSComparator) block`	Sorts the array according to the comparison performed by the block `block`

The `NSValue` Class

As you have seen, a Foundation collection like an array can only store objects. Therefore, you cannot store a basic data type like an `int` inside them. To get around this problem, you make arrays of `NSNumber` objects rather than arrays of `int`s.

You will want to store other types inside collections as you start to develop iOS applications. These types are structures, which are derived data types from the C language, and not objects. For example, you will be using a `CGPoint` (a `typedef`'ed name) to define an (x, y) coordinate in your application. That is how you specify the origin of a rectangle, for example. In fact, a rectangle is a `CGRect` type, and itself is a structure containing two other structures: a `CGPoint` structure that defines the rectangle's origin, and a `CGSize` structure that defines its width and height.

The point of this discussion is for you to note that these are structures that you may want to store in a collection. You can't do that directly. The `NSValue` class comes to the rescue by allowing you to convert one of these structures into an object, which then allows you to store it inside a collection. The process of taking a data type like a structure and then converting it into an object is sometimes referred to as *wrapping*. As you might expect, the inverse process of taking an object and extracting its underlying data type is often referred to as *unwrapping*.

Table 15.6 shows some of the wrapper methods for converting C data types into objects and the corresponding inverse methods to unwrap the object. For more information, look at the documentation for the NSValue class.

Table 15.6   **Some** NSValue **Wrapper and Unwrapper Methods**

Typedef'ed data type	Description	Wrapper Method	Unwrapper Method
CGPoint	A point consisting of an x and y value	valueWithPoint:	pointValue
CGSize	A size consisting of a width and height	valueWithSize:	sizeValue
CGRect	A rectangle consisting of an origin and size	valuewithRect:	rectValue
NSRange	A range describing location and size	valueWithRange:	rangeValue

Here's a code fragment that takes a CGPoint structure and adds it into a mutable array called touchPoints:

```
CGPoint  myPoint;
NSValue  *pointObj;
NSMutableArray *touchPoints = [NSMutableArray array];
    . . .
myPoint.x = 100;        // set the point to (100, 200)
myPoint.y = 200;
    . . .
pointObj = [NSValue valueWithPoint: myPoint];  // make it an object
[touchPoints  addObject: pointObj];
```

Make sure that you realize the need for doing this. Because myPoint is a structure, you can't store it directly inside the touchPoints array. So, you have to convert it to an object first. We use the valueWithPoint: method to do that.

If you subsequently want to get the last point from your touchPoints array and convert it back to a CGPoint structure, this line does the trick:

```
myPoint = [[touchPoints lastObject] pointValue];
```

Dictionary Objects

A *dictionary* is a collection of data consisting of key-object pairs. Just as you would look up the definition of a word in a dictionary, you obtain the value (object) from an Objective-C dictionary by its key. The keys in a dictionary must be unique, and they can be of any object type, although they are typically strings. The value associated with the key can also be of any object type, but it cannot be nil.

Dictionaries can be mutable or immutable; mutable ones can have entries dynamically added and removed. Dictionaries can be searched based on a particular key, and their contents can be enumerated. Program 15.16 sets up a mutable dictionary to be used as a glossary of Objective-C terms and fills in the first three entries.

Program 15.16

```
#import <Foundation/Foundation.h>

int main (int argc, char * argv[])
{
    @autoreleasepool {
        NSMutableDictionary *glossary = [NSMutableDictionary dictionary];

        // Store three entries in the glossary

        [glossary setObject: @"A class defined so other classes can inherit from it"
                     forKey: @"abstract class" ];
        [glossary setObject: @"To implement all the methods defined in a protocol"
                     forKey: @"adopt"];
        [glossary setObject: @"Storing an object for later use"
                     forKey: @"archiving"];

        // Retrieve and display them

        NSLog (@"abstract class: %@", [glossary objectForKey: @"abstract class"]);
        NSLog (@"adopt: %@", [glossary objectForKey: @"adopt"]);
        NSLog (@"archiving: %@", [glossary objectForKey: @"archiving"]);
    }
    return 0;
}
```

Program 15.16   **Output**

```
abstract class: A class defined so other classes can inherit from it
adopt: To implement all the methods defined in a protocol
archiving: Storing an object for later use
```

The expression

```
[NSMutableDictionary dictionary]
```

creates an empty mutable dictionary. You can add key-value pairs to the dictionary using the setObject:forKey: method. After the dictionary has been constructed, you can retrieve the value for a given key using the objectForKey: method. Program 15.16 shows how the three entries in the glossary were retrieved and displayed. In a more practical application, the user types in the word to define, and the program searches the glossary for its definition.

Note that some recent syntax additions have been added to Objective-C for working with dictionaries. Writing the expression

```
dict[key]
```

is the same as writing

```
[dict objectForKey: key]
```

And to store a key/object pair into a dictionary, you can use the expression

```
dict[key] = object
```

in place of writing

```
[dict setObject: object forKey: key]
```

Program 15.17 is rewrite of Program 15.16 showing the alternate syntax for adding and retrieving entries from a dictionary.

Program 15.17

```
#import <Foundation/Foundation.h>

int main (int argc, char * argv[])
{
    @autoreleasepool {
        NSMutableDictionary *glossary = [NSMutableDictionary dictionary];

        // Store three entries in the glossary

        glossary[@"abstract class"] =
                @"A class defined so other classes can inherit from it";
        glossary[@"adopt"] =
                @"To implement all the methods defined in a protocol";
        glossary[@"archiving"] = @"Storing an object for later use";

        // Retrieve and display them

        NSLog (@"abstract class: %@", glossary[@"abstract class"]);
        NSLog (@"adopt: %@", glossary[@"adopt"]);
        NSLog (@"archiving: %@", glossary[@"archiving"]);
    }
    return 0;
}
```

Enumerating a Dictionary

Program 15.18 illustrates how a dictionary can be defined with initial key-value pairs using the `dictionaryWithObjectsAndKeys:` method. An immutable dictionary is created, and the program also shows how a fast enumeration loop can be used to retrieve each element from a dictionary one key at a time. Unlike array objects, dictionary objects are not ordered, so the first key-object pair placed in a dictionary might not be the first key extracted when the dictionary is enumerated.

Program 15.18

```
#import <Foundation/Foundation.h>

int main (int argc, char * argv[])
{
   @autoreleasepool {
      NSDictionary *glossary =
        [NSDictionary dictionaryWithObjectsAndKeys:
         @"A class defined so other classes can inherit from it",
         @"abstract class",
         @"To implement all the methods defined in a protocol",
         @"adopt",
         @"Storing an object for later use",
         @"archiving",
         nil
      ];

      // Print all key-value pairs from the dictionary

      for ( NSString *key in glossary )
         NSLog (@"%@: %@", key, [glossary objectForKey: key]);

   }
   return 0;
}
```

Program 15.18   **Output**

```
abstract class: A class defined so other classes can inherit from it
adopt: To implement all the methods defined in a protocol
archiving: Storing an object for later use
```

The argument to `dictionaryWithObjectsAndKeys:` is a list of object-key pairs (yes, in that order), each separated by a comma. The list must be terminated with the special `nil` object.

After the program creates the dictionary, it sets up a loop to enumerate its contents. As noted, the keys are retrieved from the dictionary in turn, in no special order.

You can also use the special syntax

```
@{ key1 : object1, key2 : object2, ..., keyn : objectn }
```

to create an immutable dictionary initialized with the listed key/object pairs. So, the dictionary created in Program 15.18 could be written like this:

```
NSDictionary *glossary = @{
    @"abstract class" :
            @"A class defined so other classes can inherit from it",
    @"adopt" : @"To implement all the methods defined in a protocol",
    @"archiving" : @"Storing an object for later use"
};
```

If you want to display the contents of a dictionary in alphabetic order, you could retrieve all the keys from the dictionary, sort them, and then retrieve all the values from the dictionary for each of those sorted keys in order. You can first use NSDIctionary's allKeys method to extract all the keys from the dictionary into an array and then sort that array. Next, you could enumerate the array of sorted keys and retrieve the corresponding values from the dictionary. For example, assume you have a dictionary called states that contains the names of U.S. states as the keys and their corresponding capitals as the objects. The following code fragment displays each state name in alphabetic order along with its corresponding capital:

```
NSArray *keys = [states allKeys];

keys = [keys sortedArrayUsingComparator:
        ^(id obj1, id obj2) {
            return [obj1 compare: obj2];
        } ];

for (NSString *aState in keys)
    NSLog (@"State: %@  Capital: %@", aState, states[aState]);
```

We have just shown some basic operations with dictionaries here. Tables 15.7 and 15.8 summarize some of the more commonly used methods for working with immutable and mutable dictionaries, respectively. Because NSMutableDictionary is a subset of NSDictionary, it inherits its methods.

In Tables 15.7 and 15.8, *key*, *key1*, *key2*, *obj*, *obj1*, and *obj2* are any objects, and *size* is an NSUInteger unsigned integer.

Table 15.7   **Common** NSDictionary **Methods**

Method	Description
+(id) dictionaryWithObjectsAndKeys:*obj1*, *key1*, *obj2*, *key2*, ..., nil	Creates a dictionary with key-object pairs {*key1*, *obj1*}, {*key2*, *obj2*}, ...
-(id) initWithObjectsAndKeys: *obj1*, *key1*, *obj2*, *key2*, ..., nil	Initializes a newly allocated dictionary with key-object pairs {*key1*, *obj1*}, {*key2*, *obj2*}, ...
-(NSArray *) allKeys	Returns an array containing all the keys from the dictionary
-(NSUInteger) count	Returns the number of entries in the dictionary
-(NSEnumerator *) keyEnumerator	Returns an NSEnumerator object for all the keys in the dictionary
-(NSArray *) keysSortedByValueUsingSelector: (SEL) *selector*	Returns an array of keys in the dictionary whose corresponding values are sorted according to the comparison method *selector*
-(NSEnumerator *) objectEnumerator	Returns an NSEnumerator object for all the values in the dictionary
-(id) objectForKey: *key*	Returns the object for the specified *key*

Table 15.8   **Common** NSMutableDictionary **Methods**

Method	Description
+(id) dictionaryWithCapacity: *size*	Creates a mutable dictionary with an initial specified *size*
-(id) initWithCapacity: *size*	Initializes a newly allocated dictionary to be of an initial specified *size*
-(void) removeAllObjects	Removes all entries from the dictionary
-(void) removeObjectForKey:*key*	Removes the entry for the specified *key* from the dictionary
-(void) setObject: *obj* forKey: *key*	Adds *obj* to the dictionary for the key *key* and replaces the value if *key* already exists

Set Objects

A *set* is a collection of unique objects, and it can be mutable or immutable. Operations include searching, adding, and removing members (mutable sets); comparing two sets; and finding the intersection and union of two sets.

In this section, we take a quick look at three set classes: NSSet, NSMutableSet, and NSIndexSet. We also mention the class NSCountedSet in passing so that you will know when you might need or want to use that set.

Program 15.19 shows some basic operations on sets. Suppose, for instance, that you want to display the contents of your sets several times during execution of the program. You therefore decide to create a new method called print. You add the print method to the NSSet class by creating a new category called Printing. NSMutableSet is a subclass of NSSet, so mutable sets can use the new print method as well.

Program 15.19

```
#import <Foundation/Foundation.h>

// Add a print method to NSSet with the Printing category

@interface NSSet (Printing)
-(void) print;
@end

@implementation NSSet (Printing)
-(void) print {
    printf ("{ ");

    for (NSNumber *element in self)
        printf (" %li ", (long) [element integerValue]);

    printf ("} \n");
}
@end


int main (int argc, char * argv[])
{
    @autoreleasepool {

        NSMutableSet *set1 = [NSMutableSet setWithObjects:
            @1, @3, @5, @10, nil];
        NSSet *set2 = [NSSet setWithObjects:
            @-5, @100, @3, @5, nil];
        NSSet *set3 = [NSSet setWithObjects:
```

368 Chapter 15 Numbers, Strings, and Collections

```
                @12, @200, @3, nil];

        NSLog (@"set1: ");
        [set1 print];
        NSLog (@"set2: ");
        [set2 print];

        // Equality test
        if ([set1 isEqualToSet: set2] == YES)
            NSLog (@"set1 equals set2");
        else
            NSLog (@"set1 is not equal to set2");


        // Membership test

        if ([set1 containsObject: @10] == YES)
            NSLog (@"set1 contains 10");
        else
            NSLog (@"set1 does not contain 10");

        if ([set2 containsObject: @10] == YES)
            NSLog (@"set2 contains 10");
        else
            NSLog (@"set2 does not contain 10");

        // add and remove objects from mutable set set1

        [set1 addObject: @4];
        [set1 removeObject:@10];
        NSLog (@"set1 after adding 4 and removing 10: ");
        [set1 print];

        // get intersection of two sets

        [set1 intersectSet: set2];
        NSLog (@"set1 intersect set2: ");
        [set1 print];

        // union of two sets

        [set1 unionSet:set3];
        NSLog (@"set1 union set3: ");
        [set1 print];

    }
    return 0;
}
```

Program 15.19 **Output**

```
set1:
{  3 10 1 5 }
set2:
{  100 3 -5 5 }
set1 is not equal to set2
set1 contains 10
set2 does not contain 10
set1 after adding 4 and removing 10:
{  3 1 5 4 }
set1 intersect set2:
{  3 5 }
set1 union set3:
{  12 3 5 200 }
```

The print method uses the fast enumeration technique previously described to retrieve each element from the set. Of course, your print method is not that general because it works only with sets that have integer members in them. But it's a good reminder here of how to add methods to a class through a category.[5] (Note that the C library's printf routine is used in the print method to display the elements of each set on a single line.)

setWithObjects: creates a new set from a nil-terminated list of objects. After creating three sets, the program displays the first two using your new print method. The isEqualToSet: method then tests whether set1 is equal to set2. It isn't.

The containsObject: method sees first whether the integer 10 is in set1 and then whether it is in set2. The Boolean values the method returns verify that it is in the first set, not in the second.

The program next uses the addObject: and removeObject: methods to add and remove 4 and 10 from set1, respectively. Displaying the contents of the set verifies that the operations were successful.

You can use the intersect: and union: methods to calculate the intersection and union of two sets. In both cases, the result of the operation replaces the receiver of the message.

The Foundation framework also provides a class called NSCountedSet. These sets can represent more than one occurrence of the same object; however, instead of the object appearing multiple times in the set, a count of the number of times is maintained. So, the first time an object is added to the set, its count is 1. Subsequently adding the object to the set increments the count, whereas removing the object from the set decrements the count. If it reaches zero, the actual

---

[5] A more general method could invoke each object's description method for displaying each member of the set. That would allow sets containing any types of objects to be displayed in a readable format. Also note that you can display the contents of any collection with a single call to NSLog, using the "print object" format characters "%@".

object itself is removed from the set. The `countForObject:` retrieves the count for a specified object in a set.

One application for a counted set might be a word counter application. Each time a word is found in some text, it can be added to the counted set. When the scan of the text is complete, each word can be retrieved from the set along with its count, which indicates the number of times the word appeared in the text.

We have just shown some basic operations with sets. Tables 15.9 and 15.10 summarize commonly used methods for working with immutable and mutable sets, respectively. Because `NSMutableSet` is a subclass of `NSSet`, it inherits its methods.

In Tables 15.9 and 15.10, *obj*, *obj1*, and *obj2* are any objects; `nsset` is an `NSSet` or `NSMutableSet` object; and *size* is an `NSUInteger` integer.

Table 15.9   **Common** `NSSet` **Methods**

Method	Description
`+(id)  setWithObjects: obj1, obj2, ..., nil`	Creates a new set from the list of objects
`-(id)  anyObject`	Returns any object from the set
`-(id)  initWithObjects: obj1, obj2, ..., nil`	Initializes a newly allocated set with a list of objects
`-(NSUInteger) count`	Returns the number of members in the set
`-(BOOL)  containsObject: obj`	Determines whether the set contains *obj*
`-(BOOL)  member: obj`	Determines whether the set contains *obj* (using the `isEqual:` method)
`-(NSEnumerator *)  objectEnumerator`	Returns an `NSEnumerator` object for all the objects in the set
`-(BOOL)  isSubsetOfSet: nsset`	Determines whether every member of the receiver is present in *nsset*
`-(BOOL)  intersectsSet: nsset`	Determines whether at least one member of the receiver appears in *nsset*
`-(BOOL)  isEqualToSet: nsset`	Determines whether the two sets are equal

Table 15.10   **Common** NSMutableSet **Methods**

Method	Description
+(id) setWithCapacity: *size*	Creates a new set with an initial capacity to store
-(id) initWithCapacity: *size*	Sets the initial capacity of a newly allocated set to *size* members
-(void) addObject: *obj*	Adds *obj* to the set
-(void) removeObject: *obj*	Removes *obj* from the set
-(void) removeAllObjects	Removes all members of the receiver
-(void) unionSet: *nsset*	Adds each member of *nsset* to the receiver
-(void) minusSet: *nsset*	Removes all members of *nsset* from the receiver
-(void) intersectSet: *nsset*	Removes all members from the receiver that are not also in nsset

NSIndexSet

Let's take a look at another type of set: the NSIndexSet. This class is used to store ordered indexes into some other data structure, typically an array. You can use this class, for example, to efficiently generate a list of index numbers from an array of objects, where each object satisfies some criteria that you specify. Note that there is no mutable version of the NSIndexSet class.

For example, the NSArray method indexOfObjectPassingTest: takes a block as its argument. The block gets executed for each element in the array, passing in the array element, the index number, and a *pointer* to a BOOL variable. The code in the block will presumably test the element against some criteria and return YES if the array element satisfies the criteria, and NO if it does not. You can stop processing at any time by setting the value the BOOL pointer reference to YES. (Refer back to Chapter 13, for a discussion on pointers.)

If the indexOfObjectPassingTest: finds a match (meaning you returned YES from your block on one occasion), it returns the lowest matching index from the set. Otherwise, if no match is found, it returns NSNotFound.

Here's a modified version of the lookup: method from our AddressBook class.

```
-(AddressCard *) lookup: (NSString *) theName
{
    NSUInteger result = [book indexOfObjectPassingTest:
      ^ (id obj, NSUInteger idx, BOOL *stop)
      {
          if ([[obj name] caseInsensitiveCompare: theName] == NSOrderedSame) {
              return YES;
          }
```

```
            else
                return NO;    // keep looking
        } ];


    // See if we found a match

    if (result != NSNotFound) // there should only be one element
        return book[result];
    else
        return nil;

}
```

If you're looking for more than one match from an array, you can use the
indexesOfObjectsPassingTest: method. This method returns an NSIndexSet containing
the indexes of all the elements from the array that matched the criteria. The following uses this
new method to find and return the index numbers of all matching address cards:

```
-(NSIndexSet *) lookupAll: (NSString *) theName
{
    NSIndexSet *result = [book indexesOfObjectsPassingTest:
      ^(id obj, NSUInteger idx, BOOL *stop)
        {
            if ([[obj name] caseInsensitiveCompare: theName] == NSOrderedSame)
                return YES;   // found a match, keep going
            else
                return NO;    // keep looking
        } ];


    // Return the result

    return result;

}
```

It's left as an exercise for you to change the lookupAll: method to also return an
array of the matching address cards as the first version does. (Hint: After the
indexesOfObjectsPassingTest: method is done, enumerate each index for the index set and
add the corresponding element to an array that you will return. Better yet, look at the NSArray
method objectsAtIndexes:.)

Table 15.11 describes some representative NSIndexSet methods. In the table, *idx* is an
NSUInteger integer. You are encouraged to look up this class in your documentation and learn
more about it.

Table 15.11 **Some** NSIndexSet **Methods**

Method	Description
+(NSIndexSet) indexSet	Creates an empty index set.
-(BOOL) containIndex: idx	Returns YES if the index set contains the index idx, NO otherwise.
-(NSUinteger) count	Returns the numbers of indexes in the indexed set.
-(NSUinteger) firstIndex	Returns the first index in the set or NSNotFound if the set is empty.
-(NSUinteger) indexLessThanIndex: idx	Returns the closest index in the set less than idx or NSNotFound if none is less than idx (see also indexLessThanOrEqualToIndex:, indexGreaterThanIndex:, and indexGreaterThanOrEqualIndex:).
-(NSUinteger) lastIndex	Gives the last index in the set or NSNotFound if the set is empty.
-(NSIndexSet *) indexesPassingTest: (BOOL) (^) (NSUinteger idx, BOOL *stop) block	Block is applied to each element in the set. Return YES to have idx added to the resultant NSIndexSet, NO otherwise. Set the variable pointed to by stop to YES to end processing.

Exercises

1. Look up the NSDate class in your documentation. Then add a new category to NSDate called ElapsedDays. In that new category, add a method based on the following method declaration:

   -(unsigned long) elapsedDays: (NSDate *) theDate;

   Have the new method return the number of elapsed days between the receiver and the argument to the method. Write a test program to test your new method.

2. Modify the lookup: method developed in this chapter for the AddressBook class so that partial matches of a name can be made. The message expression [myBook lookup: @"steve"] should match an entry that contains the string steve anywhere within the name.

3. Using the result from Exercise 2, modify the lookup: method to search the address book for all matches. Have the method return an array of all such matching address cards, or nil if no match is made. (Note that the example presented at the end of this chapter returns an NSIndexSet result, but we want an array of AddressCards here.)

4. Add new fields of your choice to the `AddressCard` class. Some suggestions are separating the name field into first and last name fields, and adding address (perhaps with separate state, city, ZIP, and country fields) and phone number fields. Write appropriate setter and getter methods, and ensure that the `print` and `list` methods properly display the fields.

5. After completing Exercise 4, modify the `lookup:` method from Exercise 3 to perform a search on all the fields of an address card. Can you think of a way to design your `AddressCard` and `AddressBook` classes so that the latter does not have to know all the fields stored in the former?

6. Add the method `removeName:` to the `AddressBook` class to remove someone from the address book given this declaration for the method:

   `-(BOOL) removeName: (NSString *) theName;`

   Use the `lookup:` method developed in Exercise 3. If the name is not found or if multiple entries exist, have the method return `NO`. If the person is successfully removed, have it return `YES`.

7. Using the `Fraction` class defined in Part I, "The Objective-C Language," set up an array of fractions with some arbitrary values. Add a description method for your `Fraction` class as described in the text. Then use three different techniques to display the values of your fractions: 1) a regular `for` loop, 2) fast enumeration, and finally, 3) just using `%@`.

8. Using the `Fraction` class defined in Part I, set up a mutable array of fractions with arbitrary values. Then sort the array using the `sortUsingSelector:` method from the `NSMutableArray` class. Add a `Comparison` category to the `Fraction` class and implement your comparison method in that category.

9. Define three new classes, called `Song`, `Playlist`, and `MusicCollection`. A `Song` object will contain information about a particular song, such as its title, artist, album, and playing time. A `Playlist` object will contain the name of the playlist and a collection of songs. A `MusicCollection` object will contain a collection of playlists, including a special master playlist called `library` that contains every song in the collection. Define these three classes and write methods to do the following:

   Create a `Song` object and set its information.

   Create a `Playlist` object, and add songs to and remove songs from a playlist. A new song should be added to the master playlist if it's not already there. Make sure that if a song is removed from the master playlist, it is removed from all playlists in the music collection as well.

   Create a `MusicCollection` object, and add playlists to and remove playlists from the collection.

   Search and display the information about any song, any playlist, or the entire music collection.

   Make sure that none of your classes leak memory!

Note

This might be the most instructive exercise in the entire text, but it's not easy! Figure 15.6 shows what a sample `MusicCollection` called `myMusic` might look like. It has three playlists, which include the main playlist `library`. The library contains five songs. `playlist1` has two songs, and `playlist2` has one. Here are some hints: Make good use of the `NSMutableArray` class and just store references (and not copies) of your songs in each new playlist. (Use the `addObject:` method to do that.)

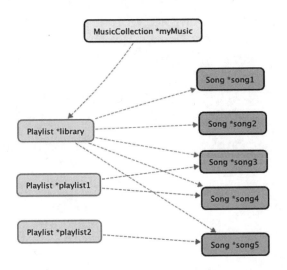

Figure 15.6   Example music collection data structures

10. Write a program that takes an `NSArray` of `NSNumber` objects (where each `NSNumber` represents an integer) and produces a frequency chart that lists each integer and how many times it occurs in the array. Use an `NSCountedSet` object to construct your frequency counts.

11. When the `addCard:` method is used to add an address card to the address book, who owns that address card? Can any of the information on that card be later changed that would affect the card stored in the address book? Can you think of a safer way to implement the `addCard:` method?

16

Working with Files

The Foundation framework enables you to get access to the file system to perform basic operations on files and directories. This is provided by NSFileManager, whose methods include the capability to

- Create a new file
- Read from an existing file
- Write data to a file
- Rename a file
- Remove (delete) a file
- Test for the existence of a file
- Determine the size of a file as well as other attributes
- Make a copy of a file
- Test two files to see whether their contents are equal

Many of these operations can also be performed on directories. For example, you can create a directory, read its contents, or delete it. Another feature is the ability to *link* files. That is, the ability to have the same file exist under two different names, perhaps even in different directories.

To open a file and perform multiple read-and-write operations on the file, you use the methods provided by NSFileHandle. The methods in this class enable you to

- Open a file for reading, writing, or updating (reading and writing)
- Seek to a specified position within a file
- Read or write a specified number of bytes from and to a file

The methods provided by NSFileHandle can also be applied to devices or sockets. However, we focus only on dealing with ordinary files in this chapter.

The NSURL class allows you to work with URLs in your applications. We take a look at this class with a simple example that shows how you can read data from the Internet.

The NSBundle class provides methods that allow you to work with your *application's bundle*. This includes the ability to search the bundle for specific resources (for example, all JPEG images). We touch on this class lightly toward the end of the chapter.

Managing Files and Directories: NSFileManager

A file or directory is uniquely identified to NSFileManager using a *pathname* to the file. A path-name is an NSString object that can either be a relative or full pathname. A *relative* pathname is one that is relative to the current directory. So, the filename copy1.m would mean the file copy1.m in the current directory. Slash characters separate a list of directories in a path. The filename ch16/copy1.m is also a relative pathname, identifying the file copy1.m stored in the directory ch16, which is contained in the current directory.

Full pathnames, also known as *absolute* pathnames, begin with a leading /. Slash is actually a directory, called the *root* directory. On my Mac, the full pathname to my home directory is /Users/stevekochan. This pathname specifies three directories: / (the root directory), Users, and stevekochan.

The special tilde character (~) is used as an abbreviation for a user's home directory. ~linda would, therefore, be an abbreviation for the user linda's home directory, which might be the path /Users/linda. A solitary tilde character indicates the current user's home directory, meaning the pathname ~/copy1.m would reference the file copy1.m stored in the current user's home directory. Other special UNIX-style pathname characters, such as . for the current directory and .. for the parent directory, should be removed from pathnames before they're used by any of the Foundation file-handling methods. An assortment of path utilities are available that you can use for this, and they're discussed later in this chapter.

Try to avoid hard-coding pathnames into your programs. As you'll see in this chapter, methods and functions are available that enable you to obtain the pathname for the current directory, a user's home directory, and a directory that can be used for creating temporary files. You should avail yourself of these as much as possible. You'll see later in this chapter that Foundation has a function for obtaining a list of special directories, such as a user's Documents directory. This function is useful for developing both OS X and iOS applications.

Table 16.1 summarizes some basic NSFileManager methods for working with files. In that table, *path*, *path1*, *path2*, *from*, and *to* are all NSString objects; *attr* is an NSDictionary object; and *err* is a pointer to an NSError object that you can provide to get more information about a particular error. If you specify NULL for *err*, the default action will be taken, which for methods that return a BOOL is to return YES if the operation succeeds and NO if it fails. We do not cover the use of this object in this chapter.

Table 16.1   **Common NSFileManager File Methods**

Method	Description
-(NSData *) contentsAtPath: *path*	Reads data from a file
-(BOOL) createFileAtPath: *path* contents: (NSData *) *data* attributes: *attr*	Writes data to a file
-(BOOL) removeItemAtPath: *path* error: *err*	Removes a file
-(BOOL) moveItemAtPath: *from* toPath: *to* error: *err*	Renames or moves a file (*to* cannot already exist)
-(BOOL) copyItemAtPath: *from* toPath: *to* error: *err*	Copies a file (*to* cannot already exist)
-(BOOL) contentsEqualAtPath: *path1* andPath: *path2*	Compares contents of two files
-(BOOL) fileExistsAtPath: *path*	Tests for file existence
-(BOOL) isReadableFileAtPath: *path*	Tests whether file exists and can be read
-(BOOL) isWritableFileAtPath: *path*	Tests whether file exists and can be written
-(NSDictionary *) attributesOfItemAtPath: *path* error: *err*	Gets attributes for file
-(BOOL) setAttributesOfItemAtPath: *attr* error: *err*	Changes file attributes

Each of the file methods is invoked on an NSFileManager object that is created by sending a defaultManager message to the class, like so:

```
NSFileManager *fm;
   ...
fm = [NSFileManager defaultManager];
```

For example, to delete a file called todolist from the current directory, you first create the NSFileManager object as shown previously and then invoke the removeItemAtPath: method, like so:

```
[fm removeItemAtPath: @"todolist" error: NULL];
```

You can test the result that is returned to ensure that the file removal succeeds:

```
if ([fm removeItemAtPath: @"todolist" error: NULL] == NO) {
   NSLog (@"Couldn't remove file todolist");
   return 1;
}
```

The attributes dictionary enables you to specify, among other things, the permissions for a file you are creating or to obtain or change information for an existing file. For file creation, if you specify `nil` for this parameter, the default permissions are set for the file. The `attributesOfItemAtPath:traverseLink:` method returns a dictionary containing the specified file's attributes. The `traverseLink:` parameter is YES or NO for symbolic links. If the file is a symbolic link and YES is specified, the attributes of the linked-to file are returned; if NO is specified, the attributes of the link itself are returned.

For preexisting files, the attributes dictionary includes information such as the file's owner, its size, its creation date, and so on. Each attribute in the dictionary can be extracted based on its key, all of which are defined in `<Foundation/NSFileManager.h>`. For example, `NSFileSize` is the key for a file's size.

Program 16.1 shows some basic operations with files. This example assumes you have a file called `testfile` in your current directory with the following three lines of text:

```
This is a test file with some data in it.
Here's another line of data.
And a third.
```

Program 16.1

```
// Basic File operations
// Assumes the existence of a file called "testfile"
// in the current directory

#import <Foundation/Foundation.h>

int main (int argc, const char * argv[]) {
    @autoreleasepool {
        NSString           *fName = @"testfile";
        NSFileManager      *fm;
        NSDictionary       *attr;

        // Need to create an instance of the file manager

        fm = [NSFileManager defaultManager];

        // Let's make sure our test file exists first

        if ([fm fileExistsAtPath: fName] == NO)  {
            NSLog(@"File doesn't exist!");
            return 1;
        }

        //now let's make a copy

        if ([fm copyItemAtPath: fName toPath: @"newfile" error: NULL] == NO) {
            NSLog(@"File Copy failed!");
            return 2;
```

```
        }

        // Now let's test to see if the two files are equal

        if ([fm contentsEqualAtPath: fName andPath: @"newfile"] == NO) {
            NSLog(@"Files are Not Equal!");
            return 3;
        }

        // Now  lets rename the copy

        if ([fm moveItemAtPath: @"newfile" toPath: @"newfile2"
                error: NULL] == NO){
            NSLog(@"File rename Failed");
            return 4;
        }

        // get the size of the newfile2

        if ((attr = [fm attributesOfItemAtPath: @"newfile2" error: NULL])
            == nil)   {
            NSLog(@"Couldn't get file attributes!");
            return 5;
        }

        NSLog(@"File size is %llu bytes",
            [[attr objectForKey: NSFileSize] unsignedLongLongValue]);

        // And finally, let's delete the original file

        if ([fm removeItemAtPath: fName error: NULL] == NO)   {
            NSLog(@"file removal failed");
            return 6;
        }

         NSLog(@"All operations were successful");

         // Display the contents of the newly created file

        NSLog(@"%@", [NSString stringWithContentsOfFile:
              @"newfile2" encoding:NSUTF8StringEncoding error:NULL]);
    }
    return 0;
}
```

Program 16.1   **Output**

```
File size is 84 bytes
All operations were successful!

This is a test file with some data in it.
Here's another line of data.
And a third.
```

The program first tests whether `testfile` exists. If it does, it makes a copy of it and then tests the two files for equality. Experienced UNIX users should note that you can't move or copy a file into a directory simply by specifying the destination directory for the `copyItemAtPath:toPath:error:` and `moveItemAtPath:toPath:error:` methods; the file-name within that directory must be explicitly specified.

> **Note**
>
> You can create `testfile` with Xcode by selecting File, New, New File. In the left pane that appears, highlight Other, and then select Empty in the right pane. Enter **testfile** as the name of the file, and be sure to create it in the same directory as your executable file. If you have trouble locating the directory, use the `currentDirectoryPath:` method as described later in this section. Or, you can use a full pathname to the file, as in /Users/steve/testfile (substituting your username for steve).

The `moveItemAtPath:toPath:` method can be used to move a file from one directory to another. (It can also be used to move entire directories.) If the two paths reference files in the same directory (as in our example), the effect is to simply rename the file. So, in Program 16.1, you use this method to rename the file `newfile` to `newfile2`.

As noted in Table 16.1, when you are performing copying, renaming, or moving operations, the destination file cannot already exist. If it does, the operation will fail.

The size of `newfile2` is determined by using the `attributesOfItemAtPath:error:` method. You test to make sure a non-`nil` dictionary is returned and then use the `NSDictionary` method `objectForKey:` to get the file's size from the dictionary using the key `NSFileSize`. The integer value from the dictionary is then displayed.

The program uses the `removeItemAtPath:error:` method to remove your original file `testfile`.

Finally, `NSString`'s `stringWithContentsOfFile:encoding:error:` method is used to read the contents of the file `newfile2` into a `string` object, which is then passed as an argument to `NSLog` to be displayed. The encoding argument specifies how the character data in the file is represented. The choices to use for this argument are defined in the header file `NSString.h`. `NSUTF8StringEncoding` can be used to specify a file containing normal UTF8 ASCII characters.

Each of the file operations is tested for success in Program 16.1. If any fails, an error is logged using `NSLog`, and the program exits by returning a nonzero exit status. Each nonzero value, which by convention indicates program failure, is unique based on the type of error. If you write command-line tools, this is a useful technique because another program can test the return value, such as from within a shell script.

Working with the NSData Class

When working with files, you often need to read data into a temporary storage area, often called a *buffer*. When collecting data for subsequent output to a file, a storage area is also often used. Foundation's NSData class provides an easy way to set up a buffer, read the contents of the file into it, or write the contents of a buffer out to a file. And just in case you're wondering, for a 32-bit application, an NSDATA buffer can store up to 2GB. For a 64-bit application, it can hold up to 8EB (that's exabytes) or 8 billion gigabytes of data!

As you would expect, you can define either immutable (NSData) or mutable (NSMutableData) storage areas. We introduce methods from this class in this chapter and in succeeding chapters as well.

Program 16.2 shows how easily you can read the contents of a file into a buffer in memory.

The program reads the contents of your file newfile2 and writes it to a new file called newfile3. In a sense, it implements a file copy operation, although not in as straightforward a fashion as the copyItemAtPath:toPath:error: method.

Program 16.2

```
// Make a copy of a file
#import <Foundation/Foundation.h>

int main (int argc, char * argv[])
{
    @autoreleasepool {
        NSFileManager      *fm;
        NSData             *fileData;

        fm = [NSFileManager defaultManager];

        // Read the file newfile2

        fileData = [fm contentsAtPath: @"newfile2"];

        if (fileData == nil) {
            NSLog (@"File read failed!");
            return 1;
        }

        // Write the data to newfile3

        if ([fm createFileAtPath: @"newfile3" contents: fileData
                    attributes: nil] == NO) {
```

```
            NSLog (@"Couldn't create the copy!");
            return 2;
    }


    NSLog (@"File copy was successful!");
  }
  return 0;
}
```

Program 16.2   **Output**

```
File copy was successful!
```

The `contentsAtPath:` method simply takes a pathname and reads the contents of the specified file into a storage area that it creates, returning the storage area object as the result or `nil` if the read fails (for example, if the file doesn't exist or can't be read by you).

The `createFileAtPath:contents:attributes:` method creates a file with the specified attributes (or uses the default if `nil` is supplied for the `attributes` argument). The contents of the specified `NSData` object are then written to the file. In our example, this data area contains the contents of the previously read file.

Working with Directories

Table 16.2 summarizes some of the methods provided by `NSFileManager` for working with directories. Many of these methods are the same as those for ordinary files, as listed in Table 16.1.

Table 16.2   **Common** `NSFileManager` **Directory Methods**

Method	Description
`-(NSString *) currentDirectoryPath`	Gets the current directory
`-(BOOL) changeCurrentDirectoryPath:` *path*	Changes the current directory
`-(BOOL) copyItemAtPath:` *from* `toPath:` *to* `error:` *err*	Copies a directory structure (*to* cannot previously exist)
`-(BOOL) createDirectoryAtPath:` *path* `withIntermediateDirectories:` `(BOOL)` *flag* `attributes:` *attr*	Creates a new directory
`-(BOOL) fileExistsAtPath:` *path* `isDirectory:` `(BOOL *)` *flag*	Tests whether the file exists and is a directory (`YES`/`NO` result is stored in *flag*)

Method	Description
-(NSArray *) contentsOfDirectoryAtPath: *path* error: *err*	Lists the contents of the directory
-(NSDirectoryEnumerator *) enumeratorAtPath: *path*	Enumerates the contents of the directory
-(BOOL) removeItemAtPath: *path* error: *err*	Deletes an empty directory
-(BOOL) moveItemAtPath: *from* toPath: *to* error: *err*	Renames or moves a directory (*to* cannot previously exist)

Program 16.3 shows basic operations with directories.

Program 16.3

```
// Some basic directory operations

#import <Foundation/Foundation.h>

int main (int argc, char * argv[])
{
  @autoreleasepool {
    NSString        *dirName = @"testdir";
    NSString        *path;
    NSFileManager   *fm;

    // Need to create an instance of the file manager

    fm = [NSFileManager defaultManager];

    // Get current directory

    path = [fm currentDirectoryPath];
    NSLog (@"Current directory path is %@", path);

    // Create a new directory

    if ([fm createDirectoryAtPath: dirName withIntermediateDirectories: YES
            attributes: nil error: NULL] == NO) {
        NSLog (@"Couldn't create directory!");
        return 1;
    }

    // Rename the new directory
```

```
    if ([fm moveItemAtPath: dirName toPath: @"newdir" error: NULL] == NO) {
        NSLog (@"Directory rename failed!");
        return 2;
    }

    // Change directory into the new directory

    if ([fm changeCurrentDirectoryPath: @"newdir"] == NO) {
        NSLog (@"Change directory failed!");
        return 3;
    }

    // Now get and display current working directory

    path = [fm currentDirectoryPath];
    NSLog (@"Current directory path is %@", path);

    NSLog (@"All operations were successful!");
  }
  return 0;
}
```

Program 16.3   **Output**

```
Current directory path is /Users/stevekochan/progs/ch16
Current directory path is /Users/stevekochan/progs/ch16/newdir
All operations were successful!
```

Program 16.3 is relatively self-explanatory. The current directory path is first obtained for informative purposes.

Note

The output shows what I got for my current directory when I ran the program using Terminal. If I run this program with Xcode, I get this as my current directory: /Users/steve_kochan/ Library/Developer/Xcode/DerivedData/prog2-cnoljvycenoopiddzwoyraybqlza/ Build/Products/Debug. Your current directory path will be different from mine and that shown in the output. On an iOS device, your program runs in what's known as a *sandbox,* where it has restricted access to files. If you run this program on such a device, you'll see that the current directory is listed as /. That's the root folder for the application running in its sandbox and not the root of the entire iOS device's file system.

Next, a new directory called testdir is created in the current directory. The program then uses the moveItemAtPath:toPath:error: method to rename the new directory from testdir to `newdir`. Remember that this method can also be used to move an entire directory structure (that means including its contents) from one place in the file system to another.

After renaming the new directory, the program makes that new directory the current directory using the `changeCurrentDirectoryPath:` method. The current directory path is then displayed to verify that the change was successful.

Enumerating the Contents of a Directory

Sometimes you need to get a list of the contents of a directory. This enumeration process can be accomplished using either the `enumeratorAtPath:` or the `contentsOfDirectoryAtPath:error` method. In the former case, each file in the specified directory is enumerated one at a time and, by default, if one of those files is a directory, its contents are also recursively enumerated. During this process, you can dynamically prevent this recursion by sending a `skipDescendants` message to an enumeration object so that its contents will not be enumerated.

In the case of `contentsOfDirectoryAtPath:error:`, the contents of the specified directory are enumerated, and the file list is returned in an array by the method. If any of the files contained in a directory is itself a directory, its contents are not recursively enumerated by this method.

Program 16.4 shows how you can use either method in your programs.

Program 16.4

```
// Enumerate the contents of a directory

#import <Foundation/Foundation.h>

int main (int argc, char * argv[])
{
    @autoreleasepool {
        NSString            *path;
        NSFileManager       *fm;
        NSDirectoryEnumerator *dirEnum;
        NSArray             *dirArray;

        // Need to create an instance of the file manager

        fm = [NSFileManager defaultManager];

        // Get current working directory path

        path = [fm currentDirectoryPath];

        // Enumerate the directory
```

```
        dirEnum = [fm enumeratorAtPath: path];

        NSLog (@"Contents of %@", path);

        while ((path = [dirEnum nextObject]) != nil)
            NSLog (@"%@", path);

        // Another way to enumerate a directory
        dirArray = [fm contentsOfDirectoryAtPath:
                [fm currentDirectoryPath] error: NULL];
        NSLog (@"Contents using contentsOfDirectoryAtPath:error:");

        for ( path in dirArray )
            NSLog (@"%@", path);
    }
    return 0;
}
```

Program 16.4   **Output**

```
Contents of /Users/stevekochan/mysrc/ch16:
a.out
dir1.m
dir2.m
file1.m
newdir
newdir/file1.m
newdir/output
path1.m
testfile

Contents using contentsOfDirectoryAtPath:error:
a.out
dir1.m
dir2.m
file1.m
newdir
path1.m
testfile
```

Note

On your system, your output will differ from that shown.

Let's take a closer look at the following code sequence:

```
dirEnum = [fm enumeratorAtPath: path];

NSLog (@"Contents of %", path);
while ((path = [dirEnum nextObject]) != nil)
    NSLog (@"%@", path);
```

You begin enumeration of a directory by sending an `enumeratorAtPath:` message to a file manager object (in this case, `fm`). An `NSDirectortyEnumerator` object gets returned by the `enumeratorAtPath:` method, which is stored inside `dirEnum`. Now, each time you send a `nextObject` message to this object, you get returned a path to the next file in the directory you are enumerating. When no more files are left to enumerate, you get `nil` returned.

You can see the difference between the two enumeration techniques from the output of Program 16.4. The `enumeratorAtPath:` method lists the contents of the `newdir` directory, whereas `contentsOfDirectoryAtPath:error:` does not. If `newdir` had contained subdirectories, they too would have been enumerated by `enumeratorAtPath:`.

As noted, during execution of the `while` loop in Program 16.4, you could have prevented enumeration of any subdirectories by making the following change to the code:

```
while ((path = [dirEnum nextObject]) != nil) {
    NSLog (@"%@", path)

    [fm fileExistsAtPath: path isDirectory: &flag];

    if (flag == YES)
        [dirEnum skipDescendents];
}
```

Here `flag` is a `BOOL` variable. The `fileExistsAtPath:` stores `YES` in `flag` if the specified path is a directory; otherwise, it stores `NO`.

Incidentally, as a reminder, you can display the entire `dirArray` contents with this single `NSLog` call
```
NSLog (@"%@", dirArray);
```

instead of using fast enumeration as was done in the program.

Working with Paths: `NSPathUtilities.h`

`NSPathUtilities.h` includes functions and category extensions to `NSString` to enable you to manipulate pathnames. You should use these whenever possible to make your program more independent of the structure of the file system and locations of particular files and directories. Program 16.5 shows how to use several of the functions and methods provided by `NSPathUtilities.h`.

Program 16.5

```
// Some basic path operations

#import <Foundation/Foundation.h>

int main (int argc, char * argv[])
{
    @autoreleasepool {
        NSString         *fName = @"path.m";
        NSFileManager    *fm;
        NSString         *path, *tempdir, *extension, *homedir, *fullpath;

        NSArray          *components;

        fm = [NSFileManager defaultManager];

        // Get the temporary working directory

        tempdir = NSTemporaryDirectory ();

        NSLog (@"Temporary Directory is %@", tempdir);

        // Extract the base directory from current directory

        path = [fm currentDirectoryPath];
        NSLog (@"Base dir is %@", [path lastPathComponent]);

        // Create a full path to the file fName in current directory

        fullpath = [path stringByAppendingPathComponent: fName];
        NSLog (@"fullpath to %@ is %@", fName, fullpath);

        // Get the filename extension

        extension = [fullpath pathExtension];
        NSLog (@"extension for %@ is %@", fullpath, extension);

        // Get user's home directory

        homedir = NSHomeDirectory ();
        NSLog (@"Your home directory is %@", homedir);

        // Divide a path into its components

        components = [homedir pathComponents];
```

```
        for ( path in components )
            NSLog (@"%@", path);
    }
    return 0;
}
```

Program 16.5 **Output**

```
Temporary Directory is /var/folders/HT/HTyGLvSNHTuNb6NrMuo7QE+++TI/-Tmp-/
Base dir is examples
fullpath to path.m is /Users/stevekochan/progs/examples/path.m
extension for /Users/stevekochan/progs/examples/path.m is m
Your home directory is /Users/stevekochan
/
Users
stevekochan
```

> ### Note
> On your system, your output will differ from that shown.

The function NSTemporaryDirectory returns the pathname of a directory on the system you can use for the creation of temporary files. If you create temporary files in this directory, be sure to remove them when you're done. Also, make sure that your filenames are unique, particularly if more than one instance of your application might be running at the same time. (See Exercise 5 at the end of this chapter.) This can easily happen if more than one user logged on to your system is running the same application. Note that temporary files are just that. If you don't remove them when you're with them, the system will remove them for you at some point. You shouldn't rely on that, however, and should remove them yourself.

The lastPathComponent method extracts the last file in a path. This is useful when you have an absolute pathname and just want to get the base filename from it.

The stringByAppendingPathComponent: is useful for tacking on a filename to the end of a path. If the pathname specified as the receiver doesn't end in a slash, the method inserts one in the pathname to separate it from the appended filename. By combining the currentDirectoryPath method with the method stringByAppendingPathComponent:, you can create a full pathname to a file in the current directory. Program 16.5 shows this technique.

The pathExtension method gives the file extension for the provided pathname. In the example, the extension for the file path.m is m, which is returned by the method. If the file does not have an extension, the method simply returns an empty string.

The NSHomeDirectory function returns the home directory for the current user. You can get the home directory for any particular user by using the NSHomeDirectoryForUser function instead, supplying the user's name as the argument to the function.

The pathComponents method returns an array containing each of the components of the specified path. Program 16.5 sequences through each element of the returned array and displays each path component on a separate line of output.

Common Methods for Working with Paths

Table 16.3 summarizes many of the commonly used methods for working with paths. In this table, *components* is an NSArray object containing string objects for each component in a path; *path* is a string object specifying a path to a file; and *ext* is a string object indicating a path extension (for example, @"mp4").

Table 16.3   **Common Path Utility Methods**

Method	Description
+(NSString *) pathWithComponents: *components*	Constructs a valid path from elements in *components*
-(NSArray *) pathComponents	Deconstructs a path into its constituent components
-(NSString *) lastPathComponent	Extracts the last component in a path
-(NSString *) pathExtension	Extracts the extension from the last component in a path
-(NSString *) stringByAppendingPathComponent: *path*	Adds *path* to the end of an existing path
-(NSString *) stringByAppendingPathExtension: *ext*	Adds the specified extension to the last component in the path
-(NSString *) stringByDeletingLastPathComponent	Removes the last path component
-(NSString *) stringByDeletingPathExtension	Removes the extension from the last path component
-(NSString *) stringByExpandingTildeInPath	Expands any tildes in the path to the user's home directory (~) or a specified user's home directory (~*user*)
-(NSString *) stringByResolvingSymlinksInPath	Attempts to resolve symbolic links in the path
-(NSString *) stringByStandardizingPath	Standardizes a path by attempting to resolve ~, .. (parent directory), . (current directory), and symbolic links

Table 16.4 presents *functions* available to obtain information about a user, her home directory, and a directory for storing temporary files.

Table 16.4 **Common Path Utility Functions**

`NSString *NSUserName (void)`	Returns the current user's login name
`NSString *NSFullUserName (void)`	Returns the current user's full username
`NSString *NSHomeDirectory (void)`	Returns the path to the current user's home directory
`NSString *NSHomeDirectoryForUser (NSString *user)`	Returns the home directory for *user*
`NSString *NSTemporaryDirectory (void)`	Returns the path to a directory that can be used for creating a temporary file

You might want to also look at the Foundation function `NSSearchPathForDirectoriesInDomains`, which you can use to locate special directories on the system or on your device, such as the Application and Documents directories. For example, the following defines a method called `saveFilePath` that returns a path to a file called `saveFile` in the Documents directory. You could use a method like this if you want to save some data from your application into a file:

```
-(NSString *) saveFilePath
{
    NSArray *dirList = NSSearchPathForDirectoriesInDomains
                        (NSDocumentDirectory, NSUserDomainMask, YES);
    NSString *docDir = dirList[0];

    return [docDir stringByAppendingPathComponent: @"saveFile"];
}
```

> **Note**
>
> You can use the Documents directory for storing data that will last from one run of your application to the next. Each iOS application gets its own Documents directory that it can write data into. The first argument to the `NSSearchPathForDirectoriesInDomains` function specifies the directory whose path you want to locate. Another directory you might want to use in your application is Caches. You can also use that directory for storing data. As of iOS 5, Apple is encouraging developers to store persistent data in the cloud. See Table 16.5 for a list of commonly used iOS directories.

Table 16.5 **Common iOS Directories**

Directory	Purpose
Documents (NSDocumentDirectory)	Directory for writing application-specific data files. Files written here under iOS can be shared and accessed from iTunes. Files stored here are automatically backed up to iCloud.
Library/Caches (NSCachesDirectory)	Directory for writing application-specific support files to persist between launches of the application. Files created in this directory are not backed up by iTunes.
tmp (use NSTemporaryDirecory())	Directory to write temporary files that can be removed after your application terminates. You should remove files from this directory when no longer needed.
Library/Preferences	This directory contains application-specific preference files. Preference files are created, read, and modified using the NSUserDefaults class.

The second argument to the function can be one of several values that specifies the directories to list, such as the user's (as shown in the example), the system's, or all directories. The last argument specifies whether to expand ~ characters in the path.

The NSSearchPathForDirectoriesInDomains returns an array of paths. The array will contain a single element if you're just looking for the user's directory and can contain more than one element based on the value specified by the second argument.

> **Note**
>
> When writing iOS applications, the second argument to the NSSearchPathForDirectoriesInDomains function should be NSUserDomainMask, and you should expect to get an array containing a single path back in return.

Copying Files and Using the NSProcessInfo Class

Program 16.6 illustrates a command-line tool to implement a simple file copy operation. Usage of this command is as follows:

```
copy from-file to-file
```

Unlike NSFileManager's copyPath:toPath:handler: method, your command-line tool enables *to-file* to be a directory name. In that case, the file is copied into the *to-file* directory under the name *from-file*. Also unlike the method, if *to-file* already exists, you allow its contents to be overwritten. This is more in line with the standard UNIX copy command cp.

You can get the filenames from the command line by using the argc and argv arguments to main. These two arguments are populated, respectively, with the number of argument types on the command line (including the command name), and a pointer to an array of C-style character strings.

Instead of having to deal with C strings, which is what you have to do when you work with `argv`, use instead a Foundation class called `NSProcessInfo`. `NSProcessInfo` contains methods that allow you to set and retrieve various types of information about your running application (that is, your *process*). Table 16.6 summarizes these methods.

Table 16.6   `NSProcessInfo` **Methods**

Method	Description
`+(NSProcessInfo *) processInfo`	Returns information about the current process.
`-(NSArray *) arguments`	Returns the arguments to the current process as an array of `NSString` objects.
`-(NSDictionary *) environment`	Returns a dictionary of variable/value pairs representing the current environment variables (such as `PATH` and `HOME`) and their values.
`-(int) processIdentifier`	Returns the process identifier, which is a unique number assigned by the operating system to identify each running process.
`-(NSString *) processName`	Returns the name of the current executing process.
`-(NSString *) globallyUniqueString`	Returns a different unique string each time it is invoked. This could be used for generating unique temporary filenames (see Exercise 5).
`-(NSString *) hostName`	Returns the name of the host system (returns `Steve-Kochans-Computer.local` on my OS X system).
`-(NSUInteger) operatingSystem`	Returns a number indicating the operating system (returns the value `5` on my Mac).
`-(NSString *) operatingSystemName`	Returns the name of the operating system (returns the constant `NSMACHOperatingSystem` on my Mac, where the possible return values are defined in `NSProcessInfo.h`).
`-(NSString *) operatingSystemVersionString`	Returns the current version of the operating system (returns `Version 10.6.7 (Build 10J869)` on my Mac OS X system).

Method	Description
-(void) setProcessName: (NSString *) name	Sets the name of the current process to name. Should be used with caution because some assumptions can be made about the name of your process (for example, by the user default settings).

Program 16.6

```
// Implement a basic copy utility

#import <Foundation/Foundation.h>

int main (int argc, char * argv[])
{
   @autoreleasepool {
      NSFileManager      *fm;
      NSString           *source, *dest;
      BOOL               isDir;
      NSProcessInfo      *proc = [NSProcessInfo processInfo];
      NSArray            *args = [proc arguments];

      fm = [NSFileManager defaultManager];

      // Check for two arguments on the command line

      if ([args count] != 3) {
         NSLog (@"Usage: %@ src dest", [proc processName]);
         return 1;
      }

      source = args[1];
      dest = args[2];

      // Make sure the source file can be read

      if ([fm isReadableFileAtPath: source] == NO) {
         NSLog (@"Can't read %@", source);
         return 2;
      }

      // See if the destination file is a directory
      // if it is, add the source to the end of the destination

      [fm fileExistsAtPath: dest isDirectory: &isDir];

      if (isDir == YES)
```

```
        dest = [dest stringByAppendingPathComponent:
                [source lastPathComponent]];

    // Remove the destination file if it already exists

    [fm removeItemAtPath: dest error: NULL];

    // Okay, time to perform the copy

    if ([fm copyItemPath: source toPath: dest error: NULL] == NO) {
        NSLog (@"Copy failed!");
        return 3;
    }

    NSLog (@"Copy of %@ to %@ succeeded!", source, dest);
    }
    return 0;
}
```

Program 16.6   **Output**

```
$ ls -l            see what files we have
total 96
-rwxr-xr-x 1 stevekoc staff 19956 Jul 24 14:33 copy
-rw-r--r-- 1 stevekoc staff 1484  Jul 24 14:32 copy.m
-rw-r--r--1  stevekoc staff 1403  Jul 24 13:00 file1.m
drwxr-xr-x 2 stevekoc staff    68 Jul 24 14:40 newdir
-rw-r--r--1  stevekoc staff 1567  Jul 24 14:12 path1.m
-rw-r--r--1  stevekoc staff    84 Jul 24 13:22 testfile
$ copy             try with no args
Usage: copy src dest
$ copy foo copy2
Can't read foo
$ copy copy.m backup.m
Copy of copy.m to backup.m succeeded!
$ diff copy.m backup.m   compare the files
$ copy copy.m newdir     try copy into directory
Copy of copy.m to newdir/copy.m succeeeded!
$ ls -l newdir
total 8
-rw-r—r— 1 stevekoc staff 1484 Jul 24 14:44 copy.m
$
```

Note

The output shown will differ on your system based on the files you have stored in your current directory when you run this program.

`NSProcessInfo`'s `arguments` method returns an array of string objects. The first element of the array is the name of the process, and the remaining elements contain the arguments typed on the command line.

You first check to ensure that two arguments were typed on the command line. This is done by testing the size of the array `args` that is returned from the `arguments` method. If this test succeeds, the program then extracts the source and destination filenames from the `args` array, assigning their values to `source` and `dest`, respectively.

The program next checks to ensure that the source file can be read, issuing an error message and exiting if it can't.

The statement

```
[fm fileExistsAtPath: dest isDirectory: &isDir];
```

checks the file specified by `dest` to see whether it is a directory. As you've seen previously, the answer (`YES` or `NO`) is stored in the variable `isDir`.

If `dest` is a directory, you want to append the last path component of the source filename to the end of the directory's name. You use the path utility method `stringByAppendingPathComponent:` to do this. So, if the value of `source` is the string `ch16/copy1.m` and the value of `dest` is `/Users/stevekochan/progs` and the latter is a directory, you change the value of `dest` to `/Users/stevekochan/progs/copy1.m`.

The `copyPath:ToPath:handler:` method doesn't allow files to be overwritten. Thus, to avoid an error, the program tries to remove the destination file first by using the `removeFileAtPath:handler:` method. It doesn't really matter whether this method succeeds because it will fail anyway if the destination file doesn't exist.

Upon reaching the end of the program, you can assume all went well and issue a message to that effect.

Basic File Operations: `NSFileHandle`

The methods provided by `NSFileHandle` enable you to work more closely with files. At the beginning of this chapter, we listed some of the things you can do with these methods.

In general, follow these three steps when working with a file:

1. Open the file and obtain an `NSFileHandle` object to reference the file in subsequent I/O operations.

2. Perform your I/O operations on the open file.

3. Close the file.

Table 16.7 summarizes some commonly used `NSFileHandle` methods. In this table `fh` is an `NSFileHandle` object, `data` is an `NSData` object, `path` is an `NSString` object, and `offset` is an unsigned long long.

Table 16.7   **Common** NSFileHandle **Methods**

Method	Description
+(NSFileHandle *) fileHandleForReadingAtPath: *path*	Opens a file for reading
+(NSFileHandle *) fileHandleForWritingAtPath: *path*	Opens a file for writing
+(NSFileHandle *) fileHandleForUpdatingAtPath: *path*	Opens a file for updating (reading and writing)
-(NSData *) availableData	Returns data available for reading from a device or channel
-(NSData *) readDataToEndOfFile	Reads the remaining data up to the end of the file (UINT_MAX) bytes max
-(NSData *) readDataOfLength: (NSUInteger) *bytes*	Reads a specified number of *bytes* from the file
-(void) writeData: *data*	Writes *data* to the file
-(unsigned long long) offsetInFile	Obtains the current file offset
-(void) seekToFileOffset: *offset*	Sets the current file offset
-(unsigned long long) seekToEndOfFile	Positions the current file offset at the end of the file
-(void) truncateFileAtOffset: *offset*	Sets the file size to *offset* bytes (pad if needed)
-(void) closeFile	Closes the file

Not shown here are methods for obtaining NSFileHandles for standard input, standard output, standard error, and the null device. These are of the form fileHandleWithDevice, where Device can be StandardInput, StandardOutput, StandardError, or NullDevice.

Also not shown here are methods for reading and writing data in the background (that is, asynchronously).

Note that the NSFileHandle class does not provide for the creation of files. That has to be done with NSFileManager methods, as already described. So, both fileHandleForWritingAtPath: and fileHandleForUpdatingAtPath: assume the file exists and return nil if it doesn't. In both cases, the file offset is set to the beginning of the file, so writing (or reading for update mode) begins at the start of the file. Also, if you're used to programming under UNIX, you know that opening a file for writing does not truncate the file. You have to do that yourself if that's your intention.

Program 16.7 opens the original testfile file you created at the start of this chapter, reads in its contents, and copies it to a file called testout.

Program 16.7

```
// Some basic file handle operations
// Assumes the existence of a file called "testfile"
// in the current working directory

#import <Foundation/Foundation.h>

int main (int argc, char * argv[])
{
    @autoreleasepool {
        NSFileHandle      *inFile, *outFile;
        NSData            *buffer;

        // Open the file testfile for reading

        inFile = [NSFileHandle fileHandleForReadingAtPath: @"testfile"];

        if (inFile == nil) {
            NSLog (@"Open of testfile for reading failed");
            return 1;
        }

        // Create the output file first if necessary

        [[NSFileManager defaultManager] createFileAtPath: @"testout"
            contents: nil attributes: nil];

        // Now open outfile for writing

        outFile = [NSFileHandle fileHandleForWritingAtPath: @"testout"];

        if (outFile == nil) {
            NSLog (@"Open of testout for writing failed");
            return 2;
        }

        // Truncate the output file since it may contain data

        [outFile truncateFileAtOffset: 0];

        // Read the data from inFile and write it to outFile

        buffer = [inFile readDataToEndOfFile];

        [outFile writeData: buffer];
```

```
    // Close the two files

    [inFile closeFile];
    [outFile closeFile];

    // Verify the file's contents

    NSLog(@"%@", [NSString stringWithContentsOfFile: @"testout" encoding:
                  NSUTF8StringEncoding error: NULL]);
    }
    return 0;
}
```

Program 16.7 **Output**

```
This is a test file with some data in it.
Here's another line of data.
And a third.
```

The method `readDataToEndOfFile:` reads up to `UINT_MAX` bytes of data at a time, which is defined in `<limits.h>` and equal to $FFFFFFFF_{16}$. This will be large enough for any application you'll have to write. You can also break up the operation to perform smaller-sized reads and writes. You can even set up a loop to transfer a buffer full of bytes between the files at a time, using the `readDataOfLength:` method. Your buffer size might be 8,192 (8KB) or 131,072 (128KB) bytes, for example. A power of 2 is normally used because the underlying operating system typically performs its I/O operations in chunks of data of such sizes. You might want to experiment with different values on your system to see what works best.

If a read method reaches the end of the file without reading any data, it returns an empty `NSData` object (that is, a buffer with no bytes in it). You can apply the `length` method to the buffer and test for equality with zero to see whether any data remains to be read from the file.

If you open a file for updating, the file offset is set to the beginning of the file. You can change that offset by seeking within a file and then perform your read or write operations on the file. So, to seek to the 10th byte in a file whose handle is `databaseHandle`, you can write the following message expression:

```
[databaseHandle seekToFileOffset: 10];
```

Relative file positioning is done by obtaining the current file offset and then adding to or subtracting from it. So, to skip over the next 128 bytes in the file, write the following:

```
[databaseHandle seekToFileOffet:
        [databaseHandle offsetInFile] + 128];
```

And to move back the equivalent of five integers in the file, write this:

```
[databaseHandle seekToFileOffet:
        [databaseHandle offsetInFile] - 5 * sizeof (int)];
```

Program 16.8 appends the contents of one file to another. It does this by opening the second file for writing, seeking to the end of the file, and then writing the contents of the first file to the second.

Program 16.8

```
// Append the file "fileA" to the end of "fileB"

#import <Foundation/Foundation.h>

int main (int argc, char * argv[])
{
   @autoreleasepool {
      NSFileHandle           *inFile, *outFile;
      NSData                 *buffer;

      // Open the file fileA for reading

      inFile = [NSFileHandle fileHandleForReadingAtPath: @"fileA"];

      if (inFile == nil) {
          NSLog (@"Open of fileA for reading failed");
          return 1;
      }

      // Open the file fileB for updating

      outFile = [NSFileHandle fileHandleForWritingAtPath: @"fileB"];

      if (outFile == nil) {
          NSLog (@"Open of fileB for writing failed");
          return 2;
      }

      // Seek to the end of outFile

      [outFile seekToEndOfFile];

      // Read inFile and write its contents to outFile

      buffer = [inFile readDataToEndOfFile];
      [outFile writeData: buffer];
```

```
    // Close the two files

    [inFile closeFile];
    [outFile closeFile];

    // verify its contents

    NSLog(@"%@", [NSString stringWithContentsOfFile: @"fileB"
        encoding: NSUTF8StringEncoding error: NULL]);
  }
  return 0;
}
```

Contents of `fileA` before running Program 16.8:

```
This is line 1 in the first file.
This is line 2 in the first file.
```

Contents of `fileB` before running Program 16.8:

```
This is line 1 in the second file.
This is line 2 in the second file.
```

Program 16.8 **Output**

```
Contents of fileB
This is line 1 in the second file.
This is line 2 in the second file.
This is line 1 in the first file.
This is line 2 in the first file.
```

You can see from the output that the contents of the first file were successfully appended to the end of the second file. Incidentally, `seekToEndOfFile` returns the current file offset after the seek is performed. We chose to ignore that value; you can use that information to obtain the size of a file in your program if you need it.

The NSURL Class

The NSURL class provides an easy way for you to work with URL addresses in your program. For example, given an HTTP address that is a path to a file on the Internet, you can easily read the contents of that file with a few method calls. You'll find many methods in Foundation that take NSURL objects as arguments. Just remember that an NSURL object is not a string object such as @"http:/www.apple.com", but it's easy to create one from a string object using the URLWithString: method.

Program 16.9 shows how the HTML contents from a Web address can be read into a program.

Program 16.9

```
// Read the contents of a file stored at a URL

#import <Foundation/Foundation.h>

int main (int argc, const char * argv[]) {
    @autoreleasepool {
        NSURL *myURL = [NSURL URLWithString: @"http://classroomM.com"];

        NSString *myHomePage = [NSString stringWithContentsOfURL: myURL
                    encoding: NSASCIIStringEncoding error: NULL];

        NSLog(@"%@", myHomePage);

    }
    return 0;
}
```

Program 16.9 **Partial Output**

```
<!DOCTYPE html PUBLIC "-//W3C//DTD XHTML 1.0 Transitional//EN"
"http://www.w3.org/TR/xhtml1/DTD/xhtml1-transitional.dtd">
<html xmlns="http://www.w3.org/1999/xhtml"><head>
<meta http-equiv="Content-Type" content="text/html; charset=iso-8859-1" />
<meta http-equiv="Content-Style-Type" content="text/css" />
<meta name="google-site-verification" content=
"J75b1yb6mDQItzHDxWDph1bNC8rVuc0OzLj8gzlj9y8" />
<title>iPhone Online Course and iPhone Programming Training - Home</title>
  ...
```

You can see how easy it is to get data from the Internet. And if you have a dictionary stored as a property list at a Web address, you can read that in as well, using the `dictionaryWithContentsOfURL:` method. Or if it's an array stored as a property list, you use the `arrayWithContentsOfURL:` method instead. You may also want to look into the `dataWithContentsOfURL:` method for reading any type of data from a Web address.

The NSBundle Class

When you create an application, the system stores all the data associated with that application—which includes resources such as images, localized strings, icons, and so on—into a package known as an *application bundle*. To access those resources from within your application, you want to become familiar with the NSBundle class.

It's easy to add a resource like an image or a text file to your application: You just drag the file into the left pane in Xcode. When prompted, you'll usually want to copy the resource into your project folder so that your project is all self-contained.

Here's a statement that returns the path to a file called `instructions.txt` that's stored in your application bundle:

```
NSString *txtFilePath = [[NSBundle mainBundle]
              pathForResource: @"instructions" ofType: @"txt"];
```

The `mainBundle` method gives the directory where the application bundle is located. You can use this method for OS X or iOS applications. The `pathForResource:ofType:` method locates the specified file within that directory and returns a path to that file. You can subsequently read the contents of that file into your application with a statement like this:

```
NSString *instructions = [NSString stringWithContentsOfFile: txtFilePath
    encoding: NSUTF8StringEncoding error: NULL];
```

If you want to locate all the JPEG images with the file extension .jpg in the images directory of your application bundle, you can use the `pathsForResourcesOfType:inDirectory:` method like so:

```
NSArray *birds = [[NSBundle mainBundle] pathsForResourcesOfType:@"jpg"
              inDirectory: @"birdImages"];
```

The method returns an array of pathnames. If your JPEG's are not stored in a subdirectory in your application, you can specify `@""` as the value of the `inDirectory:` parameter.

There are more methods in the `NSBundle` class that you'll want to learn about. Check your documentation for details.

Exercises

1. Modify the copy program developed in Program 16.6 so that it can accept more than one source file to be copied into a directory, like the standard UNIX `cp` command. So, the command

   $ copy copy1.m file1.m file2.m progs

   should copy the three files `copy1.m`, `file1.m`, and `file2.m` into the directory progs. Be sure that when more than one source file is specified, the last argument is, in fact, an existing directory.

2. Write a command-line tool called `myfind` that takes two arguments. The first is a starting directory to begin the search, and the second is a filename to locate. So, the command line

   $ myfind /Users proposal.doc
   /Users/stevekochan/MyDocuments/proposals/proposal.doc
   $

   begins searching the file system from `/Users` to locate the file `proposal.doc`. Print either a full path to the file if it's found (as shown) or an appropriate message if it's not.

3. Write your own version of the standard UNIX tools `basename` and `dirname`.

4. Using `NSProcessInfo`, write a program to display all the information returned by each of its getter methods.

5. Given the `NSPathUtilities.h` function `NSTemporaryDirectory` and the `NSProcessInfo` method `globallyUniqueString` described in this chapter, add a category called `TempFiles` to `NSString`, and in it define a method called `temporaryFileName` that returns a different and unique filename every time it is invoked.

6. Modify Program 16.7 so that the file is read and written `kBufSize` bytes at a time, where `kBufSize` is defined at the beginning of your program. Be sure to test the program on large files (that is, files larger than `kBufSize` bytes).

7. Open a file, read its contents 128 bytes at a time, and write it to the terminal. Use `NSFileHandle`'s `fileHandleWithStandardOutput` method to obtain a handle for the terminal's output.

8. A dictionary is stored as a property list at this URL: `http://bit.ly/aycNwd`. Write a program to read the contents of this dictionary and display its contents. What data does the dictionary contain?

17

Memory Management and Automatic Reference Counting

Recall the NSMutableArray class that enables you to create an array that you can add objects to and remove objects from. Suppose that at the start of execution of your program you need to read the contents of a file into an array. Assume you want to call new array myData and you want to initialize its contents from a file that is stored in the form of a *property list* (covered in more detail in Chapter 19, "Archiving"). You can do this with a single method call using NSArray's arrayWithContentsOfFile: method like so:

```
NSSArray *myData = [NSArray arrayWithContentsOfFile: @"database1"];
```

This reads and parses the file and stores the resulting elements into a newly created array, returning the reference to the array back to you. That reference is then stored into the variable myData.

Suppose that after processing the data in myData you want to read the data from a different file and process its contents in a similar manner; you execute the following statement:

```
myData = [NSArray arrayWithContentsOfFile: @"database2"];
```

Here the variable myData is changed so that it now references a different array whose contents were set from the second file. But what happened to the first array? You no longer have a reference to it. (You lost the reference when you overwrote myData.) And what about all the elements in that first array? What happened to them? And assume you need to repeat this process of reading data from different files hundreds or perhaps thousands of times. What happens to all those array objects and their elements that are no longer referenced and therefore no longer needed by the application? Those objects might still be sitting in memory somewhere, even though you're no longer using them. Well, without some sort of "cleanup" process, memory continues to fill with unreferenced objects, potentially taking your application to the breaking point, where it literally had no available memory left to do any more work.

This chapter covers the idea of memory management, albeit at a fairly high level. Memory management is all about cleaning up (recycling) unused memory so that it can be used again. If an object is no longer being used, let's reuse its memory. That sounds simple enough. However, it's not quite that simple. Somebody has to figure out that simple fact. That is, somebody—and that somebody can be you, the computer, or both—has to be able to somehow determine when an object is no longer being used and that the memory it occupies can therefore be reclaimed.

Several different memory management strategies have been developed to assist in these efforts. Two of them are automated methods; that is, the computer keeps track of the objects and frees their memory as necessary. The third method is a hybrid approach; the system does some of the work for you, but also requires that you, the programmer, be diligent and take care of telling the system when an object is no longer being used.

Up until the release of Xcode 4.2 memory management was the subject of great consternation, one that required a great deal of understanding and forethought on the part of the programmer. Programmers had to carefully navigate the world of reference counts, retains, releases, and autoreleases to produce applications that judiciously used memory and weren't subject to crashing at the most inopportune times, often as the result of trying to reference an object that had inadvertently been destroyed before its time had really passed.

With the release of a feature known as *Automatic Reference Counting,* or ARC, in Xcode 4.2, programmers no longer have to think about memory management issues; it's all taken care of for you! There are a couple of special cases you have to learn about (and we respectfully refer you to Apple's documentation for details on those). But overall, ARC is truly a godsend to iOS developers. The proof of that is that I haven't really had to mention memory management at all up until this chapter. In earlier editions of this book, I took great pains throughout the entire text to make sure that readers fully understood and judiciously applied proper memory management techniques.

In this chapter, you get an overview of the different memory management schemes that exist for Cocoa and iOS developers. We also briefly describe how manual memory management works. That's in case you have to support older code or for some reason decide not to avail yourself of the currently available automatic memory management features.

Although you no longer have to worry about the life span of your objects (and things like releasing their memory when you're done using them), depending on the type of application you're writing judicious use of memory is still important. For example, if you're writing an interactive drawing application that creates many objects during the execution of the program, you must take care that your program doesn't continue to consume more memory resources as it runs. In such cases, it becomes your responsibility to intelligently manage those resources and make sure you're not unnecessarily allocating objects.

Three basic memory management models are supported for Objective-C developers:

1. Automatic garbage collection

2. Manual reference counting and the autorelease pool

3. Automatic Reference Counting (ARC)

Automatic Garbage Collection

As of Objective C 2.0, a form of memory management known as *garbage collection* became available. With garbage collection, the system automatically determines which objects own which other objects, automatically freeing up (or garbage-collecting) objects that are no longer referenced as space is needed during the program's execution.

The iOS runtime environment doesn't support garbage collection, so you don't have the option to use it when developing programs for that platform. And, as of OS X 10.8 (Mountain Lion), garbage collection is *deprecated* (meaning at some point in the near future it will no longer be supported). Apple therefore now discourages its use and advises you to use ARC instead.

Manual Reference Counting

If you are going to create applications without the use of garbage collection or ARC, or if you have to support code that you can't migrate to run with ARC, then you need to know how to manage memory. That is, you need to learn about how to work with *reference counts*.

The general concept is as follows: When an object is created, its initial reference count is set to 1. Each time you need to ensure that the object be kept around, you effectively create a reference to it by incrementing its reference count by 1. This is done by sending the object a retain message, like so:

```
[myFraction retain];
```

When you no longer need an object, you decrement its reference count by 1 by sending it a release message, like this:

```
[myFraction release];
```

When the reference count of an object reaches 0, the system knows that the object is no longer being used (because, in theory, it is no longer being referenced anywhere in the application), so it frees up (*deallocates*) its memory. This process gets initiated by sending the object a dealloc message. In many cases, you use the dealloc method inherited from NSObject. However, you might need to override dealloc to release any instance variables or other objects that your object may have allocated or retained. For example, if your class has an NSArray object as one of its instance variables and you alloc the array, you are responsible for releasing that array when your object is to be destroyed. You do that in dealloc.

Successful operation of this manual reference counting strategy requires diligence by you, the programmer, to ensure that reference counts are appropriately incremented and decremented during program execution. The system handles some, but not all, of this for you.

When using manual reference counting, you should note that some of the methods in the Foundation framework might increment the reference count of an object, such as when an object is added to an array using NSMutableArray's addObject: method or when a view is added as a subview using UIView's addSubview: method. Likewise, methods might decrement the reference count of an object. `removeObjectAtIndex:` and `removeFromSuperview` are two such methods.

After an object has been destroyed (that is, its reference count has been decremented to zero and `dealloc` called), further references to that object become invalid. If you have such a reference, that is often referred to as a *dangling pointer* reference. Sending that dangling pointer a message often causes unexpected behavior, including your application crashing. Sometimes programmers send an object that's already been deallocated a `release` message because they haven't accurately tracked the object's retains and releases. This is known as *over-releasing an object,* and it often results in a crash.

Object References and the Autorelease Pool

You might need to write a method that first creates an object (say with `alloc`) and then returns that object as the result of the method call. Here's the dilemma: Even though the method is done using the object, it can't release it, because it needs to return its value. The `NSAutoreleasePool` class was created in order to help solve problems like these by keeping track of objects to be released at a later time in an object known as an autorelease pool. That later time is when the pool gets *drained,* which is done by sending the autorelease pool object a `drain` message.

To add an object to the list of objects maintained by the autorelease pool, you send that object an `autorelease` message, like so:

```
[result autorelease];
```

When dealing with programs that use classes from the Foundation, UIKit, or AppKit frameworks, you must create an autorelease pool because classes from these frameworks can create and return autoreleased objects. You do that in your application using the `@autoreleasepool` directive like so:

```
@autoreleasepool {
    statements
}
```

Xcode generates a template file with this directive at the start of `main`, even if you create a new project without ARC enabled.

When the end of an `autorelease` block is reached, the system drains the pool. This has the effect of sending a `release` message to every object that was sent an `autorelease` message and therefore added to the pool. And as you know, if any of those objects ends up getting their reference counts decremented to zero, those objects will be sent a `dealloc` message and their memory released.

Note that the autorelease pool doesn't contain the actual objects themselves, only a reference to the objects that are to be released when the pool is drained.

Not all newly created objects are added to the autorelease pool. In fact, any object created by a method whose name starts with the word `alloc`, `copy`, `mutableCopy`, or `new` is one that is not autoreleased. In such a case, you are said to *own* that object. When you own an object, you become responsible for releasing the memory taken up by that object when you're done using it. This is done by sending the object a `release` message. Or you can add it to the autorelease pool yourself by sending it an `autorelease` message.

This is what the `main` routine from Program 3.3 would look like if we used manual reference counting:

```
int main (int argc, char * argv[]) {
    @autoreleasepool {
        Fraction *frac1 = [[Fraction alloc] init];
        Fraction *frac2 = [[Fraction alloc] init];

        // Set 1st fraction to 2/3
        [frac1 setNumerator: 2];
        [frac1 setDenominator: 3];

        // Set 2nd fraction to 3/7
        [frac2 setNumerator: 3];
        [frac2 setDenominator: 7];

        // Display the fractions

        NSLog (@"First fraction is:");
        [frac1 print];

        NSLog (@"Second fraction is:");
        [frac2 print];

        [frac1 release];
        [frac2 release];

    }

    return 0;
}
```

Note the we `release` the two `alloc`'ed fraction objects at the end of `main`. Even though all your memory gets freed up when your application terminates anyway, the example illustrates the idea of releasing objects you own when you're done using them.

Let's take another look at the `Fraction` class's `add:` method used in Program 7.5:

```
-(Fraction *) add: (Fraction *) f
{
    // To add two fractions:
    // a/b + c/d = ((a*d) + (b*c)) / (b * d)
    // result will store the result of the addition

    Fraction *result = [[Fraction alloc] init];
```

```
    result.numerator = numerator * f.denominator + denominator *
            f.numerator;
    result.denominator = denominator * f.denominator;

    [result reduce];
    return result;
}
```

When using manual memory management, this method presents a problem. The result object is alloc'ed and returned from the method after the calculations have been performed. Because the method has to return that object, it can't release it—that would cause it to be destroyed right then and there. Probably the best way to resolve this issue is to autorelease the object so that its value can be returned, with its release delayed until the autorelease pool is drained. You can take advantage of the fact that the autorelease method returns its receiver and embeds it in expressions like this:

```
Fraction *result = [[[Fraction alloc] init] autorelease];
```

or like this:

```
return [result autorelease];
```

The Event Loop and Memory Allocation

Cocoa and iOS applications run inside what's called a *run* or *event loop*. Think of an event as something that typically occurs by your performing some action (for example, you press a button on the iPhone) or by an implicit action (for example, something arrives over the network). To process the new event, the system creates a new autorelease pool and might call some method in your application to process it. When you're done handling the event, you return from your method and the system waits for the next event to occur. Before doing so, however, the system drains the autorelease pool. That means that any autoreleased objects you have created in processing that event will be destroyed, unless you have retained those objects so they will survive the draining of the pool. When using manual reference counting, you need to think about the autorelease pool and your objects surviving the draining of the pool at the end of the event loop.

Take a look at the following interface section that comes from an iOS application. Here we define a class called MyView containing one property named data:

```
#import <UIKit/UIKit.h>

@interface myView : UIView
@property (nonatomic, retain) NSMutableArray *data;
@end
```

The retain attribute for the data property (only recognized for non-ARC compiled code) says that the setter method should retain any objects that are assigned to the property, releasing the old value first. Assume we synthesize the accessor methods for our `data` property in the implementation section. Further assume we have a method called `viewDidLoad` that gets called by the system whenever our view gets loaded into memory. (You'll learn more about this when you study iOS application programming. For now, such details are not important.)

Let's say that inside your `viewDidLoad` method you want to allocate your `data` array. You insert the following line inside that method:

```
data = [NSMutableArray array];
```

As we've described how Foundation methods created autoreleased objects by default, the `array` method creates an autoreleased *array,* which you directly assign to your instance variable `data`. The problem is that the array will be destroyed as soon as the processing of the current event is completed. That's because it's created in an autorelease pool that will be drained at the end of the event loop. To ensure the array's survival through event loops, you have a few alternatives. Here are three different lines of code you could use instead that would work:

```
data = [[NSMutableArray array] retain];   // survives draining of pool
```

or

```
data = [[NSMutableArray alloc] init];    // not autoreleased
```

or

```
self.data = [NSMutableArray array];     // uses the setter method
```

In the last case, because the `data` property has the `retain` attribute, the autoreleased array will be retained. (Recall that assigning to `self.data` will cause the setter method to be used.) Note that in all three cases you must override `dealloc` to release your array when your `myView` object is to be destroyed:

```
-(void) dealloc {
   [data release];
   [super dealloc];
}
```

(The call to `super` allows for any inherited objects to be released. One other annoyance of using manual memory management has been having to remember to do the `[super dealloc]` *last* after releasing your own objects). In many cases, when creating a new object using a framework method, you can choose between either creating an autoreleased object or creating an `alloc`'ed one. If your application will create many objects before the event loop ends and the pool will get drained, you might want to use the `alloc` approach. In that way, you can release your objects as soon as you're done using them, without having to wait for the end of event processing.

When dealing in a manual reference counting environment, in addition to properties being given attributes of `atomic` (default) or `nonatomic`, they can also be given attributes of `assign` (default), `retain`, or `copy`.

Here's how to think about how the last three mentioned attributes are implemented when using a setter method to set the value of a property, for example:

```
self.property = newValue;
```

The `assign` attribute works like this:

```
property = newValue;
```

The `retain` attribute works like this:

```
if (property != newValue) {
   [property release];
   property = [newValue retain];
}
```

And the `copy` attribute works like this:

```
if (property != newValue) {
   [property release];
   property = [newValue copy];
}
```

Summary of Manual Memory Management Rules

Here are some rules to remember when working with a project compiled without ARC or garbage collection:

- If you need to hold on to an object to make sure it doesn't get destroyed by someone else, you should `retain` it. Make sure to `release` the object when you're done with it.

- Sending a release message does not necessarily destroy an object. When an object's reference count is decremented to 0, the object is destroyed. The system does this by sending the `dealloc` message to the object to free its memory.

- Release any objects that you have retained or have created using a `copy`, `mutableCopy`, `alloc`, or `new` method. This includes properties that have the `retain` or `copy` attribute. You can override `dealloc` to release your instance variables at the time your object is to be destroyed.

- The autorelease pool provides for the automatic release of objects when the pool itself is drained. The system does this by sending a `release` message to each object in the pool for each time it was autoreleased. Each object in the autorelease pool whose reference count goes down to `0` is sent a `dealloc` message to destroy the object.

- If you no longer need an object from within a method but need to return it, send it an `autorelease` message to mark it for later release. The `autorelease` message does not affect the reference count of the object.

- When your application terminates, all the memory your objects take up is released, regardless of whether they were in the autorelease pool.

- When you develop Cocoa or iOS applications, autorelease pools will be created and drained throughout execution of the program. (This will happen each time an event occurs.) In such cases, if you want to ensure that an autoreleased object survives automatic deallocation when the autorelease pool is drained, you need to retain it. All objects that have a reference count greater than the number of autorelease messages they have been sent will survive the release of the pool.

Automatic Reference Counting

ARC eliminates all the potential pitfalls associated with manual reference counting. Under the hood, reference counts are still being maintained and tracked. However, the system determines when to retain an object and when to autorelease or release it. You don't have to worry about it at all.

And you don't have to worry about returning allocated objects from methods. The compiler figures out how that object's memory needs to be managed by generating the correct code to autorelease or retain the returned object as necessary.

Strong Variables

By default, all object pointer variables are strong variables. That means that assigning an object reference to such a variable causes that object to be automatically retained. Further, the old object reference will be released before the assignment is made. Finally, strong variables are initialized to zero by default. And that's true whether it's an instance variable or a local or global variable.

Look at this code, which creates and sets two Fraction objects.

```
Fraction *f1 = [[Fraction alloc] init];
Fraction *f2 = [[Fraction alloc] init];

[f1 setTo: 1 over: 2];
[f2 setTo: 2 over: 3];
```

Now when you write the following using manual memory management

```
f2 = f1;
```

the effect is to just copy the reference to the Fraction object f1 into f2. The Fraction object referenced by f2 would be lost as a result, as its value is overwritten. This creates what's known as a *memory leak* (a variable that is no longer referenced and therefore can't be released).

If you're using ARC, f1 and f2 are both strong variables. So, the previous assignment actually works like this:

```
[f1 retain];  // retain new value
[f2 release]; // release the old value
f2 = f1;      // copy the reference
```

Of course, you don't see this happening because the compiler does all the work for you. You just the write the assignment statement and forget about it.

Because all object variables are strong variables by default, you don't need to declare them as such. However, you can explicitly do so by using the `__strong` keyword for a variable:

```
__strong  Fraction *f1;
```

It's important to note that properties are *not* strong be default. Their default attribute is `unsafe_unretained` (or, equivalently `assign`). You've seen how to declare the `strong` attribute for a property:

```
@property (strong, nonatomic)  NSMutableArray *birdNames;
```

The compiler makes sure that strong properties survive the event loop by retaining them on assignment. No such action is taken for properties that are `unsafe_unretained` (a.k.a. `assign`) or weak.

Weak Variables

Sometimes you set up a relationship between two objects where each object needs to reference the other. (This could be as simple as two objects or as complex as a chain of objects that create a cycle.) For example, iOS applications present graphics on the screen through objects known as *views*. Views are maintained in a hierarchy. So one view might present an image, and inside that image view you might want to display a title for that image. You can set this up where the image view is the main view, and the title is a *subview*. When the main view is shown, the subview is automatically shown as well. You can think of the main image view as the parent view and the title view as the child view. The main image view owns the subview.

When working with this view hierarchy, the parent view certainly will want to hold a reference to its subview. But it's also useful when working with a subview for it to know whom its parent view is as well. So, the parent view will hold a reference to the subview, and the subview will in turn hold a reference to the parent view. This circular reference could create problems. For example, what happens when we destroy the parent view? The reference from the subview to the parent would no longer be valid. In fact, trying to reference that non-existent parent view could cause the application to crash.

When two objects have strong references to each other, you create what's known as a *retain* cycle. The system will not destroy an object if there's still a reference to it. So, if two objects have strong references to each other, neither can ever be destroyed.

The way this problem can be resolved is by creating another type of object variable that allows a different type of reference, known as a *weak* reference, to be made between two objects. In this case, the weak reference would be made from the child to the parent. Why? Because we consider an object that *owns* another object (in this case the parent view) to be the strong reference, and the other object to be the weak reference.

By making the parent view hold a strong reference to its subview, and the subview a weak reference to its parent view, no retain cycle is created. A weak variable does not prevent deallocation of the object it references.

When you declare a weak variable a few things happen; the system tracks the reference that is made on assignment to that variable. And when that referenced object gets deallocated, the weak variable gets automatically set to `nil`. That prevents any crashes that might occur by inadvertently sending a message to that variable. Because the variable will be set to `nil`, sending a message to a `nil` object does nothing, thus preventing a crash.

To declare a weak variable, you use the __weak keyword:

```
__weak  UIView *parentView;
```

or you use the `weak` attribute for a property:

```
@property (weak, nonatomic)  UIView *parentView;
```

Weak variables are also useful when working with delegates. By making the variable that holds the reference to the delegate a weak variable, you're assured that the variable will be zeroed if the delegate object gets deallocated. Again, this can prevent the kind of system crashes that have caused headaches for many a programmer prior to the invention of ARC.

Note that weak variables are not supported in iOS 4 or Mac OS X 10.6. In such cases, you can still use the `unsafe_unretained` (or `assign`) property attribute or declare your variable to be __unsafe_unretained. However, realize that these variables are not zeroed automatically when the referenced object is deallocated.

@autoreleasepool Blocks

You've seen in every example in this book so far how the compiler generates an `@autoreleasepool` directive inside your main routine. This directive encloses a block of statements that define an autoreleasepool context. Any objects created in that context that are autoreleased will be destroyed by default at the end of that autoreleasepool block (unless the compiler has taken care to guarantee their survival past the end of the block).

If your program generates a lot of temporary objects (which can easily happen when executing code inside a loop), you might want to create multiple autoreleasepool blocks in your program. For example, the following code fragment illustrates how you can set up autoreleasepool blocks to manage the temporary objects created by each iteration of the `for` loop:

```
for (i = 0; i < n; ++i) {
   @autoreleasepool {
      ... // lots of work with temporary objects here
   }
}
```

As noted earlier in this chapter, Cocoa and iOS applications run inside an *event loop*. In preparation for processing a new event, the system creates a new autoreleasepool context and might call some method in your application to handle the event. When you're done handling the event, you return from your method and the system waits for the next event to occur. Before doing so, however, the autoreleasepool context ends, which means that autoreleased objects may then be destroyed.

Note that this discussion of the autoreleasepool applies equally to programs compiled with or without ARC.

Method Names and Non-ARC Compiled Code

ARC works with code that has not been compiled with ARC. This can happen if you're linking with an older framework, for example. As long as the non-ARC code has conformed to the standard Cocoa naming conventions, all will be okay. That is, when ARC sees a method call, it checks the method's name. If the name begins with the words `alloc`, `new`, `copy`, `mutableCopy`, or `init`, it assumes that the method returns ownership of the object back to the method caller.

When we talk about "words" here, we refer to the words being written in what's known as `camelCase`. That's where the first letter of each new word in the name begins with a capital letter. So, the compiler assumes methods named `allocFraction`, `newAddressCard`, and `initWithWidth:andHeight:` returns ownership of the objects, whereas `newlyWeds`, `copycat`, and `initials`, do not. Again, this happens automatically with ARC, so you don't need to worry about this, unless you're using methods that don't follow these standard naming conventions. In those cases, there are ways to explicitly tell the compiler whether a method returns ownership of an object despite its name.

Note that the compiler gives you an error if you try to synthesize properties whose names begin with any of the special words mentioned in the first paragraph of this section.

18

Copying Objects

This chapter discusses some of the subtleties involved in copying objects. We introduce the concept of shallow versus deep copying and discuss how to make copies under the Foundation framework.

Chapter 8, "Inheritance," discussed what happens when you assign one object to another with a simple assignment statement, such as here:

```
origin = pt;
```

In this example, `origin` and `pt` are both `XYPoint` objects with two integer instance variables called x and y.

Recall that the effect of the assignment is to simply copy the address of the object `pt` into `origin`. At the end of the assignment operation, both variables point to the same location in memory. Making changes to the instance variables with a message such as

```
[origin setX: 100 andY: 200];
```

changes the x, y coordinate of the `XYPoint` object referenced by both the `origin` and `pt` variables because they both reference the same object in memory.

The same applies to Foundation objects: Assigning one variable to another simply creates another reference to the object. So, if `dataArray` and `dataArray2` are both `NSMutableArray` objects, the following statements remove the first element from the same array that both variables reference:

```
dataArray2 = dataArray;
[dataArray2 removeObjectAtIndex: 0];
```

The `copy` and `mutableCopy` Methods

The Foundation classes implement methods known as `copy` and `mutableCopy` that you can use to create a copy of an object. This is done by implementing a method in conformance with the `<NSCopying>` protocol for making copies. If your class needs to distinguish between making mutable and immutable copies of an object, you must implement a method according to the `<NSMutableCopying>` protocol as well. You learn how to do that later in this section.

Getting back to the copy methods for the Foundation classes, given the two `NSMutableArray` objects `dataArray2` and `dataArray`, as described in the previous section, the statement

```
dataArray2 = [dataArray mutableCopy];
```

creates a new copy of `dataArray` in memory, duplicating all its elements. Subsequently, executing the statement

```
[dataArray2 removeObjectAtIndex: 0];
```

removes the first element from `dataArray2` but not from `dataArray`. Program 18.1 illustrates this.

Program 18.1

```
#import <Foundation/Foundation.h>

int main (int argc, char * argv[])
{
   @autoreleasepool {
      NSMutableArray    *dataArray = [NSMutableArray arrayWithObjects:
         @"one", @"two", @"three", @"four", nil];
      NSMutableArray    *dataArray2;

      // simple assignment

      dataArray2 = dataArray;
      [dataArray2 removeObjectAtIndex: 0];

      NSLog (@"dataArray:  ");
      for ( NSString *elem in dataArray )
         NSLog (@"   %@", elem);

      NSLog (@"dataArray2: ");

      for ( NSString *elem in dataArray2 )
         NSLog (@"   %@", elem);

      // try a copy, then remove the first element from the copy

      dataArray2 = [dataArray mutableCopy];
      [dataArray2 removeObjectAtIndex: 0];

      NSLog (@"dataArray:  ");
```

```
        for ( NSString *elem in dataArray )
            NSLog (@"   %@", elem);

        NSLog (@"dataArray2: ");

        for ( NSString *elem in dataArray2 )
            NSLog (@"   %@", elem);

    }
    return 0;
}
```

Program 18.1   **Output**

```
dataArray:
    two
    three
    four
dataArray2:
    two
    three
    four
dataArray:
    two
    three
    four
dataArray2:
    three
    four
```

The program defines the mutable array object `dataArray` and sets its elements to the string objects `@"one"`, `@"two"`, `@"three"`, and `@"four"`. As we've discussed, the assignment

```
dataArray2 = dataArray;
```

simply creates another reference to the same array object in memory. When you remove the first object from `dataArray2` and subsequently print the elements from both array objects, it's no surprise that the first element (the string `@"one"`) is gone from both array object references.

Next, you create a mutable copy of `dataArray` and assign the resulting copy to `dataArray2`. This creates two distinct mutable arrays in memory, both containing three elements. Now when you remove the first element from `dataArray2`, it has no effect on the contents of `dataArray`, as verified by the last output for `dataArray`.

Note that making a mutable copy of an object does not require that the object being copied be mutable. The same applies to immutable copies: You can make an immutable copy of a mutable object.

Shallow Versus Deep Copying

Program 18.1 fills the elements of dataArray with immutable strings. (Recall that constant string objects are immutable.) In Program 18.2, you fill it with mutable strings instead so that you can change one of the strings in the array. Take a look at Program 18.2 and see whether you understand its output.

Program 18.2

```
#import <Foundation/Foundation.h>

int main (int argc, char * argv[])
{
   @autoreleasepool {
      NSMutableArray    *dataArray = [NSMutableArray arrayWithObjects:
         [NSMutableString stringWithString: @"one"],
         [NSMutableString stringWithString: @"two"],
         [NSMutableString stringWithString: @"three"],
         nil
      ];
      NSMutableArray    *dataArray2;
      NSMutableString   *mStr;

      NSLog (@"dataArray:  ");
      for ( NSString *elem in dataArray )
        NSLog (@"   %@", elem);

      // make a copy, then change one of the strings

      dataArray2 = [dataArray mutableCopy];

      mStr = dataArray[0];
      [mStr appendString: @"ONE"];

      NSLog (@"dataArray:  ");
      for ( NSString *elem in dataArray )
        NSLog (@"   %@", elem);

      NSLog (@"dataArray2:  ");
      for ( NSString *elem in dataArray2 )
        NSLog (@"   %@", elem);
   }
   return 0;
}
```

Program 18.2   **Output**

```
dataArray:
   one
   two
   three
dataArray:
   oneONE
   two
   three
dataArray2:
   oneONE
   two
   three
```

You retrieved the first element of `dataArray` with the following statement:

```
mStr = dataArray[0];
```

Then you appended the string `@"ONE"` to it with this statement:

```
[mStr appendString: @"ONE"];
```

Notice the value of the first element of both the original array and its copy: Both were modified. Perhaps you can understand why the first element of `dataArray` was changed but not why its copy was as well. When you get an element from a collection, you get a new reference to that element but not a new copy. So, when you write `dataArray[0]`, the retrieved object points to the same object in memory as the first element in `dataArray`. Subsequently modifying the string object `mStr` has the side effect of also changing the first element of `dataArray`, as you can see from the output.

But what about the copy you made? Why is its first element changed as well? This has to do with the fact that copies, by default, are *shallow* copies. Therefore, when the array was copied with the `mutableCopy` method, space was allocated for a new array object in memory and the individual elements were copied into the new array. But copying each element in the array from the original to a new location meant just copying the reference from one element of the array to another. The net result was that the elements of both arrays referenced the same strings in memory. This is no different from assigning one object to another, as covered at the beginning of this chapter.

To make distinct copies of each element of the array, you must perform a *deep* copy. This means making copies of the contents of each object in the array, not just copies of the references to the objects (and think about what that implies if an element of an array is itself an array object). But deep copies are not performed by default when you use the `copy` or `mutableCopy` methods with the Foundation classes. In Chapter 19, "Archiving," you learn how to use the Foundation's archiving capabilities to create a deep copy of an object.

When you copy an array, a dictionary, or a set, for example, you get a new copy of those collections. However, you might need to make your own copies of individual elements if you want to make changes to one collection but not to its copy. For example, if you want to change the first element of dataArray2 but not dataArray in Program 18.2, you could make a new string (using a method such as stringWithString:) and store it into the first location of dataArray2, as follows:

```
mStr = [NSMutableString stringWithString: dataArray2[0]];
```

Then you could make the changes to mStr and add it to the array using the replaceObject:atIndex:withObject: method, as follows:

```
[mStr appendString @"ONE"];
[dataArray2 replaceObjectAtIndex: 0 withObject: mStr];
```

Hopefully, you realize that even after replacing the object in the array, mStr and the first element of dataArray2 refer to the same object in memory. Therefore, subsequent changes to mStr in your program will also change the first element of the array.

Implementing the <NSCopying> Protocol

If you try to use the copy method on one of your own classes (for example, on your address book) as follows

```
newBook = [myBook mutableCopy];
```

you'll get an error message that looks something like this:

```
*** -[AddressBook copyWithZone:]:  selector not recognized
*** Uncaught exception:
*** -[AddressBook copyWithZone:]: selector not recognized
```

As noted, to implement copying with your own classes, you have to implement one or two methods according to the <NSCopying> protocol.

We now show how you can add a copy method to your Fraction class, which you used extensively in Part I, "The Objective-C Language." Note that the techniques we describe here for copying strategies work fine for your own classes. If those classes are subclasses of any of the Foundation classes, you might need to implement a more sophisticated copying strategy. You'll have to account for the fact that the superclass might have already implemented its own copying strategy.

Recall that your Fraction class contains two integer instance variables, called numerator and denominator. To make a copy of one of these objects, you must allocate space for a new fraction and then simply copy the values of the two integers into the new fraction.

When you implement the <NSCopying> protocol, your class must implement the copyWithZone: method to respond to a copy message. (The copy message just sends a copyWithZone: message to your class with an argument of nil.) If you want to make a distinction between mutable and immutable copies, as we noted, you'll also need to implement the mutableCopyWithZone: method according to the <NSMutableCopying> protocol. If you implement both methods, copyWithZone: should return an immutable copy and mutableCopyWithZone: should return a mutable one. Making a mutable copy of an object does not require that the object being copied also be mutable (and vice versa); it's perfectly reasonable to want to make a mutable copy of an immutable object (consider a string object, for example).

Here's what the @interface directive should look like:

```
@interface Fraction: NSObject <NSCopying>
```

Fraction is a subclass of NSObject and conforms to the NSCopying protocol.

In the implementation file Fraction.m, add the following definition for your new method:

```
-(id) copyWithZone: (NSZone *) zone
{
   Fraction *newFract = [[Fraction allocWithZone: zone] init];

   [newFract setTo: numerator over: denominator];
   return newFract;
}
```

The zone argument has to do with different memory zones that you can allocate and work with in your program. You need to deal with these only if you're writing applications that allocate a lot of memory and you want to optimize the allocation by grouping them into these zones. You can take the value passed to copyWithZone: and hand it off to a memory allocation method called allocWithZone:. This method allocates memory in a specified zone.

After allocating a new Fraction object, you copy the receiver's numerator and denominator variables into it. The copyWithZone: method is supposed to return the new copy of the object, which you do in your method.

Program 18.3 tests your new method.

Program 18.3

```
// Copying fractions

#import "Fraction.h"

int main (int argc, char * argv[])
{
    @autoreleasepool {
        Fraction *f1 = [[Fraction alloc] init];
        Fraction *f2;

        [f1 setTo: 2 over: 5];
        f2 = [f1 copy];

        [f2 setTo: 1 over: 3];
```

```
        [f1 print];
        [f2 print];
    }
    return 0;
}
```

Program 18.3   **Output**

```
2/5
1/3
```

The program creates a Fraction object called f1 and sets it to 2/5. It then invokes the copy method to make a copy, which sends the copyWithZone: message to your object. That method makes a new Fraction, copies the values from f1 into it, and returns the result. Back in main, you assign that result to f2. Subsequently setting the value in f2 to the fraction 1/3 verifies that it had no effect on the original fraction f1. Change the line in the program that reads

```
f2 = [f1 copy];
```

to simply

```
f2 = f1;
```

to see the different results you will obtain.

If your class might be subclassed, your copyWithZone: method will be inherited. In that case, you should change the line in the method that reads

```
Fraction *newFract = [[Fraction allocWithZone: zone] init];
```

to read

```
id newFract = [[[self class] allocWithZone: zone] init];
```

That way, you allocate a new object from the class that is the receiver of the copy. (For example, if it has been subclassed to a class named NewFraction, be sure to allocate a new NewFraction object in the inherited method instead of a Fraction object.)

If you are writing a copyWithZone: method for a class whose superclass also implements the <NSCopying> protocol, you should first call the copy method on the superclass to copy the inherited instance variables and then include your own code to copy whatever additional instance variables (if any) you might have added to the class.

You must decide whether you want to implement a shallow or a deep copy in your class. Just document it for other users of your class so that they know.

Copying Objects in Setter and Getter Methods

Whenever you implement a setter or getter method, think about what you're storing in the instance variables, what you're retrieving, and whether you need to protect these values. For example, consider this when you set the name of one of your `AddressCard` objects using the corresponding setter method:

```
newCard.name = newName;
```

Assume that `newName` is a string object containing the name for your new card. Assume that inside the setter routine you simply assigned the parameter to the corresponding instance variable:

```
-(void) setName: (NSString *) theName
{
    name = theName;
}
```

Now, what do you think would happen if the program later changed some of the characters contained in `newName` in the program? (This could happen if `newName` were a mutable string object; such an object can be used in places where an `NSString` object is specified, as the former is a subclass of the latter.) It would also unintentionally change the corresponding field in your address card because both would reference the same string object.

As you have already seen, a safer approach is to make a copy of the object in the setter routine, to prevent this inadvertent effect.

If you weren't synthesizing the setter, you could also write a version of the `setName:` method to use `copy`, like this:

```
-(void) setName: (NSString *) theName
{
    name = [theName copy];
}
```

As you saw in Chapter 15, "Numbers, Strings, and Collections," if you specify the `copy` attribute in a property declaration, the synthesized method will use the class's `copy` method (the one you wrote or the one you inherited). So, the following `property` declaration

```
@property (nonatomic, copy) NSString *name;
```

when combined with the appropriate `@synthesize` directive, generates a method that behaves like this:

```
-(void) setName: (NSString *) theName
{
    if (theName != name)
        name = [theName copy];
}
```

Use of `nonatomic` here tells the system not to protect the property accessors with a *mutex* (*mut*ually *ex*clusive) lock. People writing thread-safe code use mutex locks to prevent two threads from executing in the same code at the same time, a situation that can often lead to dire problems. However, these locks can slow programs down, and you can avoid using them if you know this code will only ever be running in a single thread.

If `nonatomic` is not specified or `atomic` is specified instead (which is the default), your instance variable will be protected with a mutex lock. This ensures exclusive access to an instance variable and prevents potential race conditions that could occur if more than one thread in a multithreaded application is trying to simultaneously access the same instance variable.

> **Note**
>
> There is no `mutableCopy` attribute for a property. So, using the `copy` attribute, even with a mutable instance variable, results in the `copyWithZone:` method being executed which, as mentioned, produces an immutable copy of the object by convention.

The same discussion about protecting the value of your instance variables applies to the getter routines. If you return a mutable object, ensure that changes to the returned value will not affect the value of your instance variables. In such a case, you can make a copy of the instance variable and return that instead of the original value.

Getting back to the implementation of a `copy` method, if you are copying instance variables that contain immutable objects (for example, immutable string objects), you might not need to make a new copy of the object's contents. It might suffice to simply make a new reference to the object by assigning it. For example, if you are implementing a copy method for the `AddressCard` class, which contains `name` and `email` members, the following implementation for `copyWithZone:` suffices:

```
-(AddresssCard *) copyWithZone: (NSZone *) zone
{
    AddressCard *newCard = [[AddressCard allocWithZone: zone] init];

    [newCard assignName: name andEmail: email];
    return newCard;
}

-(void) assignName: (NSString *) theName andEmail: (NSString *) theEmail
{
    name = theName;
    email = theEmail;
}
```

The `setName:andEmail:` method isn't used here to set the instance variables because that method makes new copies of its arguments, which would defeat the whole purpose of this exercise. Instead, you just assigned the two variables using a new method called `assignName:andEmail:`.

Realize that you can get away with assigning the instance variables here (instead of making complete copies of them) because the owner of the copied card can't affect the `name` and `email` members of the original card. (Those contain immutable string objects.) Because our two instance variables are "strong" variables by default, doing a simple assignment to them creates another reference to the object, as explained in more detail in Chapter 17, "Memory Management and Automatic Reference Counting."

Exercises

1. Implement a copy method for the `AddressBook` class according to the `NSCopying` protocol. Would it make sense to also implement a `mutableCopy` method? Why or why not? Also, think about what happens if someone uses the setter method for the book property in the `AddressBook` class. Who should own the address book that gets passed as the argument to the setter? How can you fix this?

2. Modify the `Rectangle` and `XYPoint` classes defined in Chapter 8 to conform to the `<NSCopying>` protocol. Add a `copyWithZone:` method to both classes. Make sure that the `Rectangle` copies its `XYPoint` member origin using the `XYPoint`'s copy method. Does it make sense to implement both mutable and immutable copies for these classes? Explain.

3. Create an `NSDictionary` object and fill it with some key/object pairs. Then make both mutable and immutable copies. Are these deep copies or shallow copies that are made? Verify your answer.

19

Archiving

In Objective-C terms, archiving is the process of saving one or more objects in a format so that they can later be restored. Often this involves writing the objects to a file so that they can subsequently be read back in. We discuss two methods for archiving data in this chapter: *property lists* and *key-valued coding.*

Archiving with XML Property Lists

Mac OS X applications use XML property lists (or *plists*) for storing things such as your default preferences, application settings, and configuration information, so it's useful to know how to create them and read them back in. Their use for archiving purposes, however, is limited because when creating a property list for a data structure, specific object classes are not retained, multiple references to the same object are not stored, and the mutability of an object is not preserved.

> **Note**
>
> So-called "old-style" property lists store the data in a different format than XML property lists. Stick to using XML property lists in your program, if possible.

If your objects are of type NSString, NSDictionary, NSArray, NSDate, NSData, or NSNumber, you can use the writeToFile:atomically: method implemented in these classes to write your data to a file. In the case of writing out a dictionary or an array, this method writes the data to the file in the format of an XML property list. Program 19.1 shows how the dictionary you created as a simple glossary in Chapter 15, "Numbers, Strings, and Collections," can be written to a file as a property list.

Program 19.1

```
#import <Foundation/Foundation.h>

int main (int argc, char * argv[])
{
```

Program 19.1   **Continued**

```
@autoreleasepool {
    NSDictionary *glossary = @{
        @"abstract class":
            @"A class defined so other classes can inherit from it.",
        @"adopt":
            @"To implement all the methods defined in a protocol",
        @"archiving":
            @"Storing an object for later use. "
    };
    if ([glossary writeToFile: @"glossary"  atomically: YES] == NO)
        NSLog (@"Save to file failed!");


}
return 0;
}
```

The writeToFile:atomically: message is sent to your dictionary object glossary, causing the dictionary to be written to the file glossary in the form of a property list. The atomically parameter is set to YES, meaning that you want the write operation to be done to a temporary backup file first; once successful, the final data is to be moved to the specified file named glossary. This is a safeguard that protects the file from becoming corrupt if, for example, the system crashes in the middle of the write operation. In that case, the original glossary file (if it previously existed) isn't harmed.

If you examine the contents of the glossary file created by Program 19.1, it looks like this:

```
<?xml version="1.0" encoding="UTF-8"?>
<!DOCTYPE plist PUBLIC "-//Apple Computer//DTD PLIST 1.0//EN"
          "http://www.apple.com/DTDs/PropertyList-1.0.dtd">
<plist version="1.0">
<dict>
    <key>abstract class</key>
    <string>A class defined so other classes can inherit from it.</string>
    <key>adopt</key>
    <string>To implement all the methods defined in a protocol</string>
    <key>archiving</key>
    <string>Storing an object for later use. </string>
</dict>
</plist>
```

You can see from the XML file that was created that the dictionary is written to the file as a set of key (<key>...</key>) value (<string>...</string>) pairs.

When you create a property list from a dictionary, the keys in the dictionary must all be NSString objects. The elements of an array or the values in a dictionary can be NSString, NSArray, NSDictionary, NSData, NSDate, or NSNumber objects.

To read an XML property list from a file into your program, you use the dictionaryWithContentsOfFile: or arrayWithContentsOfFile: methods. To read back data, use the dataWithContentsOfFile: method; to read back string objects, use the stringWithContentsOfFile: method. Program 19.2 reads back the glossary written in Program 19.1 and then displays its contents.

Program 19.2

```
#import <Foundation/Foundation.h>

int main (int argc, char * argv[])
{
   @autoreleasepool {
      NSDictionary *glossary;

      glossary = [NSDictionary dictionaryWithContentsOfFile: @"glossary"];

      for ( NSString *key in glossary )
         NSLog (@"%@: %@", key, glossary[key]);
   }
   return 0;
}
```

Program 19.2   **Output**

```
archiving: Storing an object for later use.
abstract class: A class defined so other classes can inherit from it.
adopt: To implement all the methods defined in a protocol
```

Your property lists don't need to be created from an Objective-C program; the property list can come from any source. You can make your own property lists using a simple text editor, or you can use the Property List Editor program located in the /Developer/Applications/ Utilities directory on OS X systems. If you plan to work with property lists in your applications, you may want to take a look at the NSPropertyListSerialization class, which allows property lists to be written to and read from files in a machine-portable manner.

Archiving with NSKeyedArchiver

A more flexible approach enables you to save any type of objects to a file, not just strings, arrays, and dictionaries. This is done by creating a *keyed* archive using the NSKeyedArchiver class.

Mac OS X has supported keyed archives since version 10.2. Before that, *sequential* archives were created with the NSArchiver class. Sequential archives require that the data in the archive be read back in precisely the same order in which it was written.

A keyed archive is one in which each field of the archive has a name. When you archive an object, you give it a name, or *key*. When you retrieve it from the archive, you retrieve it by the same key. In that manner, objects can be written to the archive and retrieved in any order. Furthermore, if new instance variables are added or removed to a class, your program can account for it.

Program 19.3 shows that the glossary can be saved to a file on disk using the method archiveRootObject:toFile: from the NSKeyedArchiver class.

Program 19.3

```
#import <Foundation/Foundation.h>

int main (int argc, char * argv[])
{
   @autoreleasepool {
      NSDictionary *glossary = @{
         @"abstract class":
            @"A class defined so other classes can inherit from it.",
         @"adopt":
            @"To implement all the methods defined in a protocol",
         @"archiving":
            @"Storing an object for later use. "
      };
      [NSKeyedArchiver archiveRootObject: glossary toFile: @"glossary.archive"];
   }
   return 0;
}
```

Program 19.3 does not produce any output at the terminal. However, the statement

```
[NSKeyedArchiver archiveRootObject: glossary toFile: @"glossary.archive"];
```

writes the dictionary glossary to the file glossary.archive. Any pathname can be specified for the file. In this case, the file is written to the current directory.

The archive file created can later be read into your program by using NSKeyedUnarchiver's unarchiveObjectWithFile: method, as is done in Program 19.4.

Program 19.4

```
#import <Foundation/Foundation.h>

int main (int argc, char * argv[])
{
   @autoreleasepool {
      NSDictionary *glossary;

      glossary = [NSKeyedUnarchiver unarchiveObjectWithFile:
                     @"glossary.archive"];

      for ( NSString *key in glossary )
         NSLog (@"%@: %@", key, [glossary[key]]);
   }
   return 0;
}
```

Program 19.4   **Output**

```
abstract class: A class defined so other classes can inherit from it.
adopt: To implement all the methods defined in a protocol
archiving: Storing an object for later use.
```

The statement

```
glossary = [NSKeyedUnarchiver unarchiveObjectWithFile:
               @"glossary.archive"];
```

causes the specified file to be opened and its contents to be read. This file must be the result of a previous archive operation. You can specify a full pathname for the file or a relative pathname, as in the example.

After the glossary has been restored, the program simply enumerates its contents to verify that the restore was successful.

Writing Encoding and Decoding Methods

Basic Objective-C class objects such as NSString, NSArray, NSDictionary, NSSet, NSDate, NSNumber, and NSData can be archived and restored in the manner just described. That includes nested objects as well, such as an array containing a string or even other array objects.

This implies that you can't directly archive your AddressBook that we developed in Chapter 15, using this technique because the Objective-C system doesn't know how to archive an AddressBook object. If you try to archive it by inserting a line such as

```
[NSKeyedArchiver archiveRootObject: myAddressBook toFile:  @"addrbook.arch"];
```

into your program, you get the following message if you run the program:

```
*** -[AddressBook encodeWithCoder:]: selector not recognized
*** Uncaught exception: <NSInvalidArgumentException>
*** -[AddressBook encodeWithCoder:]: selector not recognized
archiveTest: received signal: Trace/BPT trap
```

From the error messages, you can see that the system was looking for a method called encodeWithCoder: in the AddressBook class, but you never defined such a method.

To archive objects other than those listed, you must tell the system how to archive, or *encode,* your objects, and also how to unarchive, or *decode,* them. This is done by adding encodeWithCoder: and initWithCoder: methods to your class definitions, according to the <NSCoding> protocol. For our address book example, you'd have to add these methods to both the AddressBook and AddressCard classes.

The encodeWithCoder: method is invoked each time the archiver wants to encode an object from the specified class, and the method tells it how to do so. In a similar manner, the initWithCoder: method is invoked each time an object from the specified class is to be decoded.

In general, the encoder method should specify how to archive each instance variable in the object you want to save. Luckily, you have help doing this. For the basic Objective-C classes described previously, you can use the encodeObject:forKey: method. For basic underlying C data types (such as integers and floats), you use one of the methods listed in Table 19.1. The decoder method, initWithCoder:, works in reverse: You use decodeObject:forKey: to decode basic Objective-C classes and the appropriate decoder method shown in Table 19.1 for the basic data types.

Table 19.1 Encoding and Decoding Basic Data Types in Keyed Archives

Encoder	Decoder
encodeBool:forKey:	decodeBool:forKey:
encodeInt:forKey:	decodeInt:forKey:
encodeInt32:forKey:	decodeInt32:forKey:
encodeInt64: forKey:	decodeInt64:forKey:
encodeFloat:forKey:	decodeFloat:forKey:
encodeDouble:forKey:	decodeDouble:forKey:

Program 19.5 adds the two encoding and decoding methods to both the AddressCard and AddressBook classes.

Program 19.5 Addresscard.h Interface File

```
#import <Foundation/Foundation.h>

@interface AddressCard: NSObject <NSCoding, NSCopying>

@property (copy, nonatomic) NSString *name, *email;

-(void) setName: (NSString *) theName andEmail: (NSString *) theEmail;
-(NSComparisonResult) compareNames: (id) element;
-(void) print;

// Additional method for NSCopying protocol
-(void) assignName: (NSString *) theName andEmail: (NSString *) theEmail;

@end
```

These are the two new methods used for your AddressCard class to be added to the implementation file:

```
-(void) encodeWithCoder: (NSCoder *) encoder
{
   [encoder encodeObject: name forKey: @"AddressCardName"];
   [encoder encodeObject: email forKey: @"AddressCardEmail"];
}

-(id) initWithCoder: (NSCoder *) decoder
{
   name = [decoder decodeObjectforKey: @"AddressCardName"];
   email = [decoder decodeObjectforKey: @"AddressCardEmail"];

   return self;
}
```

The encoding method encodeWithCoder: is passed an NSCoder object as its argument. Because your AddressCard class inherits directly from NSObject, you don't need to worry about encoding inherited instance variables. If you did, and if you knew the superclass of your class conformed to the NSCoding protocol, you should start your encoding method with a statement like the following to make sure your inherited instance variables are encoded:

```
[super encodeWithCoder: encoder];
```

Your address book has two instance variables, called name and email. Because these are both NSString objects, you can use the encodeObject:forKey: method to encode each of them in turn. These two instance variables are then added to the archive.

The encodeObject:forKey: method encodes an object and stores it under the specified key for later retrieval using that key. The key names are arbitrary, so as long you use the same name to retrieve (decode) the data as you did when you archived (encoded) it, you can specify any key you like. The only time a conflict might arise is if the same key is used for a subclass of an object being encoded. To prevent this from happening, you can insert the class name in front of the instance variable name when composing the key for the archive, as was done in Program 19.5.

Note that encodeObject:forKey: can be used for any object that has implemented a corresponding encodeWithCoder: method in its class.

The decoding process works in reverse. The argument passed to initWithCoder: is again an NSCoder object. You don't need to worry about this argument; just remember that it's the one that gets sent the messages for each object you want to extract from the archive.

Again, because the AddressCard class inherits directly from NSObject, you don't have to worry about decoding inherited instance variables. If you did, you would insert a line like this at the start of your decoder method (assuming the superclass of your class conformed to the NSCoding protocol):

```
self = [super initWithCoder: decoder];
```

Each instance variable is then decoded by invoking the decodeObject:ForKey: method and passing the same key that was used to encode the variable.

Similarly to your AddressCard class, you add encoding and decoding methods to your AddressBook class. The only line you need to change in your interface file is the @interface directive to declare that the AddressBook class now conforms to the NSCoding protocol. The change looks like this:

```
@interface AddressBook: NSObject <NSCoding, NSCopying>
```

Here are the method definitions for inclusion in the implementation file:

```
-(void) encodeWithCoder: (NSCoder *) encoder
{
    [encoder encodeObject: bookName forKey: @"AddressBookBookName"];
    [encoder encodeObject: book forKey: @"AddressBookBook"];
}

-(id) initWithCoder: (NSCoder *) decoder
{
    bookName = [decoder decodeObjectForKey: @"AddressBookBookName"];
    book = [decoder decodeObjectForKey: @"AddressBookBook"];

    return self;
}
```

The test program is shown next as Program 19.6.

Program 19.6   **Test Program**

```
#import "AddressBook.h"

int main (int argc, char * argv[])
{
    @autoreleasepool {
        NSString  *aName = @"Julia Kochan";
        NSString  *aEmail = @"jewls337@axlc.com";
        NSString  *bName = @"Tony Iannino";
        NSString  *bEmail = @"tony.iannino@techfitness.com";
        NSString  *cName = @"Stephen Kochan";
        NSString  *cEmail = @"steve@steve_kochan.com";
        NSString  *dName = @"Jamie Baker";
        NSString  *dEmail = @"jbaker@hitmail.com";

        AddressCard *card1 = [[AddressCard alloc] init];
        AddressCard *card2 = [[AddressCard alloc] init];
        AddressCard *card3 = [[AddressCard alloc] init];
        AddressCard *card4 = [[AddressCard alloc] init];

        AddressBook  *myBook = [AddressBook alloc];

        // First set up four address cards

        [card1 setName: aName andEmail: aEmail];
        [card2 setName: bName andEmail: bEmail];
        [card3 setName: cName andEmail: cEmail];
        [card4 setName: dName andEmail: dEmail];

        myBook = [myBook initWithName: @"Steve's Address Book"];

        // Add some cards to the address book

        [myBook addCard: card1];
        [myBook addCard: card2];
        [myBook addCard: card3];
        [myBook addCard: card4];

        [myBook sort];

        if ([NSKeyedArchiver archiveRootObject: myBook toFile:
                @"addrbook.arch"] == NO)
```

```
        NSLog (@"archiving failed");
    }
    return 0;
}
```

This program creates the address book and then archives it to the file `addrbook.arch`. In the process of creating the archive file, realize that the encoding methods from *both* the `AddressBook` and `AddressCard` classes were invoked. You can add some `NSLog` calls to these methods if you want proof.

Program 19.7 shows how you can read the archive into memory to set up the address book from a file.

Program 19.7

```
#import "AddressBook.h"

int main (int argc, char * argv[])
{
    AddressBook          *myBook;
    @autoreleasepool {
        myBook = [NSKeyedUnarchiver unarchiveObjectWithFile: @"addrbook.arch"];

        [myBook list];
    }
    return 0;
}
```

Program 19.7 **Output**

```
======== Contents of: Steve's Address Book =========
Jamie Baker         jbaker@hitmail.com
Julia Kochan        jewls337@axlc.com
Stephen Kochan      steve@steve_kochan.com
Tony Iannino        tony.iannino@techfitness.com
====================================================
```

In the process of unarchiving the address book, the decoding methods added to your two classes were automatically invoked. Notice how easily you can read the address book back into the program.

As noted, the `encodeObject:forKey:` method works for built-in classes and classes for which you write your encoding and decoding methods according to the `NSCoding` protocol. If your instance contains some basic data types, such as integers or floats, you need to know how to encode and decode them (see Table 19.1).

Here's a simple definition for a class called `Foo` that contains three instance variables: One is an `NSString`, another is an `int`, and the third is a `float`. The class has one setter method, three getter methods, and two encoding/decoding methods to be used for archiving:

```
@interface Foo: NSObject <NSCoding>

@property (copy, nonatomic) NSString *strVal;
@property int intVal;
@property float floatVal;
@end
```

The implementation file follows:

```
@implementation Foo

@synthesize strVal, intVal, floatVal;

-(void) encodeWithCoder: (NSCoder *) encoder
{
   [encoder encodeObject: strVal forKey: @"FoostrVal"];
   [encoder encodeInt: intVal forKey: @"FoointVal"];
   [encoder encodeFloat: floatVal forKey: @"FoofloatVal"];
}

-(id) initWithCoder: (NSCoder *) decoder
{
    strVal = [decoder decodeObjectForKey: @"FoostrVal"];
    intVal = [decoder decodeIntForKey: @"FoointVal"];
    floatVal = [decoder decodeFloatForKey: @"FoofloatVal"];

    return self;
}
@end
```

The encoding routine first encodes the string value `strVal` using the `encodeObject:forKey:` method, as was shown previously.

In Program 19.8, a `Foo` object is created, archived to a file, unarchived, and then displayed.

Program 19.8   Test Program

```
#import <Foundation/Foundation.h>
#import "Foo.h"      // Definition for our Foo class

int main (int argc, char * argv[])
{
   @autoreleasepool {
      Foo *myFoo1 = [[Foo alloc] init];
```

```
        Foo *myFoo2;

        myFoo1.strVal = @"This is the string";
        myFoo1.intVal = 12345;
        myFoo1.floatVal = 98.6;

        [NSKeyedArchiver archiveRootObject: myFoo1 toFile: @"foo.arch"];

        myFoo2 = [NSKeyedUnarchiver unarchiveObjectWithFile: @"foo.arch"];
        NSLog (@"%@\n%i\n%g", myFoo2.strVal, myFoo2.intVal,
              myFoo2.floatVal);
    }
    return 0;
}
```

Program 19.8   **Output**

```
This is the string
12345
98.6
```

The following messages archive the three instance variables from the object:

```
[encoder encodeObject: strVal forKey: @"FoostrVal"];
[encoder encodeInt: intVal forKey: @"FoointVal"];
[encoder encodeFloat: floatVal forKey: @"FoofloatVal"];
```

Some of the basic data types, such as char, short, long, and long long, are not listed in
Table 19.1; you must determine the size of your data object and use the appropriate routine.
For example, a short int is normally 16 bits, an int and long can be 32 or 64 bits, and a
long long is 64 bits. (You can use the sizeof operator, described in Chapter 13, "Underlying
C Language Features," to determine the size of any data type.) So to archive a short int, store
it in an int first and then archive it with encodeIntForKey:. Reverse the process to get it
back: Use decodeIntForKey:, and then assign it to your short int variable.

Using NSData to Create Custom Archives

You might not want to write your object directly to a file using the
archiveRootObject:ToFile: method, as was done in the previous program examples. For
example, perhaps you want to collect some or all of your objects and store them in a single
archive file. You can do this in Objective-C using the data object class called NSData, as
touched on briefly in Chapter 16, "Working with Files."

As mentioned in Chapter 16, an NSData object can be used to reserve an area of memory into
which you can store data. Typical uses of this data area might be to provide temporary storage

for data that will subsequently be written to a file or perhaps to hold the contents of a file read from the disk. The simplest way to create a mutable data area is with the data method:

```
dataArea = [NSMutableData data];
```

This creates an empty buffer space whose size expands as needed as the program executes.

As a simple example, let's assume that you want to archive your address book and one of your Foo objects in the same file. Assume for this example that you've added keyed archiving methods to the AddressBook and AddressCard classes (see Program 19.9).

Program 19.9

```
#import "AddressBook.h"
#import "Foo.h"


int main (int argc, char * argv[])
{
    @autoreleasepool {
        Foo             *myFoo1 = [[Foo alloc] init];
        NSMutableData   *dataArea;
        NSKeyedArchiver *archiver;
        AddressBook     *myBook;

        // Insert code from Program 19.7 to` create an Address Book
        // in myBook containing four address cards

        myFoo1.strVal = @"This is the string";
        myFoo1.intVal = 12345;
        myFoo1.floatVal = 98.6];

        // Set up a data area and connect it to an NSKeyedArchiver object
        dataArea = [NSMutableData data];

        archiver = [[NSKeyedArchiver alloc]
                initForWritingWithMutableData: dataArea];
        // Now we can begin to archive objects
        [archiver encodeObject: myBook forKey: @"myaddrbook"];
        [archiver encodeObject: myFoo1 forKey: @"myfoo1"];
        [archiver finishEncoding];

        // Write the archived data area to a file
        if ([dataArea writeToFile: @"myArchive" atomically: YES] == NO)
            NSLog (@"Archiving failed!");
    }
    return 0;
}
```

After allocating an NSKeyedArchiver object, the initForWritingWithMutableData: message is sent to specify the area in which to write the archived data; this is the NSMutabledata area dataArea that you previously created. The NSKeyedArchiver object stored in archiver can now be sent encoding messages to archive objects in your program. In fact, until it receives a finishEncoding message, it archives and stores all encoding messages in the specified data area.

You have two objects to encode here: The first is your address book, and the second is your Foo object. You can use encodeObject:forKey: for these objects because you previously implemented encoder and decoder methods for the AddressBook, AddressCard, and Foo classes. (It's important to understand that concept.)

When you finish archiving your two objects, you send the archiver object the finishEncoding message. No more objects can be encoded after that point, and you need to send this message to complete the archiving process.

The area you set aside and named dataArea now contains your archived objects in a form that you can write to a file. The message expression

```
[dataArea writeToFile: @"myArchive" atomically: YES]
```

sends the writeToFile:atomically: message to your data stream to ask it to write its data to the specified file, which you named myArchive.

As you can see from the if statement, the writeToFile:atomically: method returns a BOOL value: YES if the write operation succeeds and NO if it fails (perhaps an invalid pathname for the file was specified or the file system is full).

Restoring the data from your archive file is simple: You just do things in reverse. First, you need to allocate a data area like before. Next, you need to read your archive file into the data area; then you have to create an NSKeyedUnarchiver object and tell it to decode data from the specified area. You must invoke decode methods to extract and decode your archived objects. When you finish, you send a finishDecoding message to the NSKeyedUnarchiver object.

This is all done in Program 19.10.

Program 19.10

```
#import "AddressBook.h"
#import "Foo.h"

int main (int argc, char * argv[])
{
    @autoreleasepool {
        NSData            *dataArea;
        NSKeyedUnarchiver *unarchiver;
        Foo               *myFoo1;
        AddressBook       *myBook;
        // Read in the archive and connect an
```

```
    // NSKeyedUnarchiver object to it

    dataArea = [NSData dataWithContentsOfFile: @"myArchive"];

    if (! dataArea) {
       NSLog (@"Can't read back archive file!");
       return 1;
    }

    unarchiver = [[NSKeyedUnarchiver alloc]
                 initForReadingWithData: dataArea];

    // Decode the objects we previously stored in the archive
    myBook = [unarchiver decodeObjectForKey: @"myaddrbook"];
    myFoo1 = [unarchiver decodeObjectForKey: @"myfoo1"];

    [unarchiver finishDecoding];

    // Verify that the restore was successful
    [myBook list];
    NSLog (@"%@\n%i\n%g", myFoo1.strVal, myFoo1.intVal,
          myFoo1.floatVal);
  }
  return 0;
}
```

Program 19.10   **Output**

```
======== Contents of: Steve's Address Book =========
Jamie Baker        jbaker@hitmail.com
Julia Kochan       jewls337@axlc.com
Stephen Kochan     steve@steve_kochan.com
Tony Iannino       tony.iannino@techfitness.com
===================================================
This is the string
12345
98.6
```

The output verifies that the address book and your Foo object were successfully restored from the archive file.

Using the Archiver to Copy Objects

In Program 18.2, you tried to make a copy of an array containing mutable string elements and you saw how a shallow copy of the array was made. That is, the actual strings themselves were not copied—only the references to them were copied.

You can use the Foundation's archiving capabilities to create a deep copy of an object. For example, Program 19.11 copies dataArray to dataArray2 by archiving dataArray into a buffer and then unarchiving it, assigning the result to dataArray2. You don't need to use a file for this process; the archiving and unarchiving process can all take place in memory.

Program 19.11

```
#import <Foundation/Foundation.h>

int main (int argc, char * argv[])
{
    @autoreleasepool {
        NSData       *data;
        NSMutableArray  *dataArray = [NSMutableArray arrayWithObjects:
            [NSMutableString stringWithString: @"one"],
            [NSMutableString stringWithString: @"two"],
            [NSMutableString stringWithString: @"three"],
            nil
          ];

        NSMutableArray   *dataArray2;
        NSMutableString  *mStr;

        // Make a deep copy using the archiver

        data = [NSKeyedArchiver archivedDataWithRootObject: dataArray];
        dataArray2 = [NSKeyedUnarchiver unarchiveObjectWithData: data];

        mStr = dataArray2[0];
        [mStr appendString: @"ONE"];

        NSLog (@"dataArray: ");
        for ( NSString *elem in dataArray )
          NSLog (@"%@", elem);

        NSLog (@"\ndataArray2: ");
        for ( NSString *elem in dataArray2 )
            NSLog (@"%@", elem);

    }
    return 0;
}
```

Program 19.11   **Output**

```
dataArray:
one
two
three

dataArray2:
oneONE
two
three
```

The output verifies that changing the first element of `dataArray2` had no effect on the first element of `dataArray`. That's because a new copy of the string was made through the archiving/unarchiving process.

The copy operation in Program 19.11 is performed with the following two lines:

```
data = [NSKeyedArchiver archivedDataWithRootObject: dataArray];
dataArray2 = [NSKeyedUnarchiver unarchiveObjectWithData: data];
```

You can even avoid the intermediate assignment and perform the copy with a single statement, like this:

```
dataArray2 = [NSKeyedUnarchiver unarchiveObjectWithData:
              [NSKeyedArchiver archivedDataWithRootObject: dataArray]];
```

You might want to keep this technique in mind next time you need to make a deep copy of an object or of an object that doesn't support the `NSCopying` protocol.

Exercises

1. In Chapter 6, "Making Decisions," Program 6.10A generated a table of prime numbers. Modify that program to store the numbers inside an `NSMutableArray` object. Then write the resulting array as an XML property list to the file `primes.pl`. Examine the contents of the file.

2. Write a program to read in the XML property list created in Exercise 1 and store the values in an array object. Display all the elements of the array to verify that the restore operation was successful.

3. Modify Program 19.2 to display the contents of one of the XML property lists (.plist files) stored in the /Library/Preferences folder.

4. Write a program to read in an archived `AddressBook` and look up an entry based on a name supplied on the command line, like so:

    ```
    $ lookup gregory
    ```

20

Introduction to Cocoa and Cocoa Touch

Throughout this book, you developed programs that had a simple user interface. You relied on the NSLog routine to display your output in the form of simple lines of text. However, as useful as this routine is, it is very limited in its capabilities. Certainly, other programs you use on the Mac or iPhone aren't as unfriendly. In fact, the Mac's reputation is based on its user-friendly dialogs and ease of use. Lucky for you, this is where Xcode and its built-in user interface design tool come to the rescue. Not only does this combination offer a powerful environment for program development, consisting of editing and debugging tools, and convenient access to online documentation, but it also provides an environment for easily developing sophisticated graphical user interfaces (GUIs).

The frameworks that provide the support for your Mac OS X applications to provide a rich user experience are called Cocoa, which actually consists of three frameworks: the Foundation framework, with which you are already familiar; the Core Data framework, for easily storing and managing data that is database driven; and the Application Kit (AppKit) framework. This last framework provides the classes associated with windows, buttons, lists, and so on.

Framework Layers

A diagram is often used to illustrate the different layers that separate the application at the topmost level from the underlying hardware. Figure 20.1 depicts one such representation.

The *kernel* provides the low-level communication to the hardware in the form of *device drivers*. It manages the system's resources, which includes scheduling programs for execution, managing memory and power, and performing basic I/O operations.

As its name implies, *Core Services* provides support at a lower or "core" level than that provided in the layers above it. For example, here you find support for collections, networking, debugging, file management, folders, memory management, threads, time, and power.

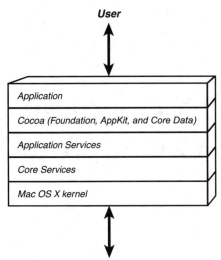

User

Application
Cocoa (Foundation, AppKit, and Core Data)
Application Services
Core Services
Mac OS X kernel

Computer Resources (memory, disk, display, etc.)

Figure 20.1   The application hierarchy

The *Application Services* layer includes support for printing and graphics rendering, including Quartz, OpenGL, and QuickTime.

Directly below your application sits the Cocoa layer. As noted, *Cocoa* includes the Foundation, Core Data, and AppKit frameworks. Foundation offers classes for working with collections, strings, memory management, the file system, archiving, and so on. AppKit provides classes for managing views, windows, documents, and the rich user interface for which Mac OS X is well known.

From this description, there seems to be duplication of functionality between some of the layers. Collections exist in both the Cocoa and Core Services layers. However, the former builds on support of the latter. Also, in some cases, a layer can be bypassed or "bridged." For example, some Foundation classes, such as those that deal with the file system, rely directly on functionality in the Core Services layer and so bypass the Application Services layer. In many cases, the Foundation framework defines an object-oriented mapping of data structures defined in the lower-level Core Services layer (which is written primarily in the procedural C language).

Cocoa Touch

iOS devices like the iPhone, the iPod touch, and the iPad contain a computer that runs a scaled-down version of Mac OS X. Some features found in iOS devices, such as accelerometers and proximity sensors, are unique to these devices and are not found in other Mac OS X computers, such as MacBook Pros or iMacs.

Note

Actually, Mac notebooks contain an accelerometer so that the hard drive can be parked if the computer gets dropped; however, you can't access this accelerometer directly from your programs.

Whereas the Cocoa frameworks are designed for application development for Mac OS X desktop and notebook computers, the Cocoa Touch frameworks are for applications targeted for iOS devices.

Both Cocoa and Cocoa Touch have the Foundation and Core Data frameworks in common. However, the UIKit replaces the AppKit framework under Cocoa Touch, providing support for many of the same types of objects, such as windows, views, buttons, text fields, and so on. In addition, Cocoa Touch provides classes for working with the accelerometer, gyroscope, triangulating your location with GPS and Wi-Fi signals, and the touch-driven interface, and also eliminates unneeded classes.

That concludes this brief overview of Cocoa and Cocoa Touch. In the next chapter, you learn how to write an application for the iPhone, using the simulator that is part of the iOS software development kit (SDK).

Writing iOS Applications

In this chapter, you develop two simple iPhone applications. The first illustrates some fundamental concepts related to using the interface design tool built in to Xcode, making connections, and understanding *delegates, outlets,* and *actions.* For the second iPhone application, you build a fraction calculator. It combines what you learned while developing the first application with what you learned throughout the rest of the book. The same principles you learn here can be used to develop applications for other iOS devices as well.

The iOS SDK

To write an iPhone application, you have to install Xcode and the iOS software development kit (SDK). This SDK is available free of charge from Apple's Web site. To download the SDK, you must first register to be an Apple Developer. That process is also free. To get the appropriate links, you can start at developer.apple.com and navigate to the appropriate point. It's a great idea to become familiar with that site.

The discussions in this chapter are based on Xcode 4.5 and the iOS SDK for iOS 6. Later versions of either should be compatible with what's described here. If you notice your screens look different from those shown, you might be using a different version of Xcode. In that case, check the forum at classroomM.com/objective-c for current information.

Your First iPhone Application

The first application shows how you can put a black-colored window on the iPhone's screen, allow for the user to press a button, and then display some text in response to the pressing of that button.

> **Note**
>
> The second application is more fun! You use the knowledge gained from your first application to build a simple calculator that does operations with fractions. You can use your `Fraction` class that you worked with earlier in the book, as well as a modified `Calculator` class. This time, your calculator needs to know how to work with fractions.

Let's dive right into the first program. This chapter does not cover all the details; as noted, there's simply not enough space to do that here. Instead, we walk you through the steps to give you the necessary foundation for you to explore and learn more concepts on your own with a separate Cocoa or iOS programming text.

Figure 21.1 shows the first application you develop for the iPhone running on the iPhone simulator (more about that shortly).

Figure 21.1   First iPhone application

This application is designed so that when you press the button labeled 1 the corresponding digit appears in the display (see Figure 21.2). That's all it does! This simple application lays the groundwork for the second fraction calculator application.

Figure 21.2   iPhone application results

By this point in this book, you should be comfortable using Xcode if you've been using it to enter and test your programs. This time, we also use a feature of Xcode that lets you design your user interface (UI) by placing UI elements such as tables, labels, and buttons in a window that resembles the iPhone's screen. Like any powerful development tool, this feature takes some getting used to.

> **Note**
>
> Before the release of Xcode 4, the UI was designed using a separate application called Interface Builder.

Apple distributes an iPhone simulator as part of the iOS SDK. The simulator replicates much of your iPhone environment, including its home screen, Safari web browser, Contacts application, and so on. The simulator makes it much easier to debug your applications; you don't have to download each iteration of your application to an actual iPhone device and then debug it there. This can save you a lot of time and effort.

To run applications on an iOS device, you need to register for the iOS Developer Program and pay a $99 fee (as of the time of this writing) to Apple. In turn, you receive an activation code for an iOS Development Certificate that allows you to test and install applications on an iOS device. Unfortunately, you cannot develop applications (even for your own iOS device) without going through this process. Note that the application we develop in this chapter will be loaded and tested on the iPhone simulator and not on an iPhone device.

Creating a New iPhone Application Project

Let's return to developing your first application. After you install the iOS SDK, start up the Xcode application. Select File, New, New Project. Under iOS (and if you don't see this in the left pane, you haven't installed the iOS SDK), click Application. You should see a window like that shown in Figure 21.3.

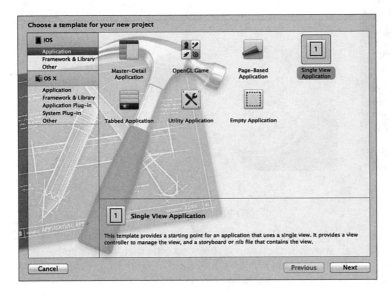

Figure 21.3   Starting a new iOS project

Here, you see templates that provide starting points for different types of applications, as summarized in Table 21.1.

Table 21.1   iOS Application Templates

Application Type	Description
Master-Detail	For an application that uses a navigation controller. Contacts is a sample application of this type. Generates a split view-based application for a large-screen device such as an iPad.
OpenGL Game	For OpenGL ES graphics-based applications such as games.
Page-Based Application	For an application that uses a page view controller to manage the display of pages.

Application Type	Description
Single View Application	For an application starting with a single view. You draw into the view and then display that view in the window.
Tabbed Application	For applications that use a tab bar. An example is the Music application.
Utility Application	For an application that has a flipside view. The Stock Quote application is an example of this type.
Empty Application	For an application that starts with just the main iPhone window. You can use this as the starting point for any application.

Returning to your New Project window, select Single View Application in the top rightmost pane and then click the Next button. Type in **iPhone_1** for the product name, whatever you choose as the organization name and company identifier, set Devices to iPhone, check the Use Automatic Reference Counting check box, and uncheck Use Storyboards and Include Unit Tests. Your screen should resemble Figure 21.4.

Note

You may want to follow the typical route and specify com.*company* as the Company Identifier. This is known as *reverse domain name* and forms the basis for what's known as the *bundle identifier* in your application.

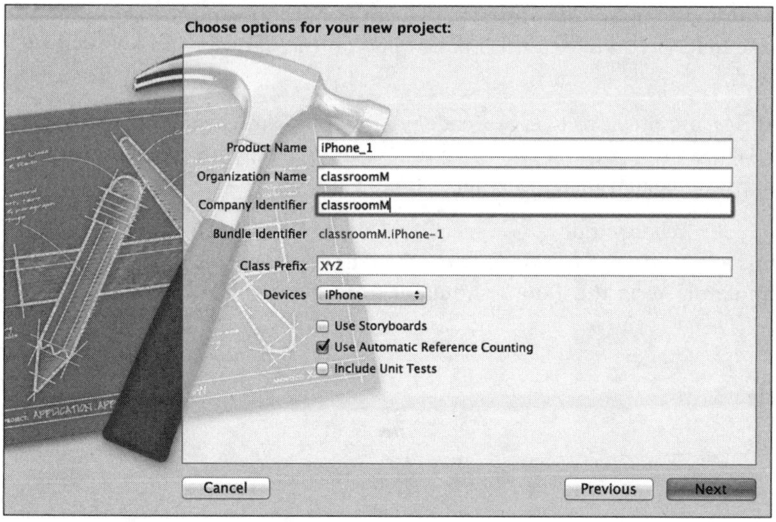

Figure 21.4   Selecting project options

Click Next. You can specify where to create your new project folder; don't worry about whether the Source Control box is checked. Your screen should now look like Figure 21.5.

Figure 21.5   Specifying where to store the project folder

Now, click Create. As you know from previous projects you created with Xcode, a new project is now created for you that contains templates for files you'll want to use. This is shown in Figure 21.6, where the iPhone_1 folder reveals five files: `AppDelegate.h`, `AppDelegate.m`, `ViewController.h`, `ViewController.m`, and `ViewController.xib`. The rightmost pane contains, among other things, orientations supported by your application and the application's icon. We ignore this pane here. If you have a third pane open on the right, you can close it for now; we don't need it yet.

Depending on your settings and previous uses of Xcode, your window might not appear precisely as depicted in Figure 21.6. You can choose to follow along with whatever your current layout resembles or else try to make it match the figure more closely.

In the top-left corner of your Xcode window, you see a drop-down labeled Scheme. Because we're not developing this application to run directly on the iPhone, you want the SDK set up to run with the iPhone simulator. Select the iPhone simulator from the Scheme window as shown in Figure 21.7.

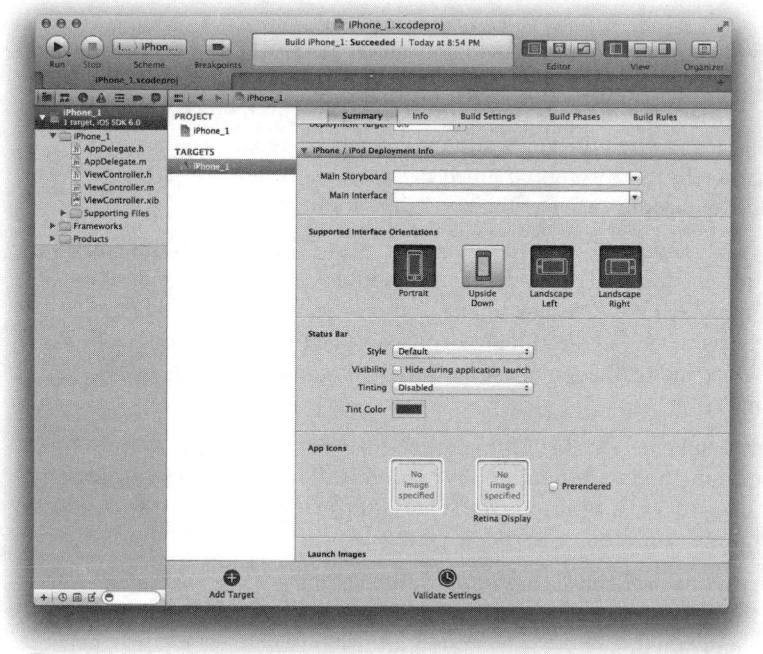

Figure 21.6   New iOS project iPhone_1 is created

Figure 21.7   Selecting the iPhone simulator

Entering Your Code

Now we're ready to modify some of your project files. Notice that a class called `AppDelegate` was created for you. An application delegate subclass is created for every new iOS application you create. In general, in this class are methods that control the application's execution. This includes such things as what to do when the application starts, when it enters and leaves the background, when the system tells it it's using too much memory, and when it terminates. We won't make any changes to this class in either of the two examples in this chapter.

A second class was also created for you called `ViewController`. As you can see, Xcode creates interface and implementation sections for you in the corresponding `.h` and `.m` files. A view controller is responsible for managing the display of one or more "views" on your iPhone's display. We have only one view in this application, as depicted in Figure 21.1. It's not uncommon for applications to present many different views and to therefore have multiple view controllers to manage them.

So, our view controller class will be responsible for handling the event of pressing the button labeled 1. There we'll define a method to respond to that action when it occurs in the iPhone's window, in our example, the pressing of a button. You'll see shortly how you make the connection between that event and the execution of a specific method.

Your objects can also have instance variables whose values correspond to some control in your iPhone's window, such as the name on a label or the text displayed in an editable text box. These are known as *outlets,* and you'll see how you connect an instance variable to an actual control (outlet) in the iPhone's window.

For our first application, we need a method that responds to the action of the pressing of the button labeled 1. We also need an outlet variable that contains (among other information) the text to be displayed in the label that we create at the top of the iPhone's window.

Edit the file `ViewController.h` to add a new `UILabel` property called `display` and declare an action method called `click1` to respond to the pressing of the button. Your interface file should appear as shown in Program 21.1. (The comment lines automatically inserted at the head of the file are not shown here.)

Program 21.1 ViewController.h

```
#import <UIKit/UIKit.h>

@interface ViewController : UIViewController

@property (strong, nonatomic) IBOutlet UILabel *display;

-(IBAction) click1;

@end
```

Notice that iPhone applications import the header file `<UIKit/UIKit.h>`. This header file, in turn, imports other UIKit header files, in a similar way that the `Foundation.h` header file imported other header files you needed, such as `NSString.h` and `NSObject.h`.

You added a property belonging to the UILabel class called display. This will be an outlet property that will be connected to a label. When you set this property's text field, it updates the corresponding text for the label in the window. Other methods defined for the UILabel class allow you to set and retrieve other attributes of a label, such as its color, the number of lines, and the size of the text.

You'll want to use other classes in your interface as you learn more about iOS programming that we won't describe here. The names of some of these give you a clue as to their purpose: UITextField, UIFont, UIView, UITableView, UIImageView, UIImage, UISlider, and UIButton.

The display property is an outlet, and in the property declaration, note the use of the IBOutlet identifier. IBOutlet is really #defined as nothing in the UIKit header file UINibDeclarations.h. (That is, it is literally replaced by nothing in the source file by the preprocessor.) However, it's needed because Xcode looks for IBOutlets when it reads your header file to determine which of your variables can be used as outlets and can be connected to the appropriate UI elements in the interface.

The click1 method is defined to return a value of type IBAction. (This is defined as void in the UINibDeclarations.h header file.) Like IBOutlet, Xcode uses this identifier when it examines your header file to identify methods that can be used as actions, that is, that can respond to events that occur from activating controls you laid out in the user interface editor.

Now it's time to modify the corresponding ViewController.m implementation file for your class. Here you synthesize the accessor methods for your display property.

Now edit your implementation file and add the @synthesize directive and click1 method definition as shown in Program 21.1. (Note that Xcode added some "stub" methods in your implementation file that we won't be modifying.)

Program 21.1 ViewController.m

```
#import "ViewController.h"

@interface ViewController ()

@end

@implementation ViewController

@synthesize display;

-(IBAction) click1
{
    display.text = @"1";
}

- (void)viewDidLoad
{
```

```
    [super viewDidLoad];
    // Do any additional setup after loading the view, typically from a nib.
}


- (void)didReceiveMemoryWarning
{
    [super didReceiveMemoryWarning];
    // Dispose of any resources that can be recreated.
}


@ends
```

Note that Xcode added a class extension to your class that you can use to define private methods and properties:

```
@interface ViewController ()
@end
```

Private methods are methods that will be used only from within the implementation section of your class. (Chapter 11, "Categories and Protocols," covered class extensions.)

The `click1` method sets the outlet variable `display` to the string `1` by setting `UILabel`'s `text` property. After you connect the pressing of the button to the invocation of this method, it can perform the desired action of putting a `1` into the display in the iPhone's window. To make the connection, you must now learn how to use the interface design tool built into Xcode.

Designing the Interface

In Figure 21.4, and in your Xcode main window, notice a file called `ViewController.xib`. An `xib` file (traditionally referred to as a *nib* file because the extension used to be `nib`) contains information about the user interface for your program, including information about its windows, buttons, labels, tab bars, text fields, and so on. Of course, you don't have a user interface yet! That's the next step.

Select the `ViewController.xib` file from the left pane. This causes the interface design tool to appear, as shown in Figure 21.8. The right pane shows the iPhone's main window, which starts out empty and with a gray background by default.

Note
The window depicted here is for the longer screen offered on the iPhone 5. If you want to write an application that also supports the iPhone 4 (or earlier models), consider the layout of your window to accommodate the smaller screen length.

From the View menu, select Utilities, Show Attributes Inspector. Your window should appear as depicted in Figure 21.9 in one of its display formats.

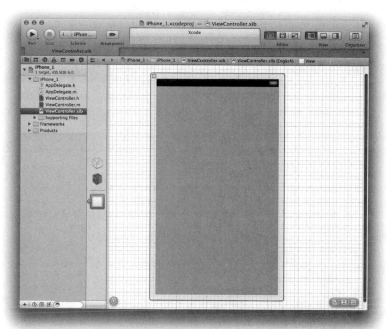

Figure 21.8   UI design pane

Figure 21.9   `ViewController.xib`

(Look at the various options selected in the Editor and View bars if you want to try to match your screen to the figure. This figure shows the Attributes Inspector in the top rightmost pane and the Objects Library in the bottom rightmost pane in icon view mode.)

The first thing we do is set the iPhone's window to black. To do this, first click inside the iPhone's window in the middle pane.

If you glance down to the View section of the Inspector pane, you'll see an attribute labeled Background. Click inside the gray-filled rectangle next to Background to bring up a color picker panel for you. Choose the black crayon, which changes the rectangle next to the Background attribute in the Inspector from gray to black.

If you take a look at the middle pane, which represents the iPhone's window, you see that it has changed to black, as shown in Figure 21.10.

Figure 21.10   iPhone's window changes to black

You can create new objects in your iPhone interface window by dragging an object from the Objects Library pane into the iPhone window. Drag a Label now. Release the mouse when the label is near the left of the window, close to the top, as shown in Figure 21.11.

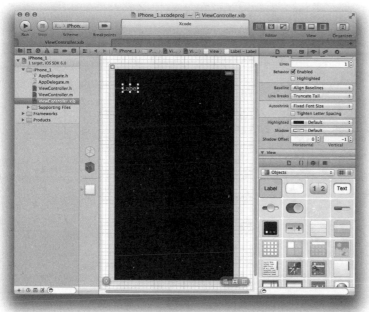

Figure 21.11   Adding a label

Blue guide lines appear as you move the label around inside your window. Sometimes they help you align objects with other objects previously placed in the window. At other times, they ensure that your objects are spaced far enough apart from other objects and from the edges of the window to be consistent with Apple's human interface guidelines.

You can always reposition the label in the window at any time in the future by selecting it and dragging it to another spot inside the window.

Let's now set some attributes for this label. In your iPhone window, if it's not currently selected, click the label you just created to select it. Notice that the Inspector pane gives you information about the currently selected object in your window.

Change the background color for the label to blue (or any other color you choose), like you changed the window's background color to black. We don't want any text to appear by default for this label, so change the Text value to an empty string. (That is, delete the string `Label` from the text field shown in the Inspector's pane.)

For the Alignment attribute, select the right-justified icon. Finally, let's now change the size of the label. Go back to the window and simply resize the label by pulling out along its corners and sides. Resize and reposition the label so that it looks like the one shown in Figure 21.12.

Now we'll add a button to the interface. From the Object Library pane, drag a Round Rect Button object into your interface window, placing it toward the lower-left corner of the window, as shown in Figure 21.13. (Note that this figure shows the Object Library pane changed from icon to list view.) You can change the label on the button in one of two ways: by double-clicking on the button and then typing your text, or by setting the second row of the Title field in the Inspector pane. Either way you choose, make your window match the one shown in Figure 21.13.

Figure 21.12   Changing the label's attributes and size

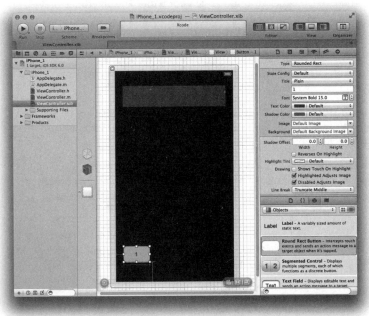

Figure 21.13   Adding a button to the interface.

Now we have a label that we want to connect to our `display` instance variable in our program so that when we set the variable in our program the label's text will be changed.

We also have a button labeled 1 that we want to set to invoke our `click1` method whenever it gets pressed. That method sets the value of `display`'s text field to 1. And because that variable will be connected to the label, the label will then be updated. As a recap, here's the sequence we want to set up:

1. The user presses the button labeled 1.

2. This event causes the `click1` method to be executed.

3. The `click1` method changes the text property of the instance variable `display` to the string 1.

4. Because the `UILabel` object `display` connects to the label in the iPhone's window, this label updates to the corresponding text value, or to the value 1.

For this sequence to work, we just need to make the two connections. You can do this in several different ways, but here we just describe one method.

First, let's get the source code displayed in the rightmost pane. To do this, we first hide the utilities pane by pressing the third icon grouped in the toolbar under View. This un-highlights it and closes the utilities pane. Next, we open an editor in the rightmost pane by selecting the middle icon in the Editor grouping on the toolbar. Your Xcode window should now resemble that shown in Figure 21.14.

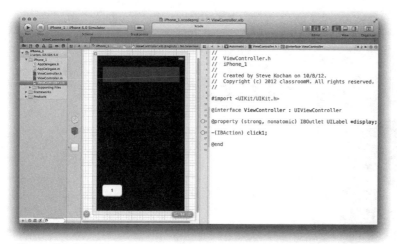

Figure 21.14   Displaying source code alongside the interface

Let's connect the button to the `IBAction` method `click1`. You do this by holding down the Control key while you click the button and drag the blue line that appears on the screen to the `click1` method displayed in the rightmost pane (and you can drag it to either the method where it's declared in the interface section or where it's defined in the implementation section). This is shown in Figure 21.15.

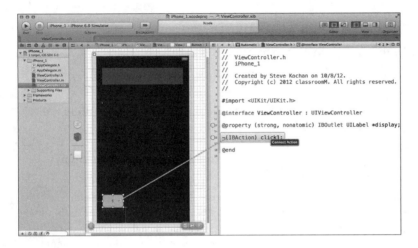

Figure 21.15   Adding an action for a button

Now, let's connect the `display` variable to the label. Select the label in the iPhone's window, hold down the Control key, and click-drag the blue line that appears to the `display` property declaration in the interface file. This is shown in Figure 21.16.

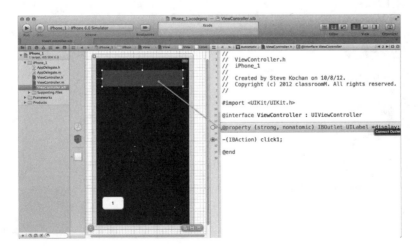

Figure 21.16   Connecting an outlet variable

When you release the mouse, the connection is made.

That's it; you're done! Select Run from the Product menu or from the toolbar. If all goes well, the program successfully builds and begins execution. When execution begins, your program is loaded into the iPhone simulator, which appears on your computer's display. The simulator window should appear as shown in Figure 21.1 at the start of this chapter. You simulate pressing a button with the simulator by simply clicking it. When you do that, the sequence of steps we outlined and the connections you made should result in the appearance of a 1 at the top of the display, as shown in Figure 21.2.

An iPhone Fraction Calculator

The next example is a bit more involved, but the concepts from the previous example apply here as well. We do not show all the steps to create this example, but rather give a summary of the steps and an overview of the design methodology. Of course, we also show all the code.

First, let's see how the application works. Figure 21.17 shows what the application looks like in the simulator just after launching.

Figure 21.17   Fraction calculator after launch

The calculator application allows you to enter fractions by first keying in the numerator, pressing the key labeled Over, and then keying in the denominator. So, to enter the fraction 2/5, you press 2, followed by Over, followed by 5. Note that, unlike other calculators, this one actually shows the fraction in the display, so 2/5 is displayed as 2/5.

After keying in one fraction, you then choose an operation (addition, subtraction, multiplication, or division) by pressing the appropriately labeled key +, −, ×, or ÷, respectively.

After keying-in the second fraction, you then complete the operation by pressing the = key, just as you would with a standard calculator.

> **Note**
>
> This calculator is designed to perform just a single operation between two fractions. It's left as an exercise at the end of this chapter for you to remove this limitation.

The display continuously updates as keys are pressed. Figure 21.18 shows the display after the fraction 4/6 has been entered and the multiplication key has been pressed.

Figure 21.18   Keying in an operation

Figure 21.19 shows the result of multiplying the fractions 4/6 and 2/8 together. Note that the result of 1/6 indicates that the result has been reduced.

Figure 21.19   The result of multiplying two fractions

Starting the New Fraction_Calculator Project

For this second program example, you'll start by creating a new project. As before, select Single View Application from the New Project window. Call your new project **Fraction_Calculator**.

When your project is created, this time you'll notice you get two class templates defined for you. `AppDelegate.h` and `AppDelegate.m` define the application's delegate class for your project, and `ViewController.h` and `ViewController.m` define the view controller class for your project. As with the first example in this chapter, it's in this latter class where you perform all your work.

Defining the View Controller

Now, let's write the code for the view controller class `ViewController`. We start with the interface file Program 21.2.

Program 21.2   `ViewController.h` **Interface File**

```
#import <UIKit/UIKit.h>

@interface ViewController : UIViewController

@property (strong, nonatomic) IBOutlet UILabel *display;

-(void) processDigit: (int) digit;
-(void) processOp: (char) theOp;
-(void) storeFracPart;

// Numeric keys

-(IBAction) clickDigit: (UIButton *) sender;

// Arithmetic Operation keys

-(IBAction) clickPlus;
-(IBAction) clickMinus;
-(IBAction) clickMultiply;
-(IBAction) clickDivide;

// Misc. Keys

-(IBAction) clickOver;
-(IBAction) clickEquals;
-(IBAction) clickClear;

@end
```

There are housekeeping variables for building the fractions (`currentNumber`, `firstOperand`, and `isNumerator`) and for building the string for the display (`displayString`). There is also a `Calculator` object (`myCalculator`) that can perform the actual calculation between the two fractions. We associate a single method called `clickDigit:` to handle the pressing of any of the digit keys 0–9. This method takes an argument that indicates the actual digit key that was pressed, as you'll shortly see. Finally, we define methods to handle storing the operation to be performed (`clickPlus`, `clickMinus`, `clickMultiply`, `clickDivide`), carrying out the actual calculation when the = key is pressed (`clickEquals`), clearing the current operation (`clickClear`), and separating the numerator from the denominator when the Over key is pressed (`clickOver`). Several methods (`processDigit:`, `processOp:`, and `storeFracPart`) are defined to assist in the aforementioned chores.

Program 21.2 shows the implementation file for this controller class. Note that we declare the instance variables in the implementation section. We could have declared properties and synthesized them instead. Either approach works fine. The approach we use here keeps the instance variables private and makes it clear they're used within the class.

Program 21.2 `ViewController.m` **Implementation File**

```objc
#import "ViewController.h"
#import "Caculator.h"

@implementation ViewController
{
    char                op;
    int                 currentNumber;
    BOOL                firstOperand, isNumerator;
    Calculator          *myCalculator;
    NSMutableString     *displayString;
}

@synthesize display;


-(void) viewDidLoad {

    // Override point for customization after application launch

    firstOperand = YES;
    isNumerator = YES;
    displayString = [NSMutableString stringWithCapacity: 40];
    myCalculator = [[Calculator alloc] init];
}

-(void) processDigit: (int) digit
{
    currentNumber = currentNumber * 10 + digit;

    [displayString appendString:
        [NSString stringWithFormat: @"%i", digit]];
    display.text = displayString;
}

- (IBAction) clickDigit: (UIButton *) sender
{
    int digit = sender.tag;

    [self processDigit: digit];
}

-(void) processOp: (char) theOp
{
    NSString *opStr;
```

```
    op = theOp;

    switch (theOp) {
        case '+':
            opStr = @" + ";
            break;
        case '-':
            opStr = @" - ";
            break;
        case '*':
            opStr = @" x ";
            break;
        case '/':
            opStr = @" ÷ ";
            break;
    }

    [self storeFracPart];
    firstOperand = NO;
    isNumerator = YES;

    [displayString appendString: opStr];
    display.text = displayString;
}

-(void) storeFracPart
{
    if (firstOperand) {
        if (isNumerator) {
            myCalculator.operand1.numerator = currentNumber;
            myCalculator.operand1.denominator = 1; // e.g. 3 * 4/5 =
        }
        else
            myCalculator.operand1.denominator = currentNumber;
    }
    else if (isNumerator) {
        myCalculator.operand2.numerator = currentNumber;
        myCalculator.operand2.denominator = 1; // e.g. 3/2 * 4 =
    }
    else {
        myCalculator.operand2.denominator = currentNumber;
        firstOperand = YES;
    }

    currentNumber = 0;
}
```

```
-(IBAction) clickOver
{
    [self storeFracPart];
    isNumerator = NO;
    [displayString appendString: @"/"];
    display.text = displayString;
}

// Arithmetic Operation keys

-(IBAction) clickPlus
{
    [self processOp: '+'];
}

-(IBAction) clickMinus
{
    [self processOp: '-'];
}

-(IBAction) clickMultiply
{
    [self processOp: '*'];
}

-(IBAction) clickDivide
{
    [self processOp: '/'];
}

// Misc. Keys

-(IBAction) clickEquals
{
    if ( firstOperand == NO ) {
        [self storeFracPart];
        [myCalculator performOperation: op];

        [displayString appendString: @" = "];
        [displayString appendString: [myCalculator.accumulator
          convertToString]];
        display.text = displayString;

        currentNumber = 0;
        isNumerator = YES;
        firstOperand = YES;
        [displayString setString: @""];
```

```
        }
}

-(IBAction) clickClear
{
    isNumerator = YES;
    firstOperand = YES;
    currentNumber = 0;
    [myCalculator clear];

    [displayString setString: @""];
    display.text = displayString;
}

@end
```

The calculator's window still contains just one label as in the previous application, and we still call it `display`. As the user enters a number digit by digit, we need to build the number along the way. The variable `currentNumber` holds the number in progress, while the BOOL variables `firstOperand` and `isNumerator` keep track of whether this is the first or second operand entered and whether the user is currently keying in the numerator or the denominator of that operand.

When a digit button is pressed on the calculator, we set it up so that some identifying informa-tion is passed to the `clickDigit:` method to identify which digit button was pressed. This is done by setting the button's Tag value in the Attributes Inspector pane to a unique value for each digit button. In this case, we want to set the tag to the corresponding digit number. So, the tag for the button labeled 0 will be set to 0, the tag for the button labeled 1 to 1, and so on. The `sender` argument sent to the `clickDigit:` method is the actual UIButton object that was pressed in the iPhone's window. By accessing the `tag` property of this object, you can retrieve the value of the button's tag. This is done in the `clickDigit:` method, as shown here:

```
- (IBAction) clickDigit: (UIButton *) sender
{
    int digit = sender.tag;

    [self processDigit: digit];
}
```

Program 21.2 has a lot more buttons than in the first application. Most of the complexity in the view controller's implementation file revolves around building the fractions and display-ing them. As noted, as a digit button 0–9 gets pressed, the action method `clickDigit:` gets executed. That method calls the `processDigit:` method to tack the digit on to the end of the number that's being built in the variable `currentNumber`. That method also adds the digit to the current display string that's kept in the variable `displayString`, and updates the display:

```
-(void) processDigit: (int) digit
{
    currentNumber = currentNumber * 10 + digit;

    [displayString appendString:
        [NSString stringWithFormat: @"%i", digit]];
    display.text = displayString;
}
```

When the = key is pressed, the `clickEquals` method gets invoked to perform the operation. The calculator performs the operation between the two fractions, storing the result in its accumulator. This accumulator is fetched inside the `clickEquals` method, and the result is added to the display.

The `Fraction` Class

The `Fraction` class remains largely unchanged from earlier examples in this text. A new `convertToString` method was added to convert a fraction to its equivalent string representation. Program 21.2 shows the `Fraction` interface file followed immediately by the corresponding implementation file.

Program 21.2   `Fraction.h` **Interface File**

```
#import <UIKit/UIKit.h>

@interface Fraction : NSObject

@property int numerator, denominator;

-(void)         print;
-(void)         setTo: (int) n over: (int) d;
-(Fraction *)   add: (Fraction *) f;
-(Fraction *)   subtract: (Fraction *) f;
-(Fraction *)   multiply: (Fraction *) f;
-(Fraction *)   divide: (Fraction *) f;
-(void)         reduce;
-(double)       convertToNum;
-(NSString *)   convertToString;

@end
```

Program 21.2   Fraction.m Implementation File

```objectivec
#import "Fraction.h"

@implementation Fraction

@synthesize numerator, denominator;

-(void) setTo: (int) n over: (int) d
{
    numerator = n;
    denominator = d;
}

-(void) print
{
    NSLog (@"%i/%i", numerator, denominator);
}

-(double) convertToNum
{
    if (denominator != 0)
        return (double) numerator / denominator;
    else
        return NAN;
}

-(NSString *) convertToString
{
    if (numerator == denominator)
        if (numerator == 0)
            return @"0";
        else
            return @"1";
    else if (denominator == 1)
        return [NSString stringWithFormat: @"%i", numerator];
    else
        return [NSString stringWithFormat: @"%i/%i",
                numerator, denominator];
}

// add a Fraction to the receiver

-(Fraction *) add: (Fraction *) f
{
    // To add two fractions:
```

```
    // a/b + c/d = ((a*d) + (b*c)) / (b * d)

    // result will store the result of the addition
    Fraction    *result = [[Fraction alloc] init];

    result.numerator = numerator * f.denominator +
            denominator * f.numerator;
    result.denominator = denominator * f.denominator;

    [result reduce];
    return result;
}

-(Fraction *) subtract: (Fraction *) f
{
    // To sub two fractions:
    // a/b - c/d = ((a*d) - (b*c)) / (b * d)

    Fraction *result = [[Fraction alloc] init];

    result.numerator = numerator * f.denominator -
         denominator * f.numerator;
    result.denominator = denominator * f.denominator;

    [result reduce];
    return result;
}

-(Fraction *) multiply: (Fraction *) f
{
    Fraction *result = [[Fraction alloc] init];

    result.numerator = numerator * f.numerator;
    result.denominator = denominator * f.denominator;
    [result reduce];

    return result;
}

-(Fraction *) divide: (Fraction *) f
{
    Fraction *result = [[Fraction alloc] init];

    result.numerator = numerator * f.denominator;
    result.denominator = denominator * f.numerator;
    [result reduce];
```

```
        return result;
}

- (void) reduce
{
    int u = numerator;
    int v = denominator;
    int temp;

    if (u == 0)
        return;
    else if (u <0)
        u = -u;

    while (v != 0) {
        temp = u % v;
        u = v;
        v = temp;
    }

    numerator /= u;
    denominator /= u;
}
@end
```

The `convertToString:` method checks the numerator and denominator of the fraction to produce a more eye-pleasing result. If the numerator and denominator are equal (but not zero), we return `@"1"`. If the numerator is zero, the string `@"0"` is returned. If the denominator is 1, it's a whole number: there's no need to show the denominator.

Recall that the `stringWithFormat:` method used inside `convertToString:` returns a string given a format string (akin to `NSLog`) and a comma-separated list of arguments. You pass arguments to a method that takes a variable number of arguments by separating them with commas, just as you did when passing the arguments to the `NSLog` function.

A `Calculator` Class That Deals with Fractions

Next, it's time to take a look at the `Calculator` class. The concept is similar to the class of the same name we developed earlier in this book. However, in this case, our calculator must know how to deal with fractions. Here are our new `Calculator` class interface and implementation files.

Program 21.2   `Calculator.h` **Interface File**

```
#import <UIKit/UIKit.h>
#import "Fraction.h"

@interface Calculator : NSObject

@property (strong, nonatomic) Fraction *operand1, *operand2, *accumulator;

-(Fraction *) performOperation: (char) op;
-(void) clear;

@end
```

Program 21.2   `Calculator.m` **Implementation File**

```
#import "Calculator.h"

@implementation Calculator

@synthesize operand1, operand2, accumulator;

-(id) init
{
    self = [super init];

    if (self) {
        operand1 = [[Fraction alloc] init];
        operand2 = [[Fraction alloc] init];
        accumulator = [[Fraction alloc] init];
    }

    return self;
}


-(void) clear
{
    accumulator.numerator = 0;
    accumulator.denominator = 0;
}


-(Fraction *) performOperation: (char) op
{
    Fraction *result;
```

```
    switch (op) {
        case '+':
            result = [operand1 add: operand2];
            break;
        case '-':
            result = [operand1 subtract: operand2];
            break;
        case '*':
            result = [operand1 multiply: operand2];
            break;
        case '/':
            result = [operand1 divide: operand2];
            break;
    }

    accumulator.numerator = result.numerator;
    accumulator.denominator = result.denominator;

    return accumulator;
}

@end
```

Designing the User Interface

For this project, your nib file is called `ViewController.xib`. You'll design your interface by selecting this file and laying out the buttons and label as depicted in Figure 21.17. (Of course, feel free to design the interface to your liking.)

Make the connection from each digit button you lay out in your view to the `clickDigit:` method. Do this by Control-click-dragging each button in turn to the `clickDigit:` method either in the interface or implementation file for your view controller. Also, for each digit button, in the Inspector pane set the Tag value to the number that corresponds to the button's title. So, for the digit button labeled 0, set the Tag value to 0, for the digit button labeled 1, set the Tag value to 1, and so on.

Draw the remaining buttons in the View window and make the corresponding connections. That's it! Your interface design is done, and your fraction calculator application is ready for action.

Summary

Figure 21.20 shows the Xcode project window so that you can see all the files related to the fraction calculator project.

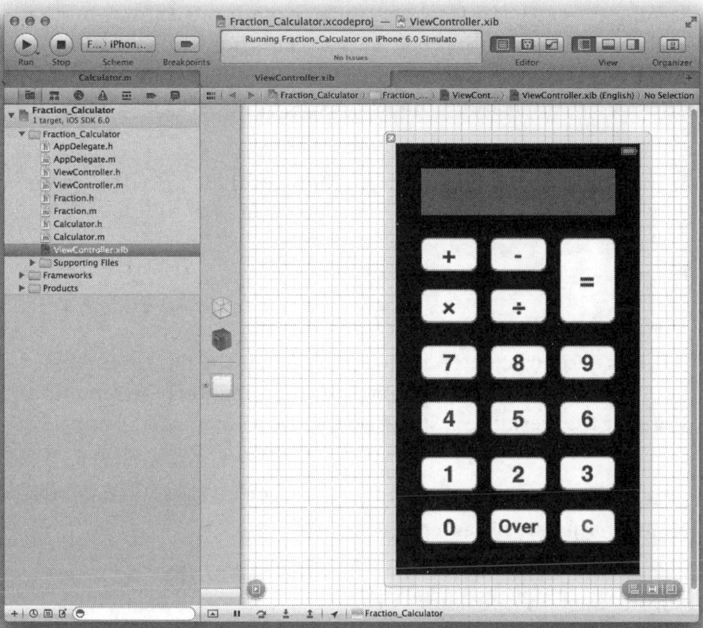

Figure 21.20   Fraction calculator project files

The following summarizes the steps you followed to create your iPhone fraction calculator application:

1. Created a new Single View Application.

2. Entered your UI code into the `ViewController` .h and .m files.

3. Added the `Fraction` and `Calculator` classes to the project.

4. Opened `ViewController.xib` to create the UI.

5. Made the View window's background black.

6. Created a label and buttons and position them inside the View window.

7. Control-click-dragged from the label you created in the View window to the `UILabel` `IBOutlet` property `display`.

8. Control-click-dragged from each button in the View window to the appropriate `IBAction` method. For each digit button, you selected the `clickDigit:` method. Also, for each digit button, you set the `tag` property to the corresponding digit 0–9 so that the `clickDigit:` method could identify which button was pressed.

It was a worthwhile exercise learning how to use a view controller, even though it was more work than simply doing everything in the application delegate object. I hope this brief introduction to developing iOS applications gives you a good start for writing your own iPhone applications. As noted earlier, there are many features offered in UIKit and lots for you to explore!

Several limitations apply to our fraction calculator application. Many of these are addressed in the exercises that follow.

Exercises

1. Add a Convert button to the fraction calculator application. When the button is pressed, use the `Fraction` class's `convertToNum` method to produce the numeric representation of the fractional result. Convert that result to a string and show it in the calculator's display.

2. Modify the fraction calculator application so that a negative fraction can be entered if the – key gets pressed before a numerator is entered.

3. If the value of zero is keyed in for a denominator for either the first or second operand, display the string `Error` in the fraction calculator's display.

4. Modify the fraction calculator application so that calculations can be chained. For example, allow for the following operation to be keyed:

   `1/5 + 2/7 - 3/8 =`

5. You can add an icon to your application that will appear on the iPhone's home screen. You can do so by dragging it to the App Icons section as shown in Figure 21.6. For a normal-sized icon (iPhone 3GS and earlier), the icon size should be 57x57 pixels large. For a Retina display iPhone (iPhone 4 and later), the icon image file should be 114x114 pixels.

   Find a suitable calculator image on the Internet that you can use and set up the fraction calculator to use this image as its application icon.

6. Give your calculator's buttons a custom look by using your own image for a button. You first add the image to your project (drag it into the left pane). Next, set the button's type to Custom in the Inspector window and set the image to the file you just copied into your project. Figure 21.21 shows a fraction calculator that uses such a custom image. This calculator is available at no charge from Apple's App Store, and the source code is posted on the forum for this book (http://classroomM.com/objective-c).

Figure 21.21   Fraction calculator with custom buttons

Appendix A

Glossary

This appendix contains informal definitions for many of the terms you will encounter. Some of these terms have to do directly with the Objective-C language itself, whereas others gain their etymology from the discipline of object-oriented programming. In the latter case, the meaning of the term as it specifically applies to the Objective-C language is provided.

abstract class   A class defined to make creating subclasses easier. Instances are created from the subclass, not of the abstract class. *See also* concrete subclass.

accessor method   A method that gets or sets the value of an instance variable. Using accessor methods to set and retrieve the values of instance variables is consistent with the methodology of data encapsulation.

Application Kit   A framework for developing an application's user interface, which includes objects such as menus, toolbars, and windows. Part of Cocoa and more commonly called AppKit.

ARC   *See* Automatic Reference Counting.

archiving   Translating the representation of an object's data into a format that can later be restored (unarchived).

array   An ordered collection of values. Arrays can be defined as a basic Objective-C type and are implemented as objects under Foundation through the `NSArray` and `NSMutableArray` classes.

Automatic Reference Counting (ARC)   A feature added as of Xcode 4.2 whereby the compiler manages the memory associated with an object. Before Xcode 4.2, iOS programmers were required to use manual techniques to manage memory. This required the use of retain, release, autorelease, and dealloc methods.

automatic variable   A variable that is automatically allocated and released when a statement block is entered and exited. Automatic variables have scope that is limited to the block in which they are defined and have no default initial value. They are optionally preceded by the keyword `auto`.

autorelease pool   An object that before ARC was managed by the `NSAutoreleasePool` class. Now it is implemented through the `@autoreleasepool` directive. The autorelease pool keeps track of objects that are targeted for delayed release by the system. For iOS and Cocoa applications, that is typically at the end of the run loop.

bitfield   A structure containing one or more integer fields of a specified bit width. Bitfields can be accessed and manipulated the same way other structure members can.

block   An extension to the C language added by Apple, Inc. A block has a function-like syntax, captures the values of variables within its scope when defined, and can be assigned to a variable or passed as an argument to a method or function. A block can be efficiently dispatched to another thread or processor for execution.

category   A set of methods grouped together under a specified name. Categories can modularize the method definitions for a class and can be used to add new methods to an existing class.

character string   A null-terminated sequence of characters.

class   A set of instance variables and methods that have access to those variables. After a class is defined, instances of the class (that is, objects) can be created.

class method   A method (defined with a leading + sign) that is invoked on class objects. *See also* instance method.

class object   An object that identifies a particular class. The class name can be used as the receiver of a message to invoke a class method. In other places, the `class` method can be invoked on the class to create a class object.

cluster   An abstract class that groups a set of private concrete subclasses, providing a simplified interface to the user through the abstract class.

Cocoa   A development environment that consists of the Foundation, Core Data, and Application Kit frameworks.

Cocoa Touch   A development environment that consists of the Foundation, Core Data, and UIKit frameworks.

collection   A Foundation framework object that is an array, a dictionary, or a set used for grouping and manipulating related objects.

compile time   The time during which the source code is analyzed and converted into a lower-level format known as object code.

composite class   A class that is composed of objects from other classes; often it is used as an alternative to subclassing.

concrete subclass   A subclass of an abstract class. Instances can be created from a concrete subclass.

conform   A class conforms to a protocol if it adopts all the required methods in the protocol, either directly through implementation or indirectly through inheritance.

constant character string   A sequence of characters enclosed inside a pair of double quotation marks. If preceded by an @ character, it defines a constant character string object of type NSConstantString.

data encapsulation   The notion that the data for an object is stored in its instance variables and is accessed only by the object's methods. This maintains the integrity of the data.

delegate   An object directed to carry out an action by another object.

designated initializer   The method that all other initialization methods in the class, or in subclasses (through messages to super), will invoke.

dictionary   A collection of key-value pairs implemented under Foundation with the NSDictionary and NSMutable Dictionary classes.

directive   In Objective-C, a special construct that begins with an at sign (@). @interface, @implementation, @end, and @class are examples of directives.

distributed objects   The capability of Foundation objects in one application to communicate with Foundation objects in another application, possibly running on another machine.

dynamic binding   Determining the method to invoke with an object at runtime instead of at compile time.

dynamic typing   Determining the class to which an object belongs at runtime instead of at compile time. *See also* static typing.

encapsulation   *See* data encapsulation.

extern variable   *See* global variable.

factory method   *See* class method.

factory object   *See* class object.

formal protocol   A set of related methods grouped together under a name declared with the @protocol directive. Different classes (not necessarily related) can adopt a formal protocol by implementing (or inheriting) all its required methods. *See also* informal protocol.

forwarding   The process of sending a message and its associated arguments to another method for execution.

Foundation framework   A collection of classes, functions, and protocols that form the foundation for application development, providing basic facilities such as memory management, file and URL access, the tasks of archiving and working with collections, strings, and number and date objects.

framework   A collection of classes, functions, protocols, documentation, and header files and other resources that are all related. For example, the Cocoa framework is used in developing interactive graphical applications under OS X.

function   A block of statements identified by a name that can accept one or more arguments passed to it by value and can optionally return a value. Functions can be either local (static) to the file in which they're defined or global, in which case they can be called from functions or methods defined in other files.

garbage collection   A runtime memory-management system that automatically releases the memory used by unreferenced objects. Garbage collection is not supported in the iOS runtime environment.

gcc   The name of the compiler developed by the Free Software Foundation (FSF). gcc supports many programming languages, including C, Objective-C, and C++.

gdb   The standard debugging tool for programs compiled with gcc.

getter method   An accessor method that retrieves the value of an instance variable. *See also* setter method.

global variable   A variable defined outside any method or function that can be accessed by any method or function in the same source file or from other source files that declare the variable as extern.

header file   A file that contains common definitions, macros, and variable declarations that is included in a program using either an #import or an #include statement.

id   The generic object type that can hold a pointer to any type of object.

immutable object   An object whose value cannot be modified. Examples from the Foundation framework include NSString, NSDictionary, and NSArray objects. *See also* mutable object.

implementation section   The section of a class definition that contains the actual code (that is, implementation) for the methods declared in the corresponding interface section (or as specified by a protocol definition).

informal protocol   A logically related set of methods declared as a category, often as a category of the root class. Unlike formal protocols, all the methods in an informal protocol do not have to be implemented. *See also* formal protocol.

inheritance   The process of passing methods and instance variables from a class, starting with the root object, down to subclasses.

instance   A concrete representation of a class. Instances are objects that are typically created by sending an alloc or new message to a class object.

instance method   A method that can be invoked by an instance of a class. *See also* class method.

instance variable   A variable declared in the interface section (or inherited from a parent) that is contained in every instance of the object. Instance methods have direct access to their instance variables.

Interface Builder   A tool under OS X for building a graphical user interface for an application.

interface section   The section for declaring a class, its superclass, instance variables, and methods. For each method, the argument types and return type are also declared. *See also* implementation section.

internationalization   *See* localization.

isa   A special instance variable defined in the root object that all objects inherit. The isa variable is used to identify the class to which an object belongs at runtime.

linking   The process of converting one or more object files into a program that can be executed.

local variable   A variable whose scope is limited to the block in which it is defined. Variables can be local to a method, function, or statement block.

localization   The process of making a program suitable for execution within a particular geographic region, typically by translating messages to the local language and handling things such as local time zones, currency symbols, date formats, and so on. Sometimes *localization* is used just to refer to the language translation, and the term *internationalization* is used to refer to the rest of the process.

message   The method and its associated arguments that are sent to an object (the receiver).

message expression   An expression enclosed in square brackets that specifies an object (the receiver) and the message to send to the object.

method   A procedure that belongs to a class and can be executed by sending a message to a class object or to instances from the class. *See also* class method and instance method.

mutable object   An object whose value can be changed. The Foundation framework supports mutable and immutable arrays, sets, strings, and dictionaries. *See also* immutable object.

nil   An object of type id, which is used to represent an invalid object. Its value is defined as 0. nil can be sent messages.

notification   The process of sending a message to objects that have registered to be alerted (notified) when a specific event occurs.

NSObject   The root object under the Foundation framework.

null character   A character whose value is 0. A null character constant is denoted by '\0'.

null pointer   An invalid pointer value, normally defined as 0.

object   A set of variables and associated methods. An object can be sent messages to cause one of its methods to be executed.

object-oriented programming   A method of programming based on classes and objects, and performing actions on those objects.

parent class   A class from which another class inherits. Also referred to as the *superclass*.

pointer   A value that references another object or data type. A pointer is implemented as the address of a particular object or value in memory. An instance of a class is a pointer to the location of the object's data in memory.

polymorphism   The capability of objects from different classes to accept the same message.

preprocessor   A program that makes a first pass through the source code processing lines that begin with a #, which presumably contain special preprocessor statements. Common uses are for defining macros with #define, including other source files with #import and #include, and conditionally including source lines with #if, #ifdef, and #ifndef.

procedural programming language   A language in which programs are defined by procedures and functions that operate on a set of data.

property declaration A way to specify attributes for instance variables that enables the compiler to generate leak-free and thread-safe accessor methods for instance variables. Property declarations can also be used to declare attributes for accessor methods that will be dynamically loaded at runtime.

property list A representation of different types of objects in a standardized format. Property lists are typically stored in XML format.

protocol A list of methods that a class must implement to conform to or adopt the protocol. Protocols provide a way to standardize an interface across classes. *See also* formal protocol and informal protocol.

receiver The object to which a message is sent. The receiver can be referred to as `self` from inside the method that is invoked.

reference count *See* retain count.

retain count A count of the number of times an object is referenced. It is incremented by sending a `retain` message to the object, and it is decremented by sending a `release` message to it.

root object The topmost object in the inheritance hierarchy that has no parent.

runtime The time when a program is executing; also the mechanism responsible for executing a program's instructions.

selector The name used to select the method to execute for an object. Compiled selectors are of type `SEL` and can be generated using the `@selector` directive.

self A variable used inside a method to refer to the receiver of the message.

set An unordered collection of unique objects implemented under Foundation with the `NSSet`, `NSMutableSet`, and `NSCountedSet` classes.

setter method An accessor method that sets the value of an instance variable. *See also* getter method.

statement One or more expressions terminated by a semicolon.

statement block One or more statements enclosed in a set of curly braces. Local variables can be declared within a statement block, and their scope is limited to that block.

static function A function declared with the `static` keyword that can be called only by other functions or methods defined in the same source file.

static typing Explicitly identifying the class to which an object belongs at compile time. *See also* dynamic typing.

static variable A variable whose scope is limited to the block or module in which it is defined. Static variables have default initial values of 0 and retain their values through method or function invocations.

structure An aggregate data type that can contain members of varying types. Structures can be assigned to other structures, passed as arguments to functions and methods, and returned by them as well.

subclass Also known as a *child class,* a subclass inherits the methods and instance variables from its parent or superclass.

super A keyword used in a method to refer to the parent class of the receiver.

superclass The parent class of a particular class. *See also* `super`.

synthesized method   A setter or getter method that the compiler automatically creates for you. It was added to the Objective C 2.0 language.

UIKit   A framework for developing applications for iOS devices. In addition to providing classes for working with usual UI elements such as windows, buttons, and labels, it defines classes for dealing with device-specific features such as the accelerometer and the touch interface. UIKit is part of Cocoa Touch.

Unicode character   A standard for representing characters from sets containing up to millions of characters. The NSString and NSMutableString classes work with strings containing Unicode characters.

union   An aggregate data type, such as a structure containing members that share the same storage area. Only one of those members can occupy the storage area at any point in time.

Xcode   A compiling and debugging tool for program development with OS X and iOS.

XML   Extensible Markup Language. The default format for property lists generated on OS X.

zone   A designated area of memory for allocating data and objects. A program can work with multiple zones to more efficiently manage memory.

Appendix B

Address Book Example
Source Code

For your reference purposes, here are the complete interface and implementation files for the address book example you worked with throughout Part II, "The Foundation Framework." This includes the definitions for the AddressCard and AddressBook classes. You should implement these classes on your system; then extend the class definitions to make them more practical and powerful. This is an excellent way for you to learn the language and become familiar with building programs, working with classes and objects, and working with the Foundation framework.

AddressCard Interface File

```
#import <Foundation/Foundation.h>

@interface AddressCard  : NSObject <NSCopying, NSCoding>

@property (nonatomic, copy) NSString *name, *email;

-(void) setName: (NSString *) theName andEmail: (NSString *) theEmail;
-(void) assignName: (NSString *) theName andEmail: (NSString *) theEmail;
-(NSComparisonResult) compareNames: (id) element;

-(void) print;

@end
```

AddressBook Interface File

```
#import <Foundation/Foundation.h>
#import "AddressCard.h"

@interface AddressBook: NSObject <NSCopying, NSCoding>

@property (nonatomic, copy) NSString *bookName;
@property (nonatomic, strong) NSMutableArray *book;

-(id)    initWithName: (NSString *) name;
-(void) sort;
-(void) sort2;
-(void) addCard: (AddressCard *) theCard;
-(void) removeCard: (AddressCard *) theCard;
-(NSUInteger) entries;
-(void) list;
-(AddressCard *) lookup: (NSString *) theName;

@end
```

AddressCard Implementation File

```
#import "AddressCard.h"

@implementation AddressCard

@synthesize name, email;

-(void) setName: (NSString *) theName andEmail: (NSString *) theEmail
{
    self.name = theName;
    self.email = theEmail;
}          ,

// Compare the two names from the specified address cards
-(NSComparisonResult) compareNames: (id) element
{
    return [name  compare: [element name]];
}

-(void) print
{
    NSLog (@"==================================");
    NSLog (@"|                                |");
    NSLog (@"|  %-31s |", [name  UTF8String]);
    NSLog (@"|  %-31s |", [email UTF8String]);
```

```
    NSLog (@"|                                     |");
    NSLog (@"|                                     |");
    NSLog (@"|                                     |");
    NSLog (@"|          O               O          |");
    NSLog (@"=====================================");
}


-(id) copyWithZone: (NSZone *) zone
{
    id newCard = [[[self class] allocWithZone: zone] init];

    [newCard assignName: name andEmail: email];
    return newCard;
}


-(void) assignName: (NSString *) theName andEmail: (NSString *) theEmail
{
    name = theName;
    email = theEmail;
}


-(void) encodeWithCoder: (NSCoder *) encoder
{
    [encoder encodeObject: name forKey: @"AddressCardName"];
    [encoder encodeObject: email forKey: @"AddressCardEmail"];
}


-(id) initWithCoder: (NSCoder *) decoder
{
    name = [decoder decodeObjectForKey: @"AddressCardName"];
    email = [decoder decodeObjectForKey: @"AddressCardEmail"];

    return self;
}
@end
```

AddressBook Implementation File

```
#import "AddressBook.h"

@implementation AddressBook

@synthesize book, bookName;
```

```objectivec
// set up the AddressBook's name and an empty book

-(id) initWithName: (NSString *) name
{
    self = [super init];

    if (self) {
        bookName = [NSString stringWithString: name];
        book = [NSMutableArray array];
    }

    return self;
}

-(id) init
{
    return [self initWithName: @"Unnamed Book"];
}

// Write our own book setter to create a mutable copy

-(void) setBook: (NSArray *) theBook
{
   book = [theBook mutableCopy];
}

-(void) sort
{
    [book sortUsingSelector: @selector(compareNames:)];
}

// Alternate sort using blocks

-(void) sort2
{
   [book sortUsingComparator:
      ^(id obj1, id obj2) {
          return [[obj1 name] compare: [obj2 name]];
       }];
}
-(void) addCard: (AddressCard *) theCard
{
    [book addObject: theCard];
}

-(void) removeCard: (AddressCard *) theCard
{
```

```objc
    [book removeObjectIdenticalTo: theCard];
}

-(NSUInteger) entries
{
    return   [book count];
}

-(void) list
{
    NSLog (@"======== Contents of: %@ =========", bookName);

    for ( AddressCard *theCard in book )
        NSLog (@"%-20s    %-32s", [theCard.name UTF8String],
            [theCard.email UTF8String]);

    NSLog (@"=================================================");
}

// lookup address card by name — assumes an exact match

-(AddressCard *) lookup: (NSString *) theName
{
    for ( AddressCard *nextCard in book )
        if ( [[nextCard name] caseInsensitiveCompare: theName]
           == NSOrderedSame )
              return nextCard;

    return nil;
}

-(void) encodeWithCoder: (NSCoder *) encoder
{
    [encoder encodeObject:bookName forKey: @"AddressBookBookName"];
    [encoder encodeObject:book forKey: @"AddressBookBook"];
}

-(id) initWithCoder: (NSCoder *) decoder
{
    bookName = [decoder decodeObjectForKey: @"AddressBookBookName"];
    book = [decoder decodeObjectForKey: @"AddressBookBook"];

    return self;
}

// Method for NSCopying protocol
```

```
-(id) copyWithZone: (NSZone *) zone
{
    id newBook = [[[self class] allocWithZone: zone] init];

    [newBook setBookName: bookName];

    // The following will do a shallow copy of the address book

    [newBook setBook: book];

    return newBook;
}
@end
```

Index

Developer's Library

ESSENTIAL REFERENCES FOR PROGRAMMING PROFESSIONALS

Objective-C Phrasebook, Second Edition

David Chisnall

ISBN-13: 978-0-321-81375-6

Programming in C

Stephen G. Kochan

ISBN-13: 978-0-672-32666-0

The Core iOS 6 Developer's Cookbook

Erica Sadun

ISBN-13: 978-0-321-88421-3

Other Developer's Library Titles

TITLE	AUTHOR	ISBN-13
The Object-Oriented Thought Process	Matt Weisfeld	978-0-321-86127-6
Python Essential Reference	David M. Beazley	978-0-672-32978-4
Test-Driven iOS Development	Graham Lee	978-0-321-77418-7
PHP & MySQL Web Development	Luke Welling / Laura Thomson	978-0-672-32916-6

Developer's Library books are available at most retail and online bookstores. For more information or to order direct visit our online bookstore at **informit.com/store**

Online editions of all Developer's Library titles are available by subscription from Safari Books Online at **safari.informit.com**

Developer's Library

informit.com/devlibrary

Programming in Objective-C

Stephen G. Kochan

Updated for Xcode 4.5 and iOS 6

Fifth Edition

Developer's Library

Safari
Books Online

FREE
Online Edition

Addison Wesley   AdobePress   ALPHA   Cisco Press   FT Press   IBM Press   Microsoft Press   New Riders   O'REILLY

Peachpit Press   PRENTICE HALL   QUE   Redbooks   SAMS   SAS Publishing   vmware PRESS   WILEY   wrox